THE LAST BRITISH LIBERALS IN AFRICA

Michael Blundell
and
Garfield Todd

Dickson A. Mungazi

Westport, Connecticut
London

Library of Congress Cataloging-in-Publication Data

Mungazi, Dickson A.
　　The last British liberals in Africa : Michael Blundell and
　Garfield Todd / Dickson A. Mungazi.
　　　　p.　　cm.
　　Includes bibliographical references and index.
　　ISBN 0–275–96283–0 (alk. paper)
　　　1. Todd, Garfield, 1908–　. 2. Zimbabwe—Politics and
　government—1890–1965.　3. Zimbabwe—Politics and
　government—1965–1979.　4. Blundell, Michael, Sir, 1907– .
　5. Kenya—Politics and government—To 1963.　6. Kenya—Politics and
　government—1963–1978.　7. Great Britain—Colonies—Africa—
　Administration.　8. Liberalism—Great Britain—History—20th
　century.　9. Liberalism—Africa, Sub-Saharan—History—20th century.
　I. Title.
　DT2979.T63M86　1999
　325'.341'09226762—dc21　　　　　　98–39876

British Library Cataloguing in Publication Data is available.

Copyright © 1999 by Dickson A. Mungazi

All rights reserved. No portion of this book may be
reproduced, by any process or technique, without the
express written consent of the publisher.

Library of Congress Catalog Card Number: 98–39876
ISBN: 0–275–96283–0

First published in 1999

Praeger Publishers, 88 Post Road West, Westport, CT 06881
An imprint of Greenwood Publishing Group, Inc.
www.praeger.com

Printed in the United States of America

The paper used in this book complies with the
Permanent Paper Standard issued by the National
Information Standards Organization (Z39.48–1984).

10　9　8　7　6　5　4　3　2　1

To L. Kay Walker, my co-author, colleague, and friend, whose interest and service in Africa extended far beyond the ordinary

We cannot avoid the African majority government and therefore our policies should simply and clearly be designed to see that this great mass of people is well educated.
—Michael Blundell in 1957
[cited in Blundell, 1994]

The Africans are aware that educated people can be governed but they cannot be enslaved forever. They are no longer willing to be controlled in the manner in which they have been controlled in the past.
—Garfield Todd, 1947

Contents

Illustrations	xi
Preface	xiii
Acknowledgments	xv
Introduction	1
1. The Political History of Kenya	21
2. The Political History of Zimbabwe	51
3. Michael Blundell: The Man and His Mission	81
4. Garfield Todd: The Man and His Mission	103
5. Michael Blundell's Role in the Political Development of Kenya	135
6. Garfield Todd's Role in the Political Crisis in Zimbabwe	161
7. Blundell's Relations with Africans	191
8. Michael Blundell and Garfield Todd as the Last British Liberals in Africa: Summary, Conclusion, and Implications	223
Selected Bibliography	255
Index	277

Illustrations

MAPS

1.	Kenya	18
2.	Zimbabwe	19

TABLES

1.	Casualties of the War of 1896	60
2.	Expenditures for White Education and African Education Compared, 1909–49	69

PHOTOS *(photo essay follows p. 133)*

1. Winston Churchill
2. Michael Blundell, 1957
3. Garfield Todd and Emory Rose, 1953
4. H. K. Nyongesa and Ruth Waswa, 1995
5. The big four of politics in Kenya: Harry Thuku, Philip E. Mitchell, Jomo Kenyatta, and Evelyn Baring
6. Garfield Todd and Guy Clutton-Brock, 1978

7. D. N. Pritt, QC, 1952
8. The arrest of Dedan Kimathi, 1956
9. Mellyse Otieno, 1977
10. Sir Peter Tapsell

Preface

PURPOSE OF THE STUDY

The purpose of this book is to present evidence that substantiates the following arguments: From 1948 to 1962 Michael Blundell played a major role in the political transformation of Kenya. From 1946 to 1980 Garfield Todd played a similar role in Zimbabwe. The two men were motivated by the liberal philosophy that had been evolved early in the 20th century in Britain. Blundell and Todd understood that philosophy to mean that political leaders had a responsibility to serve the needs of the people as a condition of national development. The colonization of Africa by European nations beginning with the conclusion of the Berlin Conference in February 1885 had a profoundly negative impact on the lives of the Africans.

By the time that Blundell and Todd became involved in the politics of Kenya and Zimbabwe in 1948 and 1946, respectively, they sought to correct that negative impact by putting their positive views of Africans into practice. The events that were taking place in 1907, the year that Blundell was born, and in 1908, the year that Todd was born, laid the foundation upon which these two men built a set of ideas and philosophy that they utilized in their endeavors to bring about the transformation of these two countries for the benefit of all. These two men succeeded in accomplishing what they did only because they were liberals. This enabled them to see the need for change far more than their fellow settlers did.

QUESTIONS ANSWERED AND EVIDENCE PRESENTED

In furnishing the evidence that will substantiate this conclusion, this book furnishes answers to the following questions: Who were Michael Blundell and Garfield Todd? What kinds of environments produced them? What conditions prevailed in the world at the time of their birth to suggest their liberal views? Who are some of the people who influenced them? What conditions prevailed in both Kenya and Zimbabwe that demanded their involvement? What difficulties did they encounter? How did their fellow settlers and Africans respond to their initiatives? How did they respond to British policy? In furnishing answers to these and other questions, the book utilizes various sources, both primary and secondary, that the author obtained during three trips to Kenya and Zimbabwe between 1985 and 1997.

CONCLUSIONS AND IMPLICATIONS

The violent manner in which European nations subjected Africa to colonial rule remained a black spot in the history of colonial adventure in Africa. As colonization was effected, the colonial systems sought to control the Africans in order to control their action. There was serious conflict between European perception of Africans and Africans' perception of themselves as a people. This cultural conflict led to political conflict after the Second World War. This is the period of the rise of African consciousness. Blundell and Todd fully recognized it and suggested taking it into account in designing colonial policy.

Because the colonial governments failed to see things from the perspective that Blundell and Todd did, colonial policy led to serious conflict within the colonial establishment itself. While colonial governments designed strategies for controlling Africans to serve their own political and economic interests, Africans themselves designed their own effective strategy not only to ensure their survival in the colonial setting, but also to initiate a process for the restoration of their sense of self. In doing so they found reliable allies in Michael Blundell and Garfield Todd. Although in recent years democracy in both Kenya and Zimbabwe has been brought to the test, it is alive and well today. Thanks to the democratic traditions that Blundell and Todd established for them, Kenya and Zimbabwe have a challenge to honor these traditions. They must not betray them.

Acknowledgments

The task of conducting a study about the political philosophy and action of two leading characters in two major countries under colonial control is hard enough in itself. But given the complicating factor of the dynamics of human interaction in colonial settings, that task becomes a challenge that only those who desire to know can accept. This is the perspective from which the author undertakes this study. However, in order to take all relevant aspects of this study into account in recording accurately all the pertinent information about the roles that Michael Blundell and Garfield Todd played in the political transformation of Kenya and Zimbabwe, the author utilized original materials on these two men supplemented by secondary sources.

It is for this reason that the author wishes to express his special appreciation to the Kenya National Archives for letting him have access to materials on Michael Blundell and the Zimbabwe National Archives for those on Garfield Todd. He also wishes to thank Ruth Washa, his research assistant in Nairobi, for collecting and dispatching the materials he requested from various sources in Kenya; and Mellyse Otieno, a secretary in Nairobi, for her insights into political developments in Kenya—especially the contribution that some members of her ethnic group, the Luo, made to the political transformation of Kenya.

The author would like to record his special appreciation to Judith Todd, daughter of Garfield Todd, for furnishing him with information that he requested about her father and the Todd family in general, as well as photographs that are used in this book. He is particularly thankful to her for sending him a copy of her book, *The Right to Say No: Rhodesia 1972*, and her "The Thoughts of Ian Smith," both of which offer some penetrating and troubling insights about the character of the Rhodesia Front government that Smith led from 1964 to 1979, and which placed both her and her father in prison in 1972 for expressing opposition to its policy and for their liberal views on the future of Zimbabwe.

The author would also like to express his appreciation to the National Social Science Association for critique of parts of the manuscript offered while he was presenting papers at conferences from 1995 to 1998. He also wishes to thank his secretary, Charlene Wingo, for helping to type parts of the manuscript, and to Linda Gregonis, indexer and proofreader; Betty Russell, computer specialist at Northern Arizona University, for her technical assistance in the production of the manuscript; and Karl Doerry, Director of International Education and the Office of Regents Professors at Northern Arizona University, for financial support of the project to enable him to travel to Britain and Africa to conduct the research needed to complete the study. Finally, the author wishes to thank William G. and Vernah Kodzai for their hospitality extended while he was conducting research for this study in Zimbabwe from 1995 to 1997.

Introduction

THE SETTING

In 1944, when Swedish sociologist and researcher Gunnar Myrdal concluded in his study, *An American Dilemma: The Negro Problem and Modern Democracy*, that the American social problems rose from the conflict between idealism and practice, he was recognizing the cruelty of the struggle between white America and black America. That white America and black America perceived the structure of the American society from two opposing points of view suggests the elusiveness of human thought process and action to project a future different from the past. It is this conflict of perception that often translates into social conflict of major proportions posing fundamental questions as to what organized society is all about.

Myrdal could have chosen colonial Africa as a setting for his study. In 1944 the elements of social conflict that he discussed relative to the United States were present in Africa. At that time South Africa, for example, was going through a painful period of trying to structure the future different from the past. In 1944 the Nationalist Party, led by Daniel F. Malan, was putting together components of a policy that became known across the world as apartheid. Until April 1994 South Africa experienced social conflict in a way that threatened to disintegrate its social institutions. This is why in 1990 the government of South Africa, led by F. W. de Klerk, and the African National Congress, led by Nelson Mandela, made a gallant effort to search their own minds to put society back on track because apartheid was destroying the most valued resources that the country needed to ensure not only its survival, but also its development.

It is important to remember that the character of society is determined by the action of individuals, who, while acting on their own, must remember that they are part of a society in which collective action is necessary. Individual action and collective initiative both require the observance of rules of conduct and behavior that have been evolved over an extended period of time. In this behavior individuals are either liberal, conservative, or moderate. How one adopts one of these three forms of political ideology depends upon their orientation and background. Some are influenced by members of their families. For example, in the United States, the Kennedy and Roosevelt family members seem invariably to subscribe to the liberal philosophy of the Democratic party, while members of the Goldwater and Lodge families have subscribed to the conservative philosophy of the Republican party, and members of the Rockefeller family have subscribed to the moderate philosophy of the same party.

These three forms of political ideology exist, as they must, in countries that espouse democracy. This allows the voters to exercise their free choice of the kind of political leaders they believe should hold public office. Without this choice the government that emerges can only be regarded as a dictatorship. The purpose of this study is to present a line of argument that suggests the conclusion that in their respective roles in Kenya and Zimbabwe, Michael Blundell and Garfield Todd subscribed to the liberal political philosophy that enabled them to make a unique and rare contribution to the political transformation of these two British colonies. In furnishing the evidence that substantiates this conclusion, the book begins with a brief discussion of both men cast in the historical context of both countries. The convening of the Berlin Conference in December 1884 is the proper place to start.

THE COLONIZATION OF AFRICA

In order to have a clear picture of the role that Blundell and Todd played in the political transformation of Kenya and Zimbabwe, it is important to have an understanding of broader events that were unfolding in Africa during their time. The knowledge among Europeans that Africa contained large quantities of raw materials needed to improve the standard of living in Europe strengthened the myth that had started during the Enlightenment that Africans were less intelligent than Europeans. The reality that came out of this conclusion is that Africans and their continent were now being subjected to a new form of campaign by European colonial enthusiasts. The publication in 1859 of Charles Darwin's

Origin of Species and of Charles Dickens's *A Tale of Two Cities* provided new ammunition to colonial forces as they now braced themselves to engage in the battle to control Africans and the raw materials. Dickens's concept of the best of times and Darwin's view of the survival of the fittest were utilized to strengthen the belief among colonial enthusiasts in the perception that Europeans had never had it so good in their strategy for dominance of the presumed intellectually weak Africans. When Darwin published his *The Descent of Man* in 1871, colonial enthusiasts hailed it as a blueprint of their opinion of the people of the "Dark Continent" that they lacked intellectual potential. It did not worry these colonial enthusiasts that they were reading into Darwin's book things that he never intended. What was important was the effect that they were exploiting his ideas to promote their own political agenda. It was open season for European nations in Africa, anything that stirred was fair game.

By the time the Berlin Conference was held at the end of 1884 to map out the colonization of Africa, Africans had been reduced to the level where European nations could manipulate them in a way that served their own political and economic interests. The brutality and the lack of concern for the welfare of Africans became a distinct characteristic behavior of colonial entrepreneurs. The process of control of Africans was now under way as the game of the survival of the intellectually fittest started in a deadly combat of wills. For European colonial adventurers the best of times was here and now, as nothing seemed to stand between them and the goals they had set. To them it was an exciting feeling to know that the vast resources in Africa and its people were at their disposal to do with as they pleased, because Africans were presumed not to understand what was happening.

As the colonization of Africa became *fait accompli*, the colonial systems designed policies to govern their African empires in accordance with the specifications of the Berlin Conference and their own colonial principles and policies. By the beginning of the First World War only three countries were politically independent in Africa. The first country was Liberia, which was founded in 1823 by the American Colonization Society as a country for freed slaves from the United States. It is ironic that in 1990 Liberia subjected itself to a brutal betrayal of itself in form of a cruel civil war that left it devastated. The second independent country in Africa by 1914 was Ethiopia, which claimed its independence from biblical times. It is equally a tragic fact that in 1974 Ethiopia endured the agony of the betrayal of itself by deposing Emperor Haile Selassie in a military coup and installing a Marxist regime that was so oppressive that it was turned out of office in 1990. The civil war that had been raging for years over Eritrea's claim of independence reached a decisive stage when the Marxist regime was removed from power. But the end of the civil war did not result in the restoration of Ethiopia, a definite pattern of events in Africa.

The third independent country in Africa by 1914 was South Africa, the land of the infamous policy of apartheid until 1994. South Africa had gained independence in May 1910 following a bitter war between the British and Boers in which the Boers were slaughtered. The introduction of the policy of apartheid was intended to ensure full control of Africans. But, again in 1990, South Africa was paying the price of trying to sustain a political and social system that left a trail of racial bitterness unparalleled by that of any other country of Africa. These three examples of countries that gained independence prior to 1914 illustrate a very important consideration presented in this book: the colonization of Africa was effected at a high price in that material comfort, not human relations, became the major focus of colonial entrepreneurs.

During the height of the colonial systems, from 1885 to 1914 and from 1920 to 1939, the colonial governments formulated policies that can only be understood in the context of their effect on their intent to control Africans through the application of various forms of colonial policy. For example, Germany formulated the policy of Deutsche Kolonialbund; France and Belgium introduced the policy of *evolué*; Britain developed a policy known as indirect rule; Portugal had a policy known as Estado Novo; and the Boers had apartheid. In addition to seeking full control of Africans, these policies had two other components in common. The first was to instill upon the Africans that they were inferior to the white man. The myth that had been evolved during the Age of Reason was now being relived in the Africans in painful ways. For the colonial governments happy days were here again. The second component was that at no time would the Africans ever hope to achieve equal status with settlers.

To strengthen their hold on their African empires, the colonial governments enacted laws that left no room for doubt as to the place of Africans in the colonial society. As Ethel Tawse Jollie, one of the first women to sit in a colonial legislature, put it bluntly in 1927, the purpose of the colonial policy was to strengthen the position of whites and weaken that of Africans. Nothing else mattered. Severe penalties were meted out to those Africans who dared question their subjection. Thus began a period that theoreticians have appropriately called "the colonial culture of violence." The imprisonment of Nelson Mandela for 27 years for suggesting that apartheid was wrong furnishes one of the clearest examples of the concept of colonial culture of violence. The supply of labor to produce the materials needed to enhance the standard of life in Europe was the only function Africans were required to fulfill.

The control of Africans was now complete and the colonial establishments looked to the future with great expectations to create a social utopia. Once the control of Africans was fully established, the colonial governments did not worry about their action because, so they believed, Africans had been tamed and broken like horses controlled by the bridle of psychological conditioning. This is what Godfrey Huggins, who was prime minister of colonial Zimbabwe from 1933 to 1952, had in mind when he argued in 1954 that the policy of his government was designed to promote partnership between the Africans and the whites, the kind of partnership similar to the one that "exists between the horse and the rider."

The maps of Kenya and Zimbabwe at the end of this chapter show demographic and political conditions in these countries in 1940, when Blundell and Todd were becoming active in their respective nations.

THE RISE OF AFRICAN CONSCIOUSNESS AND THE STRUGGLE FOR SELF

Huggins's definition of the place of Africans in the colonial society is one reason that Africans used to arouse a new level of consciousness among them. In 1939 the hope that the colonial governments had expressed at their inception, following the conclusion of the Berlin Conference that they would last at least a millennium, was shattered by events in Europe, not in Africa. The outbreak of the war in 1939 permanently altered the course of events in Africa as well as in the rest of the world, and changed the relationships that colonial governments had established between themselves and Africans. The rise of Adolf Hitler and his Third Reich was a phenomenon whose impact was profoundly felt on the African continent in ways far more serious than European nations could imagine.

Having invaded Poland and paralyzed France and the Low Countries in rapid succession, Nazi forces launched a relentless blitz on Britain in an effort to force it to sue for peace on Hitler's terms. By 1941 the Nazi forces were within striking distance of bringing Britain to its knees, as the second stage of Hitler's objective of bringing the entire world under his rule. Winston Churchill, the beleaguered British leader who had succeeded Neville Chamberlain who died suddenly in 1940, felt that Britain was fighting the battle for democracy alone and requested the support of the United States in the war against the Axis powers. On August 11, 1941, still feeling the pressure to do something dramatic to turn the war around in favor of the Allies, Churchill and President Franklin Roosevelt met secretly and issued the famous Atlantic Charter, stating that their governments respected the right of all people to choose the form of government under which they would live and that they wished to see sovereign rights and self-determination restored to those who had been forcibly deprived of them.

With this statement the Allied nations that had colonies in Africa began a vigorous campaign to recruit Africans into the ranks of their armed forces, promising improved conditions of life as a reward of their part in defeating the forces of the Axis powers. The Africans could not believe what they were hearing in both the Atlantic Charter and the recruitment campaign. They regarded both as a solemn promise to allow them an opportunity to exercise the concept of self-determination. Although the war was not their own making, the Africans responded enthusiastically. Some joined the colonial armies from the desire to see Europe. Others did so from the compulsion of curiosity. Some did so to gain for themselves the respect of the white man. The response of the Africans in deciding to join the colonial forces against the Axis powers raised a fundamental question: Did the colonial governments now think that the Africans had an intellect that could be utilized to eliminate the threat of Nazi domination? There was no point in the Africans trying to find an answer to the question in the climate of the war, but as soon as the conflict was over in 1945, the colonial governments could no longer avoid the question because it was foremost in the minds of Africans.

As soon as the war was over and the threat of Nazi domination was finally eliminated, Africans turned their attention to the restoration of their rights as human beings in accordance with the pledge made in the Atlantic Charter and the promise made by the colonial governments of improved conditions of life. Africans had at last come of age, the genie was out of the bottle and could not be put back in. While in the war service, the Africans learned as much as they could about life in Europe and came to two basic conclusions: the white man had both positive attributes and negative features that characterized life everywhere, and contrary to his claim of intellectual superiority, the white man had nothing more than a political strategy to subject Africans to oppressive conditions. One of the Africans who participated in the war, Waruhiu Itote from Kenya, used the knowledge he gained in the jungle of Burma to launch a military attack on the colonial establishments as a Mau Mau leader.

This development represents the rise of African consciousness, which manifested itself in the political activity that was fundamental to the Africans' political aspirations and to their awareness of the need to restore their position in colonial settings. Meeting in London to design a strategy for action to realize their new political objectives, Africans recognized that the war had an impact on their thought processes in ways that the colonial governments could not expect to understand. Once they put that strategy in place, Africans were determined to put it into effect and expected to see the results they had anticipated. First, they demanded an improvement in the conditions of their lives as promised by the Atlantic Charter. But when the colonial governments declined to initiate that improvement, Africans decided to adopt the next phase of that strategy, which was to demand political independence. They knew that they risked imprisonment and death in adopting the strategy of confrontation with the colonial governments. The colonial culture of violence found an expression and a target in Africans' demand for fundamental change.

Twelve years following the end of the war, Africans scored a resounding victory in their struggle against the colonial governments. The strategy of survival they had learned during the height of colonization and during the war now found an appropriate forum in confronting the colonial powers. The attainment of independence for Ghana in 1957 signaled a spiraling series of events that finally led to the fulfillment of the objectives Africans had designed as a result of the end of the war. Kwame Nkrumah, Jomo Kenyatta, Milton Margai, Albert Luthuli, Joshua Nkomo, Patrice Lumumba, Edwardo Mondlane, and others became undisputed leaders in a new phenomenon of the rising African political aspirations. Indeed, independence for Ghana triggered developments that led to the untimely collapse of the colonial empires in Africa, well short of the thousand years that some colonial enthusiasts, such as Cecil John Rhodes and others, had predicted as their minimum duration. In 1986 Africans knew that only the Afrikaners of South Africa were still trying to mislead them was the reason why there was an intense struggle between them and Africans. If history is any thing to go by, the Afrikaners would be well advised to listen to the voice of reason and to realize that they were fighting a losing battle. The Afrikaners failed to realize that no colonial power, no matter how oppressive and brutal, can win a struggle against the colonized once they have decided to restore their sense of pride. It is not surprising that with the independence of Namibia in 1990 following 70 years of brutal rule by South Africa, South Africa itself was now the only colonial power on the continent. The end of the apartheid system came only four years later, in April 1994.

The rise of African consciousness and the struggle for political independence following the end of the Second World War was also the result of the action taken by colonial governments themselves. Tragic as it was, the war gave Africans a new opportunity to study the behavior of the white man in relationship to his thought processes and toward them. They saw for themselves the misery and the suffering that the vast majority of people in Europe endured. The Industrial Revolution of the 19th century had helped improve conditions of life of some people, but it had also left many more sinking in the dark shadows of a social utopia and economic millennium that was envisaged

Above all else the Africans who went to war learned that the character of social institutions in Europe was determined by the character of political behavior of individuals, and that no single individual had an absolute monopoly of knowledge about human conditions and political knowledge. Winston Churchill, Clement Attlee, Charles de Gaulle, and Antonio Salazar were not Edmund Burke, Julius Caesar, Thomas Hobbes, and Machiavelli reincarnate. They were human beings of simple and ordinary political ability of questionable nature.

The conclusion that the Africans reached about the limitations of the colonial society translated into an action as a result of the high level of African intellect the colonial governments could not understand and control. Africans were now conscious of the fact that in terms of political thought process and action they were capable of measuring up to expectations. In this context the cards were on the table and the colonial systems and Africans were now ready to engage in a game of wills. The wind of change surging in the form of a breeze that turned into nationalistic storm aided Africans in charting a new course to self-determination and independence and derailed the game plan of the colonial officials. The days of the colonial domination of Africans were clearly numbered as the dawn of the rise of their political independence heralded the daybreak of a new era.

THE COLONIZATION OF KENYA AND THE CRUCIBLE OF CULTURAL CONFLICT

In presenting these features of the political conditions in Africa as a result of the Second World War, this book addresses some developments that were taking place at the time Blundell and Todd were born in 1907 and 1908, respectively, to suggest how they were exposed to that liberal philosophy. Cast in colonial setting in Africa, where the exercise of democracy was virtually impossible for Africans, Blundell and Todd responded to a call to rise up to the occasion and exercise the influence only they could exert in the Africans' struggle for freedom from colonial domination. In doing so the two men paid a heavy price for their beliefs and actions. They were condemned by their fellow settlers, they were threatened with arrest and charges of treason. While Blundell was not arrested, Todd was actually arrested and placed in detention and house arrest for nearly five years. In 1958 his entire cabinet resigned in protest of his liberal views and the efforts he was making to bring about meaningful change in the lives of Africans. In 1972 he was placed in detention for an extended period of time and was charged with treason for which he could have been hanged were it not for intervention by the British government.

Although the book begins with an account of events beginning with the colonization of Kenya in 1895, its major focus is when Blundell arrived in Kenya in 1925 at the age of 18, hardly an age when one can

Introduction 9

travel by oneself and live in a strange country. The account of the system of commissioner under Arthur Charles Hardinge from 1895 to 1900 ends with that of James Hayes Sadler from 1905 to 1909. This account is intended to give a narrative of the development of the colonial system. When Sadler provided a period of change from the system of commissioner to the beginning of that of governor in 1906, important developments began to take place, especially the evolution of the land policy which, by 1952, caused so much conflict between the colonial government and the Africans. Blundell's arrival in Kenya coincided with the appointment of Edward Grigg as governor in 1925.

Grigg, who had previously served in the British Parliament as a member of the Liberal Party, and Blundell had something in common in their backgrounds: they were introduced to liberal philosophy early in their lives. But, due to the demands of the office he held, Grigg abandoned his liberal philosophy in order to assert his authority as governor. Although Blundell and Grigg did not have an opportunity to work together, Blundell later learned about some of the mistakes Grigg made in dealing with critical national issues, especially the nature of relations between the colonial government and Africans. In 1922 Grigg's two predecessors, Edward Northey, who served from 1919 to 1922, and Robert Coryndon, who served from 1922 to 1925, came face to face with a powerful and proud African nationalist, Harry Thuku. Recognizing the arrogant manner in which Northey and Coryndon carried out their duties, Thuku refused to submit to the wishes and demands of colonial officials who showed neither understanding nor knowledge of the needs of the Africans.

In an effort to reduce Thuku's ego, Northey and Coryndon acted in a manner that invoked strong reaction from Thuku himself. On July 1, 1921, Africans formed the East African Association with Thuku as president. In 1922 Thuku was advocating civil disobedience among Africans as a response to the manner in which Northey and Coryndon carried out their responsibilities. He was arrested and imprisoned for nine years. Although Grigg finally ordered Thuku's release in 1930, he had been part of his continuing imprisonment for nearly five years after Coryndon had retired. Neither Coryndon nor Grigg nor their successors were aware that in taking this action against Thuku they were planting the seeds of a major conflict in the future. In this context the colonial government created Kenya as a crucible of cultural conflict.

From time to time since 1930 the crucible of conflict widened to include a mixture of elements that tarnished it beyond repair. By the time that Philip E. Mitchell was appointed governor in 1944, the crucible of cultural conflict was beginning to take serious dimensions. In that year Eliud Wambui Mathu was appointed the first African to sit in the legislative council. The appointment was made not so much with the purpose of having him represent the interests of the Africans, but to give the impression that he was, in effect, representing their interests. But it turned out that Mitchell, in accordance with the expectations of the appointment, expected Mathu to remember that he held office at his pleasure.

This development created a situation that Africans saw Mathu as a representative of colonial interests. Although Mathu tried to function in a manner that reflected his understanding of responsibilities to Africans, he could not eliminate the impression that he was being used to promote the interests of the colonial government. However, Africans did not turn their rage at Mathu, but at the colonial government for putting him in a position of conflict of interest. However, until 1957, when the Lyttleton constitution came into being, Mathu did his best to represent the interests of his fellow Africans. By this time Michael Blundell used the end of the Mau Mau rebellion in 1957 to make a major pronouncement of his philosophy, saying that settlers would be unable to stop the advent of the African government and that while it was still possible the colonial government must design a policy to ensure that Africans were adequately educated to assume their responsibility for the future of the country.

But in taking the position that he did toward the Mau Mau rebellion in 1952, Blundell, unlike Todd, compromised his liberal principles. The result was that the Mau Mau rebellion left a trail of racial bitterness that came to an end only with Kenya's attainment of independence in December 1963. If Blundell had remained true to his original principles, it would have been possible to minimize the effect of the Mau Mau to the extent that bridges of communication would have been built for the mutual benefit of both sides. However, Blundell tried to initiate contact with the leaders of the Mau Mau movement, but he was condemned by his fellow settlers.

Throughout his political involvement in the transformation of Kenya, Blundell walked a political tightrope. On the one hand he tried to represent the interests of the settlers. On the other hand he tried to have meaningful relations with Africans. As a result his balancing act left much to be desired, although he proved to be a gallant soldier in the struggle for political advancement of Africans. When Kenya achieved independence in December 1963 Blundell had a place of honor in Kenya, just as Todd did when Zimbabwe gained independence in April 1980.

TODD'S ROLE IN COLONIAL ZIMBABWE: SEEKING AN END TO THE CULTURE OF VIOLENCE

Although the drama of conflict between Africans and the colonial government in Zimbabwe, the former British colony of Southern Rhodesia, began at the inception of the colonial government in September 1890, it took a dramatic turn for the worse between 1964 and 1979 when Zimbabwe, then Rhodesia, was subjected to the political behavior of the Rhodesia Front (RF) government led by white men who were so obsessed with sustaining political power that nothing else mattered. In a unilateral declaration of independence on November 11, 1965, Ian Smith, unaware that he would be the last colonial leader, claimed that his government took this action because he believed that the mantle of the colonial pioneers had fallen on the shoulders of its members to sustain Western civilization in what he called a primitive country. It did not occur to him and his associates in government that the mantle had, in effect, fallen from their shoulders. The attitude and the policies of the RF government demonstrate the tragic nature of its political behavior.

One must not, therefore, conclude that this institutional conflict was a racial war, because it was not. This was a conflict between the vestiges of the colonial establishment and the rising tide of African nationalism. Race, indeed, became only an incidental factor when the RF government, by its own admission, made it so. But what is important to keep in mind is that the extreme positions which the combatants took suggests the critical role of the forces behind it and the explosive nature of the conflict. On the one hand was Ian Smith, the last colonial political leader of Zimbabwe, and, indeed the Pied Piper of the old era of colonial political objectives. He was a man whose political philosophy manifested a behavior that upheld and reflected the views that Cecil John Rhodes expressed at the height of his political power in 1896. It was Rhodes's absolute belief that the white man must retain political power for at least a thousand years, for he had concluded that Africans would take that length of time to acquire the elements of Western culture, without which, he argued, they would remain primitive and unable to run a government efficiently.

Smith's belief in Rhodes's views became an obsession in his action to formulate political objectives and policies of his own administration. For Smith and his government the alternative would be a return to what he called the days of African barbarism. Therefore, in declaring Zimbabwe independent unilaterally in an attempt to foil the efforts of Africans toward their own definition of self, Smith believed that he had a duty to launch a *kamikaze* assault on the rising tide of African nationalism unmindful of the consequences of his action. He failed to realize that this action was bound to turn out to be an ill-conceived strategy that meant his own ultimate self-deception because it proved to be the lull before the storm.

On the other hand were the African nationalists who believed that they had a solemn responsibility to liberate their people and to rescue their country from what they regarded as colonial usurpers who were exploiting them under the aegis of Victorian principles of the profitability of founding colonies. This belief inspired their determination to fight for their cause. It is this kind of setting that produced an environment ripe for a major conflict. One must now ask the question: What were the real causes of the war of independence? The answer depends on who one asks. Smith told this author in July 1983 that it was caused by the African nationalists who, he argued, were seeking to replace what he claimed was a democratic government with a Marxist dictatorship.

The African nationalists argued that the war was caused by the RF's oppressive policies, especially the denial of equal educational opportunity, through which they were denied equal opportunity in society. Assuming that the reasons advanced by both sides were plausible, one must find a more reliable basis of determining the actual causes. This author believes that there are four basic reasons why the war could not be avoided: historical precedence, the rise of African nationalism, the policies of the RF government itself, and the role that Garfield Todd played in bringing about the political transformation of colonial Zimbabwe. Let us take each one at a time and discuss briefly how it stands as a cause of the war.

As soon as the British South Africa Company established a colony in September 1890, Leander Starr Jameson, the first administrator who served from September 10, 1890, to April 1, 1896, operated under the Victorian principle that the Africans must be trained to fulfill the labor needs of the country. For the next six years a philosophy steadily developed which embraced the belief that practical training and manual labor should form a major component of the curricular content in African schools. Therefore, from the beginning of the colonial government in Zimbabwe, educational policy for Africans became an integral part of its political agenda. Until the end of the RF government in 1979, the educational process acquired political implications far beyond the level of educational policy.

During the period which Earl Grey served as administrator from April 2, 1896, to December 4, 1898, this practice had become an official government policy. Indeed, in 1898, during a debate on the first education bill which became law in 1899, Grey argued that the best way of promoting the advancement of Africans was not through the introduction of Christian values the missionaries were trying to promote, but training them to function as cheap laborers. The church-state crisis, which is discussed in Chapters 5 and 6, began to form with Grey's views and the reaction of the church leaders to them. The cooperation that had existed between the missionaries and the European entrepreneurs, and which David Livingstone so eloquently advocated in 1864 as the best means of advancing British commercial interests in Africa, suffered a severe setback as a result of Grey's attitude and the policy of his administration.

Within this context a triangle of badly strained relationships began to form at the conclusion of the war in 1897. Chapter 2 discusses a set of conditions created by the colonial government to show that the seeds of conflict between the Africans and the colonial government were sown right at the inception of the colonial system.

However, it was the administration of Godfrey Huggins from September 12, 1933, to September 6, 1953, which established a strong precedence that the RF government effectively used in designing its own set of policies making the road to conflict a truly perilous one. Huggins's definition of the policy of partnership between the Africans and the whites as "that kind of relationship which exists between the horse and the rider" is what the RF government used as the basis of its own policies and political action. Not only did Smith admire Huggins and accept him as his mentor, he also adopted all of his policies, programs, and philosophy.

Arguing that there was nothing wrong with the policies of his administration beyond the reaction of misinformed individuals, Smith told the author in 1983 that they were part of the history of policy in Zimbabwe, and that to expect his government to change history was unrealistic. He preferred to neglect the reality that because conditions from Jameson to Huggins had changed, there was need to change both attitudes and policies to suit these new conditions. The reason why the RF government did not think much of the policies of the administration of Garfield Todd from September 7, 1953, to February 16, 1958, and that of Edgar C. Whitehead from February 17, 1958, to December 16, 1962, is that both tried to reverse the policies that Huggins had pursued for many years. Smith and his RF government so admired Huggins and the policies of his administration that they used them as their own model, neglecting the fact that new conditions demanded a fresh appraisal and new policy elements. Failure to understand this basic and simple fact constituted the elements of the tragedy of the RF.

The second cause of the war is the rise of African nationalism. The Second World War had a profound effect upon the Africans and in ways that neither they nor the colonial governments could have foreseen. Indeed, the colonial governments all over Africa asked the Africans to fight against possible Nazi oppression, yet they returned home to endure old forms of colonial oppression. They had asked them to fight for the freedom and rights of all people, yet the Africans returned home to experience a lack of freedom and a continual denial of equal rights. They had asked them to fight to end racism, yet the Africans returned home to face new colonial racism. That the Africans grasped the effect of this contradiction on their lives suggests how the war had aroused a new level of consciousness among them.

The reality of this awareness had its basis in the conference that African leaders held in London at the conclusion of the war in 1945. Not only did they assess their contribution to the war efforts of the Allies, but they also made an evaluation of themselves as a people in light of the colonial conditions. From that moment out of the Africans' understanding of what it meant to be human, African Nationalism was born. The return of Kwame Nkrumah to Ghana in 1947 following the completion of his educational safari in Europe and the United States gave a new meaning to a momentum that was building up rapidly. When Nkrumah was elected prime minister of Ghana in 1950, he began to work toward its independence as a prelude to the struggle for the liberation of the African continent. Indeed, at the inauguration of independence for Ghana, Nkrumah made a solemn pledge to launch a continental campaign to rid Africa of colonialism because, he argued, the independence for Ghana was meaningless unless it was dedicated to the liberation of the African continent.

The attainment of independence for Ghana in 1957 altered the political landscape in all of Africa. Suddenly Ghana and Nkrumah became a symbol of a new era of consciousness in Africa, the twin-beacon lighthouse giving direction to the African political boat sailing in the troubled waters of colonial high waves. The British imperial ship sailing in the equally troubled waters on the Dark Continent had hit an iceberg and was now beginning to sink. Nkrumah's role in the founding of the Organization of African Unity on May 25, 1963, ushered in a new level of African Nationalism and offered the British an opportunity to make a political SOS call. It really is not surprising that the very first target of the African Nationalists was the system of education under colonial rule, because it determined every other aspect of national life, such as employment opportunity and the general standard of living.

The inauguration of African National Congress (ANC) in Zimbabwe in 1957—the year Ghana achieved independence, and Martin Luther King, Jr. and Rosa Parks were making news headlines in the struggle of African Americans for civil rights—was an event that was destined to alter the course of political events in the country. When Edgar Whitehead outlawed ANC in February 1958, the relationship between the Africans and the government entered a new phase. The formation of the National Democratic Party (NDP) in 1959, its banning, again by Whitehead, in 1960, and the formation of Zimbabwe African People's Union (ZAPU) and Zimbabwe African National Union (ZANU), also in 1960, were developments which suggest that the colonial governments failed to accept African nationalism as a major factor shaping political development of the country. The RF's failure to accept this reality would have dire consequences for the future. When two powerful forces, the rising tide of African nationalism and the might of the RF determination to preserve white political institutions, clashed the outcome was devastating.

The third cause of the war is the policies of the RF government itself.

Introduction 15

When Ian Smith told the author on July 20, 1983, that because the policies of his administration were part of the history of government policy in Zimbabwe, he justified them on that basis alone. He felt that easing them would lead to the formation of an African government, the prospects of which he detested completely. This is why the RF declined to consider changing them. But neither Smith nor his RF government would be aware that in remaining rigid about the influence of past policies on those of their own, they were inadvertently accelerating the advent of an African government itself.

The fourth cause of the war was the role that Garfield Todd played in bringing about the political transformation of Zimbabwe. In discussing this cause one must understand that Todd was responding to the irrational behavior of the RF. While Todd tried to respond in a manner that showed respect for the government under which he lived, the RF showed no respect for him as a person whose security and welfare it must protect. Todd and the colonial government came into conflict in 1958 when he was removed from the office of prime minister. In February 1959 he opposed the declaration of the state of emergency by Edgar C. Whitehead, the man who replaced him. In 1964 Todd and the RF began the saga of conflict when Winston Field was removed from the office of prime minister in a political coup that was led by Ian Smith. Smith and Todd would never agree on anything. In July 1964 Todd openly supported Bishop Ralph E. Dodge when he was deported for opposing RF policy. He also opposed the RF's extension of the state of emergency, which was in effect from 1964 to 1979. There is no question that Todd's opposition of the RF policy offered the Africans the encouragement they needed to wage a struggle against it.

When the advent of an African government became a reality on April 18, 1980, well short of the thousand years that Smith and Rhodes had predicted it would take for Africans to acquire elements of Western culture, Smith was stunned by the turn of events that he could not control. Where did he and Rhodes go wrong in their prediction? It is clear that the historical significance which the RF used as a basis of its own policies had a profound effect on the relationships between itself and the church, and between itself and the Africans. That this conflict began with the announcement of a new educational policy and the enactment of the infamous Land Tenure Act, both in 1969, shows how the RF government's policy was at the center of the triangle of badly strained institutional relationships. The reason why this study addresses the conflict that emerged between Todd and the church and the RF is that each wanted to exercise dominant influence on the position of the Africans. But the effect of that conflict readily translated into conflict between the RF and the Africans.

In reacting to the church's and Todd's support of the Africans' demands for better opportunity, the RF once more proved that its policies were influenced by history. It could not afford to extend that opportunity to the Africans without putting the political interests of the whites in jeopardy. It could not remain unmoved without igniting a new crisis. How was the RF government going to resolve this dilemma? In the context of badly strained relationships which emerged between the Africans, the church, Todd, and the RF government, the action of the church leaders, including Todd, manifested the behavior of an institution which recognized the imperative nature of change and the need to preserve its own position in the future. The RF's educational policy only served the purpose of aggravating an already bad situation.

There is another factor which influenced the deterioration of the relationships between the RF government and the church leaders. On the one hand the church leaders believed that they had a responsibility to identify themselves with the aspiration of the Africans. On the other hand, the RF government believed that there was nothing wrong with its policies even though it was fully aware, as Smith told the author on July 22, 1983, that the Africans were unhappy with them. What actually led to the war of independence is a combination of these four critical factors: the influence of history, the rise of African nationalism, the policies of the RF government itself, and the role that Todd played. The crisis between the Africans and the RF was an outcome of the interaction of these factors. That the RF faced a dilemma of choice helps to explain the difficulties which it faced.

Finally the RF was different from previous colonial administrations in two critical respects. The first is that its obsession with white control of the government stood in the way of any effort to design a policy which would help solve the problems the country was facing. When this obsession collided with the rise of African nationalism, the inevitable outcome was a confrontation of major proportions. The second respect is that the RF administration was the first government to reverse the development efforts of the Africans to ensure that it remained in what it called responsible, meaning white, hands. Leading members of the RF all became spokesmen of a policy that was designed to control and limit the development of the Africans as the most effective means of preserving white political control. In the end, the mantle of the pioneers that they thought fell on their shoulders actually fell from their hands as the African government which they had dreaded so much, and which they had dedicated their lives to stop from becoming a reality, became their nightmare. How this happened is the subject of this book.

CONCLUSION AND IMPLICATIONS

If there are some things that can be learned from the roles that Blundell and Todd played in the political transformation of Kenya and Zimbabwe, they must include the fact that no government can long endure which tries to preserve a system that serves the interests of a minority at the expense of the majority. There is no doubt that the colonial governments up to Evelyn Baring in Kenya and the RF in Zimbabwe felt so committed to the policies of past administrations that they were not able to see themselves as playing a role in bringing about change to accommodate African advancement in the evolvement of national policy which responded to the conditions of the times.

This author takes the position that there is also a lesson for the current governments of Kenya and Zimbabwe in preserving the roles that Blundell and Todd played: democracy demands that the people be involved at every stage and phase of developing a national policy. Both Blundell and Todd dedicated themselves to this course of development and refused to compromise their principles. Many countries of Africa have yet to learn the truth that failure to recognize this reality is the reason why African nations have experienced enormous problems, even worse than those that existed during the colonial period.

Finally, both Blundell and Todd had daughters who shared their fathers' enthusiasms in their efforts to bring about meaningful change in their respective countries. But Judith, Todd's daughter, went much further than Blundell's daughter in living by the principles that her father defined in 1946 when he first went into politics. She has shared his belief that those who hold public office must at all times remember that they do so in order to serve the needs of the people. In 1997 the author sent Judith a small amount money to help with the cost of mailing materials to him. She immediately passed it on to a young African student who was struggling to secure an education. That is the kind of people Judith and her father have been, the kind of people needed anywhere in the world. Zimbabwe should consider itself fortunate have both of them.

It is important to remember that this study is not about the inner personality of these two great liberals, but an attempt to present their perceptions of society and the principles that motivated them to seek its transformation for the benefit of all. It is imperative that African nations come together in an effort to find new solutions to old problems by following their examples. The problems are many and complex: rising population, economic decay, political disintegration, to name only a few. These problems can be resolved, not by using old methods, but by designing new strategies to suit conditions of the times. What must remain constant is the ability of Kenya and Zimbabwe to remain loyal to democratic principles. For Kenya and Zimbabwe this course of action demands new commitment and dedication so that they do not dishonor the efforts of two men whose roles left legacies that have placed both countries on the road to democracy and development.

Map 1
Kenya

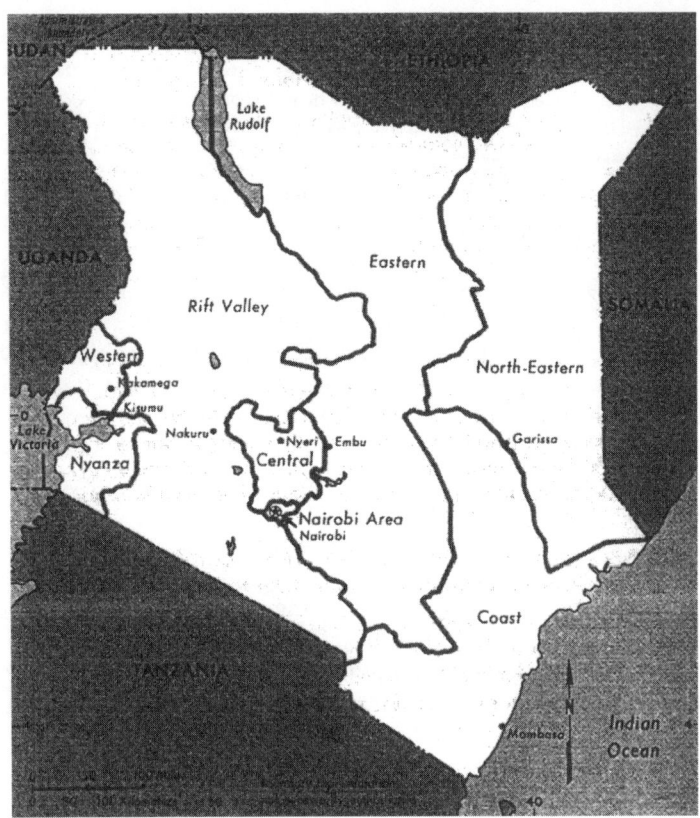

Some Facts About Kenya of Blundell's Time, 1940

Date of colonization	June 1895
Colonizing nation	Britain
Area	224,960 square miles
Population	7.6 million Africans
	260,000 whites
Annual population growth rate	3.1%
Literacy	19.1% Africans
	78.2% whites
Annual per capita income	$47.00 Africans
	$2,900 whites
Total amount spent on education	$200,110 for Africans
	$6.3 million for whites
Leading towns	Nairobi (capital), Mombassa (chief port), Kisumu, Nakuru
Leading industries	Agriculture (maize, cotton, coffee, cassava, dairy, meat, skins, hides), mining (copper, silver)
Form of government	Legislative Council of 20 whites
Leader of the government	Henry Monck-Mason Moore (1940–44)

Map 2
Zimbabwe

Some Facts About Zimbabwe of Todd's Time, 1940

Date of colonization	September 1890
Colonizing nation	Great Britain
Area	150,333 square miles
Population	3.1 million Africans 123,000 whites
Annual population growth rate	2.7%
Literacy	21.0% Africans 79.0% whites
Annual per capita income	$48.00 Africans $3,000 whites
Total amount spent on education	$204,212 for Africans $7.3 million for whites
Leading towns	Salisbury (Harare), Bulawayo, Mutare, Gweru, Kadoma
Leading industries	Mining, agriculture
Form of government	Parliament of 30 white members elected by white voters
Leader of the government	Godfrey Huggins (1933–52)

1
The Political History of Kenya

> We consider that we are pledged by undertakings given in the past to reserve the highlands of East Africa exclusively for European settlers, and that we do not intend to depart from that pledge.
> —Winston Churchill in 1922
> [cited in Grigg, 1956]

The arrival of Michael Blundell in Kenya in 1925 and of Garfield Todd in Zimbabwe in 1934 marked the beginning of the political transformation of those two British colonies in ways that had not been envisaged. Blundell was born and raised in London during a period of history in Britain that witnessed great liberal traditions coming out of the Industrial Revolution. Todd was born in New Zealand when similar developments were taking place. Because of their unique roles in the development of the two British colonies, these two men occupy a special place in their histories. Their adoption of liberal ideas came out of the thinking that the interests of society were best served by the action of those in position of power and influence to serve the needs of the people. The British governments that came out of this period recognized the imperative of the Industrial Revolution as a factor of human development. A central tenet of the thinking of the British governments of that time was that governments are instituted for a simple purpose: to serve the needs of the people. They saw the Industrial Revolution as an opportunity to bring out the best in human potential and combine it with technology for the benefit of society.

In discussing the roles of Blundell and Todd in Kenya and Zimbabwe, this book attempts to furnish answers to the following questions: Who were Michael Blundell and Garfield Todd? What kinds of background did they have? How did they come to hold the views that they did about Kenya and Zimbabwe? How did their fellow settlers react to these ideas? What kinds of relationships did they have with Africans as a result of holding these ideas? How did these ideas influence the future of these two countries? Who are some of the people with whom they worked? Exactly what problems did they encounter which they did not cause but which they had to respond to?

In attempting to answer these questions the book will show that over an extended period of time these two men gained new experiences that they needed in order to play their roles well. In doing so they also demonstrated that they were human beings whose knowledge of the issues they addressed was limited by a combination of forces beyond their control. But in their efforts to surmount these problems, they demonstrated beyond a doubt that they were equal to the task. This book, therefore, is a story of two individuals who had a vision of both themselves and of Kenya and Zimbabwe that compelled them to do nothing less than they felt called upon to do to make a difference in the lives of all people. One must remember that both Kenya and Zimbabwe had some things in common, and that they were also different. Both were colonies of Britain. Both had ideal climatic conditions that attracted British settlers. Settlers in both countries hoped to utilize cheap labor which Africans provided to elevate their standard of living to new and unprecedented level of comfort.

The central highlands in Kenya and the eastern highlands in Zimbabwe offered the settlers an ideal social and physical environment that gave them a life of ease. Both countries had a tremendous agricultural potential that settlers believed would provide them a better opportunity than they had in Britain. But the two countries were also different. Kenya had a number of African ethnic groups that, though similar in some respects, were also different. The Kikuyu, the Embu, the Luo, and the Masai exhibited cultural traditions that made them unique. While they were not hostile to each other, each group had distinctive cultural features that made them different. In Zimbabwe, the Ndebele and the Shona were hostile to each other, a fact that the British exploited to entrench the principle of divide and rule. In trying to function under these varying conditions, beginning in 1946, Blundell and Todd walked political tightropes. In the end they succeeded in accomplishing their missions during a period of political turbulence following the conclusion of the war in 1945.

THE INFLUENCE OF THE BERLIN CONFERENCE

From the time that James Bruce of Scotland explored the interior of Ethiopia and the Nile River in 1770 to the time that the Berlin Conference was convened in December 1884, European interest in Africa was based on the perceptions that quasi-researchers had generated beginning in the Enlightenment. Since the days of the Portuguese exploration of the sea routes to India, Bruce's expedition represented a new European adventure into the interior of Africa in an effort to scale the vast resources of the continent for possible extraction and shipment to Europe. In 1852 a number of European explorers ventured into the interior of Africa, returning with valuable information that was later utilized to facilitate colonization of the continent. Among these explorers were Richard Burton and John Hanning Speke, two British men who traveled across the eastern part of Africa and discovered Lake Victoria.

Among the more famous British explorers was David Livingstone, who went to Africa in 1841 in the service of the London Missionary Society. This organization had sent Robert Moffat to Africa in 1825. In 1866 Livingstone began an expedition to find the source of the Nile. This mysterious and sacred river also represented the mysteries of the African continent itself. In his endeavor to discover its source, Livingstone was, in essence, trying to discover the Africans themselves. But it was his discovery in 1855 of the Victoria Falls and the Zambezi River between the present Zambia and Zimbabwe that made him famous. However, Livingstone, as well as other European explorers, was never quite able to discover the true nature of the African people. This fact played a critical role in shaping relationships between Africans and the colonial adventurers. All European explorers and colonial entrepreneurs could do was to speculate on the character of the Africans, just as S. T. von Soemmering (a German anatomist) and Charles White (a British doctor) had done during the Enlightenment.

The Europeans who have written the history of 19th-century Africa have portrayed Livingstone as a dedicated Christian missionary who had a vision of the continent, its people, and their lives and culture radically and permanently transformed by Christianity and European cultural values. But these writers seem to neglect a very important aspect of Livingstone's work in Africa: his impact on Africans was not in things religious, but in things material. With the advent of the Industrial Revolution the message that Livingstone and other Western missionaries tried to persuade Africans to accept, that of conversion to Christianity, was lost in the confusion and conflict that emerged between their pursuit of new religious values for Africans and the search for new material comforts for Europeans. The Christian message had become a victim of the search for material wealth and commercial entrepreneurial adventure that even the most enthusiastic missionaries found difficult to resist, including Livingstone himself.

This reality is exactly why, speaking at Oxford University in October 1864, Livingstone went to great lengths to explain why he and other Western missionaries were reversing their objective from seeking the conversion of Africans to Christianity to ensuring the success of commercial enterprise. Livingstone went on to argue:

Sending the Gospel to the heathens of Africa must include more than is implied in the usual practice of a missionary, namely, a man going about with a Bible under his arms. The promotion of commerce ought to be specially attended to as this, more than anything else, makes the heathen tribes depend on commercial intercourse among civilized nations. I go back to Africa to open a new path to commerce, do you carry on the work I have started?[1]

There is no question that Livingstone and other missionaries had failed to understand Africans, and that their response to their Christian message had been negative, not because they did not see its meaning to their lives, but because it was camouflaged in efforts to exploit them and the resources of the continent for the benefit of Europeans. For Livingstone and his missionary colleagues to expect Africans to understand that the white man himself was a victim of his own conflicting values was unrealistic. Besides, the enthusiasm among Western missionaries for material comfort was not limited to this group of Europeans, it was shared by colonial enthusiasts who now began to believe that Africa must be colonized in order to bring its vast resources under their control because Europe lacked such materials.

The change of objectives by Western missionaries from the pursuit of establishing Christianity in Africa to that of promoting Western commercial enterprise was a development that had a profoundly negative influence on Africans' response to the message the missionaries were trying to have them accept. This is why, in 1882, Robert Moffat expressed total disappointment with his failure to persuade the Africans to accept Christianity, saying "a few individuals may have been influenced for good, but there is no organic result. There does not seem to be two people of the tribe who recognize each other as Christians. There is no indication that life in the tribe is in any way touched by the Gospel."[2]

Moffat's reaction suggests the conclusion that in all their enthusiasm to promote Christianity as a new way of life in Africa, Western missionaries lost touch with the real cause of African negative response: contradiction in their behavior and that of the colonial entrepreneurs. The only way the Africans could be receptive to the missionary message was for the white man himself to resolve this conflict. One can see that while

Africans were subjected to pressure to accept the values of the white man, their ability to retain their distinct character placed the white man in a difficult situation. This ability would prove crucial to the survival of Africans and to retaining their cultural identity when the colonial systems were fully established.

By 1875 interest among nations of Europe in various aspects of Africa was slowly turning into intense competition, creating an environment of conflict. Otto von Bismarck, the disciple of von Soemmering and the charismatic chancellor of Germany following the Franco-Prussian war of 1870–71, realizing that Germany was not ready for a major conflict over Africa, decided to play his political cards carefully. He persuaded other European nations to go slow in their desire to establish spheres of influence and control in Africa in order to secure the materials they needed to improve the standard of living in Europe. Bismarck concluded that a major conflict in Europe over materials in Africa would undermine the very purpose of the Industrial Revolution and the objectives they were trying to accomplish toward the "Dark Continent." Bismarck then concluded that there was a better course of action to follow relative to the need among European nations to have total access to the materials of Africa.

In 1884, utilizing his newly acquired influence and power following the defeat of France in the Franco-Prussian war, Bismarck convened a conference at Berlin to be attended by major European nations that were interested in launching a colonial adventure in Africa. By that time the knowledge among European nations that they needed colonies as a source of raw materials and as markets for their products accentuated the need for the conference to avoid conflict in Africa. The need for such a conference was also enhanced in 1875 when British Prime Minister Benjamin Disraeli ensured British control of the Suez Canal, which was completed in 1869, by buying shares from the khedive of Egypt.[3] That Bismarck and other leaders of European nations saw this action as threatening larger European security and economic interests emphasized the importance and urgency of holding such a conference so that they would coordinate their activities in Africa.

The success of the Berlin Conference is seen in two specific decisions. The first was that its participants recognized that the success of the colonizing enterprise lay in a collective action in accordance with the principles they agreed upon in order to avoid conflict. The second decision is that they established what they called spheres of influence demarcated on the map of Africa and created boundary lines that paid no regard to ethnic and tribal groupings of the Africans.[4] The participants of the Berlin Conference concluded that seeking to sustain their colonial and commercial interests was a far more important objective than trying to preserve the ethnic and cultural integrity of the Africans. They hoped that in this action they would control them far more effectively than in any other way.

To give further effect to their intent, European nations tried to manipulate the African chiefs into having them sign treaties whose terms and implications they thought the Africans did not fully understand.[5] But to their surprise the colonial governments soon discovered that Africans could not so easily be misled. However, the action of European nations to control Africans shows their determination to convert the resources of the continent into a means of sustaining their own political and socioeconomic purposes and needs in Europe. The success of the Berlin Conference could also be measured in terms of how European nations managed to subdue Africans and convert them into an instrument of fulfilling their grand plan of extending the notion that in order for them to survive, Africans had to function under new conditions created by European nations under colonial settings. In this basic element of colonial thought process, the perils of colonial adventure had now been put in place. That European nations used raw and brutal force to subject Africans to colonial rule would later play a critical role after 1945 when they sought to liberate themselves from colonial domination.

The conclusion of the Berlin Conference in February 1885 signaled the beginning of a new and decisive phase in European adventure to colonize Africa in order to control its resources. The machinery of that control was now in place. After narrowly averting conflict among themselves over colonial possessions in Africa, European nations now began in earnest the process of colonization. It was open season for them and anything that moved was fair game. While this phase represented the best of times for European nations, it ushered in the worst of times for Africans. The resources of the continent and the Africans themselves were now at the mercy of the European fortune hunters. For them the season of hope was here, but for Africans it was a season of despair. While the colonial entrepreneurs were going directly to an economic heaven, Africans were forced to march the other way. Their future, mired in the dark shadows of colonial exploitation, could only be salvaged by their own ability to utilize the strength of their willpower and the concept of self.

In their determination to bring Africans under colonial control, European entrepreneurs were as callous as they were brutal in their treatment of them. This is what led Kenneth Knorr to the conclusion that European colonial governments systematically sought to reduce Africans to a position where they were forced to become "raw material to be employed in the service of the white man. The Africans were not allowed to decide for themselves because they were considered incapable of doing so. It was therefore decided for them, to serve the white men as their masters."[6] In this basic colonial philosophy the conclusions reached by von Soemmering and White now found an appropriate form of application as Africans were being forced to become an instrument with which European colonial masters sought to fulfill their own grand objectives.

The principal architect of the new era of colonization of Africa was none another than Cecil John Rhodes, the faithful and devoted disciple of the emotional Wynwood Read, a principal character in the colonization of Africa. On arriving in South Africa in 1870, Rhodes quickly sought to make his way to the top rung of the political ladder by seeking to control the African mind in ways that had not been done in the past. He played a psychological game that he had learned to perfect as soon as he arrived in South Africa. In the process he formulated a racial philosophy that he used as a basis of his action. Its principal component was that because Africans were uncivilized and possessed less intellectual potential than Europeans, they must be afforded a treatment less than that given to the whites.

In 1891 Rhodes was quite candid in arguing to support the opinion expressed by the von Soemmering-White school of thought that as adults Africans had the minds of children. Rhodes was quickly recognized as the new spokesman of the knowledge that Europeans claimed to have about the African mind and was immediately elevated to new political pronouncements when he said in that year, "I say that the Natives are like children. They are just merging from barbarism. They have human mind, but they are like children, and we ought to do something to develop that mind."[7]

Indeed, in 1896, speaking in Parliament in Cape Town during a debate on the position of Africans in colonial society, Rhodes received an extended standing ovation when he argued that the only function Africans could fulfill was to accept the argument that because they possessed less intellectual ability they must serve as servants of the whites. Fully conscious of the impact of what he was about to say, Rhodes deliberately chose his words as he went on to argue, "We have got to treat the Natives where they are, in a state of barbarism. We are to be lords over them. We will continue to treat them as a subject race as long as they continue to be in the state of barbarism."[8] With Rhodes's pronouncements the mission among European colonial entrepreneurs to control the African mind now acquired new powerful dimensions. That Rhodes, like his mentor Wynwood Read, was never quite able to comprehend the character of the African mind and the richness of the African culture, cast a long shadow of doubt about his own mind.[9]

It is, indeed, a tragic fact that Rhodes never came to know the mind of George Washington Carver, a major 20th-century American black scientist who invented more than 300 products from peanuts. He never came to know the mind of the South African Albert Luthuli, who was awarded the Nobel Peace Prize in 1960, raising the conscience of the international community about the slavery of apartheid in South Africa; nor that of Stanlake Samkange of Zimbabwe, a distinguished historian, freelance journalist, and social critic who, through his works, posed fundamental questions about the oppression of colonial conditions in Africa. But that reality is beside the point, the point is that Rhodes used his devotion to the views of his mentor to place Africans at a level never known before.

THE COLONIZATION OF KENYA

These are the factors that motivated Europeans to found colonies in Africa. In October 1885 Britain and Germany signed an agreement in London that defined British and German spheres of influence in Africa in accordance with provisions of the Berlin Conference. The two nations agreed that Germany would occupy Tanganyika and Britain would occupy the territory that later became known as Kenya. The formation in 1877 of the British East Africa Association under the leadership of William Mackinnon now began to play a decisive role in the colonization of Kenya. In September 1888 Mackinnon received a Royal Charter from Queen Victoria enabling him to convert the association into the Imperial British East Africa Company.[10]

In October 1888 Queen Victoria granted Rhodes a Royal Charter giving him power to colonize Zimbabwe. On June 15, 1895, Mackinnon declared Kenya a British protectorate and appointed Arthur Charles Hardinge first commissioner to govern the territory that was now beginning to expand a network of the British empire in Africa. The British government immediately approved a loan of 3 million pounds sterling for the construction of a railway line running from the coastal town of Mombasa to Lake Victoria. When the section of the railway line from Kenya to Uganda was completed in 1901, the imperial administration began to plan moving the administrative headquarters from Mombasa to Nairobi in 1907, the year that Blundell was born. Hardinge served as commissioner until 1900 when he was succeeded by Charles Eliot. In 1902 the present boundaries between Uganda and Kenya were redrawn.

In deciding to move the administrative headquarters from Mombasa to Nairobi the British Colonial Office knew that the central highlands offered ideal climatic conditions far healthier than the humid weather conditions in Mombasa. Even before the move from Mombasa was made, Eliot had made a strong appeal for more British settlers to protect the railway and to begin developing the colony for their own benefit. In moving the administrative headquarters from Mombasa to Nairobi the British settlers and the British East Africa Company that offered them security created a serious conflict situation with Africans. When this conflict finally broke open 50 years later it permanently changed the political landscape and marked the beginning of the end of the British colonial rule of Kenya. Robert L. Tignor concludes that the central highlands were the home of three powerful and fiercely proud ethnic groups: the Kamba, the Kikuyu, and the Masai.[11] From the very beginning of colonization, these three groups bitterly resented the manner in which the British usurped their land. Later one of their leaders, Jomo Kenyatta, would lead a successful campaign to get rid of the British colonial system. Michael Blundell would feature prominently in seeking an equitable solution to this conflict. But in the end, he resigned himself to the fact that Africans would no longer be able to compromise on the occupation of their country.

It is clear that both the settlers and the members of the colonial administration knew the implications of their actions on their relationships with Africans. In 1922, wishing to convince Africans that settlers were in Kenya to stay, Winston Churchill, then colonial secretary, affirmed the British determination to preserve the central highlands for exclusive occupation by the settlers. With a sense of self-assuredness and the rightness of the British cause in Kenya, Churchill stated the policy of his government toward the central highlands, saying

We consider that were are pledged by undertakings given in the past to reserve the highlands of East Africa exclusively for European settlers, and we do not intend to depart from that pledge. We shall apply broadly and comprehensively Mr. Rhodes's principles of equal rights for all civilized men.[12] We consider that the interests of British settlers and Native population alike require that all future immigration of Indians should be strictly regulated.[13]

Once a decision was made in 1907 to move the administrative headquarters from Mombasa to Nairobi, tremendous effort was made to attract new settlers from Britain. In that same year, a legislative council was established in order to provide appropriate political expression for settlers.[14] There, from 1948 to 1962, Blundell would play his role well in shaping the future of Kenya. In 1904 Eliot introduced a system of hut and poll tax for Africans without making representations in the legislative council. The decision to bar Africans from political participation was based on two fundamental considerations that are characteristically European and colonial behavior. The first consideration was that settlers believed Africans would not understand operational and functional principles of Western democracy. This consideration was based on the belief that Africans were not sufficiently educated to understand European political processes.

The second consideration presented a far more serious problem for settlers. This was the question of the kind of relationships that they should have with both the Kikuyu and the Masai. The appointment of Donald Stewart in 1904 to succeed Charles Eliot as commissioner was made primarily because he had served with distinction as a soldier in the Afghanstan war from 1879 to 1880 and in the Transvaal from 1884 to 1885. The settlers were, however, uncomfortable with the fact that they had violated the grazing lands of the Masai and wanted Stewart to move them elsewhere by force or persuasion. Upon his arrival to assume his duties as the new commissioner, Stewart was reported to have adopted a hard-line attitude toward the Masai, expressing his view that the colony could not be governed effectively until Africans "had been knocked into shape."[15] This is the language settlers wanted to hear, but it would cost Stewart dearly later.

Before Eliot retired he was trying to convince the British Colonial Office to understand that the task of governing the colony from Mombasa was compounded by distance and the dual role that the commissioner had to play in being both chief administrator and commander in chief of the East Africa Protectorate. He suggested a separation of the positions to improve efficiency. This separation meant that Stewart was named commissioner to administer the colony. This decision allowed sufficient time to seek solution to the problem of the Masai's continuing to occupy the central highlands. Stewart had been given a clear understanding by both the Colonial Office and the settlers that the Masai must move from the highlands. The Colonial Office instructed him to study the nature of relationships that was likely to emerge between the settlers and the Masai and report it to the Colonial Office so that some decision could be made and appropriate action taken beyond the removal of the Masai from the highlands.

As soon as he arrived in Kenya in July 1904 to assume his duties as commissioner, Stewart began this task.[16] His study led him to the conclusion that efforts had been made in 1903 to move the Masai from the central highlands to reserved areas in the Rift Valley to allow new settlers to move in. Stewart decided to act quickly. On August 2, 1904, he sent a telegram from Mombasa to the Colonial Office stating that he had decided to go immediately to Nairobi to take decisive action of removing the Masai from the highlands to make room for settlers. The Colonial Office responded immediately to warn Stewart of irrational action that was likely to aggravate relationships between the settlers and the Masai. On August 16 Stewart dispatched yet another telegram to the Colonial Office to say that he had concluded an agreement with some Masai that meant that they would move from the highlands to Laikipia in the Rift Valley. The remainder would move to Ngong along the Mbagathi River.

Needless to say, Stewart's telegrams took the Colonial Office by total surprise. Since 1895, when Arthur Charles Hardinge was appointed first commissioner, the question of relationships between the Africans and the settlers had been a very difficult issue to handle. Neither Hardinge nor his successor, Charles Eliot, was able to find a quick solution to the problem of land occupation because Africans refused to give up their land for occupation by British settlers. How could Stewart, a professional soldier who saw solutions to problems of human relationships only in military terms, suddenly achieve diplomatic breakthrough in an area that his predecessors had no viable solution?

The Colonial Office concluded that a further review of the so-called agreement between Stewart and the Masai was necessary. Officials at the Colonial Office also concluded that Stewart had employed unorthodox strategies to compel the Masai to agree to move from the highlands to Laikipia and that the use of these methods would later cause problems in the relationships between the two sides. Because of the element of acquiescence on the part of the Masai, the Colonial Office decided to allow Stewart to implement the agreement but it was not pleased with the method he used to reach it. However, because Stewart conducted the business of the colony in military fashion, rather than in political ways, the Colonial Office removed him from office in 1905 and replaced him with James Hayes Sadler, who served until 1909. As soon as the Masai moved from the highlands they expressed their feeling that they had been forced to accept terms of an agreement under the threat of military force. In that manner, relationships between the Africans and the settlers in general were marred beyond repair. This means that at the beginning of the colonial rule Africans learned a hard lesson about the behavior of the colonial government: it was quick to utilize military force to solve social problems. Beginning in October 1952 when Africans adopted the same strategy, major conflict became inevitable.

Although the Colonial Office doubted the authenticity of a clause attributed to the Masai in the so-called agreement, stating "We would ask that the settlement now arrived at shall be enduring as long as the Masai as a race shall exist, and that Europeans or other settlers shall not be allowed to take up land in the settlement,"[17] the Colonial Office permitted Sadler to honor the so-called agreement. Stewart argued that the Masai were pleased with the agreement because they considered the land in the Laikipia area essential to their survival and the practice of their culture. In a memo dated September 5, 1904, addressed to the Colonial Office Stewart assured his superiors about the legitimacy of the agreement he had concluded with the Masai: "The Laikipia lands are well known to the Masai and will suit them well. They are a good way from the railway and not tempting to the present settler. In the future it is quite possible that when the Masai have grazed down the grass and got it used, need will be felt on their lands."[18]

Although Stewart had managed to have the Masai move from the central highlands without violent reaction, officials at the Colonial Office did not place total confidence in his ability to ensure long-term interests of settlers in Kenya. A series of unfortunate events further convinced the Colonial Office that Stewart was more prone to resort to military action to solve social problems. A case in point: in September 1905 Stewart received a report stating that some Kavirondo tribesmen[19] had been murdered by the members of the Kisii tribe. The two tribes had come into contact in a way that was triggered by the move that the Masai made. What actually happened was that by having the Masai move from the highlands Stewart made no provision for the allocation of more land elsewhere to enable different tribes to live in freedom from interference from each other. That the Kavirondo and the Kisii were compelled by conditions that Stewart had created to share land caused friction and conflict. Within a year there was less land to graze their livestock and grow food. Stewart was unable to see the conflict between the Kavirondo and the Kisii as an inevitable consequence his racial policy.

On September 12, 1905, Stewart dispatched a patrol of 100 troops and 50 policemen from Fort Kericho. In a military campaign that lasted a month the patrol captured 3,000 herd of cattle and killed over 100 members of the Kisii tribe.[20] He had forgotten that the killing of Africans by the colonial military force was prohibited by the Berlin Conference except in cases of self-defense. Although this prohibition was never fully observed, it was, nevertheless, expected of all colonial governments. Stewart had hoped that this incident would compel Africans all over Kenya to respect the colonial government and its laws. Further, Stewart used the Kisii massacre to dictate conditions of discussion with other tribes. For example, in August 1905 he held meetings with chiefs of the Iraini tribe after he had threatened them with military action if they did not agree to the conditions he had outlined. The Colonial Office did not take this action kindly.

In January 1905 A. G. Anderson, one of the leaders of the settler community in Mombasa, wrote a long letter to the Colonial Office to complain about the inadequate system of administration under Stewart. Anderson compared the administrative styles of Eliot and Stewart and concluded that Stewart had nothing to qualify him for the position of administrator other than his tendency to use military force to seek solutions to social problems. E. S. Grogan, a romantic figure who had spent a lot of time walking through a large part of East Africa, wrote an open letter to *The Times* to criticize Stewart's economic policy. In May 1905 Stewart sent a report of the land commission in which he said that he did not have sufficient time to make good recommendations. These were the conditions that compelled the Colonial Office to reach the conclusion that Stewart must be replaced by James Hayes Sadler, who assumed office on December 12, 1905. Stewart's term of office had at best been controversial. He was unable to come to terms with Africans in a way that would demonstrate lasting peace.

Sadler had impressive credentials. A lieutenant colonel, he distinguished himself as a soldier. In 1898 he served as British consul-general in British Somalia. In 1901 he served as commissioner in Uganda. Now, in 1905 he was appointed commissioner for Kenya. In that year the legislative council was introduced. In 1906 the position of commissioner was eliminated and that of governor, directly responsible, like the commissioner, to the Colonial Office, was created and Sadler was the first person to serve as governor. G. H. Mungeam concludes that Sadler "was very industrious, kind, and hospitable, but weak and vacillating, and quite unable to cope with unruly settlers"[21] and with the increasing discontent among the Africans. From the beginning of his term of office as commissioner and as governor, Sadler found the question of relationships with the Africans difficult to handle. He was frustrated by the Colonial Office's inability to formulate a policy that would work.

The change of status from protectorate to colony and from the position of commissioner to governor coincided with the replacement of the Conservative government led by Arthur James Balfour[22] by the Liberal government led by three great liberals, Henry Campbell-Bannerman, Herbert Henry Asquith, and David Lloyd George. As soon as he was defeated Balfour resigned on December 4, 1905, and on December 5 Campbell-Bannerman, the leader of the Liberal Party, became the new prime minister. These three men helped establish liberal traditions whose influenced extended far beyond the borders of Britain. Their approach to national problems was based on a simple fundamental tenet: applying the principle of responding to the needs of the people. Michael Blundell and Garfield Todd were born during this time. By the time they were adults they had both embraced liberals ideas that they could not abandon even under very difficult conditions when they became involved in politics.

The Liberal Party under Campbell-Bannerman had an impressive agenda based on an effective program to respond to the needs of the people in both Britain and in the British colonial empire. There is no question that the Liberal Party was on its way to establish great traditions that future generations of politicians would utilize in carrying out their own functions. Campbell-Bannerman had established a reputation of a leader who was sensitive to the needs of the people in every way. The British people had learned to trust him as a leader who built his entire program on the basis of seeking to serve their needs. When he died suddenly in 1908 Campbell-Bannerman was succeeded by Herbert Henry Asquith, who carried the liberal traditions to new levels of commitment to meeting the needs of the people.

The change of government from the Conservative to Liberal, and from the administration of Arthur Balfour to that of Campbell-Bannerman, brought corresponding change in policy both in Britain and its colonial empire in Africa. In 1906 the administration of Campbell-Bannerman eliminated the office of commissioner in Kenya and created that of governor. The purpose of the change was to bring the administrative structure of the colonial government into line with expected standards of conduct which were being applied in Britain. The governor was also expected to carry out his duties in accordance with principles that the Liberal Party had outlined as its modus operandi. Sadler was therefore the only man to hold both the office of commissioner and governor. The new colonial secretary, the Ninth Earl of Elgin, and his undersecretary, Winston Churchill, were demanding men.

Bethwell A. Ogot concludes that the creation of the legislative council meant that Sadler would no longer rule by decree as his predecessors and he himself had done previously as commissioners from 1895 to 1906.[23] Although the office of governor brought with it more power than the office of commissioner, Sadler was made to understand some basic principles of carrying out his duties in relation to the responsibilities of the legislative council. He would no longer be arbitrary in his action, but would seek consensus and consultation with all levels of government. These changes were introduced in order to improve the efficiency of the system of communication between the colonial government and the Colonial Office in London. They were also meant to improve the administrative system of the colonial government itself. Members of the Asquith administration also believed that these changes would also help to resolve problems that had existed between Stewart and officials at the Colonial Office about the development and implementation of policy.

It is important to note that although Asquith believed that these changes were intended to improve efficiency in the system of administration, colonial systems had never been intended to become humanitarian organizations because profit, both political and economic, was always its primary intent, not to serve the interests of Africans. Colonial systems are never designed to serve the interests of the colonized. From 1906 to 1909, when Sadler served as governor, efficiency in the implementation of colonial policy "resulted in the appreciation of African resources. Large numbers of livestock looted were partly given to collaborators, partly sold to the white settlers and the majority kept for government purposes."[24] This form of exploitation is quite common under colonial conditions anywhere. Given the liberal traditions of the Asquith administration, it is doubtful that Asquith himself would have allowed this form of colonial abuse to occur in the form that it did. While this kind of colonial activity was going on Africans were also expected to pay various forms of tax. For example, the hut tax was introduced in 1903 when Charles Eliot was commissioner.[25]

For the rest of his term of office Sadler and Elgin had serious differences about policy. In order to provide some continuity the Colonial Office under the Asquith administration decided that the policy introduced by the Balfour administration should be continued with some modification. Robert L. Tignor concludes that a dominant characteristic that was central to colonial policy was a form of racism which all organizations of European origin embraced in Africa. These organizations included members of the colonial administration, Christian organizations, and settler organizations.[26] All practiced one form of racism or another.

The missionary organizations, however, later recognized the harm that racism was inflicting on their ability to provide effective service to their people and so changed it. But the damage had been done, it would require tremendous effort to turn things around. While the Liberal Party appeared to espouse policies that seemed to show a more humane approach to colonial enterprise, in reality these policies were just as oppressive in their application as those defined and implemented by the Conservative government that it had replaced in 1905. However, it is important to recognize also that individuals approached issues relative to colonial systems differently from the approach made by officials.

Throughout the colonial period officials built military and police forces that turned the colonies in Africa into systems of a police state where oppression and brutality were their hallmark of behavior. The gun became the notorious symbol of power and brute force, disregarding the welfare of the people in the pursuit of colonial policy of exploitation. The development of human capacity to think and apply reason to resolve conflict gave way to military and police action that showed no respect for the position of Africans. Cast in an environment of cultural differences, the relationships between the colonial officials and the Africans were structured in the context of superior-inferior human beings whose roles and functions in the colonial society were determined by colonial masters in such a way that their interests were sustained at the expense of those of the Africans.

When Percy Girourd, the only governor of Kenya who was a French Canadian born in Montreal, succeeded Sadler in 1909, colonial brutality, not just British, but all over Africa, had been institutionalized in two ways. The first way was the enactment of legislation that placed unbearable burden on Africans. Examples of such legislation included hut tax, livestock tax, poll tax, pass regulations and curfews, and vagrancy laws. These were imposed to ensure more effective control of the Africans. Although the British ended slavery in 1807, colonial policy revived practices that were similar to conditions of slavery. All the colonial governments needed to do was to pass laws that reminded Africans that conditions of slavery were, indeed, back in powerful dimensions. The second way in which colonial brutality was instituted by 1909 was resorting to military and police action to force Africans to comply with the requirements of the colonial authorities. In Kenya the introduction of the Masters and Servants Ordinance in 1910 was intended to condition Africans to accept the colonial policy that they were inferior to settlers.

In the European military and technological superiority lay the whole colonial system of political operations. Whenever Africans questioned the political action of the colonial governments, those colonial governments would feel threatened and were quick to resort to military and police action to resolve social problems. But after the Second World War, the colonial governments began to realize that resorting to military action to suppress the Africans no longer worked. All over Africa Africans were rising to the occasion to challenge even the powerful military forces such as the Portuguese in Angola and Mozambique and the forces of apartheid in South Africa. Once Africans were able to neutralize the military power of the colonial governments, they succeeded in forcing them to recognize their political aspirations. Tignor concludes that in Kenya from 1900 to 1920, during a period so-called pacification, the colonial government routinely employed military and police violence to contain Africans to colonial rule.[27]

During this period three ethnic groups—the Kamba, the Kikuyu, and the Masai—protested colonial policy of maintaining them in reserved areas that were far too small to meet their needs. From time to time there were disturbances each time the colonial government ignored or belittled their request to address the issue of land distribution to respond to their needs. Tignor suggests that in response the colonial government was quick to resort to military action to silence the Africans. Tignor adds, "During the anti-colonial disturbances the British sent a contingent of troops and units of the police"[28] to ensure that the Africans were kept in their place. Once the colonial government used military force to silence Africans, it quickly turned its attention to formulate new policies that were even more oppressive. In 1919 the policy of *kipande*[29] was introduced under these conditions.

The appointment of Henry Belfield to succeed Girourd in 1912 coincided with the enactment of the Native Authority Ordinance, introduced not to give Africans a measure of authority in running their own areas, but to give the colonial government more power to regulate and control African activity in all its forms, especially social, economic, and political. In the social and cultural areas of Africans' life, that control was exercised with impunity. New regulations were imposed on marriage practices and other customs so sacred to African life. The limited role that African chiefs played in political activity was now prohibited and their role limited to few occasions in which traditional ceremony was observed.

Under the British colonial policy of indirect rule the chiefs were asked to require their people to fulfill any function the colonial government asked. This included their participation in forced labor camps that were created throughout British colonial Africa including Zimbabwe. In 1943 the author's father was one of those Africans who participated in forced labor camp projects. When Donald Stewart compelled the Masai to move from the central highlands, livestock disease inflicted severe losses when they moved to areas of low altitude. Those losses in turn ruined the economic survival of the Masai.[30] The outbreak of the First World War in July 1914 added unbearable economic difficulties to Africans as the colonial officials tried to do everything in their power to support the Allies in their war efforts. Austerity programs were introduced in a manner that hurt the Africans more than the settlers.

During the five years that Belfield served as governor from 1912 to 1917, the British colonial attitude and policy hardened in order to control the rising consciousness of Africans caused by their increasing understanding that the colonial government was there to exploit them. In 1919, during the acting governorship of Charles Bowring,[31] when the war had just ended, the colonial government made forced labor part of its institutional operation. In that year the colonial government introduced Labor Circular Number One, making the colonial government itself "acquire an unsavory reputation among humanitarian and religious bodies in Great Britain for its oppression and exploitation of the African population."[32]

In 1913 Belfield was influential in the action this administration took in forcing Africans in areas of agricultural production to increase their production by 75 percent so as to enable it to meet its export quota. Belfield hoped that the increase would also help meet railway operation costs, which were rising rapidly because of the political activity that was creating difficult economic conditions. In 1915 Belfield enacted the Crown Lands ordinance to establish a free market for settlers whose land lease he extended from 9 years to 99 years. The introduction of this latest policy meant that the burden of sustaining the economy was placed on the backs of the African farmers who were struggling for economic survival under difficult conditions. In 1919 Belfield implemented provisions of the Lands Ordinance of 1915 to make 12,000 square kilometers available to new settlers.[33] Also in 1915 the Native Registration Ordinance was passed to provide registration certificates for all Africans employed outside the African areas. Four years later the system of *kipande* came out of provisions of this ordinance. In 1917 Bowring had hoped that these measures would enhance the economy. But the drought of that year derailed that plan.

The responsibility of trying to revive the economy rested on the shoulders of Bowring's successor, Edward Northey, who served from 1919 to 1922. In June 1920 the protectorate became a Crown Colony renamed Kenya.[34] This change in the colonial status of Kenya also gave Northey an enhanced position that would enable him to deal with issues of relationships between his administration and the Colonial Office in London. As governor of a Crown Colony, rather than of a protectorate, the Colonial Office followed different procedures that demanded more respect of the views of the man who held the office of governor. However, in many ways Northey was like Donald Stewart: he sought solutions to social problems by resorting to military action. A major-general, Northey believed that more British settlers must be attracted to Kenya by offering them immediate citizenship.[35] The dissolution of the war council in 1919, which was designed to minimize damage to the economy, meant that other contingent plans must be put in place because the economy was still vulnerable to postwar conditions. Northey therefore developed a new labor policy to maximize production. In 1920 he proposed a system of income tax which was rejected by settlers. He then strengthened the hut and poll tax which the Africans had been paying since it was introduced in 1903. This means that under Northey the burden of sustaining the economy was once more placed on the shoulders of the Africans, a group of people less able to bear it. Such is the character of colonial governments anywhere.

CONFLICT BETWEEN EDWARD NORTHEY AND HARRY THUKU

Relationships between Northey and the Africans took a dramatic turn for the worse in 1921, when Harry Thuku formed the Young Kikuyu Association (YKA). This organization was a sequel to the formation in 1919 of the Kikuyu Association. Following the end of the First World War the Kikuyu, like Africans in other parts of Kenya and the rest of Africa, were faced with a number of difficulties as an outcome of the war. The outbreak of influenza in 1917, widespread famine, and a general lack of confidence in the future combined with a severe drought to cause a major social and economic disaster. Demoralized Africans were faced with additional problems of increased taxes, massive colonial government recruitment of cheap labor for new settlers, and the implementation of the Soldier Settlement Scheme, which was formulated to encourage British war veterans to come and settle in Kenya.[36]

Recognizing the seriousness of the implications of the colonial policy and action on their future, the Kikuyu chiefs formed the Kikuyu Association to protect their land from further alienation by new settlers. Chief Koinange was elected president. Philip Katanja was elected secretary, and Joseph Njonjo was elected to serve as a committee member. At its inception the Kikuyu Association enlisted the support and assistance of Christian missionary organizations because its members argued that its intent was honorable: to create a climate of a better system of communication and understanding between the Kikuyu and the colonial government about the need to preserve the land allocated to the Africans.

To demonstrate its good faith, YKA requested that a survey of farmers in Kiambe be conducted to determine flaws in issuing title deeds to landholders. In making this request YKA had reason to believe that the colonial government was practicing irregularities in order to have land available for new settlers. YKA also made representations to the colonial officials about other grievances such as the continuing practice of forced labor, stringent regulations governing registration of Africans, assignment and collection of tax, and continuing change in land policy to favor new settlers at the expense of Africans. The decision of YKA to enlist the support and assistance of Christian missionary organizations convinced the colonial government that YKA was quite prepared to act and behave appropriately under proper organizational and legal basis.

But the missionary organizations were not forthcoming in giving YKA the support and assistance that it needed to fulfill its objectives. Like oppressed people anywhere struggling to maintain their distinct cultural identity in a hostile environment, the members of the association turned to themselves to sustain their organization. Among the activities the association sought to fulfill were its decision to appear before two British parliamentary committees, the Ormsby-Gore Commission in 1924 and the Hilton-Young Commission of 1929, to present its views on the effect of colonial policy on Africans. Did the Africans really believe that these two commissions, members of which were part and parcel of the British colonial policy in Africa, would offer viable solutions to their problems? However, that was the procedure available to them even though they knew that the two commissions would not address their problems.

Membership of the association, though not exclusively for chiefs, was essentially conservative while it sought better system of communication and understanding between itself and the colonial government. YKA refused to allow the colonial government to exploit it in any way. From 1925 to 1929 the association played a major role in the activities of the Kiamba Local Native Council. In doing so it raised a new level of consciousness among Africans about the need to struggle for development. It converted the local council into an agent which it used to bring about innovation in agriculture, expansion in educational facilities, and opportunity discarding some customs which, in the opinion of its members, were detrimental to the developmental interests of the African people. For example, during the controversy surrounding female circumcision in 1929 the association supported the missionary opposition to this ancient cultural practice.

Although the reputation of YKA was tarnished considerably because its opposition to female circumcision was regarded as supporting promiscuous sexual behavior by women who did not have it, it succeeded in maintaining a high ground on most issues pertaining to the relationships between Africans and the colonial government. In many respects YKA became the spokesman and representative of the Africans in their relationship with the colonial government, especially in matters of allocation and use of land. The impressive performance of Chief Koinange in London in 1930, when he gave evidence before the British parliamentary Joint Select Committee opposing closer union of three British colonies of Uganda, Tanganyika, and Kenya, angered colonial officials, especially Edward Grigg, who was governor at the time and whose major mission was to bring closer union between the three colonies. As a result of Koinange's performance the colonial officials threatened to outlaw YKA. In 1931 the leaders of the association decided to change it name to Kikuyu Loyal Patriots. In 1931 the new organization went before the Land Commission to oppose the policies the colonial government intended to implement.

In forming the Young Kikuyu Association in 1921, Harry Thuku recognized the hard reality that since its formation in 1919 the Kikuyu Association, led by Chief Koinange, refrained from any activity that was considered political in nature. He concluded that this was the reason why the colonial government did not take it seriously. When Thuku was born in 1895 the British East Africa Protectorate was declared. From 1907 to 1911 Thuku attended the Gospel Missionary Society School at Kambui. Unhappy with the kind of education he was receiving, because he believed that the missionaries were teaching Africans to be docile to the policies of the colonial government, Thuku left the school to look for work in Nairobi where he thought that he might come into contact with Africans who may influence the development of his political education.

Thuku was employed as a composer and machinist on the European settler newspaper, *Leader of British East Africa*. There he learned a lot from what he read about politics among settlers. In 1917 Thuku left the *Leader* and was employed as telephone operator and dispatcher at the Treasury. There he made friends with many Kenyans of varied backgrounds and became spokesman for the grievances of returning servicemen from the First World War.[37] In May 1921 attempts were made to raise wages for Africans. As the spokesman for the Africans Thuku argued that the low wages the Africans were receiving made it possible for settlers to enjoy a high standard of living at their expense. He cited the example of what Marcus Garvey, leader of the Universal Negro Improvement Association, was doing in the United States to improve the living conditions of American Negroes.[38] He also encouraged Africans to be more involved in political activity of the country. In 1922 he began to advocate civil disobedience as a political response to colonial policy.

Northey took immediate exception to the aggressive nature of Thuku's leadership of the association. He ordered his arrest for threatening peace and good order. But his arrest led to riots, which caused a number of deaths resulting from clashes with the police. Thuku was imprisoned for nine years. But this crisis also brought Northey's term of office as governor to an end. He was succeeded by Robert Coryndon, who served from 1922 to 1925. While Thuku was in prison at Kismaya from 1922 to 1925 he ran a small school for Indian and Somali children. He was transferred to Lamu, Witu, and Marsabit where he was finally released in 1930, unrepentant and more determined to fight what he considered a colonial injustice.

In August 1932 Thuku was elected president of the Kikuyu Cultural Association and immediately presented a memorandum to the Morris Carter Commission on land distribution, asking for fairness in the distribution of land to settlers and Africans.[39] However, the chairman of the commission, Morris Carter, former chief justice of Tanganyika, was a true Victorian who saw Africans from the perspective of inferior human beings who must emulate the white man's civilization in order to advance themselves. Carter shared Rhodes's views that as long as Africans remained steeped in their primitive culture they denied themselves an opportunity for their own development.

With reference to racial relations in colonial Zimbabwe, Carter advocated strict racial segregation, saying "However desirable it may be that members of the two races should live together side by side with equal rights, we are convinced that in practice for generations to come such a policy is not practicable until the natives have advanced on the path of civilization."[40] Therefore, Thuku might have expended his energy trying to convince a colonial official who had already made up his mind about policy on land distribution. Further, to ask Morris Carter to exercise fairness in the distribution of land was like asking the fox to ensure that the chicken coop was safe, or asking the palace guard to investigate the conduct of the king. It simply cannot be done.

From 1933 to 1935 Thuku broke away from YKA to form the Kikuyu Provincial Association. From this point on he became a loyalist. When the Second World War broke out he joined the chiefs in assuring the colonial government of his support to recruit Africans for military service. However, his position of president of the Kikuyu Provincial Association was challenged by Jesse Kariuki and Joseph Kangethu, who thought Thuku had become too moderate at a time when Africans must adopt a strong position to face the increasing problems that the colonial government was creating for Africans. Thuku opposed the Mau Mau movement because he thought that the colonial government would kill large numbers of Africans if hostilities broke out between the two sides. Following the end of the Mau Mau, Thuku returned to farming until his death on June 14, 1970. The conflict between him and Northey helped to arouse a new level of consciousness among the Africans about the need to seek their own political salvation.

DEVELOPMENTS FROM ROBERT CORYNDON TO MALCOLM MACDONALD

Thuku's impact on the politics of Kenya was profound. In 1923 a settler organization proposed a reduction of 33 percent in the African farm wages in order to control the African workers economically and politically. But in response, Africans threatened a massive strike if such a cut was made. In the same year the first Native Local Councils were introduced. Although these councils were not political, they formed the basis of political organizations that the Africans needed to be fully functional in all areas of national life. The appointment of Robert Coryndon as governor in 1922 coincided with the beginning of a period of the creation of the African local councils that began to be active in 1924. Coryndon's unexpected death in 1925 led to the appointment of Edward Grigg as governor. Grigg served until 1930.

During his term of office Grigg encountered problems that his predecessors did not experience. He was appointed mainly to try to bring about a closer union between Tanganyika, Uganda, and Kenya. The question of closer union seemed important to settlers in all the three colonies, because they believed that they would be better able to create stronger economic and political systems that would offset the pressure from the Africans. Although the British Colonial Office supported the idea of closer union, it refrained from imposing it on the unwilling Africans. This situation provided a precedence that the British government used in 1963 to end the Federation of Rhodesia and Nyasaland.

In 1931 Grigg was succeeded by Joseph Byrne, whose term of office lasted until 1937. In 1955 Grigg published a book entitled *Kenya's Opportunity: Memories, Hopes and Ideas*. In it Grigg recorded his bitter disappointment over the failure of his main mission of bringing about closer union between the three British colonies. He was compelled to say

I left Kenya for London towards the end of 1930, a sad and disappointed man. My mission had failed so far as closer union was concerned, and I saw no light beyond the angry clouds of controversy which had gathered over Kenya's sky. Very different would have been that mood had I been able to foresee that Cameron[41] would change his earlier mind and come to favor some of East Africa union provided the central organizations were not under white control.[42]

When Joseph Byrne was appointed to succeed Grigg, the focus of the British Colonial Office was no longer closer union of the three colonies but other issues that included the question of the franchise for new settlers and Indians, the question of representation for Africans, the structure and functions of the legislative council, and the extent of their political activity. These issues had not been resolved in the past. The roles that Harry Thuku and Jomo Kenyatta were playing in raising Africans' political consciousness was a critical factor that Byrne had to take into account in designing and implementing the policy of his administration. Was he equal to the task?

In the same year, 1931, the British Labour Party published the main components of its policy and decided that any closer union of the three colonies must take place only with the support and full cooperation of the Africans. In 1953 the Labour Party took this same policy position toward the formation of the Federation of the two Rhodesias and Nyasaland, known as the Central African Federation. Ten years later, in 1963, when the Federation was under review to determine its future, the Africans in Nyasaland and Northern Rhodesia vigorously opposed it because they believed that it would stand in the way of their political advancement. The British Labour Party supported that opposition and the Federation unceremoniously came to an end in December 1963. It is surprising that the leaders of the Federation, Godfrey Huggins and Roy Welensky, never learned from the experience of Edward Grigg. Like Grigg, both Huggins and Welensky went out of office bitterly disappointed men.

Events of 1931 moved so rapidly that they put Byrne out of action. The release of the report of the commission of inquiry into Africans' affairs raised questions about future colonial policy. The commission recommended moderation of settler impatience with the desire to become wealthy as soon as they arrived in Kenya. The British parliamentary Joint Select Committee raised similar concern. Indian candidates to the legislative council pledged themselves not to take up seats on the legislative council in protest of discrimination and unrepresentative character of the system. Jomo Kenyatta, the general secretary of the Kikuyu Cultural Association, left Kenya to pursue his studies in Britain. When he returned to Kenya in 1946 the country was on the verge of a major revolution. The report of the Hilton-Young Commission published in 1929 on closer union of the three colonies took a backseat in view of the events of 1931.

Byrne was simply unable to conduct the business of the colony in a manner he was expected to. The best that he could do was to run out his term of office in 1937.

When Robert Brooke-Popham succeeded Byrne in 1937, events in Europe seemed to overshadow those in Africa. In 1936 the exploits of Jesse Owens, an African American at the Olympic Games held at Berlin, were making international news headlines. Since 1932 the rise of the Third Reich was changing the political landscape in Europe in a way that frightened Europeans. In 1937 the crisis caused in Britain by the abdication of Edward VIII created a serious problem for Stanley Baldwin. The end of Baldwin's administration in that year paved way for Neville Chamberlain, leader of the Conservative Party, to assume the office of prime minister of Britain at a period of great crisis in Europe. For the next two years Chamberlain never had a chance to pay attention to matters in the British colonies in Africa because he was consumed by the crisis that was created by Adolf Hitler in his demand for land in Europe. Brooke-Popham was totally at the mercy of events in Europe. His term of office came to an end in 1939 unable to accomplish anything of substance. The beginning of the war in September 1939 simply disabled him in any effort he tried to make to resolve a number of serious issues.

By the time that Henry Monck-Mason Moore was appointed to succeed Brooke-Popham in 1940, the world was already at war and German forces were having a good field day on the battlefront. Chamberlain's death and the assumption of the office of prime minister by Winston Churchill in 1940 put everything in the British colonies in Africa on hold. The strike by dock workers in Mombasa in 1939, the demonstration by the Kamba tribesmen at Government House in 1938 to demand change in policy, and the banning of the Kenya Central Association and the arrest of its leaders all in 1940 were issues that Moore had to deal with. During the next four years he made attempts to resolve these problems but without success. However, in 1941 Kenyan soldiers of the East African Brigade led British forces across the Kenya frontier into Italian-held territory in Somalia and Ethiopia and took it back.[43] Moore took pride in the fact that in 1942 the last Italian stronghold in Ethiopia surrendered to East African forces. In 1943 former leaders of the Kikuyu Cultural Association were released.

Moore would also take pride in the fact that on October 5, 1944, Eliud Wambui Mathu, a Kikuyu educator, was nominated as the first African member of the legislative council. From that time until 1957, Mathu distinguished himself as an efficient parliamentarian, an effective spokesman of the African people. Ogot describes Mathu as follows: "Mathu was the chief spokesman for the African masses in the colonial dominated legislature. He displayed courage, intelligence, dedication and nationalism which, in effect, laid a solid foundation for the more radical

African politics that was ushered in by the first African elections in 1957."[44] After he served in the legislature Mathu worked as an official of the United Nations from 1960 to 1970, as private secretary to President Jomo Kenyatta from 1970 to 1977, and as chairman of the Kenya Airways Board of Directors in 1978. Conditions created by the war made it difficult for Moore to accomplish anything else. The formation of the Kenya African Union in 1944 served as notice to the colonial government that Africans intended to become aggressive in seeking improvement in the political, social, and economic opportunity.

The appointment of Philip E. Mitchell to succeed Moore was made in the belief that he appeared to have impressive credentials. After graduating from Trinity College, Oxford, Mitchell was posted to Nyasaland (Malawi) in 1912 as a junior administrative officer. He was then assigned to Tanganyika after the end of the war in 1918, when it became a trusteeship under British administration. He remained there until 1935. From 1935 to 1940 he served as governor of Uganda where he played a critical role in elevating Makerere College to university status. From 1940 to 1944 he carried out various assignments on behalf of the Colonial Office in London and the colonial government in Kenya. For example, he coordinated the war effort in the three British East African territories. He also worked as British representative in Ethiopia and as high commissioner in the West Pacific territory. Mitchell's term of office was the most difficult period in the history of British colonial Africa—the period of the Mau Mau uprising. Chapter 7 of this book discusses Mitchell's response to this tragedy.

When Mitchell's term of office came to an end in 1952 he was succeeded by Evelyn Baring, later named Lord Howick, who served until 1959. But the change of governors from Mitchell to Baring came at the worst possible time. Granted that the British Colonial Office needed to initiate change in the leadership of the colonial government during a period of great crisis, the change placed Baring in a very difficult situation of not knowing exactly how to respond to the crisis caused by the Mau Mau uprising. The elements of the uprising were in place on April 8, 1952, when the colonial government imposed a collective fine of 2,500 pounds starting with Africans in two districts in the Nyeri area for causing disturbances, and for an incident of arson which Africans had engaged in their protest of the policy of the colonial government.

On June 21 Mitchell retired, setting the stage for a showdown between Baring and the Africans. On October 7, six Kikuyu and Meru tribesman were sentenced to imprisonment after they were found guilty of attacking livestock belonging to settlers in protest against the land policy of the colonial government. On that same day Chief Waruhiu was assassinated. Using the information at his disposal on October 19, Baring declared a state of emergency, and the following day he ordered the arrest of Kikuyu leaders that included Kenyatta. When these leaders were put on trial on November 25, Baring knew that the country was in a major political revolution. For the next five years unprecedented violence broke out on a scale never seen in Kenya in the past.

The appointment of Patrick Renison in 1959 to replace Baring was made to begin the process of transfer of power and government to the Africans. In 1954, while the Mau Mau uprising was still going on, Oliver Lyttleton, secretary of state for the colonies, introduced a new constitution that set Kenya on the road to independence. In 1957, soon after the Mau Mau rebellion had come to an end, Alan Lennox-Boyd, Lyttleton's successor, went a step further in working out a new constitution that allowed Africans to participate in general elections as the first step toward self-government. In 1958 six additional African members were elected to the legislative council. In 1960 the first of two constitutional conferences was held at Lancaster House in London to pave the way for independence.[45] The British Colonial Office instructed Renison to ensure the smooth transition of power from the colonial government to Africans. The granting of independence to Ghana in 1957 served as model for the decolonization of British colonies in Africa.

However, Britain was not done with appointment of colonial governors yet. There was one last governor, Malcolm J. MacDonald,[46] who was appointed in 1962 to succeed Renison and complete the transfer of power to the Africans. After Kenya gained independence on December 12, 1963, MacDonald was appointed first British high commissioner to Kenya. In 1965 he became British special representative in east Africa and central Africa. He also accepted various assignments in Africa on behalf of the British government. MacDonald's final duty in Kenya was to supervise the elections that were held in May 1963. The Kenya African National Union (KANU) led by Jomo Kenyatta, won a sweeping victory and Kenyatta became the first prime minister of independent Kenya. In 1964 Kenya became a republic and Kenyatta became the first president. Thus, the struggle that began with colonization in 1895 finally concluded with the attainment of independence in 1963.

SUMMARY AND CONCLUSION

This chapter has presented some highlights in the political history of Kenya beginning with the conclusion Berlin Conference in February 1885 to the attainment of independence in December 1963. The central tenet of this chapter is a discussion of the nature of political leadership that each British administration exercised in contributing to development of Kenya. It is quite evident that the British colonial officials approached their task from the Victorian perspective, which was based on three assumptions that were part of the perception of Europeans about Africans.

The first assumption was that the Africans lacked an intellectual potential that is characteristic of being human. In reaching this conclusion Victorian Europeans were extending the myth that originated with the Age of Reason. But in applying this myth to their relationships with Africans, colonial officials were void of any respect for Africans. Colonial officials were quite surprised to see Africans of the caliber of Harry Thuku and Eliud Wambui Mathu demonstrate a high-level intellect equal to and even higher than theirs. The reaction of the colonial officials was one of anger. They had lost it.

The second assumption was that since African culture was considered to be primitive, the Africans themselves were primitive. It was very difficult for colonial officials to recognize the contribution of the Africans to society when all they were was a group of people incapable of initiating original ideas to benefit society. In their approach to problems of development, the colonial officials adopted a paternalistic attitude and treated Africans like children. In the course of human relationships this approach simply does not work. The third assumption was that resources in Africa could be extracted cheaply by using the Africans themselves as laborers. When these three assumptions combined they formed an environment of human relationships that led to inevitable conflict as soon as Europeans and Africans came into contact with each other. This is the environment that formed Michael Blundell's approach to the politics of Kenya. How was he going to deal with it? How did it affect his relationships with his fellow settlers and Africans? This book attempts to furnish some answers.

NOTES

1. David Livingstone, *Missionary Travels in Southern Africa, 1857–1870* (Harare: Zimbabwe National Archives).

2. G. C. Grove, *The Planting of Christianity in Africa, Vol. II* (London: Murray, 1954).

3. H. T. Kimble, *Emerging Africa* (New York: Scholastic Books, 1963), p. 6.

4. Leo Marquard, *The People and Policies of South Africa* (London: Oxford University Press, 1969), p. 15.

5. For a detailed discussion of how European colonial governments put this strategy into operation, see, for example, Dickson A. Mungazi, *Colonial Policy and Conflict in Zimbabwe: A Study of Cultures in Collision, 1890–1979* (New York: Taylor and Francis, 1991), pp. 9, 143.

6. Kenneth Knorr, *British Colonial Theories* (Toronto: University of Toronto Press, 1973), p. 375.

7. British South Africa Company Records. Ref. AV/1–01. Zimbabwe National Archives.

8. Ibid.

9. Some people have questioned the level of intelligence of Rhodes himself.

Some say that he dropped out of Oxford University because of poor grades. Others say that he was asked to leave because his work fell below the minimum requirement. History seems to indicate that he was given an honorary degree by Oxford University after making a sizable donation. He was also admitted to Oriel College at Oxford in 1873 but did not graduate until 1881. See *Parade*, in *The Arizona Republic*, August 11, 1991, for details.

10. A. Marshall McPhee, *Kenya* (New York: Frederick Praeger, 1968), p. 216.

11. Robert L. Tignor, *The Colonial Transformation of Kenya: The Kamba, the Kikuyu, and the Masaai from 1900 to 1939* (Princeton, NJ: Princeton University Press, 1976), p. 3.

12. Speaking in the Cape Parliament on June 23, 1887, Rhodes said, "My motto is equal rights for every civilized man south of the Zambezi. What is a civilized man? It is a man who has sufficient education to write his name, and has some property or works, not a loafer. We will treat the Natives as long as they remain in a state of barbarism." Stanlake Samkange, *What Rhodes Really Said About Africans* (Harare: Harare Publishing House, 1982), p. 15. It seems, therefore, that Churchill quoted Rhodes accurately.

13. Edward Grigg, *Kenya's Opportunity: Memories, Hopes and Ideas* (London: Faber and Faber, 1956), p. 31. Grigg, later Lord Altrincham, served as governor of Kenya from 1925 to 1930.

14. Bethwell A. Ogot, *Historical Dictionary of Kenya* (London: The Scarecrow Press, 1981), p. 6.

15. G. H. Mungeam, *British Rule in Kenya, 1895–1912* (Oxford: Clarendon Press, 1966), p. 116.

16. Ibid., p. 119.

17. Ibid., p. 121.

18. Donald Stewart, Memo to the British Colonial Government, September 5, 1904. Ref. FO/11839. Kenya National Archives.

19. These are members of the Luo tribe.

20. Mungeam, *British Rule of Kenya*, p. 145.

21. Ibid., p. 152.

22. Balfour had been leader of the Conservative Party for over 30 years, but he served as prime minister of Britain from 1902 to 1905.

23. Ogot, *Historical Dictionary of Kenya*, p. 277.

24. Ibid., p. 6.

25. In Zimbabwe this form of taxation took new dimensions for Africans the same year. The hut tax had been introduced in 1894. For details see Mungazi, *Colonial Policy and Conflict in Zimbabwe*.

26. Tignor, *The Colonial Transformation of Kenya*, p. 6.

27. Ibid., p. 7.

28. Ibid., p. 9.

29. See Chapter 5 of this book for a more detailed discussion of the effect of introducing the policy of *kipande*.

30. Tignor, *The Colonial Transformation of Kenya*, p. 7.

31. Bowring served as acting governor for two years from 1917 to 1919, when he was succeeded by Edward Northey as governor. Northey served until 1922.

32. Tignor, *The Colonial Transformation of Kenya*, p. 9.

33. Ogot, *Historical Dictionary of Kenya*, p. 6.

34. Ibid., p. 277.

35. This practice remained in operation throughout British colonial Africa. Settlers were given citizenship rights upon their arrival in Africa. This means that they exercised the right to vote. But Africans did not have such a right, they had to struggle to qualify to citizenship, which would given them the right to vote.

36. Ogot, *Historical Dictionary of Kenya*, p. 104.

37. J. D. Hargreaves, *Decolonization in Africa* (New York: Longman, 1988), p. 18.

38. Ibid., p. 19.

39. The Morris Carter Commission also investigated the distribution of land in Zimbabwe in 1925. For details see Dickson. A. Mungazi, *Education and Government Control in Zimbabwe: A Study of the Commissions of Inquiry, 1908–1974* (New York: Praeger, 1990), pp. 30–40.

40. Southern Rhodesia, Report of the Land Commission (Morris Carter, chairman). Ref. CS R/3/26/1926 (Harare: Zimbabwe National Archives, 1926).

41. Donald Cameron, the governor of Tanganyika at the time, was opposed to closer union of the three colonies.

42. Grigg, *Kenya's Opportunity*, p. 85.

43. McPhee, *Kenya*, p. 218.

44. Ogot, *Historical Dictionary of Kenya*, p. 134.

45. McPhee, *Kenya*, p. 220.

46. Malcolm J. MacDonald was the son of James Ramsay MacDonald, who served as Labour prime minister of Britain in 1924 and from 1929 to 1935. They are the only father and son to serve as governors of Kenya.

2

The Political History of Zimbabwe

> It is true to say that the more primitive the African the easier the problem both to educate and to control.
> —Godfrey Huggins, 1954

EVENTS LEADING TO THE COLONIZATION OF ZIMBABWE

Chapter 1 presented materials leading to the conclusion that the colonization of Africa was a product of the Berlin Conference that lasted from December 1884 to February 1885. To understand the Victorian European desire for founding colonies in Africa, one needs to understand first the effect of an important period in history known as the Age of Reason, or the Enlightenment, as it is known in contemporary terminology. The Enlightenment placed heavy emphasis on human reason, rather than on religious belief alone as was the practice in the past, to find solutions to human problems. This period also placed social institutions on a level that man had not experienced before. During this period Europeans slowly substituted old customs and practices with new thinking. Up to the Renaissance nearly every aspect of life revolved around the practice of religion. One of the greatest achievements of the Enlightenment was the development of science, based on the application of scholarship or rational thought process, made possible by the Renaissance. Just as the people of the Renaissance regarded the Middle Ages as a period of intellectual stagnation and lifestyle dominated by superstitions and religious values, the people of the Enlightenment regarded people of the Renaissance as living through a period when human reason was based on knowledge of science.

As developments of the Enlightenment slowly translated into advanced knowledge of the scientific process and intellectual awakening in the 19th century, those deeply interested in research glorified the search for truth into the mysteries of life and approached their newfound interest with a religious importance of their endeavors. The study of human existence—anthropological, physical, intellectual, and social—became a major focus and a preoccupation of Victorian scientists. This is why Charles Darwin became an instant scientific celebrity when he published his *Origin of Species* in 1859 and *The Descent of Man* in 1871. Even though both books were based on scientific speculation, rather than on actual data obtained from empirical and scientific investigation,[1] Victorian science enthusiasts hailed them as touchstones of promoting their own ideas in an area that was attracting the interest and attention of members of the scientific community.

An interesting aspect of Victorian scientists is that the study of human condition in general slowly shifted to the study of people in less-developed countries of the world, especially Africa. Comparative studies of the various racial and ethnic groups became an extremely popular subject of scientific investigation. Anyone who wished to make a name for himself would do so by spending some time gathering data on some aspect of life of people in distant lands. The study of human intellect in those lands attracted the interest of many Victorian researchers, whose methods of gathering the data were as seriously flawed as the instruments they used. Therefore, the conclusions they reached in these studies were filled with gross inaccuracies. To many investigators of that time the inadequacy of both the instruments they used and the data they gathered were not as important as the belief that they were engaging in an intellectual exercise of what they considered to be of great importance.

As the Victorian scientists generated a new interest in the African intellectual potential as a distinct quality of being human, they began a new practice of basing conclusions on scientific speculation alone. This was part of the legacy of some of the leading figures of the Enlightenment itself. For example, in 1785, S. T. von Soemmering published an essay which made him an instant celebrity because he went further than anyone else at that point in speculating about African intellectual potential. After making a comparative study of the skulls of Africans and those of Europeans, von Soemmering concluded that because the cranial capacity of the former was considerably smaller than that of the latter, so was the level of their intellect.[2]

Ten years later, in 1795, a British medical doctor, Charles White, went further to speculate after studying only one skull of an Egyptian[3] that of the four races of man—white, yellow, red, and black—the white race was the most intelligent and the black race was the least.[4] However, in 1803, Thomas Winterbottom, a British medical researcher who had spent more years in Africa than any other researcher at that point, published an essay, *An Account of the Native Africans*, in which he disputed the conclusions which von Soemmering and White had reached.

Winterbottom argued that both von Soemmering and White had based their conclusions on insufficient data and on inaccurate methods of gathering them. He then stated that his own practical observations led him to the conclusion that there was no difference between the cranial capacity of the Europeans and that of the Africans.[5] This argument about cranial capacity was indeed a very important one. Many Victorian scientists believed that cranial capacity was directly related to human intelligence. The theory they overwhelmingly supported was that the larger the cranial capacity one possessed, the more brain one had, and the more brain one had, the more intelligence one possessed.[6] This line of thinking posed very serious implications for the colonization of Africa following the conclusion of the Berlin Conference. This is why, at the annual meeting of the London Anthropological Society held in 1863, James Hunt, the society's president, fully endorsed the belief that Africans were less intelligent than Europeans because their cranial capacity was smaller. Among the supporters of this belief was Wynwood Read, a popular and influential man, who was known more for his patriotic and nationalistic emotions than for his intellectual depth. Read had a young and devoted admirer, Cecil John Rhodes, who regarded him as his hero and mentor, the vanguard of the British superiority complex which victimized them as well as those people in distant lands whom the British later came in contact with during their colonial and imperial adventure. The views quoted in Chapter 1 with reference to Rhodes came from the contemporary thinking about Africans.

Two facts are important to understand with respect to Victorian perception of Africans. The first is that as the British empire builders sought to establish colonies in Africa, they justified their action by basing it on the mythical belief of the intellectual inferiority of the Africans. The second fact is that Victorian researchers ignored a very important fact in their quasi-scientific studies of the African intellectual potential: that human intelligence is a relative quality of the mind, and that to neglect the effects of the environment in which it depends for its development is, in effect, to ignore a very important factor of human development. They also ignored the fact that the environment in which the African child lived and grew was quite different from that in which a European child lived and grew, and that to measure African intellectual potential with Western criteria is to become false to scientific method. It is also important to understand that there was nothing in the Victorian so-called scientific research into human intellectual potential to suggest that the British were motivated by humanitarian considerations toward Africans in their desire to found colonies on the continent. Rather, they were driven by an economic and political desire to exploit the resources in Africa, both human and material, for their own socioeconomic gain.[7] Therefore, the colonization of Africa was based on myth, which became a justification for the action Europeans took to seek the fulfillment of their own objectives.

THE RUDD CONCESSION AND THE COLONIZATION OF ZIMBABWE

The myth that Africans were intellectually inferior became the basis on which the British colonization of Zimbabwe was effected in accordance with the specifications of the Berlin Conference. No consideration was given to the objections of the Africans to the intrusion of their society, because they were considered "incapable of formulating opinions and to define positions consistent with the application of human logic on important issues,"[8] which required a demonstration of highly developed intellect. This is exactly why, throughout colonial rule, Africans remained nothing more than what Kenneth Knorr concluded as merely a commodity or a form of raw materials to be utilized for the benefit of the white man.[9] The architect of British colonial adventure and policy in Africa, not just Zimbabwe, was none other than Cecil John Rhodes.[10]

Indeed, Rhodes became both a product and an agent of Victorian thinking toward Africans and British objectives in Africa, the vehicle by which the British government, including Queen Victoria herself, sought to fulfill their grand objective of bringing British civilization to what they believed to be the heathen and barbaric races of Africa. But in their desire to attain this objective, and in their self-appointed mission to salvage the Africans from the presumed condemnation of their equally presumed primitive culture, the British entrepreneurs, under the direction of Rhodes, created a social environment that eventually led to a serious conflict between the two cultures. This happened much sooner than colonial entrepreneurs had anticipated after colonization was effected.

The specific occasion that shows Rhodes to be the mastermind of the British objective of establishing a colony in Zimbabwe, as the first stage of establishing a colonial empire all over Africa, came in October 1888 as a result of his own schemes. Believing that he was politically and financially secure as a financial king of the Cape, Rhodes commissioned a party of men led by Charles Rudd, presumably to negotiate with King Khumalo Lobengula to allow the British fortune hunters to prospect and dig for gold in his land for a limited period of time,[11] in return for security and guaranteed delivery of a thousand rifles which the king needed for defense purposes, because the increasing number of Europeans who were coming into his land manifested hostile intentions. Rhodes also promised a payment of a hundred pounds sterling per month in fees for twelve months. King Lobengula, who had ascended the Ndebele throne in 1870, the year that Rhodes arrived in South Africa, following the death of King Mzilikazi in 1868, was extremely suspicious of the white man's ultimate intentions in his land.

Besides Rudd, who was a partner of Rhodes in the diamond diggings at Kimberly, the party included Rochfort Maguire, a leading proponent of British colonial empire in Africa, and Robert Thompson, a one-time secretary to Rhodes. Rev. Charles Helm, who had been born in South Africa and who came to Lobengula's country in 1875 in the service of the London Missionary Society, had studied African culture, including language, well enough to be recognized by the whites as an expert on African culture in general. This is why King Lobengula took him into his confidence and appointed him his official interpreter and adviser on all matters relating to his dealings with the white man. Indeed, King Lobengula thought that Reverend Helm was a good and honest Christian man who would not deceive him or allow the white man to take advantage of him in any way. Lobengula was to be bitterly disappointed to discover that Helm actually betrayed him. However, because he was not an official member of the Rudd team, Reverend Helm enjoyed the trust of both sides. Although Helm seemed genuinely interested in the welfare of the Africans, Lobengula did not know that at the same time he was secretly paid by Rhodes to provide information that he wanted to use to facilitate the colonization of Zimbabwe in accordance with provisions of the Royal Charter that Rhodes received from Queen Victoria in 1889.

As the negotiations between the two sides progressed, the Rudd party found Lobengula to be a shrewd politician and a highly intelligent man who understood the implications of the deliberations. His ability to articulate positions and to comprehend the significance of the discussions surprised the members of the Rudd team. Their Victorian belief that the African was intellectually inferior to the white man created a shocking experience for them. Peter Gibbs describes the extent to which Lobengula demonstrated his intellectual skills and as a negotiator:

Hour after hour, week after week, month after month, the king argued with remarkable success with the Cambridge men. He tore to shreds their thesis on the advantages of granting Rhodes the concession. The pillars of learning made so little headway that Rhodes felt compelled to force the issue.[12]

Indeed, Rudd later admitted that he been greatly surprised by the high level of intelligence which the king demonstrated, adding "He was as sharp as a needle, and remembered everything. If you contradicted yourself, he was down on you at once."[13] To suggest that Rhodes was irritated to learn that Lobengula's high level of intelligence proved the Victorian belief of African intellectual inferiority a myth is to conclude that for him, too, this was a shattering experience.

For Rhodes to discover that this myth had dictated his attitudes and behavior toward the Africans only existed in his mind was also a shattering experience. This helped turn his low regard of Lobengula into anger and a desire to eliminate him as quickly as possible. In Lobengula's demonstration of intelligence the Rudd team was placed on the horns of a dilemma. If it failed to manipulate him, then Rhodes's pursuit of his grand objective of building a vast British colonial empire in Africa would suffer a severe setback, because he wanted to utilize the colonization of Zimbabwe as a stepping-stone to his grand imperial goals in Africa. If it forced the issue, then Rhodes would risk the danger of a serious military confrontation with the powerful Lobengula's army, which was estimated at 6,000 strong. In his own sense of destiny, Rhodes did not make room for possible failure in his schemes, because he was convinced of the rightness of his mission to the extent that for him this was the only thing worthwhile living and dying for. He had both the political power and the financial resources to fulfill his ambitions no matter what they cost. Rhodes was prepared to go to any length to ensure the completion of his mission. Rhodes was no compromiser.

Therefore, Rhodes instructed Rudd to ensure that by fair means or foul, Lobengula must be pressured to sign a piece of paper which, in effect, seemed to carry the appearance of a properly drawn-up and legal contract.[14] With his patience running out, Rhodes demonstrated an intolerance, in a way that was so typical of Victorian Europeans, of Lobengula's ability to think logically to preserve the integrity of his society and culture. This is how he proved that the white man was wrong in holding on to the myth of African intellectual inferiority. Rhodes did not want to be the first high-level colonial official to admit that he and other Victorian individuals who shared his views were wrong about their views of the Africans. In this way, they lost a valuable opportunity to build human relationships on the foundation of mutual cultural respect. Unable to manipulate Lobengula, Rhodes secretly paid Reverend Helm to supply him information that he utilized in planning the colonization of Zimbabwe. Lobengula was, thus, betrayed by a Christian man whom he trusted.[15] Rudd also found Lotshe, Lobengula's senior counselor, so capable of exercising reason and logic that he refused to be manipulated.

On October 30, 1888, taking the advice given by Reverend Helm into consideration and without the slightest knowledge that the missionary whom he trusted so much was, in effect, Rhodes' agent, Lobengula signed a piece of paper known as the *Rudd Concession*. This pseudolegal document granted Rhodes exclusive rights supposedly to dig for minerals for a limited period of time. But Rhodes took it as a blank check to do what he always wanted to do: colonize Zimbabwe as the first stage of his grand plan to bring all of Africa under British imperial rule. By the time Lobengula knew that he had been misled and cheated, Rhodes had already obtained a Royal Charter from Queen Victoria to colonize Zimbabwe.

The charter gave Rhodes legal authority to form a colonial administration known as the British South Africa Company, which ruled Zimbabwe from 1890 to 1923. Rhodes was so pleased with the terms of the charter that he said "our concession is so gigantic that it is like giving a man the whole of Australia."[16] Soon after signing the concession and before he knew that he had been a victim of conspiracy, Lobengula remarked to Reverend Helm, "Did you ever see a chameleon catch a fly? He gets behind the fly and remains motionless for some time. Then he advances slowly. When well within reach, he darts his tongue and the fly disappears. Britain is the chameleon, and I am the fly."[17] Of course, Reverend Helm had no comment.

As soon as he knew that he had been cheated, King Lobengula repudiated the agreement and requested Queen Victoria not to honor it because Rhodes and members of the Rudd team, including Helm, were not honest with him. He did not know that the queen herself was part of the plan to colonize his land. To make matters worse, Rhodes failed to honor the terms of the agreement. The guns and ammunition, which he had promised as a condition of the agreement, were never delivered. The promise which he had made that he had no intention of colonizing Zimbabwe was also not kept. The tragic reality of all this is that Lobengula felt that the trust and confidence which he had placed in both Rudd and Helm went down the drain as the British men with whom he was dealing made him a victim of the myth they cunningly tried to maintain as the only viable means of fulfilling their own objectives.

Because Rhodes was not truthful with him, Lobengula refused to honor the terms of the Rudd Concession and so tension between the two sides was rapidly rising as the dialogue that he thought would help resolve the problems of race relations fell into the background of things. The breakdown in race relations came from the anger Rhodes showed at learning about Lobengula's ability to understand critical issues and to show the white man that intellectual potential was not his exclusive quality of human existence. Rhodes's anger and frustration with a presumably uneducated African leader translated into a strategy to eliminate him quickly if he hoped to carry out his grand plans. After all, who was Lobengula, trying to prove that he possessed an intellectual potential equal to that of the white man? Between 1889 and 1890, Rhodes made elaborately secret plans to invade Lobengula's kingdom. In 1890 Rhodes was ready to make a decisive move. In March of that year he instructed the secretary of the British South Africa Company to write a letter to the British commissioner at the Cape to say "Mr Rhodes has felt that to assure the position of the Chartered Company it is necessary to take possession of Mashonaland in the winter."[18] For this reason Rhodes urged the migration of settlers to Zimbabwe as part of the nucleus of a white community which he needed to sustain a white civilization in a land which, according to his opinion, was occupied by barbarians. The response from the commissioner was so encouraging that Rhodes felt that his plan of action was now ready to implement.

In September 1890 Rhodes secretly dispatched a squadron of 400 mounted police and troops to protect a column of 200 colonial adventurers who were going to settle in Mashonaland in central Zimbabwe. There they hoisted a Union Jack without Lobengula's knowledge or permission. With this action Rhodes officially colonized Zimbabwe. Leander Starr Jameson, his close associate and partner in the De Beers Mining Company, was appointed the first administrator and served from September 10, 1890, until April 1, 1986. But a series of unfortunate events precipitated a deterioration in the relationships between the colonial adventurers and the Africans. First, a severe outbreak of foot-and-mouth disease killed hundreds of cattle. The whites, having taken some precaution to prevent a devastation of theirs, tried to exterminate those of the Africans to stop the spread of the disease. But this is not how the African saw the situation, they simply regarded the white man's action as an example of a callous and brutal strategy to subdue them. Then a severe drought brought a crisis in the food supply. During the next two years, the Africans were in a restless state as a result of these events. While the whites were able to obtain assistance from South Africa to ease the problems caused by both the foot-and-mouth disease and the drought, they did nothing to assist the Africans.

Suddenly and without warning, Rhodes ordered his men to invade Lobengula's kingdom in October 1893. The invaders killed the king,[19] destroyed his royal village, confiscated his livestock, and declared Matabeleland a British colony. The superiority complex which became Rhodes's preoccupation had finally found a target and a channel of expressing itself in accordance with the Victorian belief of African cultural inferiority. Rhodes would no longer allow Lobengula time to learn the tactics of the white man; he had to be eliminated quickly in order to establish his own authority. To allow him more time to design his strategy of defense would greatly embarrass the proponents of the believers of African intellectual inferiority. Rhodes was not prepared to endure this agony any longer. Besides, everything pointed to the fact that, indeed, Lobengula had been framed into a situation which left him no options at all.

CONSEQUENCES OF COLONIZATION: SOWING THE SEEDS OF CONFLICT

What has been discussed so far leads to the conclusion that the European belief in the cultural inferiority of the Africans did not make it possible for Rhodes, Rudd, Queen Victoria, or Helm to consider the Africans as equal partners in the course of building human relationships. The manner in which Rhodes and his associates conspired against Lobengula demonstrates a lack of respect for African culture. Therefore, one must conclude that British colonization of Zimbabwe, and indeed other countries in Africa, constituted both cultural invasion and an act of violence. By its very nature, colonial domination is violent. These elements constitute a set of reasons to suggest why Rhodes neglected the fact that African culture was not cut out to become an instrument by which he and his associates sought to fulfill their own imperial goals. Rather, it fully embraced the freedom and the dignity which manifested themselves in universal human aspirations for self-fulfillment. This is why in the period from 1893 to 1895, the Africans were in restless state, unable to swallow their pride and a sense of self-worth in the wake of the pursuit of the fulfillment of colonial objectives by the white man. In the entry to his diary of April 24, 1893, Jameson records his argument that the rising tension between the two races was a result of the African resistance to what he characterized as a properly constituted and civilized authority.[20] Of course, Jameson never saw his own behavior as its major cause of the rising tension. Instead, he chose to blame the victims of the policy of his own administration.

This explains why between 1893 and 1896 the Africans were steadily getting ready to resist the invasion of their culture. In March 1896, after the settlers had destroyed their cattle, presumably to control the spread of foot-and-mouth disease, the Africans concluded that the settlers had gone too far. Bitter fighting broke out. In 1897 the Africans were about to win the war when the settlers received aid from South Africa and Britain. The use of the gun by the settlers, while superior to the spear, was almost reduced to minimum effect by the sheer force of numbers. However, the Africans were ruthlessly crushed, but the war had inflicted a permanent damage to the relationships between the two groups. Nothing could be done to salvage the remnants of goodwill which the Africans still hoped would be the basis of relationships between them and the white man.

Table 1
Casualties of the War of 1896

DEAD	Volunteers	Imperial Troops	B.S.A.C. Police	Total
1. in action	47	8	4	59
2. of wounds	17	3	5	25
3. killed by Africans	262	1	1	264
Total	326	12	10	348
WOUNDED				
1. in action	121	29	8	158
2. accidentally	15	1	—	16
3. at start of war	14	—	—	14
Total	150	30	8	188

Source: *Reports on Native Disturbance in Southern Rhodesia, 1896–1897* (Zimbabwe National Archives).

What was even more important is that this was not the last time the Africans would fight to end colonialism. The war of independence that lasted from 1966 to 1979 had a different outcome from that of 1896. However, casualties of the war of 1896 were an indication of how serious the conflict was. Table 1 shows white casualties of that war.

The British South Africa Company did not keep accurate figures of the African casualties for a good reason: to conceal the atrocities which it has committed in subjecting the Africans to colonial rule. It can therefore be assumed that these figures were much higher than those of the whites.

THE MISSIONARY FACTOR

The opening of the first Western school at Inyati for Africans in Zimbabwe in 1859 by Robert Moffat of the London Missionary Society was an important event in many ways. At that time neither Moffat and the organization he represented nor the Africans themselves were aware that in introducing Western education, the missionaries intended to pursue a set of religious objectives that, although designed with the intention of promoting their development, created an environment that posed serious implications for conflict in the future.

Therefore, from its inception, Western education acquired cultural and political dimensions that would affect the Africans in profound ways. That Western Christian missionaries were in the forefront of introducing Western education to the Africans does not negate the conclusion that they were seeking to promote Christianity as a new form of religious and cultural relationships between the Africans and the white man. In time, Christianity, as a basis of that new relationship, became a potent factor of cultural conflict. That Christianity and African traditional religious practices were incompatible suggests an environment of conflict between the Africans and the settlers.

One of the tragic outcomes of the colonization of Africa was the absence of dialogue between the colonial officials and the Africans, because of the basic assumption on the part of the former that the latter belonged to a primitive culture. Because the colonial officials were tragically fearful of the educational development of the Africans, they instituted a system of education that was designed to promote and protect their own socioeconomic and political interests at the expense of those of the Africans. With the passage of time, this situation created an environment from which conditions of conflict emerged. However, Western missionaries had a vision of Africa transformed by education and Christianity.

Encouraged by the modest success of his efforts, Moffat sought and secured the permission of the skeptical King Mzilikazi to open a second school at Hope Fountain in 1870. From that time until 1893, other Christian organizations, both Catholic and Protestant, opened schools for Africans in different parts of the country for the purpose of promoting Christianity, with the main objective of transforming the life of the Africans to enable them to adjust to the colonial society by accepting Christian values rooted in Western cultural traditions.[21] The introduction of Western education to the Africans by Christian organizations meant two things: it was poised to alter permanently the way of life they had known for hundreds of years, and the education of the Africans remained largely the responsibility of Christian organizations until the church-state crisis of 1969. Western education stressed the learning of Western cultural values as a more important objective than any other.[22] When applied to the conditions of human existence in African cultural settings, especially under colonial rule, Christianity itself carried an explicit message of obedience as an instrument of control. This suggested the reality that control of the Africans was under the influence of Western culture because Christianity and Western culture could not be separated. In the context of colonial conditions, that form of control became synonymous with an effort to replace African cultural values with those of Western culture. This became a contributing factor to the conflict between the two cultures when conditions were ripe.

The opening of Western schools for Africans was also a product of the Victorian enthusiasm among Western Christian missionaries to promote Christianity as the most important means of ensuring the advancement of the Africans. But, by demeaning African cultural values the missionaries created a larger problem than they could solve, because the Africans resisted any action they regarded as an intrusion of their culture. With the advent of the Industrial Revolution, the Christian message and Western culture, which Livingstone and other Western missionaries thought they were attempting to persuade the Africans to adopt as a basis of new life, seem to have been lost in the confusion and conflict that emerged between the religious values and the search for a new material comfort as a manifestation of that distinct British entrepreneurial ingenuity. It had been derailed by the pursuit of material wealth and commercial entrepreneurial adventure that even the most ardent missionaries, such as Livingstone himself, found hard to resist.

Material wealth and comfort, as the intended outcome of the Industrial Revolution, combined with the so-called British brooding spirit, which British philosopher and economist John Stuart Mill so eloquently described, compelled the missionaries to alter their objective from promoting Christianity in Africa, with its universal message of brotherhood of all men, to promoting European commercial interests as an important instrument of reducing the value of African culture in order to control the Africans politically. This is precisely why Livingstone, speaking at Cambridge University in 1864, went to great lengths to explain why he and his missionary colleagues were reversing their missionary objectives to embrace imperial objectives, saying, among other things, that sending the Gospel to the heathens of Africa must include much more than was implied in the usual meaning of a missionary, a man going about with a Bible under his arms. The promotion of commerce must be specially attended to because this, more than anything else, persuaded the Africans to seek commercial relationships with civilized people.[23]

Therefore, it is not surprising that the Africans' impression of missionaries as a group of people motivated by a religious objective of promoting their advancement through Western education and Christian values was substituted for a new impression of them as fervent British nationalists who were motivated by the objective of promoting British commercial interests as their new modus vivendi. The commercial vehicle that the European entrepreneurs were now trying to build with equally fervent determination was intended to run on the political wheels of Western cultural values fortified by the hub of socioeconomic prosperity and fueled by cheap labor, which the Africans were expected to provide. Therefore, Livingstone's change of objectives and his acquiescence to British imperial goals manifested a serious contradiction in the behavior of the Victorian Christian missionaries. This contradiction alerted the Africans to the perils that the white man posed to their culture and the obvious threat he created to the integrity of their own cultural values.

This is why, until 1899, the sole purpose of the Western Christian missionary educational effort among the Africans was the promotion of

British commercial objectives and the conversion to Christianity. This was a clear means of having them accept British cultural influence and political power. But within only a short period of time, from 1888 to 1896, the elements of conflict between the missionaries and the colonial enthusiasts became apparent when the former emphasized religious instruction and the latter emphasized manual labor as a more appropriate form of education for the Africans. How would the Africans respond to this conflict between two major Western institutions?

This change of missionary objective was a development that had a negative influence on the Africans' response to their message. Thus, in 1882, six years before the so-called Rudd Concession of 1888, Moffat expressed his disappointment with his failure to persuade the Africans to accept Christianity, saying "a few individuals may have been influenced for good, but there is no organic result. There does not seem to be two people of the tribe who recognize each other as Christians. There is no indication that life in the tribe has in any way been touched by the Gospel."[24] This shows that in all his missionary enthusiasm, Moffat appears to have lost touch with the real reason of African negative response: contradiction in the behavior of the missionaries themselves and the extent of control that the white man in general wished to exercise over the African cultural values through religious instruction and acculturation.

This leads one to the conclusion that the acquiescence of the Victorian Christian missionaries to British colonial objectives resulted in a partnership between the colonial government and the missionaries in promoting British commercial interests through the introduction of Western education to the Africans in order to control them. This may not have been the intention of Christian missionaries, but it certainly was the effect of their action on the attitudes of colonial entrepreneurs toward the Africans and their culture.

The question now arises: If Christian missionaries wanted Western education to help the Africans accept Christianity on the assumption that this meant their own advancement, why, then, did they not succeed in convincing them that this was, in effect, good for them? The answer lies in the Africans' perception of the value of Christianity itself and the culture of the white man as two distinct products of the socioeconomic and political objectives that they were trying to accomplish for themselves. That the Africans were aware of this did not help contribute anything positive to the emergence of an environment of good relationship between them.

The introduction of Christianity and Western education to the Africans of Zimbabwe also meant, in effect, the introduction of Western culture with all the negative manifestations that they believed it entailed. Viewed from the Victorian perspective, therefore, for the Africans to accept Western education, they had to accept Christianity and the white man's culture first. But to do that they would have to discard their own culture. The missionaries had always insisted that there was no room for both. That this was not easy for Africans to do is shown by their negative response to the missionary call. Nevertheless, from 1859 to 1899, the missionary educational effort among the Africans set the stage for major developments to take place, especially the action that the colonial government took toward the Africans in order to give effect to its own objectives.

CONFLICT BETWEEN CHURCH AND STATE OVER AFRICAN ADVANCEMENT

The establishment of the colonial government in Zimbabwe in September 1890 ushered in a new set of conditions that the Christian missionaries did not foresee. There is no doubt that the colonial government was pleased with the change of missionary objective, as Livingstone had outlined in his address at Cambridge University in 1864. But colonial officials were still unhappy with this change because the essential goal of missionary education was "to stabilize the faith of converts and assist in character development,"[25] as if to suggest that the Africans had no character as a product of their culture, instead of preparing them to contribute to the promotion and fulfillment of British commercial and political objectives. The difference of opinion regarding what constituted proper educational objectives for Africans between two Western institutions was as cruel as it was damaging to their educational development.

This difference was slowly but steadily leading to a major institutional controversy about the place of Africans in the colonial society and culture as an outcome of the kind of education provided them under the political control of the white man. This is evident in the events that followed. The education of the Africans became a subject of debate among the colonial officials and church leaders following the bitter war of 1896–97, not because it was in the hands of the missionaries but because of what it was designed to accomplish.

The conflicting viewpoints that various segments of the white community were expressing by 1898 about what that education should be demonstrate how controversial the education of the Africans was slowly becoming. This suggests that from its very beginning, the education of the Africans acquired powerful socioeconomic and political dimensions, which were determined by those who were conscious of its implications for the racial and institutional relationships of the future. The reality of this situation is that having come out of the scourge of slavery and being mindful of the effects of the devastating war of 1896, the Africans knew that the colonial government wanted to control their education so that it would not enable them to acquire elements of critical thinking and logic.

The question that was at the center of the debate between colonial officials and church leaders is the following: What kind of education should the Africans receive? The answer determined whether it was the government or the missionaries who should control it. The fact that colonial officials and missionaries had conflicting views about the answer suggests how critically important it was to furnish a clear answer to the question. But a clear answer was possible only if the two sides agreed, and they did not. The missionaries argued that the education of the Africans must include literary and religious instruction in order to introduce them into the universal Christian community. But the colonial officials wanted only an education that would produce cheap laborers out of them.

Among the colonial officials who felt compelled to express their opinions about this unprecedented debate between the two differing Western institutions was Earl Grey, who served as administrator from April 12, 1896, to December 4, 1898. With a sense of duty as required by the high office he held and conscious of the future implications of finding an answer to the question of what constituted good education for the Africans and who should control it, Grey argued that the government must control it because it had a responsibility for designing a policy for national development beyond the peripheral objectives of introducing the Africans to the Christian community.

Arguing in 1898, when he introduced the first bill on education, that "I am convinced that the very first step towards civilizing the Natives lies in a course of industrial and practical training which must precede the teaching of [religious] dogma,"[26] Grey was, in effect, supporting his belief that religious instruction, such as the missionaries were trying to promote as a viable form of education for Africans, must come after the policy of industrial and practical training was fully established. Because Grey's position was quite compatible with Livingstone's, he was therefore quite candid in defining the policy of industrial training as being synonymous with the policy of manual labor. This is exactly what the education ordinance that the British South Africa Company legislature enacted in 1899 was intended to do.

Illustrating the reality of the growing institutional controversy between the two institutions about the character, the main objective, and the control of African education are the views that Reverend Arthur Bathe expressed to Grey: "I am sorry that on the part of the whites there is a reluctance to encourage good education among the Natives under the pretext that they will not be useful cheap laborers when they can read and write."[27] It is clear that Bathe knew what Grey and William

Henry Milton, Grey's successor, defined as industrial training was nothing more than training the Africans as laborers. What was troubling to the missionaries about the definition of the colonial government relative to the content of education for Africans was really not that it had moved to have its own policies prevail at the expense of their own, but that in formulating such policies it would render meaningless the religious values of the educational process through the implementation of a totally secular educational policy which was alien to the Africans.

Two observations must be made at this point regarding the controversy about the educational objectives of African education as defined by both the colonial government and the missionaries. The first is that the Victorian missionaries readily recognized that if the views of the colonial officials about the character of education for the Africans prevailed, then the educational process that ensued would reduce their influence in the life of the people whom they believed only they could change for the good of the country. For the missionaries to learn otherwise was to go through a painful experience and to wonder if they had lost the major objective of their work. The views Livingstone had expressed in 1864 only helped to serve as cold comfort to their cause.

The second observation is that for the Victorian missionaries to regard African traditional religion, within the context of African culture itself, as primitive and to expect the Africans to discard the customs of their ancestors, during a period when the memories of the bitter war of 1896 were still fresh in their minds, was to expect them to discard their cultural identity and religious practices. The white man's negative attitudes toward the essentials of African culture did not help their cause either. This is how the missionaries were losing the struggle for control of the education of Africans. For them to utilize a Western cultural perspective from which to try to influence the Africans' acceptance of Western education as a condition of accepting Christianity and, thus, Western culture itself was to neglect the seriousness of the contradiction that manifested the behavior of the white man in general.

Therefore, from the time that Livingstone endorsed the general goal of colonial commercial activity in 1864 to the time that the colonial government enacted the first legislation on education in 1899, the missionaries alienated themselves from the Africans, losing the influence they should have rightly exerted in their life and the course of their advancement. It was only after they had realized that their influence had been damaged that they began to question the policies of the colonial government by critically appraising their own. Geoffrey Kapenzi, a Zimbabwean theological thinker, explains how the thinking among Victorian missionaries had become detrimental to their own cause by the time the debate between them and the colonial officials was reaching a critical point in 1899, and how they were losing the struggle for the control of the education of the Africans: "The vast majority of the missionaries referred to the Africans as the degraded descendants of Ham and Kaffir Natives. Therefore, they did not practice biblical Christianity, but colonial religion in which African-missionary relations were set in their colonial pattern of masters and servants, superiors and inferiors."[28]

Kapenzi's conclusion seems an accurate interpretation of the views that Livingstone expressed on that very same issue when he wrote, "True, the Africans, when Christianized, are not so elevated as we who have had the advantage of civilization and Christianity for ages."[29] An intriguing aspect of the Victorian missionaries is the extent of the contradiction that manifested itself in their action. On the one hand, they feared that if the colonial policy prevailed, they would lose the influence they thought they should rightly exert on the conduct of education for the Africans. On the other hand, they believed that before the educational process should begin, the Africans must show a willingness to accept Christianity. By failing to recognize that the educational process itself would eventually bring about a change in the lives of the Africans, which would mean, in essence, acceptance of Christianity, they precluded the opening of meaningful channels of communication between themselves and the Africans. There is no question that the colonial government took advantage of the weakened position of the missionaries to strengthen their own position.

EFFECT OF LEGISLATIVE ACTION ON AFRICAN EDUCATION

These developments constituted the beginning of government power to control education in accordance with its policies. In 1899, aware that it had an advantage over the missionaries, the colonial government took action to implement its own objectives of education for Africans. Therefore, the enactment of the first legislation on education[30] in that year was an event that gave the colonial government the power it had wanted to have in order to formulate its educational policy based upon the Victorian philosophy of the place of the Africans and their culture in the colonial society and the objective of training them to make a contribution to the economic development of the country by functioning as laborers.

This legislation gave the colonial government the power it did not have since its inception in 1890. This is why it moved quickly to assert its authority by introducing the policy of industrial training for Africans. Aware that the type of education that would emerge as a result of formulating a policy and regulations requiring industrial training for Africans, the colonial government, first under Earl Grey, then under

William Milton, pushed a bill into the legislature with a complete knowledge of what it was intended to accomplish. Thus, whereas government control of African education was taking shape, implications for cultural conflict were also taking shape.

Although the primary purpose of the Education Ordinance of 1899 was to assist in the development of an effective academic education for white students, its impact was greater on government power to formulate an educational policy consistent with its objective of training Africans as laborers. There is no doubt that the main provision of this legislation was, in addition to the general educational grant of $4.00 to be made for each white student who met an academic standard or proficiency in English, Latin, literature, history, mathematics, geography, science, music, and shorthand,[31] to ensure government control of African education in a way different from the way it controlled white education. All the missionaries could do now was to hope that their influence on the character of African education did not erode away.

There is no question that from the beginning of its direct involvement in the educational process, the government wanted to use the financial power that it gave itself by enacting this legislation to ensure that these subjects formed the core of the curriculum for white students, thereby ensuring that they were adequately prepared to exercise socioeconomic and political control of both the Africans and the country. It was therefore by design that Section B of the ordinance made provision for the African schools, all of them under missionary organizations, to receive aid grants of ten shillings ($1.00) per student per school year for each school that offered no less than two hours per day for practical training and manual labor, from a total of four hours per day, and in which the average daily attendance was not less than 50 during the preceding school year of 200 days.[32]

There is, therefore, no doubt that the government believed it had found a workable solution to the problem it had faced since its inception in 1890. The confused state in which missionary educational policy found itself must have come as a blessing in disguise. Now that it had finally made its move, was the future of the white man, based upon the nature of relationships between himself and the Africans, going to be what Rhodes, Jameson, Grey, and Milton had predicted, or were this legislation and the policy based on it the opening chapter of a new saga in the brutal struggle ahead? It remained to be seen. However, the euphoria that characterized the reaction of the colonial enthusiasts could be understood only in terms of what they hoped the new legislation would help accomplish—namely, to prepare Africans to function as cheap laborers.

The racially discriminatory character of the colonial educational policy that came into being with the Education Ordinance of 1899 remained a

Table 2
Expenditures for White Education and African Education Compared, 1909–49

Year	Expenditures for White Education		Expenditures for African Education		Grand Total
	Amount	% of Total	Amount	% of Total	
1909	$ 1,048,052	99.72	$ 3,000	0.28	$ 1,051,052
1919	1,855,300	98.83	22,000	1.17	1,877,300
1929	4,587,032	97.01	141,740	2.99	4,728,722
1939	7,354,208	97.30	204,212	2.70	7,558,420
1949	32,361,140	96.49	1,178,524	3.51	33,539,664

Source: Zimbabwe, *Statistical Year Book, 1983.*

permanent feature of education and national life throughout the rest of the colonial rule of Zimbabwe. Once the colonial government tasted the fruit of this bias against genuine development of the education of Africans, it would never give it up or change it in any way that would represent a departure from the need for cheap labor. Table 2 shows how government expenditure for education placed the African student at a financial, and thus educational, disadvantage.

From the Education Ordinance of 1899 two things are clearly distinguishable. The first is that the colonial government placed more restrictions on the education of the Africans than it did on that of the white students by the regulations that came from it. Whereas it required white students to show evidence of academic performance as a condition of receiving aid grants, it specified that African schools must engage their students in a rigorous manual training as a condition of receiving financial aid. Indeed, this action was quite compatible with the aim of having Africans function only as cheap laborers. Now, the colonial government was living and operating by the application of an age-old philosophy in formulating an educational policy for the Africans.

The second thing that one sees as an important outcome of the Education Ordinance of 1899 is that by instituting racism in the educational process, the government put in place an effective strategy of exercising power to design educational policies for Africans differently from those for white education. The effect of this racial discrimination is that whereas the education of whites steadily improved, that of Africans remained in a relatively undeveloped state until the advent of a black majority government in April 1980. The cultural bias that Livingstone had expressed was now yielding tangible results. Therefore, the missionaries indirectly contributed to the structure of a policy that was incompatible with their own goals.

The enactment of the Education Ordinance of 1899 had other adverse effects on the character of education for Africans. Having tasted the power that it did not have before, the government amended this ordinance in 1903 to add more conditions under which it made aid grants to African schools. These new conditions included the requirement that there must be at least forty students attending 150 days per year with four hours of manual labor per day as the core of their curriculum. In addition, the African students must be taught the basic elements of English to help them understand instructions given by their employers as well as habits of cleanliness and discipline.[33] That no such requirements were placed on the education of white students suggests a different form of control as a definite component of cultural bias.

That the colonial government was quite pleased with this amendment is evidenced by the action of one high-ranking government official who took it upon himself to write to the editor of *The Rhodesia Herald*, a daily newspaper, in 1903: "The black peril will only become a reality when the results of a misguided system of education has taken root and the veneer of European civilization struggles with the innate savage nature of the Native."[34]

It is therefore evident that the power the colonial government gave itself through the Education Ordinances of 1899 and 1903 was having a profound impact on its desire to design an educational policy that was consistent with its larger socioeconomic and political goals. This meant that the education of Africans, unable to develop along viable and dynamic academic lines, became nothing more than simply manual labor and practical training. This is exactly how Earl Grey and William Milton had defined it in 1898. Among the evidence that one sees to substantiate this conclusion is that in 1904 the chief native commissioner for Matabeleland, a high-ranking official within the hierarchy of the colonial structure, argued, "The Native in his ignorance almost invariably abuses a purely bookish education, utilizing it only as a means of defying authority. A purely literary education for Natives should not be considered for many years to come."[35]

This opinion no doubt reflected official government policy, because his counterpart in Mashonaland went further in outlining the principles that he argued must guide the government in formulating an educational policy for Africans:

It is cheap labor which we need in this country, and it has yet to be proved that the Native who can read and write turns out [to be] a good laborer. As far as we can determine, the Native who can read and write will not work on farms and in mines. The official policy must be to develop the Natives on lines least likely to lead to any risk of clashing with Europeans.[36]

One can conclude that, indeed, even basic literacy was discouraged for Africans because it was believed to enable them to become aware of the oppressive conditions under which they lived. Unable to recognize that it was reducing the education of the Africans to a level where the educational process itself had no meaning except to enable them to provide cheap labor, the government amended the Education Ordinance of 1903 by enacting Ordinance Number 133 of 1907, to require that manual labor and practical training form a major component of the curriculum in all African schools, whether or not they qualified for aid grants.[37]

TWO DECADES OF WILDERNESS: ZIMBABWE FROM 1903 TO 1946

Within only a few months of the enactment of this ordinance, the government concluded that the power it had acquired was being threatened by the formation of the Southern Rhodesia Christian Conference, which came into being in 1906, and, by 1907, was questioning its educational policy for Africans. Indeed, the formation of the Southern Rhodesia Christian Conference reopened the old debate between the two institutions about which must control African education. The refusal of the church leaders to acknowledge the claim that the colonial government had made and the action it had taken suggests that the controversy had not been resolved.

In its first annual report for 1907, the Southern Rhodesia Missionary Conference expressed regret over government pursuit of a policy that its members believed was having an adverse effect on the course of African advancement.[38] The colonial government then initiated a process of redefining its policy in a way that seemed to address the concerns that the missionaries were expressing. One such action was the naming of the Graham Commission in 1910 to investigate the character of African education. In addition to recommending that African education follow three basic lines—literacy, religion, and practical training—the Graham Commission recommended that the missionaries be allowed to operate these schools, but added "All schools for the instruction of Natives, whether in matters religious, literacy or industrial, must come under the control of the government."[39]

On July 19, 1912, wishing to implement the major recommendation of the Graham Commission, the colonial government enacted Ordinance Number 7 for the major purpose of providing for more effective control of African schools. Paragraph 5 of this ordinance states, "The Director of Education may order the closure of any Native school if he is not satisfied with the manner in which it is being conducted."[40] It is clear that the government was really not interested in any form of education for Africans besides manual labor and practical training. In a fashion typical of the attitudes of the colonial government, one official explained the reason for this policy as a means of controlling the education of the Africans: "I do not consider it right that we should educate the Native in any way which will unfit him for service. The Native is, and should always be, the hewer of wood and the drawer of water for his white master."[41]

The criticism that came from the Southern Rhodesia Missionary Conference, that the requirement of the government that African schools focus on manual labor was converting the Africans into hired slaves,[42] was actually substantiated by other organizations and studies. For example, in 1913 the Rolin Report graphically described the extent to which government obsession with labor supply had created a situation of misery for the Africans. Henri Rolin, a professor of law in Belgium, had been commissioned by his government to study the claim of the colonial government in Zimbabwe that its policy was the best that could be pursued in Africa. The Belgian colonial office had hoped that the report would shed light on some features of the colonial policy that it could adopt for its own colonies. But when Rolin reported "a white trader will not hesitate to tell you that an African is a stupid animal,"[43] the real intent of both the policy of industrial training and manual labor as a form of education for Africans became fully known and understood by international observers for what it really was, a farce.

As public opinion, both in Britain and in Zimbabwe, seemed to go against the policy of the colonial government, there was a new twist in the growing conflict. The government itself, believing that its educational policy was turning public opinion against it, decided to divert attention from things educational to things political. For the next ten years everything else was left in abeyance as the government, with the support of the white entrepreneurs who were harvesting economic and political benefit from the policy of practical training and manual labor, directed all its efforts toward negotiations with the British government about its political future. What emerged in 1923 was a new constitutional arrangement, which meant a change of status from the British South Africa Company rule to what was known in British colonial traditions as Responsible Government. However, the Southern Rhodesia Christian Conference, in its struggle to sustain the church's influence on the course of African development, did not regard the new constitutional arrangement as creating a responsible government, and so intensified its efforts to have its own views prevail in the face of an increasing conflict between the two institutions.

However, the attainment of responsible government status gave the new government a greater degree of freedom to do as it saw fit in all its internal matters, including its policy toward Africans. Although Britain retained the power to intervene when it thought that the colonial government policy toward Africans was detrimental to their interests, it elected not to exercise that power until the constitutional crisis of 1966. Therefore, one can see that the status of responsible government had nothing to do with responsible behavior of the government toward the Africans. Nonetheless, this new situation allowed the colonial government time to rethink things and to design a new strategy to deal with the new situation created by the status of responsible government. It soon became evident that instead of acting in a responsible manner, the colonial government acted in a way that proved its intent had been to place the Africans in a situation from which they would find it hard to rise again. The uprising of 1896, so thought the colonial government, must never be allowed to reoccur. The outbreak of the war of independence in 1966 proved that the colonial government was basing its policy and action on the wrong cultural, socioeconomic, and political assumptions.

As the new legislature was seated in 1924, the controversy surrounding the question of which of the two institutions should control African education intensified. A new dimension was introduced in that the question was not only what kind of curriculum must be taught in African schools as defined by the Graham Commission in 1911, but also who should control it. When this continuing controversy forced the government officials to conclude that the missionaries were no longer faithful to the spirit of institutional cooperation in the conduct of African education, which had existed from the time of Livingstone and Moffat, it felt a compelling need to reaffirm a major recommendation of the Graham Commission to claim that it should control it. When the Graham Commission suggested that "officials who directly control the Native population must be authorized and required to preach the doctrine of labor as a civilizing factor,"[44] it left no room for any other form of education for Africans. This was the argument the government used to justify its policy for many years to come.

These developments suggest the evidence that leads to the conclusion that the colonial government and the members of the white community feared the academic educational development of the Africans more than they feared anything else in their relationships with them. This is the reason why, reminding the members of the white community about the importance of the recommendation of the Graham Commission, Ethel Tawse Jollie, one of the first few women to sit in a colonial legislature, argued during a debate on African education in 1927: "We do not intend to hand over this country to the Natives, or to admit them to the same social and political position which we ourselves enjoy. Let us therefore make no pretense of educating them in the same way we educate whites."[45] In his support of Jollie's argument and motion, Hugh Williams, also a member of the colonial legislature in Zimbabwe at the time, went a step further in arguing that the schools the missionaries were opening for Africans were detrimental to the future political interests of the whites. Williams had a suggestion for solving what he thought to be a growing problem posed by the educational development of the Africans: "If we clear out every school which the missionaries are opening for Natives and stop all this fostering of education and development for them, we would much sooner become an asset to the [British] Empire."[46] Jollie and Williams expressed a fundamental colonial philosophy that the Rhodesia Front (RF) adopted and utilized as the cornerstone of its own policy, and Ian Smith had no apology as he argued that his government would not be expected to depart from the precedence of history.[47]

One sees that both Jollie and Williams had similar ideas of controlling Africans that were quite consistent with those of Grey, Milton, and other colonial officials of earlier times. Regardless of this negative attitude among government officials toward the genuine educational development of Africans, there were two developments that occurred in 1927 that had a profound impact on the future course of African education and the relationships that would emerge between the two cultural groups. The first was the report of the Hadfield Commission which recommended that the sixteen denominations that operated schools for Africans coordinate their efforts in order to formulate common educational objectives and curriculum.[48] The Hadfield Commission concluded that this was the best way of seeking an improvement in African education, which must include other components besides manual labor and practical training. This recommendation added new fuel to the existing controversy.

The second development was the establishment of the Department of Native Development with Harold Jowitt as its director. Two essential considerations were central to this development: that the government wanted to convince the missionaries that it was genuinely interested in the educational development of the Africans, and that its principal objective was to have Jowitt coordinate all programs having to do with African education. That for seven hard years Jowitt operated under a philosophy of education for Africans different from the one the government wanted proved to be a shattering experience for the missionaries and a disappointment for Jowitt himself. Having been put in a situation in which he could not discharge his responsibilities effectively, Jowitt had no alternative but to resign in 1934. The formation of the first African National Congress also in 1934 (the second was in 1957) proved to be the beginning of conflict between the colonial government and the Africans.

No significant change took place in the conduct of African education from 1905 to 1934, when George Stark succeeded Harold Jowitt. A conservative colonial official, Stark undid the progress that Jowitt had made. From that time to 1954, Stark based his entire policy on his philosophy of African education that "the fundamental objective in African education must be to make an effort to bind more closely the ties between the school and tribal life."[49] This is the philosophy that Godfrey Huggins, prime minister from 1933 to 1953, shared. Huggins felt that because the Africans belonged to a primitive culture, they must be allowed an education that would help arouse their minds. This is why, as late as 1954, Huggins defended his policy:

It is true to say that the more primitive the Africans, the easier the problem, both to educate and to control. You can deal with basic matters without having to consider complications which are eventually caused when primitive man becomes, to a certain point, sophisticated through whatever form of education he receives.[50]

SUMMARY AND CONCLUSIONS

The events which we have discussed in this chapter lead to the conclusion that the colonization of Zimbabwe constituted an invasion and an act of violence by the British against the Africans. Recognizing the futility of their resistance, they are forced to submit to the will of their invader. But in their submission, the invaded put in place the elements of a major conflict. This explains why a bitter war was fought between the Africans and the British from 1896 to 1897. The myth which became central to British formulation of colonial policy was a product of cooperative effort between social scientists, politicians, and Christian missionaries. The Berlin Conference of 1884 placed the missionaries on the horns of a dilemma: to pursue the policy of establishing Christian principles with their message of universal human brotherhood, or to promote British culture and commercial interests in the belief that they represented the highest Christian ideals. Instead of insisting on equality between the races, the missionaries preached to the Africans the gospel of accepting British rule in the belief that it was sanctioned by God as a means of ensuring their own salvation.

While it is true that the perpetuation of this myth about the African culture and the failure to engage in dialogue as a cooperative enterprise had severe consequences for both Africans and whites, the implementation of colonial policies arising from that myth was actually the work of individual enthusiasts who assumed a mission of promoting British imperialism in Africa. These individuals included Rhodes himself. Indeed, Rhodes went much further than becoming both a product and an agent of British imperialism, he became a British Machiavelli, whose racial philosophy became deeply rooted in his political beliefs. Rhodes was outspoken about the inferiority of African culture as he had no illusions about the importance of his mission in Africa. In petitioning Queen Victoria to grant him the Royal Charter, Rhodes argued that British culture would be advanced more effectively by subsequent colonization of Zimbabwe as the first stage of establishing a British colonial empire in Africa than by missionary effort alone. This is why, in the same year, 1889, Rhodes forcefully argued in the Cape Parliament, "The Natives are children, and we ought to do something for their mind."[51] Until the end of his life, Rhodes never considered changing or modifying his views of the Africans.

By adopting this attitude as a basis of his policy, Rhodes effectively eliminated the Africans from any form of dialogue. This made him a tragic figure in all of southern Africa. He set out to prove that divine providence and his daring financial adventure combined to make him one of the most patriotic and illustrious sons of Britain. The rapidity with which he amassed political power and fortune and by which his name became a household word demonstrates the assumed infallibility of his mission. But in all his power, Rhodes made two serious errors in his policy and action toward the Africans. The first is that in his treatment of the Africans, the subject race he identified them to be, he created conditions which accelerated the creation of an environment of conflict between the two racial groups. The second error is that for him to negate the role which the Africans must play in the course of human interaction was simply to imply that he did not care about the feelings of the people whom he regarded as inferior. Ignoring the feelings of a people who have been colonized is often a sure recipe for conflict. Rhodes's view that democracy was for whites only because the Africans were unable to understand its operation was the ultimate proof of his belief in their inferiority. This view was, of course, only expressed in the context of the Victorian myth. Rhodes was not suggesting that the British withdraw from Africa in order to practice democracy, but that from that point on it would be wise for the colonial governments to take a different course of action to ensure their power to control the Africans.

One can conclude that in the context of Victorian thinking, the contact between two groups of people profoundly different in physical appearance and cultural background did not constitute an ideal environment from which mutual respect would lead to an understanding between them. This is why Ian Smith[52] characterized the Africans as *uncivilized* and that they did not understand Western democracy. But it was Smith himself who was forced to preside over the transfer of political power to the Africans, a painful experience for a man who had refused even to talk with the Africans. Still, the white man's failure to appreciate African ability to question the legitimacy of the colonial system was a shattering experience and proved to be an erratic behavior on the part of the white man. In this setting lay the seeds of a major racial confrontation and cultural collision in Zimbabwe. This was the situation that Todd found as he arrived in Zimbabwe in 1934, and one that he had to deal with thirteen years later.

NOTES

1. History says that Darwin went on an expedition to the Galapagos Islands in 1835 to study the various species he saw there, but went back to Britain with no new information about his theory of evolution.

2. Vincent M. Battle and Charles H. Lyons (eds.), *Essays in the History of African Education* (New York: Teachers College Press, 1970), p. 2.

3. Ibid., p. 3.

4. Charles White, "The Gradation of Man" (London, 1795), in Philip D. Curtin (ed.), *The Images of Africa: British Ideas and Action, 1780–1850* (Madison: University of Wisconsin Press, 1964), p. 45.

5. Thomas Winterbottom, *An Account of the Native Africans*, 2 vols. (London: Richard Books, 1803).

6. Battle and Lyons, *Essays in African Education*, p. 2.

7. J. E. Penn and E. E. Thorpe, *Pioneers and Planters: Black Beginnings in America* (Middletown, CT: Xerox Corporation, 1971), p. 9.

8. W. D. McIntyre, *Colonies into Commonwealth* (New York: Walker and Company, 1967), p. 106.

9. Kenneth Knorr, *British Colonial Theories* (Toronto: University of Toronto Press, 1973), p. 378.

10. In his will Rhodes provided for annual scholarships, which began in 1902, to white students for study at Oxford University, his alma mater. The number of scholarships was specified in the will as follows: Canada—11, South Africa—9, Australia—6, the United States—32, Rhodesia—2, New Zealand—2. In 1976, one happy American recipient remarked that she was accepting the scholarship "to rectify some of the problems he created" (*The Lincoln Evening Journal*, Lincoln, Nebraska, December 20, 1976). Did she really believe that she could do that, or was she simply expressing excitement about receiving the prestigious scholarship?

11. *The Rudd Concession*, October 30, 1888 (Harare: Zimbabwe National Archives). For the complete text of *The Rudd Concession*, see Dickson A. Mungazi, *The Struggle for Social Change in Southern Africa: Visions of Liberty* (New York: Taylor and Francis, 1989), p. 115

12. Peter Gibbs, *Flag for the Matebele: An Entertainment in African History* (New York: The Vanguard Press, 1956), p. 31.

13. Ibid. p. 34.

14. J. S. Green, *Rhodes Goes North* (London: Bell and Sons, 1936), p. 95.

15. Upon learning of Helm's behavior, Lobengula reacted, "The white man is indeed the father of lies," Zimbabwe National Archives.

16. British South Africa Company Records, No. 369/2468–60, Zimbabwe National Archives.

17. British South Africa Company Records, March 1889, No. 369/24639–68, Zimbabwe National Archives.

18. British South Africa Company Records, No. 3921/1321, Zimbabwe National Archives.

19. It seems that the exact cause of Lobengula's death is not clearly known. Some say that he died while trying to escape. Others argue that he was actually killed by the colonial military forces. The author shares the latter opinion.

20. British South Africa Company Records: Leander Starr Jameson, Folio 1/11–109/111, Zimbabwe National Archives.

21. For the names of these organizations, see, for example, Southern Rhodesia: Commissions of Inquiry into Native Education (Alexander Kerr, Chairman), 1951, p. 3.

22. Harold Jowitt, "The Reconstruction of African Education in Southern Rhodesia" (master's thesis, University of Cape Town, 1927), p. 4. Jowitt was appointed director of Native Education in colonial Zimbabwe in that same year.

23. David Livingstone, *Missionary Travels in Southern Africa, 1857–1870* (Harare: Zimbabwe National Archives).

24. G. C. Grove, *The Planting of Christianity in Africa* Vol. II (London: Murray, 1952).

25. Jowitt, "The Reconstruction of African Education in Southern Rhodesia," p. 5.

26. British South Africa Company Records, Earl Grey, Ref. GR:1/1; sh11:Folios 547–48, Zimbabwe National Archives.

27. Robert John Challiss, "The Education Policy of the British South Africa Company in Southern Rhodesia, 1899–1904" (master's thesis, University of Cape Town, 1968), p. 43.

28. Geoffrey Kapenzi, *A Clash of Cultures: Christian Missionaries and the Shona of Southern Rhodesia* (Washington, DC: University Press of America, 1978), p. 21.

29. William Monk (ed.), *Dr. Livingstone's Cambridge Lectures* (London: Bull and Dadly, 1960), p. 166.

30. Southern Rhodesia, Ordinance Number 18 of 1899: The Appointment of Inspector of Schools, otherwise known as The Education Ordinance of 1899.

31. Ibid., Section A.

32. Ibid., Section B.

33. Southern Rhodesia, Ordinance Number 1, 1903, Section D: Schools for Natives, Zimbabwe National Archives.

34. *The Rhodesia Herald*, April 4, 1903.

35. Southern Rhodesia, *The Annual Report of the Chief Native Commissioner for Matabeleland*, 1904, Zimbabwe National Archives.

36. Southern Rhodesia, *The Annual Report of the Chief Native Commissioner for Mashonaland*, 1905, Zimbabwe National Archives.

37. Southern Rhodesia, Ordinance Number 133: Education Ordinance of 1907, Order D, Zimbabwe National Archives.

38. The Southern Rhodesia Christian Conference, Annual Report for 1906, Old Mutare Methodist Archives.

39. Southern Rhodesia, The Commission of Inquiry into Native Education (James Graham, chairman), 1911, p. 15, Zimbabwe National Archives.

40. Southern Rhodesia, Ordinance Number 7: Ordinance to Provide for the Control of Native Schools, July 12, 1912, Zimbabwe National Archives.

41. Letter written to the editor of *The Rhodesia Herald*, June 28, 1912.

42. Southern Rhodesia Christian Conference, Annual Report, 1912.

43. Henri Rolin, *Les Lois et l'Administration de la Rhodesie* (Brussels: l'Etablissment Emil Bruyant, 1913).

44. Report of the Graham Commission, para. 48, p. 7.

45. Southern Rhodesia, *Legislative Debates*, 1927.

46. Ibid.

47. Ian Smith, during an interview with the author, in Harare, Zimbabwe, July 20, 1983.

48. Southern Rhodesia, Commission of Inquiry into Native Education (F. L. Hadfield, chairman), 1927, para. 26, p. 7, Zimbabwe National Archives.

49. George Stark, writing an inspection report of Masasa School, in Harold Jowitt, *The Annual Report of the Director of Native Development*, 1930, p. 3. For a detailed discussion of Stark's policy see Dickson A. Mungazi, *Colonial Education for Africans: George Stark's Policy in Zimbabwe* (New York: Praeger, 1991).

50. Godfrey Huggins, "Taking Stock of African Education," an address to the Southern Rhodesia Missionary Conference held at Goromonzi School, August 26, 1954, Zimbabwe National Archives.

51. British South Africa Company Records, Ref. AV/1–01, Zimbabwe National Archives.

52. Ian Smith served as the last prime minister of colonial Zimbabwe from April 13, 1964, to March 3, 1979.

3

Michael Blundell: The Man and His Mission

> Changes in our and the African minds were to make my political days turbulent and difficult and finally to erase altogether the simple dictums which my friendly neighbor had given me for my first political speeches.
> —Michael Blundell, 1994

THE WORLD INTO WHICH BLUNDELL WAS BORN

The landslide victory that the British Labour Party under the leadership of Tony Blair scored in the elections held on May 2, 1997,[1] was a result of continuing change in politics that had been unfolding since the enactment of the Reform Act of 1867. This legislation was part of a new thinking that came out of the Industrial Revolution that national economic development was closely related to an emerging political philosophy that was greatly enhanced by the participation of the people. In this new line of thinking, democracy was being applied to social and human conditions in a way that had not been done in the past. Tony Blair's victory in 1997 was part of this application. Since Margaret Thatcher assumed the leadership of the Conservative Party in 1979, there has been a shift in thinking along lines that indicate that voters would closely watch political parties to determine which one seems to operate under the principles of relating political activity in response to the needs of the people.[2]

Although the evolution of the present political parties in Britain began to take shape with the Reform Act of 1867, the thinking that political action must relate to the needs of the people began to emerge in the 17th century. At that time the Tory Party was being transformed into the Conservative Party. Early in the 19th century its leader, Benjamin Disraeli, was the only man to be born a Jew who became prime minister of Britain. The reason for changing the name from Tory to Conservative was to strengthen the claim that the new party represented the interests of the people better than the old party and that its main goal was to conserve what was good for the people. Born of simple and humble origins, Disraeli tried to live and operate under this new principle. He was converted to the Church of England in 1817 in order to be more effective in responding to the needs of the people he represented. After trying several times to win a seat in the British Parliament, Disraeli was finally elected to the House of Commons in 1837 as a member of the Tory Party. But the transformation of political ideology was already under way. Although Disraeli had considerable difficulty adjusting to the new political philosophy, he managed to do so in a manner that left his name in the pages of the political history of Britain as a reasonably successful leader.

Disraeli then served as prime minister for ten months in 1868. During his second term as prime minister, from 1874 to 1880, he introduced bills that were intended to improve conditions of life for the masses. But the Conservative Party was viewed as one that still represented the interests of the aristocracy and the privileged. This reputation has continued to this day, and was partly the reason for the Labour Party's victory in the elections of May 1997 from which Tony Blair and the Labour Party emerged victorious. The phenomenon of Benjamin Disraeli was quite short-lived. Disraeli's political philosophy, that Britain must conserve what was good, also suggested the conclusion that he was not quite able to base political action on principle and functions of the Conservative Party on expectations of the people, a condition that the Industrial Revolution had created. This was the main reason why the Labour Party was formed in 1900

Because of its desire to be inclusive, the Labour Party, from its inception, included representatives of trade unions and socialist groups from all walks of life. It began to build itself as a party that represented the interests of the ordinary and common people. In the elections of 1906 the Labour Party presented 39 candidates for election to Parliament. Its platform had a special appeal to the workers and average people. Robert L. Tignor suggests that the political philosophy of the Labour Party reflected the liberal views that were coming from conditions of the times.[3]

During the First World War some leaders of the Labour Party alarmed the country by their pacifism and opposition to war in general. These leaders saw war as the ultimate betrayal of the common human good because, they argued, war is a result of the failure of politicians to apply human reason and exercise understanding to resolve conflict. Today politicians who make their countries go to war are considered to lack faith in humanity and, while they appear to negotiate in good faith, they are motivated by the illusion of military power as a form of security and resorting to war as a solution to international conflict. Ultimately it is the young people who make the ultimate sacrifice, not the politicians themselves. It is for this reason that the Labour Party minimized the importance of building military forces to defend the country, but operates under the belief that educating the citizens would be the best way of ensuring the security of the country.

In 1919 the Labour Party openly declared itself in favor of socialism. As a result its membership dramatically increased to make it the second largest political party in Britain after the Conservative Party. In 1924, a year before Michael Blundell left for Kenya, James Ramsay MacDonald formed the first Labour government. However, the party still depended upon the support of the Liberal Party to carry out its programs. In 1931 MacDonald and the members of the Labour Party left the party to join a coalition government which was formed to fight the Great Depression. In spite of this great economic disaster the Labour Party managed to retain its image among British voters that it was the party of the people.[4]

The Liberal Party follows policies that fall between those of the Conservative Party on the right and those of the Labour Party on the left. Following the Reform Act of 1832, the Whig Party also began to fall away. The other new party, the Liberal Party, was led by William Gladstone, an outstanding lay leader in the Church of England.[5] Elected to the British Parliament in 1833 as a conservative, Gladstone became a follower of Sir Robert Peel, who distinguished himself as a politician at the age of 21, first as a conservative, then as a liberal. Peel captured the imagination of those who were trying to transform the British social and economic systems.

During the debate on the repeal of the infamous Corn Laws in 1846, Gladstone switched to the Liberal Party because he believed that the Tory Party had become heavily influenced and controlled by the wealthy and the powerful. He also concluded that the Tory Party had become an instrument through which the privileged had their own way at the expense of the masses, who were expected to pay heavy taxes without receiving any benefit. In 1870 Gladstone succeeded in opening elementary schools to all children without regard to social background or position. During his term as prime minister from 1868 to 1886, Britain experienced a new sense of purpose as the ordinary people began to identify themselves with a government that was there to serve their needs. His term of office came to an end when opposition forces intensified their effort to put a stop to his program which they believed entailed socialism, especially his plan to give the Irish a larger measure of self-government.

At that time two German socialist thinkers, Karl Heinrich Marx and Friedrich Engels were having a profound impact on raising consciousness among Europeans about their place in society and the conditions that controlled their lives. Since the publication of their work, *The Communist Manifesto* in 1848, Marx and Engels were revered as social reformers who were trying to promote the welfare of the people, because they feared that the Industrial Revolution was likely to make the rich richer and the struggling poor masses even poorer. They concluded that if this happened then the revolutions of 1832 and 1848 would be minor in comparison to the nature of the social conflict that was likely to emerge. Although Gladstone did not fully embrace the ideas that Marx and Engels expressed, they certainly had a considerable appeal to the British masses. In 1892, at the age of 83, Gladstone once again served as prime minister of Britain, leaving a legacy for the 20th century that future leaders would admire and utilize as a basis of their own programs. Michael Blundell was born into this kind of environment.

It is an accepted historical fact that Gladstone was the first British leader to generate sensitivity among politicians to direct their action in response to the needs of the people. This new liberal perspective of politics sowed the seeds that germinated early in the 20th century. When Michael Blundell was born in 1907 the Liberal Party was under the leadership of Herbert Henry Asquith. When Asquith became prime minister in 1908, the Liberal Party put forth an impressive agenda for action in response to the needs of the people. His administration passed the Old Age Pension in 1908, the National Insurance Act in 1911, and the Parliamentary Act also in 1911. These pieces of legislation were intended to serve the interests of the people far more than had been done in the past. This was the first time that social legislation had been passed to address the needs of the people.

The Parliamentary Act limited the power of the House of Lords because as members of the aristocracy the House of Lords had a reputation of not caring about the conditions that governed the lives of the masses struggling for improvement in the conditions that governed their lives. When Asquith retired in 1916 he was succeeded by David Lloyd George, who had served as chancellor of the Exchequer since 1908. Highly sensitive to the tradition that politicians must fulfill their functions in response to the needs of the people, Lloyd George sought to honor the liberal philosophy that had become a central tenet of his party.

BLUNDELL MAPS OUT HIS FUTURE IN KENYA

By the time that David Lloyd George succeeded Asquith as prime minister of Britain, Blundell was nine years old, and was being introduced to the liberal traditions that had brought Britain a measured sense of prosperity for all people. A series of events from the conclusion of the Versailles Peace Conference in 1920 to the evolution of labor relations in 1925 had a profound impact on Blundell. The liberal trend that had started under William Gladstone and brought Britain to where it was became the basis of Blundell's own political philosophy. The Fourteen Points that President Woodrow Wilson presented at Versailles as a basis of future international relations also became the basis of the peace efforts for the world as a whole. The first four of these Fourteen Points are pertinent to British political action in Africa: (1) Covenants of peace must openly be arrived at with no secret agreements that may undermine the position or security of their people. (2) Freedom of the seas outside territorial waters in peace and war must be maintained in order to facilitate communications and trade among nations and people. (3) Nations must ensure the removal of all economic barriers to provide equal trade conditions among nations and their people. (4) Nations must endeavor to reduce their armaments to the lowest level consistent with domestic safety. While the Fourteen Points did not say so directly, the international community understood that they were also applicable to colonial conditions in Africa because they affected human life everywhere. This means that to some degree the colonial governments were expected to exercise proper consideration in designing policy toward Africans. To do so they were expected to adopt a more liberal perspective from which to initiate their colonial undertakings.

This is the perspective from which Britain signed a trade treaty with Russia in March 1921 and the Irish treaty in December of the same year. However, in 1922 Lloyd George, the pillar of liberal thinking in Britain, was defeated in the general elections and his administration was replaced by a Conservative Party.[6] Lloyd George's fall from power was the result of the action that was taken by Stanley Baldwin in leading a rebellion against him. However, Baldwin was defeated in 1924 due to his unpopular proposal for tariff reform. Nevertheless, ten months later, he was returned to power with increased majority. His second term of office, from 1924 to 1929, was noted for the social unrest that was part of the events that led to the Great Depression. Baldwin's third term of office from 1935 to 1937 is best known for the crisis surrounding the abdication of Edward VIII in 1936 because he decided to marry Wallis Simpson, the twice-divorced American woman he loved. The liberal trend of the time did not resolve this national crisis in a manner that was mutually satisfactory to all the parties.

While these events seemed unrelated, they had a profound impact on Blundell's thinking about his future. In October 1925 Blundell, then 18 years old, was somewhat confused by the rapid pace of events that were part of his life. On the one hand the six years following the end of the First World War seemed to cast a long shadow on the horizon of his dreams for the future. On the other hand the liberal trends that were accentuated by the thinking of the time meant a new opportunity for those who had a vision of the future different from the past. Blundell's father was a successful lawyer in London. He did everything possible to lay the foundation for his adventurous son to train for the profession that meant so much to him and his family. Given the liberal environment of the time, the young Blundell would have a career in law in Britain because of his successful study at Wellington College and his father had connections in high places.

During Blundell's closing days at Wellington College in 1923 the headmaster announced that there was an opening in Kenya for an interested boy to work as an associate to a graduate of Wellington College who was already engaged in agricultural operations. There was a reluctance on the part of students to respond to the announcement because they regarded all of Africa as an uninhabitable jungle infested with dangerous animals and savage African cannibals who resented the presence of Europeans. But Blundell seemed excited about the prospects of an adventure in Africa.

At that time an exhibition was being held at Wembly showing different parts of the British empire in Africa. He made a special effort to visit the Kenya pavilion and was quite impressed with what he saw. Photographs of great rolling plains and mountains graced the African landscape. The immense variety of wildlife from antelope to elephants added to the panoramic beauty unmatched by anything he had ever seen about Africa. The African people with their long spears, drums, and humped cattle gave him the impression of an attractive country. This captured his interests and imagination and decided to go.[7]

At an early age Blundell showed an intense interest in all aspects of Kenya: its history, its people, its geography. He read almost everything he could find. The Masai, the Embu, the Kikuyu, and the Luo became the center of his attention and reading. His father, having recognized his son's unusual interest in Kenya, did not discourage him, even though he reacted with shock when Blundell told him one afternoon that he had decided to go to Africa. Recognizing that at the age of 17 in 1924 Blundell might not have the necessary experience in life to make independent decisions, his father hoped that he might influence his son to see reason and change his initial decision. That was not to be. In 1924 Blundell had passed his entrance examinations into Magdalen College at Oxford University in order to prepare himself as a law student.[8] But his interest in Kenya was so intense that he abandoned both the pursuit of his studies and the scholarship that he had been offered to pursue his studies at Magdalen. Matched against his intense interest in Africa, Blundell considered prospects of enrolling at Magdalen College as nothing more routine than offering an average opportunity to students of average ability to lead a life of ordinary people struggling against difficult conditions that Britain would offer.

In October 1925 Blundell had made up his mind to leave for Kenya. With his personal things in two small trunks, a short gun, and 100 pounds sterling, he set sail for Kenya on the British India Company ship, the *SS Matiana*. He paid 80 pounds sterling for a first-class cabin. Twenty-nine days later he arrived at Kilindini, the major port in Mombasa, Kenya. There he was in the land of the enchanted, standing on the edge of a new African world. This was the Africa he had dreamed of when he was still young, the land of a people who were presumed inferior and uncivilized, the land he had imagined to be the focus of romantic vision and imagination that were so powerful that they derailed the hope and aspiration of his family for him to become a lawyer in Britain. Here he was captivated by the curiosity of a land and people that one could only read about in fiction or history. His interest and desire to see a strange land and its people had alienated him from his own culture and society.

Now that he was here, what was he going to do with this strange land and people whose culture he did not understand? How was he going to interact with the people whose language he did not understand? In spite of these obvious difficulties, this was the land that was to become his home for the rest of his life. As an African expression goes, he chose to see the baboons enough to share with them space on the mountain. Here Blundell and Kenya would shape each other's destiny for the next 70 years. From this time on Britain would represent a background to the past that shaped his future. It became a form of reference to political activities in Kenya. It would become a testing ground for some of the theoretical elements he formulated in Africa. It would become a place he would visit from time to time to express his views to captivated audiences about his political philosophy on the future of Kenya. But Kenya was home.

Indeed, Britain would become a country and place where he would argue with officials at the Colonial Office about policy in Kenya. It would never again become home to Blundell. Each time he returned there he did so to represent the Kenya that had become his home and part of his life. For the rest of his life Blundell placed the interests of Kenya above those of Britain. His entire political behavior was influenced by this simple fact. While he did not turn his back on the country of his birth, he recognized Britain only as an imperial nation he had to deal with because it had a vast colonial empire in Africa. This was the Blundell that neither he nor his old friends in Britain ever anticipated.

Blundell began to map out his future as soon as he arrived in Kenya. He traveled to Eldoret, where, by prior arrangements, he was going to stay with Captain Timothy Brodhurst-Hill,[9] a British aristocrat who had served all his life in the British army in India. Brodhurst-Hill was known wherever he went as Bronco Bill. On the way to Eldoret Blundell had the opportunity to see the real Africa he had imagined while he was still in Britain. Herds of elephants were slowly and elegantly pacing across the bush with majestic grace and dignity, unmindful of the concerns of the world. Lions were lying about in the hot, red soil believing that they were the real kings of the hill. Colobus monkeys leaped distances of thirty feet from one tree to the next in a spectacular show of athletic agility that defied human understanding. He was fascinated to see the baboons gracefully surveying their territory to ensure sufficient supply of food and the big dominant male watching and protecting his harem. He saw the Masai proudly leading their herds to the grazing areas, unmindful of events that were taking place elsewhere in the world.

This was the Africa Blundell had read about while he was student in Britain. Now it was part of this experience. He felt the gentle equatorial rain piercing through the thin air turning the vegetation below into a lush and green carpet that graced the vast landscape at his feet. He saw the unassuming Embu leading a simple and carefree lifestyle untouched by the pervasive influence of the white man. Slowly but steadily Blundell began to form new images of Kenya, the land, the Africans, the British immigrants he saw there, and himself. He saw the land as providing him an opportunity to develop agriculture because the climate was ideal. He was deeply impressed to see that amid the great contrast that he saw in the lifestyle of the Kikuyu, the Luo, the Kisii, and the Embu, between the tribal leader and the aspiring African, the Africans of Kenya had one thing in common: their desire to maintain their distinctive cultural identity.

Blundell soon recognized that his own society and culture had cast the Africans into stereotypes of blatant racial savages, imposing on themselves a brutal and cruel yoke of self-oppression, or beating the drums as simple children of nature as they led a simple and primitive lifestyle that defied a call to change and development. Indeed, Europeans of 1925 regarded African life as completely surrounded by an impenetrable veil of primitive existence cast in the jungle of human ignorance. Blundell quickly formed a new image of the British immigrants he saw in Kenya. He saw firsthand the extent of prejudice that, for example, Bronco Bill had toward the Africans. He was compelled to observe, "We had four Masai families on the farm who, between them, owned more than 600 head of cattle. Bronco Bill did not like the Masai and called them lazy and indolent, but could not understand that they had their own proud customs and traditions."[10]

Such was the kind of attitudes and the extent of prejudice that Europeans adopted toward Africans in order to justify their policies. The decisions that were made at the Berlin Conference in 1885 were based on this attitude and prejudice. Translated into policy this attitude alienated Europeans from the Africans. From the inception of the colonial systems in Africa, Europeans and Africans became strangers destined for a major confrontation in the future. In his study, *Facing Mount Kenya*, Jomo Kenyatta discusses how settlers succeeded in creating a social environment that eventually led to conflict between them and Africans:

Europeans have not been conspicuously zealous in imparting their inheritance to the Africans and seem to think that the only way to do it is by police discipline, and armed force. They speak as if it was somehow beneficial to any African to work for them instead of for himself. To make sure that he will receive this benefit they do their best to take away his land and leave him with no alternative. Along with his land they rob him of his government, condemn his religious ideas and ignore his fundamental conceptions of justice all in the name of civilization.[11]

In forming a new image of himself cast in an African setting, Blundell had to contrast himself with the other British settlers like Bronco Bill in order to map out his future. Part of that action was his recognition that

Bronco Bill and his wife Evelyn, were really people from another age. He was weak from years of colitis,[12] and could only walk short distances while she had a considerable intellect and critical nature. They were excessively class-conscious. When new visitors arrived, however nice and charming they might be, Evelyn would always wonder from what class they came, and he would refer to any non-regular army officer who had served in the 1914–8 war as temporary gentleman. Both were territorially minded.[13]

Blundell gives an account of how his relationship with Bronco Bill helped sharpen his own image of himself. Bronco Bill's farm was 5,000 acres and he assigned Blundell to ride a horse and regularly go around it to make sure that those "lazy and indolent Africans" did not continue their traditional footpath as a shortcut from one point to another through the farm. The practice of prohibiting Africans from passing through their farms was quite common among settler farmers in colonial Africa.[14] Blundell concluded that Bronco Bill never came to understand African culture, and that he himself would endeavor to acquire essential understanding of its basic elements so that he would be better able to relate to the African people. Bronco Bill never understood that the Africans did not harm his land. He would also rage at them for failing to greet him as Bwana (boss) on his regular walks or rides. Bronco Bill never came to understand a critical element of African culture that demanded a person in higher position or an older or senior person to make the first greeting.[15]

There were other things that Blundell learned from Bronco Bill's attitude toward Africans that provided a social environment that he needed to map out his future in Kenya. In the evening, when Bronco Bill, Evelyn, and Blundell were having dinner, three huge dogs lay around the table as if to protect them from possible African invaders. Bronco Bill did not expect Africans to behave in a dignified way toward British settlers. He did not understand that Africans respected all people regardless of who they were. One of the dogs, Sportsman, was a large and vicious Airedale terrier. The light from the paraffin (kerosene) lamps that were used before the advent of electricity was so dim that the African servant, Masirero,[16] was unable to see where the dogs lay. Somehow Sportsman often lay in the path of Masirero. Instead of removing the dogs from Masirero's way, Bronco Bill expected him to recognize the presence of the dogs in his way. Unsure of where Sportsman lay, Masirero could stumble over him, spilling the dish he was bringing to the dining table and invoking an angry reaction from both Bronco Bill and Sportsman. Ignoring the fact that both he and Sportsman were to blame, Bronco Bill reacted, "You clumsy, lout you!"[17]

Blundell quickly learned that the African world was what it was because the British settlers made it so. One day the key to the storage room was misplaced. After making a desperate effort to locate it, Bronco Bill decided to open it by some other means. He secured a long and large screwdriver and painfully unscrewed the steel hinges as he stood on a wooden stool. Masirero held the stool in place to make sure that Bronco Bill did not fall. After considerable effort and amount of time Bronco Bill succeeded in unscrewing the hinges. The entire process was repeated in reverse, making Masirero very uncomfortable.

A few weeks later, when Blundell was alone with Masirero at the farm, the key to the same storage room was once again misplaced. Blundell was about to start the process of unscrewing the hinges when Masirero came up to him and told him not to worry because all the keys in the house opened the storage room door. Masirero picked up one of the keys and opened the door. Why did Masirero not remind Bronco Bill of this fact the first time? The reason is that Bronco Bill was unapproachable. Masirero would rather follow instructions from Bronco Bill, than suggest solutions to problems. Blundell learned an important lesson that day: Masirero's silent world in the presence of Bronco Bill was created by Bronco Bill himself. For Blundell this was a revelation that he needed in order to map out his future in the real African world, not the one that Bronco Bill was trying to create. He immediately decided that he was going to approach the question of human communication in an open and honest way. In 1938, when Blundell sought his first political office, he applied this lesson with success.

In an indirect way Bronco Bill's attitude toward Africans helped Blundell map out his future in Africa. Six months after his arrival at Bronco Bill's farm he noticed something that had a lasting impact on him. H. B.

Swann, a young man three years older than Blundell, joined in the Bronco Bill household. Swann paid 30 pounds sterling per month for his education in agricultural operations. He was the son of a wealthy Englishman and had 10,000 pounds with which to buy a farm and settle down to farming. Swann was also a graduate of New College, Oxford with manners of an aristocrat who drank gin and smoked expensive cigarettes.

Soon after Swann's arrival Bronco Bill and Evelyn began to treat him and Blundell very differently. They regarded Blundell as a poor young man who did not have as much money as Swann, even though his father was a successful solicitor in Britain. But they regarded Swann as a distinguished young man from the upper social class. They gave Swann a bedroom much better than the one they gave Blundell. As soon as he arrived Swann received special treatment fitting his upper social class. However, Swann showed a deficiency in his habits. Blundell explained how, "when talking to Evelyn the ash on his cigarette got longer and longer until he leant forward in front of her and under her nose flicked the ash across her into the fireplace."[18]

Although Bronco Bill and Evelyn regarded this habit as the height of bad manners, they gave Swann a preferential treatment over Blundell, a young man they thought was working for room and board. Blundell began to rethink his identity within the Bronco Bill household. He became convinced that he had lost meaning given the place that Swann was enjoying. He began to feel more and more that as long as he remained there Bronco Bill would always have a limited opportunity for his efforts to gain new and meaningful experiences. In December 1926, one year after he had arrived, Blundell concluded that it was time to move to Solai, where he was hired as a farm manager at a salary of 7 pounds and 10 shillings per month. He gave Bronco Bill a notice of three months to leave. Bronco Bill was just as pleased to see him go because he believed that he lacked sufficient educational background to understand important aspects of agricultural operations in Kenya.

Blundell was so successful as manager of the farm in Solai that with his father's help he bought a quarter share in the farm three years later in 1929. But this is the year that the Great Depression started and for the next ten years it was a great struggle. However, Blundell and his older brother bought the whole farm at a price four times lower than its actual price.[19] The collapse of the price of agricultural products continued from 1929 to 1939. The price of maize, the main crop in Kenya, fell from 16 shillings to 3 shillings a bag and butterfat, which gave farmers a monthly income, fell to half a shilling per pound. Now that Blundell had his own farm, he and his brother decided to diversify their agricultural activity in order to fight the effects of the Depression. Raising livestock and diversifying crop production to include coffee, maize, wheat, oats, and other crops made it possible for them to counteract the devastation of the Depression. From 1933 to 1935, with the help of the Africans and their knowledge of agriculture, Blundell and his brother were able to produce enough to remain in operation. By 1936 they had turned the corner as the worldwide Depression began to show signs of ending. The losses they had suffered now slowly began to turn into profit.[20]

BLUNDELL'S MISSION: THE DILEMMA OF A POLITICIAN

The improvement in the economy led to the increase in confidence in the future. From 1936 to the beginning of the war in 1939, Blundell seized the opportunity to play an increasing role in the developments in Kenya. However, he took no part in political activity in those years, preferring to devote all his efforts to agricultural production. Political activity was directed at improving relationships between the settler community and the colonial government concerning the distribution of land and the rights of the individual settler. Seeking an improvement in relationships between settlers and Africans was not considered important except in the area of cheap labor to make it possible for farmers to make profit from their agricultural operations.

In 1964 Blundell observed the nature of colonial political activity, saying "Except for the long established bubble and squeak of the Kikuyu political scene, where these aggressive, industrious and sensitive people enjoyed the intrigue and the whispering of an embryonic nationalism, the scene was tranquil."[21] However, the main focus of settler political activity was the need to establish an economic system which would make it possible for settler farmers to survive and allow them to be involved in the political events of the colony.

The masses of the African people were not yet politically conscious to demand direct involvement in political activity. That would come later. They were only aroused when the colonial administration, in trying to create a climate that it considered conducive to the evolution of a modern country, ran against age-old tribal traditions that the Africans considered detrimental to their own interests. For Blundell and his fellow settlers, life encountered daily challenges of unexpected dimensions. The only certainty they enjoyed was the freedom to own vast tracts of land, bought at a very low price, and a steady supply of cheap labor that the Africans provided. This is why many of them came to Africa in the first place.

In addition to all this, settlers had an implacable sense of achievement and divine purpose to create a utopia for the future British settlers or their children and grandchildren. At least that is what they thought.

None of them, except a few that included Blundell, were ever able to see Africans as rapidly becoming politically conscious in a way that demanded fundamental change in the political process. None of them saw the possibility that in less than 20 years Africans would demand nothing less than total control of the government itself. This would become a reality in 1945 with the conclusion of the war.

The outbreak of the war in September 1939 posed a serious threat to the economic recovery that the settlers believed represented the resurgence of confidence in the future and to the efforts they were making in trying to build a social utopia in Africa. They regarded the Axis powers as the epitome of evil to be eliminated from the face of the earth, a social cancer that was trying to spread to all parts of the body of the international community. At the age of 32 Blundell was considered too old for military service. He was therefore asked to continue his agricultural operations as well as to manage several other farms in the area whose owners had already been conscripted into the army.

But in January 1940 this position would change. As Blundell was trying to settle in to assume his new duties and play his role in the economic activity, he was suddenly summoned to the military headquarters in Nairobi and was informed that the first battalion of the King's African Rifles at Isiolo in the northern frontier district had mutinied that the situation was still very unsettled. Military officials told him that because of his knowledge of African culture and language he was being asked to take command of the battalion. Following a month of training Blundell went to his new post, 70 miles to the northeast at Garbo Tule. By the time he arrived, the battalion was camped on the edge of Nyambeni Hills, right in the middle of a lava belt. There wild game freely roamed the area and scattered in the open plains in great numbers.[22]

Blundell decided that in order to end the mutiny and create confidence among members of the battalion, he needed to show appreciation of the position in which its members found themselves. He felt they believed they were being sent into action without weapons and proper training because they were Africans. He shared their concern and sought to rebuild their confidence in him and asked them to respond to what he considered a national call to join efforts to fight against the Axis powers for the freedom of all people. This was a strange claim, considering the fact that colonial conditions do not allow freedom of all people. However, in this simple military decision Blundell was unaware that he had established a social environment that would enable him and the Africans to function in the political arena only three years following the end of the war. In achieving success, where his predecessor had experienced only failure, in his attempt to end the mutiny by members of the King's African Rifles, Blundell was defining the parameters of his mission, both for the present and for the future. The success of his battalion in Ethiopia would later translate into success in other areas of his mission following the conclusion of the war in 1945.

In 1946 Blundell was released from the army to return to his farm in Solai, where there was much to be done to solve the operational problems of five years of neglect caused by the war. At that time Blundell was the most eligible bachelor at the age of 39. One evening, while dancing in Nairobi to celebrate his release from the army, a lovely girl named Gerry caught his eye. He and Gerry danced together for the rest of the evening. Before the evening was over Blundell asked Gerry to marry him. But Gerry, taking his proposal as a joke, burst into laughter and told him that he must have had too much drink.[23] However, sensing his seriousness, Gerry accepted the proposal and they were married a week later in Nairobi. Blundell and his new bride spent their honeymoon on the farm, much to Gerry's delight because she hated traveling long distances. For the rest of his life Blundell never stopped making Gerry laugh. Years later, when his political fire was extinguished, Gerry shared the twilight years of his life constantly by his side living on the memories that meant so much to both. She was trying to relight the ebbing fervor of the past as the old soldier and romantic was pacing closer to the edge of the River Jordan of his life, getting ready to cross it into eternity.

Blundell and Gerry had hardly been on the farm two weeks when he was invited to take on the responsibility of initiating a settlement scheme for new British immigrants to Kenya, most of them former soldiers. The scheme had been initiated by the colonial government in cooperation with the Colonial Office in London to encourage business development in light of the expansion of new opportunity that was expected as a result of the end of the war. In accepting the invitation Blundell was unaware that he was taking the first step toward his initiation into the political arena of colonial Kenya. After discussing details of his new responsibility with Major Ferdinand C. Cavendish-Bentinck, who was one of the elected members of the legislative council and of the government responsibility for the overall supervision of the scheme, Blundell assumed his new mission with great enthusiasm.

In explaining the task Blundell was about to assume, Cavendish-Bentinck gave him the political support that he thought he needed. As an elected member of the legislative council who represented settlers in the district of North Nairobi, Cavendish-Bentinck had considerable influence among British settlers. He was one of two candidates for the position of leader of the legislative council, a position similar to that of party chairman, who, in an independent country, would become prime minister following an election in which his party has a majority of seats. However, Cavendish-Bentinck narrowly lost the position to Alfred Vincent, another elected member of the legislative council representing another district in Nairobi.[24] With this loss Cavendish-Bentinck also lost the political influence he once exercised in colonial politics and was therefore in no position to assist Blundell in carrying out his new assignment. Blundell was left to struggle on his own because Vincent did not support him as much as Cavendish-Bentinck did. It turned out that Blundell and Vincent became political adversaries, unable to reconcile themselves to the fact that within a few years Africans would take over political control of the country.

Fearing to be regarded as a failure, Blundell struggled against formidable odds to make the scheme a success. Cavendish-Bentinck had impressive political credentials. Born in 1889, he began his political career as private secretary to the governor of Uganda from 1925 to 1927. He then moved to Kenya where he became a hard-liner in colonial politics and a powerful defender of the notion of Kenya as a white man's country. He became secretary to the Association of British Immigrants to Kenya and then an elected member of the legislative council representing the Nairobi North district. He was appointed secretary of the white-elected members organization of the council. But, in his association with Blundell, Cavendish-Bentinck began to modify his views and assumed a moderate position, realizing that at some point in time Africans would have control of the country. This is why he and Blundell had a close relationship. But Vincent would have no such Damascus Road experience, he remained solid in his view of Kenya as a white man's country.

In 1945, Philip E. Mitchell, governor from 1944 to 1952, introduced a system of membership in the legislative council in which leading unofficial members resigned their districts to join the government as members in charge of departments. Cavendish-Bentinck became the member with responsibility for agriculture, forests, and water development. He also served as the speaker of the legislative council from 1955 to 1960. He resigned in March 1960 to form the Kenya Coalition Party, whose main policy was to protect the interests of settlers, which he believed had been eroded away by the Lyttleton constitution of 1954 and the Lennox-Boyd constitution of 1957. Cavendish-Bentinck knew that he was fighting a losing battle, Kenya was on its way to independence under an African government.[25]

Blundell greatly admired Cavendish-Bentinck's political courage with which he approached his task and readily identified himself with his mission to protect the interests of settlers. Blundell was so successful in managing the settlement scheme that by 1947 it had received national attention and Blundell received all the credit. At that time he had successfully located 81 new settlers, and his office was in the process of interviewing 3,000 new applicants and had administered 2 million pounds sterling provided by the colonial development loans that came from the colonial government. Blundell became an instant celebrity whose name was associated with efforts of those former soldiers who were searching for an opportunity to establish agricultural enterprise in the famous central highlands. Blundell was the rising star shining to provide the guiding light for settlers who were seeking an opportunity in a part of the continent where land was considered plenty. Now he was ready to launch the next phase of his mission by active participation in colonial politics.

Blundell had a taste of political power in 1938 when he was elected to the Coffee Board of Kenya. As a progressive farmer who adopted methods of agriculture far different from the bad methods he observed Bronco Bill use,[26] Blundell did his best to promote the latest methods of growing quality coffee. He distinguished himself as an effective member of this important board by expressing ideas and thoughts that he believed represented the best economic interests of coffee growers. Through his efforts the price of coffee was now giving the growers the economic boost they needed to lead a comfortable life, while raising Blundell's political fortunes to new heights. The reciprocal benefit that the coffee growers and Blundell obtained later translated into a call for him to launch a more important mission in a larger national arena. Blundell would have done this earlier if the war had not broken out in 1939.

However, in 1947 Blundell felt that he was now ready to launch the most important phase of his mission. Indeed, the success he had scored as a member of the Coffee Board in 1938 and his successful military campaign combined to give him the background that he needed to attract the attention and support of the people in his district. In 1947 Walter French, a farmer in the Rift Valley, who was the elected member of the legislative council, asked Blundell to represent the district as a nominated member for six months while he was away on leave in Ireland. This gave Blundell an opportunity of a lifetime. Blundell did every thing possible to capture the moment to demonstrate his political knowledge.

On his return in 1948, French decided not to seek reelection to his seat. He appeared to have lost the support of the people while he was on leave in Ireland. He had also lost his enthusiasm for politics and preferred to attend to his farm, which had deteriorated badly while he was away. Members of his district began to compare his performance with that of Blundell and concluded that French should retire from politics. There was a considerable lack of interest in his experiences in Ireland. French had become a spent force, a forgotten warrior in the face of an energetic and enthusiastic individual who seemed to have what the district needed to offer an effective representation for the district.

Out of a sense of dejection and hopelessness, French asked Blundell to run for his seat. Blundell was somewhat surprised by French's move. Although he knew he would win, Blundell did not want to create the impression that he was acting in an underhanded manner in seeking to replace French, especially the possible feeling among members of the district that he worked hard to undermine French while he was on leave in Ireland. Therefore, Blundell's immediate reaction to French's suggestion was, as he stated later, "I was rather doubtful about this as I had paid attention to politics, but I thought perhaps it opened a door into a new world which was worth exploring."[27] After considering the suggestion Blundell did not jump to the opportunity; he was still unable to reach a decision as to what he should do. He decided to seek the advice of his neighbor and successful businessman, Major H. F. Ward. Ward encouraged him to run, saying that the district needed someone to represent it more effectively than French had done. Blundell then asked Ward what he should say during the election campaign. Ward responded, "All you need to say is that you support the sanctity of the white highlands, the communal role and separate education for each race and you will be elected."[28]

Although Blundell did not think that this strategy was particularly appealing to the voters, he adopted it and was elected. However, long before his death, Blundell had repudiated this political philosophy, and in 1992, a year before his death, he explained why he did not think such an approach would work in a vastly changing environment, saying that conditions demanded that Kenya must become independent.[29] But in doing so Blundell compromised his basic principle never to invoke racism into the political arena because he was raised by traditions that rejected it. How was he going to live with himself? What kind of values was he going to operate under in the future? Indeed, Ward was quite correct in advising Blundell to adopt an anti-African position. Throughout colonial Africa this strategy always yielded high political profit. The white politicians knew that white voters were totally against any form of racial understanding or cooperation because they believed that Africans were inferior. These white politicians knew that adopting a position against Africans gave them a ticket to political power and influence.[30]

Blundell's opponent was Lody Francis Scott, the brother of the Duke of Buccleuch. Apart from being a member of the aristocracy, Scott was a dull and unexciting campaigner whose understanding of the issues was seriously impaired by too much self-pride and class consciousness. Scott was also caught between his understanding of his responsibility to all people, including Africans, because his position demanded it, and the need to adopt the traditional negative attitude toward Africans. Scott therefore could not pass the litmus test that white voters expected politicians to take regarding their views of the place of Africans in the colonial society. Blundell exploited this situation to his advantage. But in doing so he was caught between two sets of conflicting values. On the one hand he sought political office based on what was a racist colonial philosophy.

On the other hand Blundell knew or claimed that he was not a racist.

He knew that from the time of birth in 1907 to the time that he was elected to the Kenya legislative council in 1948, the liberal traditions established during the days of James Ramsay MacDonald, Herbert Henry Asquith, David Lloyd George, Stanley Baldwin, and his own father had brought tangible benefits to ordinary people as an important prerequisite of bringing benefits to society itself. During the six weeks of campaigning Blundell was acutely aware of this form of white man's burden cast in an African setting. Where did he place his loyalty? To the traditions that had brought him to Africa and were now about to place him in the seat of power, or to the short-sighted expedience created by colonial conditions? Only he could answer the question.

Indeed, Blundell had to search his soul carefully to recognize the forces that were impacting his mental processes. He had to reexamine the values that had brought him to where he was in terms of the direction they were likely to lead him into the future. He needed to remember that the Kenya of 1948 was quite different from the Kenya of 1925. He also needed to remember that while the settler voters expected him to behave in a manner that represented their political views, especially those on race, his own background required him to scale the walls of human endeavor in order to articulate his own position consistent with the values of his upbringing and the traditions that made him who he was. Indeed, Blundell found himself facing a dilemma of choice that only he could resolve. In doing so he would be wise to project a future different from the past.

The election campaign was not based on issues associated with party principles and policy but purely on how what candidates said appealed to voters. Blundell observed on this aspect of colonial politics: "The election campaign took place over six weeks and I got bored with making the same speech at innumerable small meetings and changed it at intervals, but the other candidates stuck firmly to the same address right throughout the campaign."[31] While Blundell was bored with making the same speech to different audiences, his message got through to the voters. He saw that politicians needed to do this to be consistent in what they were saying and to have a broad acceptance of their ideas by showing what they considered knowledge of the issues based upon principles the voters could support. What really bored him, however, was the message that voters wanted him to deliver, that Africans had no place in the Kenya of the future. Blundell knew that this message was not only foolish, but it was also outright dangerous. But he had to deliver that message to get the vote. This approach simply accentuated the dilemma of choice that he was facing as a politician.

As the campaign progressed Blundell felt compelled to maintain some positive attributes of both worlds. He sought the white vote so he could represent their interests in the legislative council. In seeking to do so he also sought to maintain a semblance of communication with Africans. Although he won the election he did not seem to have much success with either world. One incident seemed to remain in his memory. On polling day Blundell was traveling around the polling stations to get some indication of how the voters were responding to the campaign. He came upon a car that had broken down with a family originally from South Africa inside and stranded. Remembering that in 1948 South Africa was under the grip of the Nationalist government led by Daniel F. Malan, this encounter carried ominous implications.

Blundell asked the occupants of the car if he could help by offering to take them in his own car to the polling station where they were going to cast their ballots. The occupants readily accepted the offer. As soon as they reached the polling station the four occupants of the car rushed out of Blundell's car into the station to cast their ballots without even taking a moment to thank him for the ride. After the election was over, Blundell learned from one of his election campaign organizers that all the people he had given a ride to had voted against him because they had learned that he had socialized with Africans by having tea with them.[32] From this experience Blundell learned an important lesson: the perils of a liberal politician come in strange turns.

Blundell's election to the colonial legislative council meant that 23 years after he arrived in Kenya he was now in the seat of power that enabled him to influence the direction that the country was going to take. Was it possible for him to focus strictly on representing the interests of British settlers and imperil their future by alienating the Africans, or was he going to devote his efforts toward seeking an improvement in the conditions of life of the Africans and so alienate the settlers, whose vote he needed to remain in office? This situation presented him with yet another dilemma of choice only a liberal politician was destined to encounter.

The question now is: What did Blundell accomplish during the 14 years that he was in the seat of power from 1948 to 1962? The list may be as impressive as it may be deceptive. From 1948 to 1957 he was the white elected member of the legislative council representing the Rift Valley doing his best to represent the interests of the settler community. In 1952 he became leader of the white elected members of the legislative council. In 1954 he was appointed minister without portfolio. In that position he played a major role in fighting against the Mau Mau uprising. From 1955 to 1959 and from 1961 to 1962 he served as minister of agriculture. From 1959 to 1963 he became leader of the New Kenya Group consisting of liberal whites and moderate Africans. From 1962 to 1967 he served as director of a multinational company operating in East Africa.[33]

There was something that weighed heavily upon Blundell's mind as he was ready to assume his mission as a full-fledged politician in 1948. He became increasingly aware of the hard reality that settlers who had fought in the war side by side with Africans realized that they had to adopt a completely different attitude toward race and race relationships if they hoped to have a future in Kenya. They had to recognize Africans as people with whom they had to share opportunity for development and political participation on the basis of equality. They also had to recognize that Africans had a new vision of themselves as a people different from the stereotypical perceptions that dictated policy and programs initiated by the colonial government. Above all the settlers were expected to recognize the fact that within a very short period of time they would have to accept the fact that Africans would have full control of the government. In recognizing the importance of adopting new attitudes toward Africans Blundell was compelled to conclude that

changes in our and the African minds were to make my political days turbulent and difficult and finally to erase altogether the simple dictums which my friendly neighbor had given me for my first political speeches. Indeed, allied also with pressures on the British government and the destruction of the imperial will as a result of the war they were to lead to independence for Kenya.[34]

This statement, made in 1992, the year of his death, is a classical example of the dilemma that Blundell faced as a politician.

SUMMARY AND CONCLUSION

This chapter has been an introduction to the role that Michael Blundell played in the developments that shaped the future of Kenya from the time he was elected to the Coffee Board of Kenya in 1938 until he was elected to the colonial legislative council in 1948. Because of the environment in which he was raised in Britain until he emigrated to Kenya in 1925, Blundell integrated elements of liberalism and moderation that placed him at the political crossroads, which made it very difficult to function effectively in an effort to satisfy members of both races. Having learned the game of political survival, Blundell approached his mission with courage and determination. In the end he seems to have accomplished his mission with a degree of measured success. But his was not an easy task by any means.

NOTES

1. In these elections the Labour Party won 419 seats, 89 more than the 330 seats needed for an absolute majority. The Conservative Party, led by John Major, won only 161 seats. The extent of the loss compelled Major to resign as leader

of the Conservative Party, raising speculation that Margaret Thatcher might once again seek its leadership.

2. On August 30, 1997, when Princess Diana was killed in a traffic accident in Paris, Blair was visibly shaken by the tragedy, saying "I feel like everyone else in this country, totally devastated." That is the kind of response of a national leader who cares about his people.

3. Robert L. Tignor, *The Colonial Transformation of Kenya: The Kamba, the Kikuyu, and the Masai from 1900 to 1939* (Princeton, NJ: Princeton University Press, 1976), p. 94.

4. G. H. Mungeam, *British Rule in Kenya, 1895–1912* (Oxford: Clarendon Press, 1966), p. 262.

5. Gladstone wrote several books on theology and was highly regarded for his views of relating political action and theology to address the needs of people.

6. Stephen Constantine, *David Lloyd George* (New York: Routledge 1992), p. ix.

7. Michael Blundell, *A Love Affair with the Sun: A Memoir of Seventy Years in Kenya* (Nairobi: Kenway Publications, 1994), p. 1.

8. Ibid., p. 7.

9. Ibid., p. 8.

10. Ibid., p. 5.

11. Jomo Kenyatta, *Facing Mount Kenya* (Nairobi: Kenway Publications, 1938), p. 317.

12. A painful inflammation of the colon that often has a negative effect on one's ability to think rationally.

13. Blundell, *A Love Affair with the Sun*, p. 6.

14. The author recalls that as he was growing up in colonial Zimbabwe, one settler farmer, B. D. Goldberg, a wealthy man who had 7,000 acres, threatened to shoot any African who passed through his land.

15. Blundell, *A Love Affair with the Sun*, p. 6.

16. Blundell does not give Masirero's family name. This was a common practice in colonial Africa to suggest the inferiority of the Africans. Blundell learned this practice as soon as he arrived in Kenya. Settlers never addressed Africans with a title such as Miss, Mr., or Mrs. They addressed them only by their first name, a practice Africans bitterly resented. In 1964 Martin Luther King, Jr. discussed how southern whites used this practice to reinforce the inferiority of African Americans and how African Americans themselves fought against as part of their struggle for civil rights. King said, "When you have to concoct an answer for a five-year-old son who is asking: 'Daddy, why do white people treat colored people so mean?'; when you take a cross-country drive and find it necessary to sleep night after night in the uncomfortable corners of your automobile because no motel will accept you; when you are humiliated day in and day out by nagging signs reading 'white' and 'colored', when your first name becomes 'nigger,' your middle name becomes 'boy' and your last name becomes 'John,' and your wife and mother are never given the respected title 'Mrs.,' then you will understand why it is difficult for us to wait." Martin Luther King, Jr, *Why We Can't Wait* (New York: New American Library, 1964), p. 81.

17. Blundell, *A Love Affair with the Sun*, p. 6.

18. Ibid., p. 9.

19. Michael Blundell, *So Rough a Wind* (London: Weidenfeld and Nicolson, 1964), p. 42.
20. Ibid., p. 43.
21. Ibid., p. 45.
22. Blundell, *A Love Affair with the Sun*, p. 48.
23. Blundell, *So Rough a Wind*, p. 61.
24. Ibid., p. 62.
25. Bethwell, A. Ogot, *Historical Dictionary of Kenya* (London: The Scarecrow Press, 1981), p. 35.
26. Blundell, *A Love Affair with the Sun*, p. 8.
27. Ibid., p. 85.
28. Ibid., p. 86.
29. Ibid., p. 85.
30. For detailed discussion of this strategy, see Dickson A. Mungazi, *Colonial Education for Africans: George Stark's Policy in Zimbabwe* (New York: Praeger, 1991).
31. Blundell, *A Love Affair with the Sun*, p. 85.
32. Ibid., p. 86.
33. Ogot, *Historical Dictionary of Kenya*, p. 31.
34. Blundell, *A Love Affair with the Sun*, p. 86.

4

Garfield Todd: The Man and His Mission

> The Africans are aware that educated people can be governed, but they cannot be enslaved forever. They are no longer willing to be controlled in the manner in which they have been controlled in the past.
>
> —Garfield Todd, 1947

THE WORLD INTO WHICH TODD WAS BORN

When Reginald Stephen Garfield Todd was born in New Zealand on July 12, 1908, the world was going through considerable change. A year before, New Zealand had achieved dominion status giving its people considerable autonomy. Although the British monarchy still exercised constitutional responsibility, the people of New Zealand, most of them immigrants from Britain, began to enjoy the responsibility of self-rule with little interference from Britain. The rise in prices for exports and increase in production, especially wool, led to corresponding increase in confidence in ability to provide a stable system of government. The conflict that had broken out in 1845 between the settlers and the Maoris had, by 1900, been transformed into peace that was needed to plan the future. Britain, having been satisfied that New Zealand was on the road to progress, granted its request for dominion status in 1907, the year that Michael Blundell was born.

Chapter 1 concluded that Britain of 1908 was going through a period of unprecedented social change because the leadership that emerged from the Industrial Revolution embraced a new concept of political philosophy and action that were directed at serving the needs of people. The leadership of Herbert Henry Asquith beginning in that year soon had a profound influence on a new progressive perception among the British people about themselves and their society. Asquith fully understood the fact that the Liberal Party had a major role to play in seeking improvement in the standard of living of the people. To accomplish this goal the Asquith administration presented to the British Parliament a set of carefully structured pieces of legislation for enactment into law.

The year 1908 is also when critical developments were taking place in South Africa. The conclusion of the Boer War in 1902 led to intense political activity that finally reestablished British domination over the Afrikaners during the next six years, forcing the humiliated Boers to recognize the British government as supreme over them. In 1908, however, the Boers signed the Treaty of Vereeniging, providing for independence in 1910 as a result of terminating hostilities.[1] In the context of the great liberal movement that was sweeping across the British empire in 1908, the Treaty of Vereeniging was signed in a political environment that made it a highly controversial document as it cast the future of South Africa in serious doubt because it did not accommodate the future of Africans. Failure to take the position of Africans in planning the future of South Africa cost it dearly as the country was caught in decades of conflict that finally came to an end in April 1994 when an African government led by Nelson Mandela was installed following elections in which all people participated.

In 1908 Canada was going through a period of political revival within the environment that Asquith, David Lloyd George, and other great liberals had created. In that year William Lyon Mackenzie King was elected to the Canadian Parliament. From the beginning of his life King was introduced to the great movement of liberal thought which stressed the theme of service to the people as a central tenet of the responsibility that politicians had to fulfill. This is why King had a great ambition to meet Jane Addams,[2] the famous founder of Hull House in Chicago. Addams attracted international attention by her efforts in settling immigrants from Europe in Chicago, and was recognized for her campaign to give women the right to vote. This was finally achieved by the passage of the Nineteenth Amendment, which went into effect on August 26, 1920.

In 1896, when King attended the University of Chicago, Addams invited him to live at Hull House. The two became close associates in the struggle for the promotion of liberal causes, which included the development of the individual human being as the most important resource any nation needed for its own development. King served as prime minister of Canada from 1921 to 1930 and from 1935 to 1948 along the Asquith-Lloyd George traditions and setting Canada on the road to rapid development. Canada would never be the same again. As a national leader King helped raise consciousness among politicians that their primary responsibility was to serve the needs of the people. This came as a reminder that politicians who failed to operate under this basic principle should not remain in office. King represented the epitome of integrity in politics that his successor, Louis S. St. Laurent, who served from 1948 to 1957, established traditions that raised Canada to an unprecedented level of national development.[3] This is the tradition that his successor as prime minister, John Diefenbaker utilized from 1957 to 1963— the same period that Harold Macmillan served as prime minister of Britain—used to place Canada on the road to rapid national development.

In 1908 dramatic developments were also unfolding in Zimbabwe, a country that became Todd's home in 1934. Two of these developments deserve mention and a brief discussion: the appointment of the Hole Commission to investigate the conduct of African education, and the election of Charles Coghlan to the legislative council. The founding of the Southern Christian Missionary Conference in 1906 was a response to rapidly moving events that were both economic and political. These were part of the movement of liberal thought that was already under way in Britain. The Southern Rhodesia Missionary Conference focused on the need to improve the position of Africans under colonial domination as a condition of national development. In their own projection, members of the Southern Rhodesia Missionary Conference saw conflict in the future if the position of Africans did not improve. Consistent with the spirit of liberal views that were in operation at the time, the missionaries felt they had a responsibility to promote the development of Africans to prepare them for the future.

In 1908 the Southern Rhodesia Missionary Conference made strong representations to the colonial government to do something soon to improve the educational opportunity for Africans. The Conference also continued to criticize the policy of the colonial government in general as biased against Africans. Unable to endure this criticism any longer William Henry Milton, who served as administrator from 1898 to 1914, responded to this criticism by naming Marshall H. Hole chairman of a commission of inquiry into education for Africans. Hole was a senior civil commissioner in Bulawayo and had participated in the first war of liberation from 1896 to 1897. He was considered knowledgeable about critical features of African culture.[4] The terms of reference the Hole Commission was "to inquire into and reporting upon the laws and system under which education is at present being provided for Natives and make such recommendations as will improve efficiency in government role."[5]

In outlining these terms of reference, Milton, a moderately liberal colonial official of the Asquith-Lloyd George tradition, addressed only the need for efficiency in the delivery system of educational programs. He did not focus on the evolution of policy elements that would promote the development of the Africans as the Southern Rhodesia Missionary Conference had suggested. Some 40 years later Todd would address the principles governing the naming of commissions of inquiry into education. As a result of what Milton failed to address, the Hole Commission simply recommended that the colonial government exercise more power to control education for Africans in accordance with the requirements of the Education Ordinance of 1899, which required that Africans receive no academic training.[6]

Therefore, the Southern Rhodesia Missionary Conference and the colonial government saw education for Africans from two completely opposite perspectives. The former wanted to see the evolution of policy that would promote the rapid advancement of Africans, and the latter wanted to exercise more power to control that development. In this setting the institutional conflict that first emerged in 1898 took perilous dimensions. Milton had been appointed to improve the efficiency of the colonial administrative system, not to provide vision in the evolution of policy needed to ensure the development of the country. This means that the difference of opinion between church leaders and leaders of the colonial government did not agree about policy. Todd would later play a major role in that controversy, helping to bring the colonial government to an end sooner than was expected.

The second dramatic development that took place in 1908 is the election of Charles Coghlan to the legislative council in colonial Zimbabwe. Born in South Africa on June 24, 1863, Coghlan studied law and practiced it in Kimberly, the city where Cecil John Rhodes made a fortune by investing in the diamond mining industry. Coghlan went to Zimbabwe in 1900 and settled in Bulawayo where he established a law practice. He was so successful that in 1908 he was elected to the legislative council. There Coghlan quickly rose to the position of leadership of the Liberal Party and distinguished himself as an effective advocate of the rights of all people. In so doing he soon came into conflict with the policy of the colonial administration led at that time by William Henry Milton. Only six months younger than David Lloyd George, Coghlan quickly adopted the political philosophy that was making Lloyd George a household name in political thought in both Britain and its empire.

Milton, who shared Coghlan's political philosophy, was placed in a restraining position by virtue of the high office he held. This allowed Coghlan to distance himself from the policy that Milton was pursuing. Through no choice of their own the two men were heading toward a showdown, a battle of wills. Milton was a colonial bureaucrat who saw his position as maintaining the status quo by implementing the policy of an unpopular system. From his unique point of view Coghlan saw the policy Milton was pursuing as posing a threat to the stability of the existing system. Coghlan also saw Milton as representing a system that was riddled with gross flaws and injustice. When Milton retired in 1914, a stalemate had existed between him and Coghlan to the extent that there was little progress made in the development of the country. In Coghlan's eyes Milton had come to represent stagnation. In Milton's eyes Coghlan had come to represent a radical approach and anarchy to national programs.

In October 1908 an opportunity presented itself for Coghlan to show skills in political leadership. A national convention was held in Durban as a follow-up to the Treaty of Vereeniging to consider reunification of the four provinces in South Africa in preparation for independence, which was to be achieved on May 31, 1910. Colonial Zimbabwe was invited to send a delegation with the right to participate in the deliberations but no right to vote.[7] Coghlan was the leader of the delegation which consisted of two other members: Milton himself and Lewis Michell, a senior member of his administration. The issue before the convention was whether the four provinces should form a federation or union. In a federation power was divided more or less equally between the states and the federal government. In a union the central government would exercise more power.

When the vote was taken delegates decided to have a union instead of a federation. Using his knowledge of South Africa Coghlan effectively argued in favor of a union, hoping that the union government would be in a much stronger position than the federal government in protecting the rights of all people. He was particularly concerned that if the issue of representation of the Africans was not fully resolved, there would be a serious conflict in the future. No one listened to him but Coghlan was quite right. Conflict began as soon as South Africa gained independence. The impact of these events was not lost on the future of colonial Zimbabwe. Coghlan had made the contribution to the convention that only he could make.

Coghlan was not through. When Milton retired in 1922 he was succeeded by Francis P. Chaplin, another graduate from the Asquith-Lloyd George school of thought. In that year the charter that Rhodes received from Queen Victoria in 1889 to form the British South Africa Company (BSAC) to administer colonial Zimbabwe was due to expire. The settlers were given two choices: to become part of South Africa as its fifth province,[8] or to assume the status of responsible government, which meant considerable self-rule but not total independence. The question was so controversial that it had to be decided by a national referendum. This is where Coghlan rose to the occasion to exercise effective leadership. He strongly advocated for responsible government, a position that Chaplin supported. On October 27, 1922, the referendum results showed that of the total settler vote of 14,673, some 8,774 voters favored responsible government and 5,899 voters favored union with South Africa. Only 60 Africans were allowed to vote.[9] On October 1, 1923, as a result of the referendum, colonial Zimbabwe was declared a British Crown colony and Coghlan was sworn in as the first prime minister. Chaplin was appointed the first governor. When Coghlan died suddenly in 1927 he was succeeded by Howard Unwin Moffat, the grandson of Robert Moffat, the famous missionary who founded the first school for Africans at Inyati in 1859. From 1927 to 1934 events began to move rapidly. The beginning of the Great Depression in 1929 played into the hands of Godfrey Huggins, a conservative medical practitioner who decided to go into politics to reverse the liberal trends that were developing in colonial Zimbabwe. From 1933 to 1952 Huggins dominated the political scene by his conservative political philosophy.

TODD DESIGNS HIS STRATEGY FOR ACTION

Throughout his work and career in colonial Zimbabwe, Todd would be influenced heavily by the momentous developments that occurred all over the British empire in the year of his birth. These events remained a constant reminder of what he must do to sustain the impact of developments that came out of these events and to live up to the true meaning of the traditions that had so much meaning to the less fortunate people of the world, and Africans of colonial Zimbabwe who had no rights at all. Todd was also heavily influenced by the work of men who came before him, including Charles Coghlan, Francis Chaplin, Howard Unwin Moffat, George Mitchell (prime minister in 1933), Harold Jowitt, Robert Tredgold, and, during his own time, by religious leaders that included Ralph E. Dodge, Kenneth Shelton, and Donal Lamont. Todd was overwhelmed by the sacrifice that these men had made to leave traditions on which to build his own work in the interest of Zimbabwe.

In 1929, when Todd was 21 years old, New Zealand, like the rest of the world, was hit severely by the Great Depression. The leader of the Labour Party, Michael J. Savage, struggled against formidable odds to maintain a semblance of economic survival and a sense of national purpose. In 1934, as economic conditions continued to deteriorate, Todd offered his services to the Church of Christ as a missionary. As he arrived at Dadaya Mission in that year, the economic situation in both New Zealand and colonial Zimbabwe took a turn for the worse. In 1935 the Savage administration was unable to contain the devastation of the Depression. In 1938 Savage tried to introduce complete social security programs that included full dental and medical care for those who had suffered through the Depression. In 1940 Peter Fraser, who succeeded Savage, extended these programs. At that time the world was at war, making it hard to measure the impact of any program that tried to limit the effects of the Depression. Todd learned a lot from the management of the crisis, both in New Zealand and colonial Zimbabwe.

In colonial Zimbabwe political developments were occurring at an alarming speed. At the time that Howard Unwin Moffat succeeded Coghlan in 1927, he was serving as deputy prime minister and minister of mines. Moffat was considered a man of integrity because of his background as the grandson of a famous missionary. He was believed to detest the character and conduct of colonial politics, especially the anti-African rhetoric that such people as Ethel Tawse Jollie, Hugh Williams, and a host of other colonial officials invoked to get the support of settler voters. Political extremists, including Godfrey Huggins, exploited Moffat's moderation and accused him of lacking in leadership that they said was needed during a period of great economic and political crisis.

From 1929 to 1935, while the Great Depression was having considerable political implications, Todd was struggling to make Dadaya a school that gave the Africans new hope for the future. Robert Blake concludes that at the time Todd arrived at Dadaya, "the missionary became a suspect figure within the white community about education which he was conducting for Africans. There were prejudices which even a man with the charisma of Garfield Todd did not surmount."[10] Todd immediately knew he and other missionaries were working under severe scrutiny and suspicion from their fellow settlers, because of what they were trying to accomplish in providing an education to Africans.

Todd also encountered other serious problems as soon as he arrived at Dadaya in 1934. In 1935 Huggins made education for white students free and compulsory, but for Africans it was neither. The schools for Africans were in a constant struggle, depending on donations and contributions from missionary organizations in overseas countries. With the Great Depression having a profound effect on the economic situation, the financial support that the schools for Africans needed simply dried out. For the next 11 years Todd encountered serious problems that nearly brought Dadaya and other schools for Africans to a grinding halt. Suddenly Todd decided to become the spokesman for the Africans, speaking out on every possible opportunity against the colonial policy that was placing them at a disadvantage. He remembered the influence of the Asquith-Lloyd George movement of thought and the ominous events that took place in 1908. He was ready to put these elements of this strategy into practice for action to change things and seek improvement. Todd was ready to act.

TODD OUTLINES THE TERMS OF HIS POLITICAL MISSION

In 1946 Todd resigned from the missionary work that he had been doing for the Church of Christ at Dadaya and went into politics. He ran for a seat in Parliament under Huggins's United Party and won. In launching his political mission Todd recognized the importance of the position that some individuals and organizations were taking in the development of Africans. To understand Todd's political mission it is important to understand developments that were taking place at the time. Todd understood these developments and took them into account as part of his mission. Let us discuss these developments briefly to understand how they became part of Todd's political mission.

In February 1947 Todd, already a senior member of Huggins's administration, surprised the country and angered Huggins himself by publicly criticizing the educational policy of a government of which he was a member. Todd never supported that policy because he believed it was unfair to Africans. Characterizing a policy that allocated an expenditure of $0.40 per African student and $20.00 per white student as a national disgrace, Todd underscored the urgent need to redesign educational policy so that it would result in equal opportunity for the students of both races.

A disturbing aspect of the postwar change of attitude among Africans and some whites is that while whites recognized the need to do something dramatic in the conduct of African education, none called for racial integration in both society and the schools. They seemed to neglect the fact that as long as the school system remained segregated by race, it was futile to talk of equal educational opportunity for all students. Todd and many other liberals fell victim to this shortcoming. Calling for an end to racial discrimination in all its forms was a risk that liberal colonial politicians did not want to take.

As a former missionary, Todd understood the educational needs of Africans better than any other politician. The problems the African students encountered due to inadequate colonial policy was the main reason he decided to enter politics. He believed he could use his missionary background and awareness of the problems Africans faced to make a difference. When he recognized Huggins's unwillingness to move toward providing equal educational opportunity to all students, Todd decided to launch a national campaign to force the issue. Speaking before the Bulawayo National Affairs Association in February 1947, Todd called for a commission of inquiry into African education and warned Huggins about the consequences of continuing his existing policy, saying "the Africans are aware that educated people can be governed, but they cannot be enslaved forever. They are no longer willing to be controlled in the manner in which they have been controlled in the past."[11] Todd went on to add that there was a spirit of urgency in African development, and urged every establishment in the country—the business community, the church, and the colonial government itself—to guide it and give it assistance. He concluded that if this happened there would develop a people who would become a credit to the country. He warned that the alternative approach to this spirit of urgency was to disregard, hinder, or cripple it in any way, and adverse effects would result with severe consequences for the entire country.[12]

While Huggins felt betrayed by a man he thought supported the official policy of his government, a typical reaction of those unwilling to adjust to new situations, Todd himself felt that the situation demanded him to say what he said. Aware that the Huggins educational policy was designed to fulfill two main objectives—to prepare Africans to function as cheap labor and to condition them to tribal settings—Todd argued that this policy was intended to ensure colonial control of Africans and, thus, of the country. Because he believed that the education the Africans received under this policy did not produce individuals who were complete, Todd concluded that it had to be changed in order to prepare the Africans for full participation in a dynamic society. He asked Huggins to appoint a commission to study the situation and come up with an answer.[13]

If Huggins had reason to believe that he was a superman in the conduct of educational policy for Africans, that image had been seriously tarnished by a widespread belief among liberal whites like Todd that his obsession with practical training and manual labor had plunged the educational process into total disarray. This explains why the views Todd expressed were shared by Africans. In an editorial one week after Todd's speech, *The African Weekly* addressed this critical question:

The African view is that since education is the complete formation of the whole man, what reason is there to classify the educational process into black education and white education? To the Africans the term "Native Education" carries with it such labels as little finances, inferior equipment, few qualified teachers. The product of this is a man ill-fitted for the economic, social, and political life in the colony. We favor a system of education based on total equality and which shapes all people so that they come into a world which gives them a hope for the future, not despair and bitterness, as the Africans are now experiencing.[14]

Like Todd, *The African Weekly* concluded by calling for a commission of inquiry into African education with the purpose of removing all inequalities that handicapped the education of Africans and of enabling them to adjust to new political and socioeconomic conditions.

The wave of continuing criticism against Huggins's educational policy aroused the indignation of many individuals who supported Todd's call for a commission of inquiry. This was the line of thinking of Reverend Kennedy Grant, a leading priest in the Anglican Church, when he argued in September 1947, "The aim of education should be to train our pupils in the art of living together. Education is a continuous process of developing a personality which is essential to human relationship. The foundations of all good living are built on man's relationship with his own fellow man."[15]

In taking this position Todd fully recognized the rapid pace of change that was taking place among Africans in viewing themselves in relation to conditions that controlled their lives. He knew that when the war came to an end in 1945, the African world was transformed in ways which the white man had failed to predict and measure. He also knew that Africans who participated in the war came to learn things about the white man and his culture, which they could not have learned in any other way. They learned to value most what was valuable: self-consciousness. This enabled them to perceive themselves as people who, though under colonial rule, deserved respect. The problems of their relationship with the white man were the primary concern and were "the key to all other problems."[16]

Todd was aware that a common thread of self-consciousness among the Africans who participated in the war was the knowledge of conditions of life in Europe. To their amazement and disbelief, the Africans discovered that European nations had both positive attributes and negative features which characterize human life all over the world. The Great Depression had left political and socioeconomic scars that could not disappear. For Africans to discover that poverty and squalor were the lot of the great number of people in Europe was a demonstration of the fallibility and inability of the white man to create socioeconomic and political utopian society in Europe itself. What was happening to the resources which European nations had been exploiting in Africa since the 19th century? The Africans also learned that for many people in Europe the centers of civilization were also the ramshackle dwelling places of the deprived masses. For Africans to discover that indeed some white people in Europe were poor was "to recognize the inability of European governments to solve human problems."[17] But what was shattering to Africans was that the European nations which had colonies in Africa, including Britain, France, Belgium, Portugal, and Spain, adopted educational policies that effectively eliminated the African population from participating in the affairs of their countries—politically, socially, and economically. This realization became more of a reality than imagination following the end of the war.

The only reason why Africans joined the ranks of the Allied armies to fight against the Axis powers was the promise made by Winston Churchill in the Atlantic Charter of August 11, 1941, on behalf of colonial governments for improvement of the conditions of their lives as a reward for their service in the war. Africans clearly understood Winston Churchill and Franklin Roosevelt proclaim in the Atlantic Charter that they would be given an opportunity for self-fulfillment after the war was over. In stating, "after the final destruction of the Nazi tyranny we hope to see established a peace which will afford all the lands and all men to live out their lives in freedom from fear and want,"[18] the two leaders were, in effect, warning against continuing colonial conditions to the detriment of the people. The inability and the unwillingness of European nations to heed this warning for a decade following the end of the war helped the Africans in raising and strengthening their self-consciousness.[19] The quest for educational opportunity was its ultimate manifestation.

While in Europe Africans saw what nations were doing to promote the development of their people through education. They saw the contradictions that were central to the way in which people lived. Some lived a life of luxury while others lived a life of poverty and deprivation. Some enjoyed an opportunity to play an effective role in society, while others had no such opportunity. The so-called Great Industrial Revolution was a mixed bag for Europeans. While it had benefited some, it had left others sunk in the mire of deprivation and want. Upon their return home the African military men shared their experiences in Europe with those who had stayed home.[20] From this informal education the Africans began to question the legitimacy of the colonial governments and the assumption that only the white man was capable of running a good government.

The meeting in London of African leaders at the conclusion of the war in 1945 was a prelude to the drama of the evolution of an African strategy to deal with the emerging situation. The lack of participation in the affairs of their countries added fuel to the fire of their rising consciousness, as they began to articulate political views which were opposed to the principles of the colonial governments. The ability Africans acquired to express views and formulate developmental objectives helped set the two racial groups on a collision course beginning in 1955. That the colonial governments failed to recognize that the war had helped arouse a new African consciousness accelerated the Africans' demand for more meaningful educational opportunity, which they felt they had earned by participating in the war.

One unfortunate development of the postwar period was that the colonial governments in Africa were unwilling to see the need for education as something that was likely to cause a serious problem within a few years, although some colonial officials seemed to recognize the potential danger for the future. For example, in April 1945 the Duke of Devonshire, the British parliamentary under-secretary for the colonies, paid tribute to "the courage and endurance of the African soldiers,"[21] and warned members of the British House of Lords that "the Africans are anxious to practice in civil life the various new skills which they have learned during the war."[22] But, by the very nature of their existence, the European colonial governments entailed a potential for their collapse. Africans dramatically realized that social institutions needed a fundamental change if conflict had to be avoided in the future.

At the beginning of the war the colonial governments had made Africans understand that they were asked to fight for human freedom by defeating the Axis powers, but they returned home to experience new forms of oppression. They were made to believe that they were fighting to ensure the liberation of the universal human being and self-fulfillment, but they returned home to find new repression. They were made to believe that they were fighting to eliminate possible Nazi dictatorship, and yet they returned home to experience new forms of colonial domination. They were made to believe that they were fighting to ensure equal rights for all people, and yet they returned home to endure new forms of racial discrimination and prejudice as well as distributive opportunity. Todd felt that the colonial governments in Africa had a solemn responsibility to address and correct this situation because Africans would no longer allow it to continue.

Therefore, tragic as the war was, there was a silver lining in the cloud which it had created for Africans. It had given them an opportunity to see themselves in relation to the manner in which colonial governments were running their countries. It soon became evident to them that the Machiavelli principles which were central to the policies of the colonial governments were indeed vulnerable to a united opposition and affront. But, unlike Machiavelli, the colonial governments did not think that the subjected Africans "will take up arms"[23] and fight sooner than they had anticipated. By colonizing Africa in the first place, the European governments created a desire for freedom among the Africans. By exploiting the resources of the continent, they inadvertently created an environment of racial and cultural conflict.

Todd also argued that by introducing Africans to new social and political systems, the colonial governments indirectly implanted the need for the freedom of self-expression. By demonstrating their political intolerance, they gave rise to a new thinking that all people must be treated equally in society. Robert July seemed to take Todd's line of thinking into account in arguing in 1974 that by providing a limited educational opportunity for Africans to serve their own socioeconomic and political purposes, the colonial governments indirectly taught them the skills that were necessary to engage in new self-directed activity in their lives.[24] Todd had seen this inadequate education while he was at Dadaya. For more than ten years he had tried under very difficult circumstances to provide meaningful educational opportunity for Africans, but with little success because he was handicapped by the policy of the Huggins administration.

The continuation of forced labor in Zimbabwe and other British colonies in Africa, even during the war years,[25] created an environment which strengthened the Africans' quest for self-fulfillment.[26] By instituting forced labor in the first place in 1894, the colonial governments indirectly implanted in the Africans an irrepressible desire to be free. By forcing them to work for the white man on public projects, such as road construction, the colonial governments strengthened their will power, not just to survive, but also to demonstrate that they were no longer available to serve as instruments of fulfilling colonial purpose. The ability of the Africans to recognize that the white man was subjecting them to a dehumanizing condition demonstrated a capability in converting adverse situations into a strategy for their liberation. The creation of the Rhodesia African Rifles during the war was an occasion which Godfrey Huggins failed to recognize as having the beginnings of a potential conflict in the future. But Huggins felt that he had to create it in order to augment the white army.[27] But he did not know the extent of the effect of this action on the rise of African political consciousness.

One important aspect of the African consciousness that Todd believed the war helped develop was a new concept of personality. He thought the war had touched this personality in a way that the colonial governments could not comprehend. In the relentless pursuit of their objectives the colonial governments failed to recognize that this generation of Africans was not afraid to take risks in assessing new possibilities for their development. This new personality enabled Africans to acquire practical perceptions of the impact of the events that were increasingly influencing their lives. To resent forced labor laws and practices of the colonial governments, to question the legitimacy of the colonial governments themselves, to value freedom of human thought and action, Africans needed to understand that they had to develop a new personality to challenge the assumed superiority of the white man.

Todd fully understood that this new African personality helped Africans reject outright the Victorian myth that had yielded some political benefits to the white man, and he looked forward to the emergence of a new society conceived in the ideals underlying the process of seeking to promote the universal human being on the basis of equality in every sphere of national life.[28] The Africans of the postwar period considered this an imperative condition for their self-fulfillment. That the colonial governments did not see things this way contributed to the rise of African political consciousness with its consequences for the colonial society.

Todd and other white liberals recognized that in their limited contact with the white man, especially through the tragedy of the war, Africans learned that personality, which elevated their sense of self-worth of ensuring future development at the highest level possible, was, in the nature of things, necessarily both collective and individual. In order to structure their quest for the future which their consciousness helped them perceive, they knew they had to base it on values that gave a new meaning to their lives. They made sacrifices and took risks to ensure their development. This level of consciousness became possible in the context of an instant death, which the war environment produced.

This sense of value of life translated into real strategies for dealing with oppressive colonial conditions after the war. Todd concluded that for Africans to value freedom, they had to recognize the environment of oppression. In this connection, Africans came to realize that only a blind person can yearn for sight. Only a sick person can appreciate good health. Only a prisoner can cherish freedom. Only a slave can dream of liberty. Therefore, Todd concluded that only the Africans fighting in the white man's war could aspire to have the reverence of a life of dignity and respect. He concluded that out of this realization Africans endeavored to develop a personality that assisted them in refusing to be treated as mere objects of the colonial officials or instruments to fulfill their own purposes. Todd fully understood that in this way, the development of a new African personality was helping elevate a new level of consciousness which caused a common concern among colonial officials, but one which they could not control. Todd felt that now it was time to address it.

Todd also observed that in developing this kind of personality the Africans knew that the successful attainment of their objectives lay in the discovery of the power that manifested itself in their will to achieve what the colonial government considered impossible: political freedom. He saw that it was the will to achieve identified goals that helped them concentrate on doing their best with the minimum educational opportunity the colonial government gave them. He knew that for this reason, Africans regarded their participation in the war not only as an opportunity to fight the potential Axis oppression, but also to struggle against the real oppression they were enduring under colonial conditions. He was aware that they knew the development of a new personality and the rise of their consciousness were inseparably linked to their search for a more meaningful opportunity for development.

Taking issue with Huggins's policy, Todd argued that this new African personality created a situation which the colonial governments failed to understand and which he and other white liberals appreciated more than any other aspect of the rise of African consciousness of the postwar period. He appreciated the fact that their restless minds, their desire for development, and an emerging sense of purpose emanated from values that only their cultural heritage could make possible. Now, the challenge before the settler community was to eliminate the Victorian attitudes toward African cultural values, because the settler community was watching the chickens coming home to roost. The ability of Africans to hold their cultural values as important to their cause helped them design strategies of seeking ways of ending colonial conditions. This strategy gave them an ability to formulate goals for the future "consistent with universal human aspirations. This became the basis of their critical examination of the settler standards of conduct and behavior."[29] In 1947 Todd recognized that blind obedience and loyalty to colonial governments was no longer possible. Instead, a new form of personality became a new channel through which Africans searched for new principles which had universal application to human conditions of life.

It really was quite easy, however, for Todd to see how Africans could overcome the disability which the colonial governments had imposed on them. He was convinced that their personality helped them not to allow the colonial establishments to pit some Africans against others, or to believe that the white man had a superior personality simply because of his ability to exploit them politically. They recognized, instead, that the colonial governments were "guilty of warping their full development and training misfits for society"[30] at the expense of their own development.

To appreciate the development of a new personality among the Africans of the postwar decade is to understand their motivation. Todd was unwavering in his belief that throughout human history, those who have no recognized cultural values on which to base self-motivation in self-directed endeavors are more unlikely than those who do to attain the basic developmental objectives which are often a measure of human aspirations and fulfillment. To do this Africans of the postwar period developed among themselves dependable qualities consistent with their new personality as proof of group-proud people and as a collective norm of identifying goals which would help fulfill their dreams and aspirations. This is why Todd recognized that the development of a new personality and the rise of consciousness among Africans of that period was evident more profoundly in their quest for the opportunity for better education. That the colonial governments were unwilling to give them this opportunity created a new problem.

In Zimbabwe, such organizations as the African Artisans Guild, the Council of African Chiefs, and the National African War Fund all did more than any other organization or institution of the postwar period to help Africans establish educational objectives for the future. The National African War Fund, for example, offered Africans an opportunity to contribute money to assist men returning from the war to secure the education they needed for the future. This African GI program elevated the new African personality to a new height. Between September 1940 and April 1945 Africans had contributed more than $52,000 to this Fund.[31] What alarmed the colonial government was not the amount of money Africans raised, but the consciousness that brought new meaning and purpose to self-directed objectives. Todd fully understood this development as part of the activity of a people who were trying to ensure their own advancement. This level of thinking placed Todd far above the level of Huggins's comprehension of what was happening in the country. The two men belonged to different ages and schools of thought.

While the colonial government in Zimbabwe welcomed the Africans' contribution toward the war effort, it did not appreciate the effect it had on the emergence of a new personality and consciousness. While it welcomed their participation in the war, Huggins did not welcome their newly acquired ability to recognize the need to promote their own educational development. This was the real meaning of self-consciousness and liberation that Todd fully appreciated. In 1983 a retired white mechanic who emigrated to Zimbabwe in 1944 told the author:

The colonial government faced a dilemma in asking Africans to fight in the war. It wanted them to help end the threat of Nazi domination without addressing the question of its own real domination at home. It wanted them to learn about the importance of liberation from possible Nazi oppression without letting them learn about the reality of its own oppression. How could the Africans recognize possible Nazi domination without questioning real colonial domination? How could they resist possible Axis oppression without raising fundamental questions about real colonial oppression? The emergence of a new personality and consciousness among the Africans as a result of their war experience compounded this colonial dilemma. How could this dilemma be resolved?[32]

As the Africans pondered the contradiction which colonial conditions manifested, they felt obligated to do something to eliminate its causes. For the first time since the war of 1896, they increasingly questioned the claimed benefits of colonialism. By exposing the weakness of the colonial system itself, they could no longer ignore it as the ultimate contradiction that characterized colonial behavior. The same retired white mechanic put this contradiction in the context of that reality when he observed:

The colonial government wanted the Africans to accept its own oppression, but have them fight against that of the Axis powers. It tried to portray them as oppressors, but wished them to accept Godfrey Huggins as a leader interested in their development. To suggest that a man who espoused Victorian political philosophy of the Africans had suddenly changed constituted an attempt to camouflage his real colonial character. That kind of logic simply did not make sense to the Africans. I guess one could say that it was one of those cultural differences. By campaigning against possible Axis domination the colonial governments exposed themselves more about the reality of their own oppression. The Africans could no longer accept that line of thinking.[33]

Earlier this chapter commented that the involvement of Africans in the war had a different effect on the attitudes of colonial officials from what it had on themselves. Africans converted the effect of the tragedy of war into something that gave them an impetus for the rise of a new self-consciousness. But colonial officials attempted to use the end of the war and the defeat of the Axis powers as a means of strengthening Victorian beliefs of the inferiority of Africans. Speaking on March 21, 1945, D. L. Smit, secretary of African affairs in South Africa, recognized the need for the colonial governments to acknowledge the fact that their preoccupation with the belief of African inferiority was detrimental to their own future and that the colonial governments themselves must pursue policies which sought to promote mutual respect in both South Africa and Zimbabwe. Smit added,

Our efforts to improve race relations should be guided not by extremes, but by a sane approach along the pathway of moderation. Before the community of mankind could be formed, the old attitudes, the old forms of social organizations must be replaced by a forward-looking attitude to bring all people into a single family of the universal man.[34]

Smit was, in effect, recognizing the fact that during the war Africans had acquired a new level of self-consciousness that no colonial government, in all its power, could stop. This is the reason why he, like Todd, urged the white community to accept this consciousness as a development that would safeguard the long-term interests of the whites by regarding it in a positive light. Unfortunately this was not the perspective from which many whites viewed African consciousness. Many saw it as a development that carried political implications that they considered detrimental to their own interests. They could not understand that in gaining a new form of awareness, Africans could "no longer remain as they were,"[35] and that this consciousness was not merely an initial stage in the process of self-liberation by only the Africans, but a necessary condition of the liberation of all people.[36]

It was not surprising that Smit's perspective was not shared by many colonial officials. This is why Sir Alfred Beit, an influential member of the Royal African Society, expressed his view that the postwar colonial government policy must not seek to emphasize the promotion of equal rights for the Africans. Beit argued that it would be a mistake for the colonial government to design educational policies "to set more importance for economic and political rights to a man who could not avail himself of them."[37] There is no question that Beit was thinking in terms of the Victorian attitudes that were becoming part of the problems the colonial governments in Africa were now facing. For Beit, a high-ranking colonial official, to make this claim was to be blind to the hard realities that the whites either pretended did not exist or attempted to ignore. This indiscretion would later prove costly to the future of colonial governments in Africa.

The knowledge that the colonial governments were not genuinely enthusiastic about accepting the rise of African consciousness as a positive national development prompted Anglican Church Bishop E. F. Paget to deliver a thought-provoking address to the African Welfare Society in January 1946, and went on to warn:

There is a growing suspicion as to our sincerity in seeking to our national objectives with specific reference to the development of the Africans. Stern days lie ahead of us when we must inevitably sow the seeds of either educational disillusionment and further racial strife, or of good neighborliness expressed in sincere efforts to bring about justice and freedom for all people. The government must resolve this dilemma by seeking to gratify the new consciousness, which has become a permanent part of the experiences of the African people as a result of the war, or seek to repress it and create conditions of further racial strife.[38]

For Paget to urge the colonial government to formulate good racial and educational policies with a sense of urgency suggests that he was painfully aware that the war had transformed the African world in a way which most white people refused to understand and accept. The prophetic warning which Paget made would not go unheeded without a price to pay. For Todd, Paget's position was an encouragement offered for a great national cause.

Unable to remain silent in the wake of a growing national controversy, various church organizations held meetings to discuss appropriate courses of action to take as a response. Many believed that the colonial government's neglect of the educational development of Africans would ultimately lead to a cultural conflict and that Huggins's government was way behind time in pursuing the kind of policy which it did toward the Africans. This is why Paget felt compelled to break ranks with a popular myth in order to urge the reconstruction of postwar society on lines that would seek to promote human understanding and better communications beyond racial boundaries. Like Todd, Paget warned that an alternative course of action would be a serious racial conflict, from which the colonial government might come off second best.[39]

In this kind of thinking among moderate and fair-minded white individuals, it was really not possible to expect Huggins and his government to break out of the confines of Victorian thinking and rise above the level of the myth of the inferiority of Africans to design a policy that would ensure the long-term interests of the white man himself. That Huggins felt it was not possible to design a policy to promote the development of Africans as a way of protecting the interests of the whites shows the dark side of colonialism itself. This failure was a demonstration of the tragedy of the educational and racial policies of his administration. This constituted part of the circumstances that compelled the Methodist Church to do something to help Huggins recognize the error of his policy. Meeting at Waddilove in February 1946, the Methodist Church passed a number of resolutions urging him to make a major review of his educational policy:

We believe that a satisfactory educational policy awaits a clearer enunciation of principles than has been the case in the past regarding the Africans' place in society, economic and political life of the country, and that the formation of definite lines of development of the Africans be initiated so that they reach the full and unrestricted citizenship which we believe is unquestionably their right.[40]

HUGGINS, NATIONAL CRISIS, AND TODD

On December 21, 1950, responding to a question following a political campaign speech, Huggins stated, "We can only build this country as partners. At the present stage of development of the backward people, it is not easy for observers to realize that we believe in a policy of racial partnership, the kind partnership that exists between the horse and the rider."[41] To understand Huggins's attitude, one must remember what George Stark had said in 1930: that it was up to the Africans to promote their own development. The irony of what Huggins said was not only that he wanted to see the Africans become a good horse, in his definition of partnership, but also that they must train themselves to be one. Where would such a policy lead the country? For the next two years there was a wave of criticism against Huggins. There were calls for his apology and for his resignation. During that time government operations came to a halt as political dissension within the ranks of the colonial hierarchy resulted in total disarray. Wherever Huggins went, Africans received him with demonstrations and jeers.

Faced with the reality that the end was near, Huggins came out swinging as he vigorously defended the policy of his government, saying in 1952, "You can call me an imperialist of the old school. I detest the attitude of the people who condemn imperialism. True imperialism entails paternalism. It would be outrageous to give the Native a so-called political partnership and equal educational opportunity when he is likely to ruin himself as a result."[42]

On September 6, 1953, Huggins resigned to become prime minister of the ill-fated Federation of Rhodesia and Nyasaland. He was succeeded by none other than Garfield Todd, the man who had criticized his policy. This is also why some colonial officials with moderate views shared the thinking that the educational advancement of the Africans was in the best interest of the white man himself. One such influential individual was General J. C. Smuts, who had commanded South African troops in both wars. Speaking in Maputo, Mozambique, at a banquet held in July 1945 in his honor, Smuts warned:

> In the long run the security of the white man in Africa will depend on a *modus vivendi* based on justice and granting the Natives opportunity for development. By their labor the Natives have provided the great progress which in the space of a generation, has helped transform the face of this region. There is room for white and black to work side by side in the spirit of mutual respect and understanding. Each makes indispensable contribution to the welfare of the country as a whole. Discrimination based upon any thinking or notion creates an environment of racial conflict which would serve the best interests of any country.[43]

What Smuts and other moderate white individuals were, in effect, doing is to suggest that the war had created a totally new social environment which compelled the white man to reevaluate his attitudes toward the development of Africans. Some were beginning to realize what Todd had been saying that there was only one hope for the survival of European culture in Africa, and that was to recognize the need to extend equal educational opportunity and political and socioeconomic rights to Africans as human beings capable of contributing to the good of the country. A. M. Tredgold, a leading farmer in the Bulawayo area and a descendent of the famous Tredgold family which settled in Zimbabwe during the 19th century, recognized this reality and urged his fellow whites to move aggressively to extend equal political rights and educational opportunity to Africans to help them play an effective role in society as a prior condition of racial cooperation, which he believed Zimbabwe needed for national development.

> The powerful force which the Africans exert must be felt in the educational, socioeconomic and political fields. If we deny them that right we're going to create in their minds a feeling of oppression. The sacrifices which they made to defeat the Axis forces must be rewarded in tangible ways. If we fail to do this we might not suffer as a result, but our children and their children will suffer.[44]

The surprising thing about this liberal thinking on the part of some white individuals was that it was taking place at all. Considering the fact that before the war the attitudes of whites toward Africans were heavily influenced by Victorian traditional thinking, this trend of thinking was slowly creating new difficult realities for the colonial government itself in its relationships with Africans, and Huggins himself knew it. However, these liberal views were expressed exclusively by the white individuals who felt a sense of compulsion and urgency because their position in society demanded of them as a demonstration of their capability to see social issues from a higher level of philanthropic consciousness. For them to think otherwise would have reduced them to the level of ordinary men. Their position in society would not allow them to do this. Therefore, General Smuts, Bishop Paget, A. M. Tredgold,[45] and Garfield Todd all belonged to this exclusive club, and its members took it upon themselves to remind their fellow whites to adopt new attitudes toward Africans or to face the increasing prospects of a racial conflict in the future.

For Tredgold to try to convince the white population that "the world opinion of 1947 is against all forms of repression"[46] of Africans, and for Sir Stewart Gore-Browne to suggest, "I think it is time a good thing was said about the Africans,"[47] was, in essence, a recognition of the fact that Africans, through the rise of their consciousness, had stirred the conscience of the white community about the conditions which controlled their life within the colonial society and had created a set of new conditions which demanded an honest and objective reappraisal. Were Huggins and his government equal to that challenge? It was not easy for these white individuals to take this position, but they felt it was something they had a duty to do. One effect of these views was that they further strengthened the consciousness that was gaining momentum among the Africans. Todd remained the leader and spokesman of this new school of thought.

Only six years following the end of the Second World War it had become evident among the members of the white community that Africans could no longer accept the view that their failure to adapt to the white man's culture and to emulate the white man were responsible for their lack of development. D. L. Yamba spoke for many Africans when he wrote a letter to the editor of "The Home Teacher" section of *The Bantu Mirror* on February 19, 1947, to say "Africans are as capable as Europeans[48] and can easily equal all that the white man does if only they had the opportunity to learn to do those things."[49]

By 1954 this controversy over the place of Africans was beginning to worry the leaders of the colonial government. They were now considering ways of putting an end to it. The debate and the position taken by liberal whites on it were having a profoundly negative effect on Huggins himself. He felt that the whole question of the educational development of Africans as perceived by the white liberals was detrimental to their own interests. On August 26, 1954, Huggins used the occasion of the annual conference of the Rhodesia Missionary Conference held at Goromonzi Secondary School for Africans as an appropriate forum to attempt to correct what he believed was an erroneous notion that Africans were equal to the white man and that they were capable of guiding their own advancement. Huggins argued:

We have the sad spectacle of many of our so-called educated Africans wasting their energies on some completely unattainable objectives such as self-government. The African with one foot in his primitive culture presents two problems for the government. The first is how to deal with the immediate situation caused by the mis-guided and so-called African intellectuals. The second is how to develop the African so that the educated ones do not waste their time on sterile and futile nationalistic agitation. The best that we can do is to formulate an educational policy to assist the African with one foot in his primitive culture. Our task as a government is to reverse the claimed consciousness which is believed to have come about as a result of the war.[50]

Therefore, Huggins regarded the education of Africans as charity which only his government could extend to them. To conclude that Huggins was a product of the Victorian thinking toward Africans is, indeed, to recognize his overwhelming negative attitude toward their educational development. It is quite clear that Huggins shared the thinking that no matter how hard they tried, Africans must never attach an exaggerated importance of education to their advancement or awareness. He saw the rise of African consciousness and nationalism as inconsequential to his policies and felt that because most Africans were not properly educated, they were unable to appreciate that, in the evolutionary process which he believed Zimbabwe was going through at that time, the white man was doing everything possible to create a social and educational environment that would offer them an opportunity for socioeconomic progress. Huggins saw the relationship between the level of educational attainment and the emergence of African consciousness as something the white man must control entirely at all times. This is why he argued that this was not incompatible with African aspirations because they were incapable of upsetting the social system as defined by the white man himself.[51] But in less than three years, in 1956, Huggins's political career came to an end as he discovered that he had made serious errors in judging the impact of the rise of African political consciousness as a result of the war.

It is a sad irony that in all his political charisma and popularity among the whites, Huggins, like his protégé Ian Smith, the last colonial prime minister who served from 1964 to 1979, was unable to understand that there was a serious cultural conflict between Africans and whites. He perceived Africans only from traditional European cultural perspectives, and the cultural arrogance which dictated both his attitudes and the policy of his government. This translated into various forms of racism which became an instrument of shattering bridges of communication between the two races. Because he failed to respect African culture, Huggins was unwilling and unable to initiate any meaningful dialogue with Africans. Without dialogue based upon mutual respect, it was virtually impossible to ease the rising racial tension which was making it hard for the two racial groups to live together in peace and cooperation in building a dynamic society.[52]

That Huggins refused to recognize that the negative attitude and flawed policy of his government were inherent in his cultural arrogance was an important factor in the cultural collision that occurred in 1966. This is why the educational policy of his administration caused one of the most serious problems that he and the white community which supported him faced as a consequence of their negative view of the Africans. Their notion of the superiority of the white man combined with their view that Africans must be so controlled that they must not be allowed to threaten the power they enjoyed. In the course of pursuing this policy, the colonial government failed to initiate a process of effective communication between itself and the Africans. Paulo Freire, the Brazilian writer, concludes that this is often an outcome of the action of politicians who speak but "are not understood because their language is not attuned to the concrete situation of the men they address."[53] Therefore, Huggins was engaging in political action which Freire says its designers are not critically aware of in the deteriorating relationships that emerge between the oppressor and the oppressed and so run "the risk of preaching in the desert"[54] of his own ignorance about the viability of the African culture. Huggins ignored the reality of the rise of the African consciousness as central to Africans' perception of their place in the colonial society.

Huggins's refusal to see the rise of African consciousness and the need for their advancement as a positive component of national development was the main reason why the Council of Non-European Trade Unions issued a statement in February 1947 in which it concluded:

It is the firm belief of this Council that the present educational policy of preserving skilled trades exclusively for white workers is not in the interests of the country as a whole, but one that is bound to lead to racial conflict. The Council urges the government to reconsider this policy in light of the adverse effects which may ensue from implementing it.[55]

That the Council felt that trade unions run by whites were actually standing in the way of national progress by supporting Huggins's denial of equal opportunity to Africans for self-improvement through education suggests the critical nature of the situation. This is why the Council called on "all progressive trade unions of whatever race and color to deplore in the strongest terms possible the attitude and reactionary action of the white trade unions and the educational policy of the government."[56] That the Council also recognized that these "reactionary moves are responsible for dragging the Africans down the road of underdevelopment"[57] is why it urged all people to work toward compelling the government to formulate an educational policy that would help in promoting equal opportunity for all people in order to prepare them to engage in any trade or profession without suffering from any restrictions imposed by an inadequate social policy.[58]

To listen to Huggins react to this call is to leave no doubt in one's mind that he was as much a victim of Victorian myth about African culture as the Africans themselves. He felt sorry for them for what he believed to be their failure to realize that total equality with the white man was impossible. That he was angry to hear the white liberals urge him to abandon his Victorian attitude is why he turned around and accused them of falsely raising hopes among the Africans that would eventually attain their educational aspirations and political rights. What Huggins preferred to neglect is that in the course of human events, as the expression goes, there is no force that can reverse the consciousness that any group of people has carved for itself. For Huggins to attempt to retard that progress was tantamount to reneging on the promise and commitment that his own government and the British government had made to Africans at the outbreak of the war that they would be given equal opportunity for advancement. Huggins had no apology at all for his negative views of the Africans and their consciousness. This is why he went on to reiterate the Victorian views when he argued in 1954:

We must unhesitatingly accept the doctrine that our superiority rests on our technical skills, education, cultural values, civilization and heredity. We must appreciate the fact that we have a paramount monopoly of these qualities and that the Natives have been denied them by their primitive culture. The best we can do is to educate only a few in the hope that they will pull the rest out of the mire of that primitive culture.[59]

That Huggins made no effort to hide his Victorian views of the Africans is really not surprising, because those were the views of a man who had come out of the Victorian era. But in his forthright negative opinion of the Africans, Huggins thought he had put an end to a growing controversy that he feared was paralyzing the ability of his government to pursue the policies he believed were designed to ensure colonial political domination of the Africans. He also believed that he had a duty to remind the Africans of their proper place in the colonial society. This is why he refused to accept the truth that he was creating serious problems for the country. Although he envisaged a slow development of Africans for the future, he concluded that total equality for the time being was impossible.

Speaking on July 26, 1945, Aldon Mwamuka, president of the African Teachers Association, observed: "During the war we have been called upon to assist in every way possible to fight against the forces of darkness, tyranny and racism. Our men in the Rhodesia African Rifles are shedding blood in order that men everywhere may be free from racial domination."⁶⁰ Mwamuka was expressing the dreams and aspirations of Africans when he added, "With the end of the European war, all liberty-loving people of the world are looking forward to the statesmen of the world to bring into being that world in which the evils and injustices which have been the cause of the war will be eliminated."⁶¹ In expressing these views Mwamuka was, in effect, criticizing the colonial government for adopting negative policies toward the educational development of the Africans. Because Huggins could not tolerate criticism of the policy of his government, and because the Africans could no longer acquiesce to the totality of that policy, the two cultural groups were heading toward a political showdown. In the context of the colonial environment, this showdown could only be avoided by a new approach.

TODD'S FIVE-YEAR EDUCATION PLAN FOR AFRICANS

When Todd succeeded Huggins as prime minister on September 7, 1953, he placed educational development for Africans at the top of his national agenda. For the next two years he formulated plans to introduce a system of education that had not been tried in the past. In 1955 his government authorized the opening of a new teacher training school in Mutare. Then on March 15, 1956, Todd announced a new five-year education plan for Africans. The plan went much further than any effort made in the past. It provided five years of schooling at the minimum for all school-age children. But no child over the age of 14 years would be permitted to enter below the Standard III (equivalent to the sixth grade in the United States) level. Facilities in the existing schools would be improved to provide eight years of training for urban children.

Teacher training facilities would also be expanded so that there would be 4,000 trained teachers for primary schools by 1960. The number of secondary schools would gradually be increased to enable all eligible students to attend. Trade courses in building, carpentry, leatherwork, and metalwork would be established at the postsecondary school level. A technical college offering five-year training courses beyond secondary school level would be established to train teachers for technical and industrial schools. With the increase in the number of trained teachers, the untrained teachers would eventually be eliminated. A second government secondary school would be opened in Gweru in 1957.⁶² The enrollment in upper primary schools would double by 1960. The new plan would start immediately with the total cost for the five-year plan to be $10.6 million.

At the beginning of the new school year in January 1957, instead of the expected 20,000 new students in primary schools in the urban areas,

45,000 students appeared. In 1958 the demand for places in school was even greater. A crisis had developed from the blueprint that was expected to solve the problems of education. Todd's policy to bar students over the age of 14 from entering classes below Standard III created a new difficult situation for those students. For a number of reasons those students had been unable to secure an opportunity for education earlier in their lives. As a result of this policy 60,000 students were denied entrance into schools.

In January 1958 African parents felt that this policy was not fair because it denied their children an opportunity for education On April 16, 1968, 300 students, unable to find places in schools in Highfield alone, marched with their mothers in heavy rain to demanded places in school from the educational officials. They were met by the deputy director of African education who promised to do something for them. The arrangements worked out by the ministry were temporary and involved double sessions, popularly known as the "hot seat system" because as some classes dismissed about noon others were ready to take their places in the same classroom in the afternoon under the same teachers. In announcing the plan in 1956 Todd appointed himself minister of African education to make sure that his plan was implemented the way he outlined it. In doing so he created confidence among the Africans in his program. However, the crisis was not over.

THE CONSEQUENCES OF TODD'S FALL FROM POWER

Suddenly and without prior warning, on January 11, 1958, Garfield Todd, the consummate liberal visionary who was so impatient to bring about change to ensure a rapid development of Africans, found himself a target of conspiracy by the inner members of his own administration. These members thought he was trying to bring about revolutionary change to expedite the end of the white man's political power in Zimbabwe. His entire cabinet resigned because its members had been increasingly worried by his liberal views regarding the place of Africans. His cabinet members recognized that while Todd had supported Huggins's policy of "partnership" between the Africans and settlers, he distanced himself from it because Huggins defined that partnership as the same kind of relationship that exists between the rider (the settlers) and the horse (the Africans).[63]

The conspiracy against Todd was led by eight senior members of his government who were at first considered to share his view that something urgent must be done to promote the advancement of Africans: Patrick Fletcher, Cyril Hatty, George Ellman-Browne, A. R. Stumbles,

H. J. Quinton, A. E. Abrahamson, A. D. Lloyd, and Ralph Cleveland. Todd brought these men into his administration because they had given him their assurances that they would support whatever policy he formulated. Except Fletcher, the other seven men had been successful businessmen and attributed their success to the faithful work that their African workers had done. But even they, liberal as they thought they were, could not keep up with the pace of change Todd had set for the country. In derailing Todd's program they became castigated by the Africans who immediately lost confidence in whatever they did and saw them as the riders in Huggins's definition of partnership between Africans and settlers. Within a short period of time their business operations came to an end, the ultimate price of betraying a man who was trying to bring meaningful change to a country and its people for the benefit of all.

In trying to explain their reason for breaking faith with Todd, the cabinet members issued a statement saying they had found that in his enthusiasm to bring about the kind of change that he had in mind, Todd "has been an authoritarian leader, who has not given us the normal opportunity to carry out our individual responsibilities."[64] Lawrence Vambe, veteran journalist who, along with other journalists, attended a press conference which the rebel members of Todd's cabinet called, concluded that their explanation did much to harden attitudes by Africans against them because they saw their action not just being against Todd, but against the advancement of Africans.[65] A. J. Peck, later a member of the RF and its spokesman, cited three reasons why the cabinet resigned, causing Todd's fall. The first reason was that Todd sought to make himself the very symbol of liberalism in Rhodesia by constantly exaggerating his own role in the introduction of liberal legislation and by minimizing the role of others. The second reason was that he was driving a wedge between the black man and white man by making it appear that he was the champion of the black man against the white man. The third reason was that Todd had completely abrogated the principle of collective cabinet responsibility by acting entirely on his own and in dictatorial fashion in most vital national matters.[66]

For several days Todd considered naming a new cabinet so that he could continue his reform program. But he finally decided to call new elections in the hope that he would have a new mandate from the voters. But to his surprise he found that the settler voters had also abandoned him and he was defeated in the elections of 1958. Within a few days Todd was expelled from the party. Edgar C. Whitehead was recalled from his position of British attaché in Washington D.C. to assume the leadership of the United Federal Party, the government, and the country. But Todd was not through, he had just began to fight, as events discussed in Chapter 6 of this study will show.

Todd's fall from power had serious consequences for the country. His five-year education plan was cast in doubt. The most important consequence was a realization by Africans that they could no longer place their trust and confidence in the so-called liberal whites who would act in the way that Todd's cabinet members did. They decided to intensify their own political activity to promote their development. The African National Congress that they had formed in 1957 took a dramatic turn in recruiting new members. Those Africans who had hoped that liberal whites would come to Todd's aid now abandoned that hope and decided to launch a full-scale nationalist movement that, within one year, came into serious conflict with Whitehead, the man who had succeeded Todd. From this point on the politics of cooperation and understanding was substituted for by the politics of confrontation. Colonial Zimbabwe would no longer be the same, as the settlers had lost their last chance to bring about change by peaceful means that Todd represented.

SUMMARY AND CONCLUSION

From what we have discussed in this chapter, one sees that by failing to recognize the reality of the rise of African consciousness, the colonial government and the settler community which supported it placed the two races on a cultural collision course. The only way to avoid that collision was for the colonial government to accept the reality that the rise of African consciousness represented a positive feature of national development. In a gallant effort Garfield Todd launched a mission to help his fellow settlers to recognize this reality. But by its very character, colonialism is unable to see things this way. Africans were willing to allow time for the settler community to make some adjustment, just as they themselves had done during the decade following the end of the war in 1945, in order for the two races to live together in peace. But the colonial government was not willing to consider that possibility, suggesting the conclusion that conflict of a major proportion could not be avoided in the future as Todd predicted.

One also sees that as long as he felt he enjoyed the support of the settler community, Huggins acted as if there was nothing the Africans could do to change things. He was quick to blame the emergence of African consciousness as the cause of deteriorating race relationships. In turn the Africans blamed him for failing to bridge the differences that ultimately led to the conflict that made headlines of international newspapers from 1966 to 1979. Indeed, besides Todd, other colonial officials recognized that the war had produced in the Africans a new determination quite different from their opposition to the colonization of their country in 1890 and the subsequent war of 1896. J. R. Taylor, a high-ranking colonial official in the government led by Ian Smith, fully recognized this fact when he said in 1970, "The change of attitude which has produced in the Africans an increasingly insistent demand for education since the post-war years stems from their broadened outlook from the war service."[67] This shows that Todd's mission had yielded some tangible results. He recognized this reality soon after the war ended. For Huggins to argue otherwise was to pretend that the war had no impact on the way Africans reflected upon their situations.

NOTES

1. Leo Marquard, *The People and Policies of South Africa* (New York: Oxford University Press, 1969), p. 10.
2. In 1931 Addams shared the Nobel Peace Prize with Nicholas Murray Butler, president of Columbia University from 1902 to 1945, for their service to humanity.
3. See Chapter 7 of this book for St. Laurent's position on the Mau Mau rebellion.
4. In 1926 Hole published *The Making of Rhodesia* in which he tried to show that he knew the African culture well.
5. Southern Rhodesia, The Report of the Commission of Inquiry into Native Education (Marshall H. Hole, chairman) (Salisbury: Government Printer, 1908), p. 2.
6. Southern Rhodesia, Ordinance No. 8: Education Ordinance, Section B, 1899. Zimbabwe National Archives.
7. Robert Blake, *A History of Rhodesia* (New York: Alfred A. Knopf, 1978), p. 167.
8. South Africa had four provinces: the Cape, Natal, the Transvaal, and the Orange Free State.
9. R. Kent Rasmussen, *Historical Dictionary of Rhodesia/Zimbabwe* (London: The Scarecrow Press, 1979), p. 263.
10. Blake, *History of Rhodesia*, p. 161.
11. Garfield Todd, "African Education in Southern Rhodesia: The Need for a Commission of Inquiry," address to the Bulawayo National Affairs Association, February 18, 1947. Zimbabwe National Archives.
12. Ibid.
13. Ibid.
14. *The African Weekly*, Vol. 3, No. 38, February 26, 1947.
15. Reverend Kennedy Grant, "Teach the Children the Art of Living Together," address to the Conference of African Teachers, Harare, September 16, 1947. Zimbabwe National Archives.
16. Southern Rhodesia, *Report of the Education Committee*, 1943, p. 55.
17. Ndabaningi Sithole, during an interview with the author in Harare, July 22, 1983.
18. Prime Minister Winston Churchill and President Franklin Roosevelt, *The Atlantic Charter*, August 11, 1941. British Embassy, Harare, Zimbabwe.
19. Sithole, interview.
20. Indeed, the author remembers that while he was a student at Old Mutare,

E. D. Chasinda, who had been a sergeant during the war, came to speak of his experiences in Europe and drew large crowds with accounts of life in Europe.

21. *The African Weekly*, April 18, 1945.
22. Ibid.
23. Christian Gauss (ed.), *Machiavelli's The Prince* (trans. Luigi Ricci) (New York, Signet Classics, 1952), p. 127.
24. Robert July, *A History of the African People* (New York: Charles Scribner and Sons, 1974), p. 28.
25. Indeed, forced labor remained a major component of colonial policy in Zimbabwe until 1943. For details, see, for example, Dickson A. Mungazi, "The Change of Black Attitude Towards Education in Rhodesia, 1900–1975." Dissertation, University of Nebraska, Lincoln, 1977, p. 52.
26. Ibid., p. 193.
27. Ibid., p. 194.
28. Rhodesia: *Parliamentary Debates* (Salisbury: Government Printer, 1947), p. 17.
29. Ibid., p. 18.
30. Ibid., p. 50.
31. *The African Weekly*, April 18, 1945.
32. Interview with the author in Mutare, August 6, 1983. The man declined to be identified because, he said, "I do not wish to appear to be a liberal man who seems to rejected his own British heritage."
33. Ibid.
34. D. L. Smit, Secretary of African Affairs in South Africa, "Black and White in Southern Africa," *The African Weekly*, Vol. 1, No. 28, April 18, 1945.
35. Paulo Freire, *Pedagogy of the Oppressed* (trans. M. B. Ramos) (New York: Continuum, 1983), p. 47.
36. Ibid., p. 40.
37. Sir Alfred Beit, "Government Policy and African Development," *The African Weekly*, Vol. 1, No. 28, December 13, 1945.
38. Bishop E. F. Paget, "Native Welfare Societies Must Act Fearlessly," an address to the African Welfare Society, January 11, 1946. Old Mutare Methodist Archives.
39. Ibid.
40. The Methodist Church, *The Waddilove Manifesto: The Education Policy of the Methodist Church*, February 9, 1946. Old Mutare Methodist Archives.
41. Godfrey Huggins, "Taking Stock of African Education," an address to the Southern Rhodesia Missionary Conference, Goromonzi, August 26, 1954. Old Mutare Methodist Archives.
42. Godfrey Huggins, speech delivered at Gueru during a political campaign, May 15, 1952. Zimbabwe National Archives.
43. J. C. Smuts, "Fair Play for the Africans," an address given at a banquet in his honor in Maputo, Mozambique, as reported in *The African Weekly*, Vol. 2, No. 9, August 1, 1945.
44. A. M. Tregold, "Recognition of Africans' Rights to Citizenship Is the Only Hope of European Survival in Africa," an address to the Farmers Union, Bulawayo, November 11, 1947. Old Mutare Methodist Archives.
45. Two other members of the Tredgold family were quite active during that

time in promoting the advancement of the Africans. Robert Tredgold, the chief justice of the Federation, often espoused liberal views and so came into conflict with the colonial government officials. Barbara Tredgold, his sister, was very active in promoting the advancement of African women as a national asset.

46. Tredgold, "Recognition of African Rights to Citizenship."

47. *The African Weekly*, Vol. 4, No. 12, November 12, 1947.

48. As it was used in colonial Africa, the term *Europeans* meant anyone who was white.

49. D. L. Yamba, "Lost Opportunities for Africans: The White Man's Problem," letter to the Editor, *Bantu Mirror*, No. 23, February 19, 1947.

50. Huggins, "Taking Stock of African Education."

51. Ibid.

52. Freire, *Pedagogy of the Oppressed*, p. 84. Freire argues that in a situation in which oppressor-oppressed relationships exist, dialogue is the only way to end the situation of oppression or conflict will result.

53. Ibid., p. 85.

54. Ibid., p. 86.

55. The Council of Non-European Trade Unions, Statement of Goals and Objectives, February 18, 1947. Old Mutare Methodist Archives.

56. Ibid.

57. Ibid.

58. Ibid.

59. Huggins, "Taking Stock of African Education."

60. Aldon Mwamuka, President of the African Teachers Conference, a presidential address, Mutare, July 26, 1945. Old Mutare Methodist Archives.

61. Ibid.

62. Fletcher Secondary School; the first government secondary school for Africans was Goromonzi, opened in 1946.

63. Larry Bowman, *Politics in Rhodesia: White Power in an African State* (Cambridge, MA: Harvard University Press, 1973), p. 25.

64. Lawrence Vambe, *From Rhodesia to Zimbabwe* (Pittsburgh: University of Pittsburgh Press, 1976), p. 255.

65. Ibid., p. 256.

66. A. J. Peck, *Rhodesia Accuses* (Boston: Western Islands Press, 1966), p. 103. In Chapter 2 of this book Peck claims that he was no admirer of the Rhodesia Front, but in Chapter 9 he attacks Todd in a way that leaves no doubt that he disliked his entire program. Peck, born in Zimbabwe in 1922, is a typical example of white conservatives who were unable to understand the need for fundamental social change. On page 53 he describes Africans as ignorant and lacking in hygiene. The book includes six photographs of Africans he claims were murdered by members of the African nationalist organizations. This leads him to conclude that Africans cannot run a responsible government.

67. J. R. Taylor, *African Education in Rhodesia* (Salisbury: Government Printer, 1970), p. 6.

Photo 1. Winston Churchill, prime minister of Britain, from 1940 to 1945 and from 1951 to 1955. "We shall apply Mr. Rhodes's principle of equal rights for all civilized men." Photo: Kenya National Archives.

Photo 2. Michael Blundell, 1957, member of the legislature of Kenya, 1948 to 1962. "We cannot stop an African government. We must therefore see that this great mass of people is well educated." Photo: Kenya National Archives.

Photo 3. Garfield Todd, prime minister of colonial Zimbabwe from 1953 to 1958, and Emory Rose, a close friend and former American missionary to the Congo and founder of African-American Institute, 1953. "The Africans are aware that educated people can be governed but they cannot be enslaved forever." Photo: Supplied by Judith Todd.

Photo 4. H. K. Nyongesa, Director of Kenya National Archives, and Ruth Waswa, a member of the staff, 1995. "Michael Blundell tried all he could to promote the political advancement of the Africans." Photo: By the author.

Photo 5. The Big Four of politics in Kenya: Harry Thuku, African nationalist; Philip E. Mitchell, governor from 1944 to 1952; Jomo Kenyatta, first prime minister of independent Kenya, 1963; and Evelyn Baring, governor from 1952 to 1959. "For these men politics was a battle of wills." Photo: Kenya National Archives.

Photo 6. Garfield Todd and Guy Clutton-Brock, 1978. Clutton-Brock was another great liberal who was deported from colonial Zimbabwe in 1971 by the RF government led by Ian Smith. Clutton-Brock shared Todd's belief expressed by the Methodist Church in 1946 that "definite lines of development of the Africans must be initiated so that they reach the full and unrestricted citizenship which is unquestionably their right." Photo: Supplied by Judith Todd.

Photo 7. D. N. Pritt, QC, 1952, who defended Jomo Kenyatta and four other defendants when they were tried for their role in the Mau Mau rebellion. "My clients are being tried for practicing nationalist politics." Photo: Kenya National Archives.

Photo 8. The arrest of Dedan Kimathi, Mau Mau rebellion leader, 1956. (He was executed in 1957.) "I do not lead terrorists, I lead freedom fighters." Photo: Kenya National Archives.

Photo 9. Mellyse Otieno, secretary, Nairobi, 1997. "Some members of the Luo have made an outstanding contribution to the development of Kenya." Photo: By the author.

Photo 10. Sir Peter Tapsell, Member of the British Parliament for 40 years, a friend of both Michael Blundell and Garfield Todd, addressing a conference at The Hague in 1998. Photo: Supplied by Sir Peter Tapsell.

5

Michael Blundell's Role in the Political Development of Kenya

> That this council notes the increasing disregard for law and order within the Colony and urges the government to take the necessary measures to improve the situation.
> —Michael Blundell, 1952

KIPANDE CONTROVERSY: DEFINING THE PARAMETERS

As soon as Michael Blundell was elected to the legislative council in Kenya in 1848, he knew that he had to establish a functional relationship with Africans, even though since 1944 there was only one African in the legislature, Harry Thuku. The occasion that gave him the opportunity to do so came only a few months following his election from the action that the colonial government under Philip E. Mitchell took to ensure a more effective system of control of Africans. The colonial government decided, as a result of strong representations made by Africans, to replace the old registration certificates which all Africans were required to carry on their person for identification purposes[1] with an identity card that people of all races would have. The reason for Africans to demand change in the national identification system was that the registration certificates were highly discriminatory and humiliating to Africans. The Africans were no longer willing to continue to endure the indignity imposed by a discriminatory system. They demanded an immediate end to it.

The demand itself is a remarkable example of how the rise of consciousness enabled Africans to recognize evidence of mistreatment, prejudice, and discrimination in the colonial law. Chapter 4 of this study has presented evidence to suggest how the war had helped arouse this consciousness. The surprising thing is that only a few liberal settlers, such as Garfield Todd, recognized it. The rest, such as Godfrey Huggins, pretended that it was not an important factor. In accepting the representations from Africans to introduce a new system of national identification, the colonial government decided that new identity cards should carry a thumbprint of the holder. This suggestion was acceptable to Africans because it meant that every citizen would be treated equally and fairly. But the settlers strongly opposed the system because they associated fingerprinting with criminal behavior and keeping records of criminals.

The old registration certificate was considered to have served a useful purpose since it was first introduced in 1919.[2] Settler employers valued it as part of keeping accurate records and economic information about Africans. Upon engaging Africans as employees, the settler employers entered on the registration certificate date of employment, monthly pay, address of employer, date of issue of the certificate, name and address, and date of birth. Like *chitupa* in colonial Zimbabwe, the employer kept the certificate in his office to minimize the chances of desertion, which was quite common because of the practice of mistreating African workers. The employer would then issue the African employee a substitute pass for identification purposes in order not to violate vagrancy regulations. Even with the knowledge that desertion was a crime punishable by six months of imprisonment with hard labor, Africans routinely deserted their places of employment to escape from mistreatment by their settler employers.

Effective as it was as a means of ensuring control of Africans, the old registration certificate was often open to abuse by settler employers who routinely made it hard for African workers to leave their employment legally for better opportunity elsewhere. Like settler employers in colonial Zimbabwe, these employers also indicated a higher rate of pay than they actually paid their workers. The Africans of 1948 argued that this abuse was a form of colonial oppression and demanded fundamental change made possible by the introduction of *kipande*. Mitchell knew that his administration faced a major problem. On the one hand Africans would not accept continuation of the old registration certificate because it was humiliating and discriminatory.[3] On the other hand settlers would not accept the proposed identification system because they associated it with criminal behavior. What was he going to do about this controversy whose origin was the policy of the colonial government itself? Unable to resolve the controversy, Mitchell decided to do nothing about it, hoping that it would go away.

At this point Michael Blundell came into the picture. After carefully studying the reasons why Africans demanded an end to the old system of registration certificates, Blundell made up his mind on which side of the controversy he was. He concluded, "It was ridiculous, for instance, to insist on an educated laboratory technician carrying an old-fashioned registration certificate just because he happened to be an African."[4] In taking this position Blundell had taken the views of some liberal settlers who had accepted the proposed system of identification because they thought its introduction would help bring about an improvement in racial relationships as a response to conditions created by the end of the war. Blundell's response was therefore not a rush to judgment about an issue where Mitchell feared to tread, but a deliberate and calculated move to respond to a possible national crisis that would not benefit anyone. He had even discussed the proposed system to make sure that he represented their opinion in his response.

Suddenly and without any prior warning, Blundell was placed in an untenable position to find that many settlers who had accepted the proposal for a new national identification later began to have doubts about possible wider implications of accepting it. Among these implications was the possibility of social equality with Africans. This was unacceptable. The thinking behind this position was that if equality was attained through a national identification system, what reason was there to maintain social distinction in other areas of national life? The settlers began to think that if Africans were granted equality in a national identification system, they would begin to demand political equality and the colonial government would have no basis to deny them this demand. If this happened, Africans would soon gain control of the government, and, thus, the country.

Unknown to the colonial government and the Colonial Office in London, a major political storm was gathering, threatening the political stability that Kenya had known since the end of the war. Mitchell, like Blundell, was placed in an uncomfortable position as he tried to downplay the magnitude of the issue.[5] Both men had few options; the Africans held all the cards. For the first time in his long and distinguished career, Mitchell was faced with the reality that he did not have absolute power to do what he had always done in the past: demonstrate a political savvy that made him unquestionable in the conduct of colonial policy. In the *kipande* controversy he had finally met his match. Mitchell tried to find inspiration from his knowledge of military history and classical Latin literature in which he excelled during his college days.[6] He tried to remember his past success in Nyasaland where he was posted in 1912 as a junior administrative officer and as secretary for native affairs, and as provincial commissioner in Tanganyika and Uganda where his claimed knowledge of the African thought process was considered to be exceptionally high. But he found nothing there to suggest a possible solution to the *kipande* controversy. Mitchell was slowly becoming a beleaguered colonial official placed on the horns of dilemma by two powerful and conflicting forces: the demand from Africans and resistance from settlers.[7]

While Mitchell remained unable to resolve the controversy, conservative settlers began to exert more influence to reject the proposed national identification system. Slowly the number of those opposed to it began to grow. They formed a civil rights movement to intensify their opposition to the proposed system. They held public meetings where they hoisted the Union Jack and sang "God Save the King"[8] before they made fiery speeches against the proposed system. The organizing members of the group toured the country in an effort to gain support for their opposition. At every meeting a resolution was passed indicating that if the proposed system was introduced through an enactment of an ordinance, settlers would ignore the law. It was quite clear that Africans and settlers were heading toward a major showdown, as each group was not willing to back down on an issue its members considered critical to their future. How was the issue to be resolved? What was Blundell going to do to help find a solution to it?

The issue was so controversial that colonial officials decided to hold public meetings to discuss it. One such meeting was held at Nakuru, right in the heart of Blundell's electoral district, to discuss it in order to find a solution to it. In deciding to convene the meeting to discuss the crisis caused by this issue, Blundell held the opinion that he failed to see what harm would be done by having one's thumbprint placed on a national identification card. He further concluded that the settlers who were so much in the practice of regarding themselves as leaders of the country should now be against a proposal challenging them to demonstrate it in the interest of promoting racial equality.[9] The town hall where the meeting was held was packed with people who came from as far as Kitale and the Trans-Nzola area. The loudspeaker system was used to ensure that everyone understood what was being said.

The man selected as chairman of the meeting was E. H. Wright, a retired settler and an individual of mixed credentials and conflicting views on the question of race relations. At some point in time Wright subscribed to the view that settlers should, for the foreseeable future, provide the leadership that Kenya needed in economic, social, and political development and that Africans had so much to learn before they could begin to demand equal treatment. In essence Wright seemed to share the views that Cecil John Rhodes expressed at the height of his power in 1896 and Winston Churchill affirmed in 1922. Now, in 1948, Wright was taking the same position. That is why he was selected to chair this meeting. Would he be realistic in understanding that the Africans of 1948 were different from those of 1896 and 1922? Could he understand that this controversy was a result of the change that Africans had gone through in recognizing the many flaws that the colonial policy represented and were now demanding change? Wright does not appear to have a complete comprehension of the magnitude of the responsibility that he carried in being asked to chair this meeting.

Wright also long took the position that the central highlands must be permanently exclusively for settlers because they were the hub that turned the economic wheels of the country. But after the war Wright seemed to modify his views and began to see the importance of according Africans some rights, though not totally equally to those of settlers, to make it possible for them to ensure their development as a condition of creating a national climate of cooperation for the benefit of the country. However, in asking Wright to chair this meeting Blundell was taking a big risk because he simply did not know what position he was going to take. Also, the settlers who came to the meeting did not know which side of the issue Wright was on because he had not expressed his opinion one way or the other.

Indeed, as soon as the meeting started Blundell discovered the unpredictable nature of Wright's behavior. He loaded himself with brandy just before the meeting started, as Blundell would later state, "experience had taught him to settle his stomach first."[10] In rambling opening remarks Wright acknowledged the concern the settlers expressed about the proposed national identification system and expressed his resentment that if it were introduced, it would mean that settlers would be treated equally with Africans. At the same time he recognized the concern the Africans were expressing about the need for equal treatment in society. In a series of rapidly moving but disjointed statements Wright sounded like Hamlet's method in madness. He invited participants of the meeting, many of whom marched up and down with pistols flapping against their thighs as they sang "Land of Hope and Glory" while he continued to speak incoherently on one issue to the next without pausing to change the topic he thought he was addressing.

Blundell watched in disbelief as confusion accentuated by the conditions that Wright was in reigned supreme. He watched helplessly and hopelessly as Wright demonstrated total inability to direct the meeting toward responsible debate and resolution. In the end there was an uproar and pandemonium that translated into division of opinion about what resolution to pass. Some argued that the proposed national identification system was an affront of the superiority of settlers. Others argued that adherence to this 19th-century myth would play into the hands of the Africans who would exploit it to their political advantage because the Africans of 1948 were quite different from those of 1895 when Kenya became a colony of Britain. Blundell watched nervously as two inconclusive ballots were taken. He was greatly relieved to see that the issue that raised so much emotion and anger disappeared into the thin winds of the central highlands and that those settlers who had come to see the issue as a threat to their notion of social superiority over the Africans was not that important.

The participants of the meeting returned home more confused and unsure of themselves than they were when they came to the meeting. Blundell seized the opportunity to bolster his own political fortunes. He took advantage of Wright's failure to generate purposeful deliberations based on collective wisdom of those who would be affected by change in the structure of colonial policy. He decided that he was going to exercise effective leadership not only of this controversial issue, but also all issues that were likely to surface in the future. He concluded, "The emotions aroused over this rather small matter were significant. However, they showed the first faint difference among settler electorate, not only on the concept of white leadership, but also in the attitude of many settler voters to African social advancement and political resentment."[11] Many of those who opposed the proposed identification system later formed a right-wing political party known as Federal Independence Party (FIP), which set its goal toward political independence for Kenya under settler control. Realistically this party had no chance of succeeding.

In considering his options Blundell was guided by what he learned in Britain as he was growing up. He remembered those things he learned at Wellington College and Magdalen College about the importance of serving human needs in a larger social context. He recalled the conversations he used to have with his father as they strolled in the local park in London about the importance of serving human needs. He remembered what he had studied about the great liberal traditions that were created early in the 20th century by great liberal leaders whose ideas had brought about meaningful change from which he was now benefiting. He recalled the philosophy of the Liberal Party and the Labour Party in Britain that the greatness of a society is realized when individuals in leadership positions endeavor to protect those who are unable to protect themselves.

Unlike Wright, Blundell had a clear concept of the legitimate place of Africans in the colonial society. He was equally conscious of the place of settlers. He believed as early as 1941, as a result of his participation in the war, that there was need to balance the interests of Africans with those of settlers. He did not subscribe to the notion that the white man was superior to the African. He saw settlers and Africans as equal partners in the struggle for national development. Each had an important contribution to make to the development of the other. Therefore, while he sought to protect the rights of settlers who had elected him to a political office, he was equally conscious of the need to protect the developmental interests of Africans. Blundell also recognized that the balance between the two was the only realistic and sane course of action to take. In this approach he was defining the parameters of his relationships with both his fellow settlers and Africans. For the rest of his political career and life Blundell operated under this basic principle.

George Bennet concludes that since the failure of the Nakuru meeting on the proposed national identification system Blundell went on the offensive, making public speeches addressing the need to destroy what he regarded as the fear complex among settlers.[12] Blundell also argued that settlers and Africans must come together to discuss their concerns. However, this suggestion was unrealistic because it was not a strategy that was adopted anywhere in British colonial Africa to bring Africans and their colonizers together to discuss issues of common concern. Nonetheless, it was worth trying and if anyone had a reasonable chance of success it was Michael Blundell. Influential as he was, Blundell was unable to persuade either group to see things the way he did. Settlers and Africans continued to drift apart as they operated under the belief that each group was trying to dominate the other. He felt strongly that this problem, if resolved, would set an excellent example that he believed could be used all over British colonial Africa.

The fact that there was no precedence did not, in Blundell's mind, mean that it should not be tried. Blundell believed that establishing lines of communication between settlers and Africans was critical if the two groups hoped to live together in peace. He took tremendous pride in his innovative approach to problems. He considered every idea put to him by anyone, and never dismissed it as unworkable before he gave it a serious try. This political action is the hallmark of a true liberal. He was also aware that solving this problem required the utilization of the dynamics of human understanding. But he was also aware that conditions coming out of the war made this task very difficult because Africans were afraid that settlers would adopt harsher attitudes toward them than they did before the war, and settlers believed that the rise of African nationalism made it hard for Africans to exercise any understanding of settlers' fears. Although there was no immediate answer, Blundell believed that an effort must be made to bring the two racial groups together in the spirit of mutual trust and confidence in their roles in shaping the future of Kenya. Although the *kipande* controversy was not fully resolved, it helped Blundell define the parameters of his relationships with both settlers and the Africans in more precise terms.

BLUNDELL ON CAUSES OF THE MAU MAU REBELLION

If Blundell thought that the crisis caused by settler negative response to the proposed national identification system brought his political influence to a test, he did not know that within four years he would encounter the greatest test of his political career yet in the Mau Mau rebellion. Although the Mau Mau movement began to form in 1947, one year after Jomo Kenyatta returned from his studies in Britain, the colonial officials ignored it because they thought Africans were incapable of organizing something of that magnitude. However, Bethwell A. Ogot concludes that in 1952 the leaders of the Mau Mau movement "believed that political goods were attainable only through a violent struggle."[13]

When the rebellion broke out in 1952 the colonial government under Evelyn Baring failed to acknowledge that Africans had legitimate reasons for their action. Instead, colonial officials argued that since the inception of the colonial government, Africans had benefited in many ways, such as education, Christianity, and economic well-being. Wunyabari O. Maloba suggests that these are the things that Africans claimed the settlers had brought to Africa to persuade them to accept in order to move away from their primitive culture and barbarism. But to their surprise Africans discovered that the settlers were not willing to allow them to share in them.[14] But as long as the settlers operated by the view that their culture and civilization were the salvation of the Africans, it was not possible for the colonial government to understand that they had legitimate reasons to be dissatisfied with colonial policies.

In 1925, the year that Blundell arrived in Kenya, recognizing that the colonial government had every intention of strengthening racial discrimination, Africans formed the Kikuyu Central Association (KCA), a militant political organization that emerged from the ashes of the East African Association. When the colonial government outlawed KCA in 1940 the Kikuyu formed the Kenya African Union (KAU). It was not coincidental that Africans formed these two militant organizations. They wanted to preserve the central highlands as their homeland because since 1904 they had watched the settlers prepare to relocate them elsewhere. This process picked up speed in 1922. From that time to 1944 the colonial government did everything in its power to evict Africans from the central highlands to make room for settlers.

The year 1944 is also when Philip E. Mitchell was appointed governor. Mitchell was an arrogant aristocrat who held a very low opinion of the African intellect. He therefore regarded the formation of KAU as a result of the action of a few frustrated educated Africans who were trying to use their uneducated people to promote their own political agenda.[15] The colonial officials also concluded that these few frustrated educated leaders were removed from the position of exercising influence on their simple people who were vulnerable to manipulation to disobey the authorities. In assuming this line of response the colonial government lacked basic knowledge of the actual extent of extensive discontent that was now becoming part of life of the Africans' response to colonial condition.

This discontent was coming from three main sources: a lack of adequate opportunity for development for both rural and urban Africans, discrimination that was most visible in education, and an absence of political participation. The colonial officials also failed to understand the profound hatred of the colonial condition itself. Basil Davidson concludes that when the Mau Mau rebellion came to an end this lack of understanding had cost the colonial government "60 million pounds sterling with the commitment of some 50,000 troops and police, and resulted in 10,000 Africans killed and 90,000 others impounded in concentration camps under appalling conditions."[16] By the time the rebellion came to an end in 1956, three basic aspects of the discontent had been identified as its principal causes: discrimination in land distribution, the rise of African nationalism, and a lack of economic opportunity.

Up to the time the Mau Mau rebellion began in October 1952, the issue of land distribution had always been a major cause of conflict between Africans and the colonial government. For example, the appointment of James Hayes Sadler as governor to succeed Donald Stewart as commissioner in 1905 convinced the British government that its representative administration in Kenya was quite secure and that it was necessary to formulate a land policy it believed would lead to the security of the settlers. And from 1908 to 1952 officials at the Colonial Office in London authorized the governor to formulate a land policy that did just that. This is why in 1922 Winston Churchill stressed the importance of reserving the central highlands for exclusive occupation by settlers. It was also the policy that angered the Africans.

In 1908 Lord Elgin, who became secretary of state in 1905 after the transfer of the administration of the East African Protectorate from the Foreign Office to the Colonial Office with Winston Churchill as his undersecretary, issued a statement on March 19, 1908:

It would not be in accordance with the policy of His Majesty's[17] Government to exclude any class of his subjects from holding land in any part of British Protectorate, but that in view of the comparatively limited areas in the protectorate suitable for European colonization, a reasonable discretion will be exercised in dealing with applications for land on the part of Natives of India and other non-Europeans.[18]

What this means is that the question of land distribution had already been decided before there was any contact between the Africans and the settlers, and that from now on Africans must be reminded that the land they had inherited from their ancestors now belonged to the white man by virtue of claimed superiority and colonization. The lack of regard with which the British pursued this policy was bound to cause a major conflict in the future. The elements of this conflict were already in place by the time that Blundell arrived in Kenya in 1925. That Elgin made it possible for natives of India and other groups to apply for land suggests the conclusion that Africans had no place in the land policy of the British government.

Speaking on January 27, 1922, at an East African dinner held in London, Winston Churchill, then undersecretary for the colonies, went further in explaining the structure of the land policy of the British government, saying that the Colonial Office would apply Rhodes's philosophy of equal rights for all civilized men in allocating land in the central highlands. Churchill had visited Kenya in 1907 and recorded his thoughts in *My African Journey* about the need to open the central highlands for exclusive settlement by British immigrants. Churchill, like Rhodes, was operating under the assumption that because Africans could not write their names, they were not civilized enough to receive equal rights. The first right the British government considered was the right to own land, which was taken from the Africans.

In 1923 the Duke of Devonshire, then British colonial secretary, stated the strategy that his office was going to utilize in implementing the land policy of his government, reiterating what previous officials had outlined in the past. He gave notice that the Kikuyu and the Masai who had occupied the central highlands must begin to make plans to move elsewhere to make room for new British settlers. He indicated that the legislative council would soon enact an ordinance under the Crown Lands Act, which Britain had been using for years to implement its land policy in its empire in Africa. The Duke of Devonshire concluded, "An area of land in the highlands which can be set aside without infringing any native requirements will be temporarily reserved in order that it may be ascertained by experience what demands there are for agriculture."[19]

But it was Malcom J. MacDonald who issued the Highlands Orders-in-Council and the Native Areas Orders-in-Council, which he presented to the British Parliament on February 21, 1939, which Britain began to implement as its land policy. For the first time in their lives Africans felt the power of the British government in carrying out its plans. Suddenly they were strangers in the land of their birth and forefathers. In losing the land that they had used for hundreds of years, Africans resented British action far more than they resented colonization itself. They determined that the only course of action left open to them was to utilize the same force that the British had used to colonize their land and to force them out of the central highlands. The sad part of all this is that the colonial officials took this action in the belief that it was good for Africans. In October 1952 the colonial government finally knew the extent of African resentment of this action.

On March 7, 1949, Creech Jones secretary of state for the colonies from 1946 to 1950, explained in the House of Commons that the Colonial Office wished to make it clear that Africans of Kenya fully understood and recognized the value of British settlement in the central highlands because the settler community brought benefits to the country. Jones concluded, "I want to stress that while we must have regard to the basic interests of the Africans that does not mean that we should sacrifice the best interests of Europeans in building up that country and making it their contribution to its economic life and political development."[20] So far, the statements made by successive officials at the Colonial Office seem to indicate a steady shift of policy from seeking to balance the land needs of the Africans to establishing a practice where settler interests became paramount. By degrees the Africans were losing their land as settlers acquired it at an unprecedented pace.

In a similar manner Jones's successor, James Griffiths, who served from 1950 to 1951, argued on December 13, 1950, that any plans to make Kenya a suitable country for British settlers must be based upon a good land policy and must make it attractive to them. He stated the position that from time to time the land policy must be reviewed to make it more appealing to prospective British settlers. This means that Africans must be ready to move from the land they were occupying to make room for these settlers whose contribution to the economy was needed to ensure the development of the country.[21] In 1952 Henry Hopkinson, who succeeded Griffiths, added that because British settlers were permanent inhabitants of Kenya, their land rights must be secured to enable them to contribute to the economy in a way that benefited the Africans. Hopkinson did not explain how, in light of the fact that Africans were used as cheap labor, they would benefit from the policy that successive British governments had designed.

On February 22, 1952, Alan Lennox-Boyd, who served as British secretary of state for the colonies from 1952 to 1959, justified the land policy of the government that he served in a way that upset the Africans during the first phase of the Mau Mau rebellion. He said "It is not alienation of land that has led to land hunger amongst the Africans. If the whole of the white highlands were handed over tomorrow to Africans it might lead to a small and temporary alleviation of the problem, but it would be at the total loss of the whole economy of the country."[22] Lennox-Boyd added that because the British settlers contributed more to the economy than the Africans, they must be permitted to own the most productive land in Kenya. During a visit to Kenya in October 1954, Lennox-Boyd was quoted as saying "Her Majesty's[23] Government is not likely to lend itself to encouraging people to come if they intend to betray them or their confidence in the possession of land and homes they have built for themselves and their children."[24]

It is ironic that while Lennox-Boyd was explaining policy elements of the British government he was also seeking to introduce a new constitution that served as the first step toward granting independence to

Kenya. In 1954 Kenya was embroiled in the Mau Mau rebellion, and it would be impossible for any official of the British government to predict the future with any degree of accuracy. The best that any colonial official could do was to try to maintain a level of confidence that things would not deteriorate. But with Mau Mau activity from both sides of the conflict it was virtually impossible to maintain that level of confidence. The visit to Kenya was meant to assure the settlers that Britain had not abandoned them during a period of major national crisis. Lennox-Boyd, a savvy politician, was trying to play it safe. The secrecy which surrounded his approach to the new constitution in 1954 can be understood in the context of his desire to assure the settlers that things were under control when he actually knew otherwise.

Speaking in the House of Commons on November 7, 1952, about a month after the Mau Mau rebellion had started, Oliver Lyttleton, who served as secretary of state for colonies from 1951 to 1954, was quite candid in stating the land policy of the government he served: "We have wide plans for the vast territories of Africa, and we want to let everyone know that in Kenya we are not to be turned aside by a band of terrorists. We are in this country to develop it and not to exploit it, to develop it for everyone. Above all we are in the country to stay. Let there be no doubt about that."[25] While he spoke in this manner, Lyttleton was part of British plan to evolve a constitutional arrangement that eventually turned over the country to Africans.

In saying what he did Lyttleton either did not say it from clear knowledge of what was happening or he did not wish to create confusion and panic among settlers that he, like Lennox-Boyd, had been charged with the responsibility of initiating transition from the colonial government to the Africans. In ten years the British settlers whom successive British policy was intended to protect would be forced to turn over power and the government to the Africans. The land policy that the British government had formulated was so oppressive that Africans were determined to fight to bring it to an end. Throughout its history the land policy of the British government and the colonial government itself lacked one fundamental consideration: the fact that Africans regarded it as land-grabbing at its worst. Successive British officials added insult to injured African feelings by claiming that the policy was intended to promote the economic development of the Africans themselves, when in reality the policy exploited them in every possible way. It is for this reason that Africans were not persuaded to see things the way the colonial government did. Alan Lennox-Boyd and Oliver Lyttleton, two British officials who were charged with the responsibility of evolving new constitutional plans setting Kenya for independence, approached their task with a sense of its enormous importance.

To understand how the economic deprivation of the Africans became one of the major causes of the Mau Mau rebellion, one needs to understand why the Africans believed that they were being exploited economically. In seeking to understand and appreciate this cause one needs to understand the economic implications of the system of *kipande*. When it was introduced at the end of the First World War by the Native Registration Ordinance, *kipande* was intended to ensure labor control and gather statistics on the extent of the contribution the Africans were making to economic development of the country. African workers were required to carry this metal tag on their necks like a dog carried an identification tag. Among other things the *kipande* showed the name of the holder, address, ethnic origin, nature of employment, and income, just like *chitupa* did in colonial Zimbabwe.

George Bennet concluded that because *kipande* was applied only to Africans who were employed in settler business establishments in Kenya, and not in Uganda and Tanganyika, the Africans of Kenya felt particularly oppressed.[26] They began to believe that the colonial governments in Uganda and Tanganyika were more humane in their treatment of the their African populations and took it upon themselves to remove the causes of that oppression. There was something that the Africans in Kenya particularly resented bitterly and this was the fact that as holders of *kipande* they were not allowed to engage in certain economic activity such as growing coffee, the principal economic activity that had sustained their livelihood in the past. By seeking employment in settler business establishments, the Africans forfeited their right to engage in any other economic activity to augment their meager wages. This policy entailed the extent of oppression that the Africans could no longer accept as time went on. On its part the colonial government made no effort to adjust the system to suite changing times.

The system of *kipande* had other devastating effects on the economic relationships between the British settlers and the Africans. The settlers tried to do what they considered reasonable in treating their African employees well. On many farms African laborers were treated in a manner that showed a degree of compassion and kindness. This was done in order to make sure that entire families were employed. Children, parents, grandparents, and members of the extended family were all engaged as employees without increasing their wages. Settlers allowed these Africans to grow their own food to supplement their poor income. Once the settler employers succeeded in creating this relationship, Africans could no longer expect to be paid for their labor. They were bonded to their master in the same way tenants were bonded to their landlord in the Middle Ages or the sharecropper to his former slave master in the southern United States soon after the Civil War. In this setting, exploitation of Africans as cheap labor acquired powerful economic dimensions of an oppressive system. This practice was so pervasive in British colonial Africa that it systematically deprived the African farm laborers of any meaningful economic livelihood.[27]

This system created serious problems for Michael Blundell as he tried to balance two conflicting systems: the one required by *kipande* regulations, and the genuine needs of the Africans to survive economically. He learned to treat his African workers different from the way B. D. Goldberg treated his in colonial Zimbabwe. Robert B. Edgerton suggested that Blundell's treatment of his African workers was "expected of him from the upper-class Britons who were used to caring for their servants and tenants with kindness and compassion."[28] This was the kind of knowledge that Blundell had acquired through liberal traditions about the importance of treating human beings as a condition of national development. In many cases the Africans who worked under these conditions often developed dependence and vulnerability because they became totally loyal to their employers, even those who behaved like B. D. Goldberg. This is why British settlers came to conclude erroneously that their African laborers were happy and faithful and that nothing should be done to disturb this mutually beneficial relationship. In her book *Out of Africa*, Karen Blixen made a major contribution to the evolution of this romantic view of the obedient and loyal African laborer. After an extensive tour of Kenya in 1955, Fenner Brockway, an influential member of the Labour Party, concluded that, as was the practice in British colonial Africa, the employment of an African man as farm laborer implied that all of his family members were also employed in the same kind of work without receiving additional pay.[29] This is how settler farmers made fortunes. B. D. Goldberg, Godfrey Huggins, and Ian Smith became wealthy from their agricultural operations in colonial Zimbabwe by resorting to this exploitation of Africans.

Although a vast majority of settler employers in Kenya maintained this traditionally negative attitude toward Africans because they thought it dangerous to trust them completely, many farmers like Blundell came to have reasonable working relationships with their African employees. However, there was a side of the so-called benevolent settler employers that remained subtle in form and sinister in application. They succeeded in persuading the colonial administration to impose taxes on Africans to improve the effectiveness of the administrative system, to enforce provisions of the *kipande* regulations, and to limit educational opportunity so that they could be more effectively controlled economically and politically.[30] This strategy made it possible for the colonial establishment to deny Africans a viable means of self-support so they would be forced to seek work on settler farms for very low pay. In 1950 the standard monthly pay for a male African laborer who worked every day of the month, including Sunday, was 14 shillings. At that time a shilling was the equivalent of $0.14.[31]

In 1952, when the Mau Mau rebellion started, Blundell paid his farm workers 12 shillings per month.[32] This revelation came as a great embarrassment for Blundell himself. The reality that he was paying his African workers 2 shillings less than the average wage suggests his acquiescence to the strategy that settler farmers recommended to the colonial government, designed to limit economic development of Africans to ensure that they we more effectively controlled. Blundell decided that he was not going to endure this embarrassment any more and tried to prove that he operated under the traditions of liberal principles that had been in use during the early part of the 20th century. He therefore raised the wages of his workers to 15 shillings a month, just a shilling above the existing average.

There were other considerations that heavily impinged upon the Africans' struggle for economic survival. In 1952 a cheap shirt cost 4 shillings and the annual poll tax was 20 shillings. With the level of income that the Africans had, a laborer was able to stay alive by raising his own food from a small piece of land that his employer allowed him to till. Edgerton concludes that in most cases "regulations required the African laborer to sell some of the produce from the small land to their employers at a price that was determined by the farmer himself. There was no negotiations about the actual price."[33]

This practice meant that no matter what an African laborer was able to do to enhance his economic survival, he was undercut by a combination of forces that were created by both the settler employers and the policy of the colonial government. It was a common practice for the employer to buy a bag of maize from his employees for 15 shillings then sell it at 32 shillings. Government subsidy made it possible for the settler farmer to exploit his African laborers in this fashion. Then, through the system of control, the colonial government would make huge profits by selling the maize flour at a price it would determine with no regard to the earning ability of the Africans. In this manner the entire African population was exploited and the Africans bitterly resented it, especially when the colonial government pretended that things were fine.

The practice adopted by settler farmers of employing African families without paying them individually was as pervasive as it was exploitive. Edgerton quotes Charity Wacuima, an educated Kikuyu woman who, as a child, worked with her parents as a laborer on a settler coffee plantation: "I rapidly grew to dislike these white men who made people work like slaves and paid them half a shilling a day, who sometimes struck the grown men as if they were children and who always treated us as if we were permanently children."[34] Edgerton then concludes that regardless of how many members of the family there were, they were paid a single wage, adding "Africans bitterly resented this economic exploitation just as they detested their treatment as inferior beings. Most white settlers believed that Africans rarely exceeded the mental development of a 12-year-old and had to be treated as irresponsible children."[35]

To add intellectual insult to economic injury, settlers adopted a 19th-century myth that Africans were intellectually inferior to Europeans. As recent as 1954 Isaac Leigh quoted a settler as saying "the uneducated African is a child in many respects. He is forgetful and often quite stupid."[36] In 1913 a noted British colonial official, Chauncy Stigand, wrote, "For the proper understanding of the savage African one must not look on him as a human being, but rather as a superior kind of animal."[37] In 1952, seeking to revive this myth, the settlers hoped that they would realize the effect of the Man Mau rebellion.

This myth was in the first place the basis of the economic and political policies the settlers and the colonial government adopted to ensure effective control of the Africans. These policies also contributed to the outbreak of the Mau Mau rebellion. In the context of developments that were taking place in the lives of the Africans, the rise of African nationalism became a powerful determining factor of relationships between them and the settlers. Once this nationalism became part of the consciousness of the Africans, it would not be destroyed no matter what the colonial government did to limit its effect. This was the reality that Blundell and other liberals like him were compelled to take into account in deciding the kind of role they played in shaping the development of Kenya. It was a challenge that had to be met, and a call that had to be answered.

EXAMPLES OF SUCCESSFUL PEASANT REBELLION

In discussing the Mau Mau rebellion from a broad context of theoretical considerations, one can make a viable contribution to the understanding of theory of peasant uprising. Various aspects that make up the Mau Mau movement can be compared to theoretical considerations relative to other rebellions. Wunyabari O. Maloba concludes that it is an amazing fact that on the eve of his retirement as governor of Kenya in 1952, Philip E. Mitchell expressed his belief that wherever he went in the country he saw nothing but happy smiling African faces and that they were contended with their lives because the government had in place a good policy.[38]

In 1954, two year after he had retired, Mitchell recorded a different reaction to conditions that caused the Mau Mau rebellion while he was governor. He even refused to give an account of these events, saying "I have no intention whatsoever of offering any explanation or defense of myself or my government for what we did or did not do. If it gives any one satisfaction to believe that what has happened since I retired is all my fault, he is welcome to do so."[39] This is not the reaction of a man who saw smiling faces only two years before. Before the Mau Mau finally broke out Mitchell either never saw the rebellion coming or he pretended it was not coming. Yet the Mau Mau movement was a nationalist and anticolonial peasant rebellion. How could he possibly fail to see it coming?

Among the examples of the successful peasant rebellion in history is the one in Britain in 1400. This rebellion was caused by the harshness of the application of the infamous Corn Laws that Britain passed in order to increase the margin of profit of the landlords, many of whom were powerful members of parliament. Ronald Webber concludes that beginning with in 1381 as a result of rapidly declining conditions of life, the peasant rebellion in Britain consisted of ordinary people. However, some members of the aristocracy and the clergy saw the cause of the oppressed as the cause of Britain itself and decided to support the rebellion, increasing its chances of success.[40] This means that for the peasant revolt to succeed it must have a broadly based operational principle. Paul Avrich discusses the Russian peasant revolt in the 17th century and concludes, "Cossacks of the steppes fought against the central government. Poor Cossacks fought against rich Cossacks. Rising gentry clashed with declining aristocracy. National minority attacked Russian colonizers. Old believers resisted new faiths. Serfs rose against landlords. Village went against town and periphery fought against the center."[41] Avrich concludes that these peasant revolts were successful because their leaders believed they were fighting a just cause and had effective leadership. Chapter 7 of this book addresses the question of leadership of the Mau Mau movement to suggest its structure and impact on the colonial society and how Blundell responded to it.

Among the well-known examples of the peasant revolt in history is the French Revolution of 1789, which was caused by declining conditions of life under the economic policy of Louis XVI, who ascended the French throne in 1774. In 1832 and 1848 Europe was hit by a series of revolutionary struggles created by the poor conditions of life among the working class. The Russian Revolution of 1917 was caused by excessively abusive policy adopted by Czar Nicholas II toward the declining position of the serfs from 1893 to 1917. Each of these examples shows that, indeed, the oppressed masses are quite capable of organizing a revolt on their own. They do not need educated elite to lead the rebellion. Leadership emerges only when the rebellion has already started. Neither Mitchell nor any other colonial official, including Blundell, fully understood this critical fact.

There are also examples of successful peasant rebellions in the Third World. These include the revolution in Cuba from which Fidel Castro emerged as leader. In China the revolution of 1949 was caused by dissatisfaction among the peasants with the economic policies of the government. Mao Tse-tung and Chou En-lai helped organize its direction. In a similar manner the revolutions in Vietnam, Angola, Mozambique, Zimbabwe, Ethiopia, Namibia, and South Africa were a result of the policies that were pursued by the colonial governments. Once discontent erupts, it will not be contained without a successful revolution. The oppressive policies initiated by the colonial governments in Africa ultimately led to their own demise much sooner than the thousand years that Cecil John Rhodes, at the height of his political power in 1896, predicted they would last.

In Africa the rise of African nationalism took powerful dimensions that the colonial governments were not quite able to understand. Two thinkers from the Third World who understand colonial conditions, Albert Memmi of Tunisia and Paulo Freire of Brazil, have outlined elements of theoretical considerations that explain the effect of the rise of nationalism on the character of the colonial society. Memmi offers some theoretical explanations to suggest reasons why nationalism was an inevitable outcome of colonial conditions that were designed to control it. Memmi goes on to observe, "In all of the colonized there is a fundamental need for change. For the colonizer to be unconscious of this need means that either his lack of an ability to understand that the effect of the colonial system on the colonized is immense or that his blind selfishness is more than he can readily believe."[42]

Memmi argues that while failure or refusal to understand the oppressive conditions that control the lives of the colonized is a universal phenomenon, it cannot serve as an excuse to perpetuate them. This is why, he goes on to conclude, nationalism "derives from the very nature of the colonial conditions themselves. The colonized now understands his fate and becomes impatient. He no longer tolerates colonization."[43] Memmi concludes that in acknowledging this reality the colonized uses the techniques and thought process of the colonizer to fully understand his mind so that he can deal with it from a complete knowledge of the consequences of his action. Because the colonizer always operates from an illusion of the inferiority of the colonized, he is never quite able to understand why the colonized are forced to resort to rebellion to bring colonization to an end.

Paulo Freire takes this same line of thinking to argue further that the reason why the colonizer refuses to understand the harshness of the conditions that control the life of the colonized is because he assumes that those colonial conditions have reduced the position of the colonized to a level where he cannot engage in a rational thought process.[44] This is why the colonizer refuses to engage in dialogue with the colonized. Without dialogue the chasm that is created between them gets wider. This is the kind of social environment that generates conflict. In his assumption that the colonized is inferior, the colonizer loses an opportunity to understand the adverse effects of the conditions that oppress the colonized.⁴⁵ These conditions and the refusal of the colonizer to understand their effect on the colonized combine to create a new situation in which confrontation becomes inevitable. Freire explains in precise terms why only the colonized can grasp the essentials of what they must do to regain their sense of self. He concludes:

The oppressed, having internalized the image of the oppressor and adopted his guidelines, are at first fearful of freedom. But sooner or later they will understand that their freedom would require them to reject the image of them imposed by the oppressor and seek to replace it with autonomy. They now realize that their freedom is acquired by conquest, and that it is not a gift from the oppressor. They understand that freedom is an indispensable condition for the quest for human completion.⁴⁶

One reaches two conclusions about the application of these theoretical considerations to peasant rebellion. The first is that sooner than later the colonized begin to reassert themselves in ways that the colonizer does not understand. Once the colonized take action to reassert themselves, it cannot be reversed, and the only form of relationship that now exists between the colonizer and the colonized is conflict. The second conclusion is that the colonizer either refuses to understand that the conditions he has imposed on the colonized will have an adverse effect on relationships between the two, or he believes that the colonized is unable to envisage and attain his destiny without his assistance or guidance. A critical theoretical element that must be regarded as essential to peasant rebellion is Freire's conclusion that freedom is acquired by conquest, not as a gift from the oppressor. In other words, Freire is arguing that the colonized must assume the right to confront the colonizer because he will not support or encourage the quest for freedom

There are other individuals who have articulated some theoretical considerations of trying to understand the Mau Mau rebellion. A few examples follow. In 1961 Mao Tse-tung outlined a theoretical perspective that had a direct application to the Mau Mau rebellion. Mao concluded that there is no successful rebellion that has occurred without unity of purpose bolstered by the willpower of both the masses and their leaders. He argued that the leaders must not seek to dominate or dictate the course of the rebellion, but must facilitate the collective action generated from consensus.⁴⁷ Mao concluded, "Without a political goal guerrilla warfare must fail, as it must if its objectives do not coincide with the aspiration of the people and their sympathy, cooperation, and assistance cannot be gained."⁴⁸ Although the rebellion encountered serious difficulties in adopting the strategy that Mao outlined, the Mau Mau participants fully recognized the important nature of cohesion in seeking to fulfill its basic objectives.

Samuel Popkin theorizes that whenever one culture imposes itself on another culture tension between them becomes inevitable because the imposing culture also imposes conditions of domination and oppression that eventually lead to a rebellion among the oppressed.[49] Popkin went on to conclude, "Peasants do not necessarily act to further their group or common interests. They often opt for individual interests over common interests."[50] But Popkin argues that in doing so the peasants sustain common interests so that individual interests are sustained. Popkin suggests that by rebelling against the capitalist system that exploits them, the peasants are not against capitalism, they are merely rebelling against its exploitive character. The rebellion is therefore directed at ending exploitation so that a new and fair system of distribution emerges. This is the context in which collective interests take precedence over individual interests.[51] It was virtually impossible to expect Mitchell to understand these theoretical perspectives of the Mau Mau rebellion.

Allen Isaacman, a noted writer of the political process in Africa, especially Mozambique, has stressed the importance of formulating goals that are attainable in a reasonable period of time if the rebellion should have a chance of success. Isaacman argues that peasants act and behave in different ways from urban workers in their relationships with the colonial authorities. He argues that the peasants usually enjoy a degree of autonomy higher than the urban worker. For example, the peasant who produces his own food, or the laborer who is allowed by his settler employer to raise grain, has a higher degree of autonomy than the worker who stands on the production line in a factory. When the peasant's autonomy is threatened or is removed by policy of a higher order, he is more likely to rebel than a factory worker who loses his job in the factory because, while the factory worker can find another job, the peasant cannot always find another piece of land to grow his food.[52]

In his study, *The Psychology of the Mau Mau*, conducted in 1954, two years before the Mau Mau rebellion came to an end and two years after it had started, J. C. Carothers attempted to explain the uprising in terms of psychological response. He suggests that the rebellion was a result of mass madness, the behavior of a people whose culture was being eroded away by a stronger and more powerful forces the Africans could not control.[53] Carothers made no effort to discuss the political and economic forces that caused the rebellion. Further, Carothers did not wait to see the net outcome to the Mau Mau rebellion to make a complete assessment of its impact. Therefore, his conclusions are incomplete and erroneous. However, in 1954, Godfrey Huggins, a sad figure in the politics of colonial Africa, endorsed Carothers's conclusion and went on to add:

In his illuminating report on the psychology of the Mau Mau Carothers classifies the environmental factors which account for the observed diversities as climate, nutrition, and culture. The last is, of course, the most vital. The task of changing the environment of the African in these connections is a stupendous one when one considers their numbers and the great changes that have to be made. But it is by no means an impossible task and we can derive great hope from this. The doctrine of segregation is based on the belief that there are certain fundamental and unchangeable differences between the races and that these differences can never be reconciled.[54]

Like Carothers, Huggins missed the real cause of the Mau Mau rebellion. As the high priest of colonial attitude and policy in Africa, Huggins behaved very much like Philip E. Mitchell. He refused to see the situation from its proper perspective, preferring, instead, to operate by the Victorian myth that had yielded tangible benefits to the colonial governments.

Three other theoretical perspectives relative to the Mau Mau deserve mention. In *We Built a Country*, F. F. Lipscomb argues that the settlers and residents of Kenya made an effort to denounce the Mau Mau rebellion as being void of any sense and without focus or purpose, and was the action taken by barbaric people who had no cause to fight.[55] In the same vein in *Defeating the Mau Mau*, L. B. Leakey suggests that the Mau Mau movement was a product of thought processes among a people who had lost proper perspective of their focus and direction.[56] Both Lipscomb and Leakey appear to confuse the economic deprivation the Africans were subjected to with their political action to end it. As members of the settler community, Lipscomb and Leakey espoused theories that were part of the problem that they could not understand and so failed to offer viable solution to the problem.

Finally, Robert B. Edgerton quotes F. C. Corfield as stressing the importance of the role that taking oaths had on strengthening bonds among members of the Mau Mau movement. Corfield goes on to argue that the evil genius of the movement was Jomo Kenyatta, who administered the oaths as the chief priest and key administrator of the entire movement. According to Corfield, Kenyatta was the principal architect of the Mau Mau movement, which "aimed against Western civilization and technology, and, in particular was against the government and Europeans as symbols of progress."[57] It is quite surprising that Western writers who were based in Africa and who were part of the system or establishment had a confused understanding of the actual causes of the Mau Mau rebellion, except to say that the Africans were against Western civilization. If the Africans were against Western civilization they would have begun the uprising in 1895 when the colonial system was put in place. Besides, no group of people has decided to rebel against another group purely on the basis of aversion to its culture, but rather on the injustice the group brings and which contravenes its interests. The plain truth that these individuals miss is that the Mau Mau rebellion was not directed against Western civilization, it was directed against the injustice of the colonial system.

BLUNDELL'S RESPONSE TO THE MAU MAU

The preceding discussion was intended to establish the fact that Blundell, in becoming involved in the politics of Kenya as a liberal, faced a difficult and unprecedented situation that no previous settler politician had encountered in the past. The Mau Mau rebellion invoked a strong reaction from settlers, one of panic among them. In 1952 Blundell was returned to the legislative council unopposed. In June of that year Mitchell retired and was succeeded as governor by Evelyn Baring. The change of guard signaled change in the political landscape considerably, because Baring tended to do things differently from Mitchell. Where Mitchell was prone to respond quickly, making errors of indiscretion, Baring was inclined to take his time and consider his options carefully.

Where Mitchell acted alone because he was the governor, Baring wanted to consult members of the legislative council and his administration to make sure that consensus was reached before any decision was made and any action was taken. Where Mitchell felt that the legislative council had a limited role in government decisions, Baring felt that it had an important role to play in seeking solutions to national problems. Where Mitchell was secretive in doing things, Baring was open because he believed that secrecy had no place in any action seeking to serve the interest of the people. Such was the character of the two men with whom Blundell had to do official business. In the last few months of Mitchell's administration the Colonial Office in London found it increasingly difficult to work with him. He would not communicate with them, and when he did the information he sent was either incomplete or inaccurate.

For several months during the year in 1950 Blundell received reports from his district of impending rebellion among the Kikuyu, the people whose land was taken to make room for settlers. Blundell later remembered, "As early as 1950 my constituency had told me of a secret society called Mau Mau which was terrorizing men and women on their farms with oaths and all the mumbo jumbo of tribal witchcraft."[58] For the next two years tension between the Africans and the settlers increased dramatically as the Mau Mau movement intensified its activity. On July 10, 1952, barely a week after Mitchell had retired, Blundell, after gathering sufficient information on the activity of the Mau Mau, introduced a motion in the legislative council, stating "that this Council notes the increasing disregard for law and order within the colony and urges the government to take the necessary measures to improve the situation."[59]

Blundell considered the motion and the debate that followed important because this was the first time that the issue of the Mau Mau was brought openly into the public debate. The purpose of the motion was also to compel the colonial government to take action to prevent a national disaster. To his surprise Blundell found the response of the colonial government was one of complacence and disbelief, not wishing to spread panic among the settlers. On August 7, 1952, Blundell and Humphrey Slade, another settler member of the legislative council, met to discuss the situation and what action to take, if any. When they presented the information before them to Baring, he showed no immediate interest in the matter. It turned out that Baring had been in touch with Mitchell, consulting with him on matters relating to policy and action. Mitchell advised Baring to do nothing that would throw the country into a state of confusion. Baring's lack of response placed Blundell on the horns of a dilemma. If he did nothing further as a result of Baring's inaction he would lose the support of the settlers for failing to represent their interest. If he became too aggressive in pursuing the matter he risked being labeled an extremist and alarmist. This would alienate him from having meaningful relations with Africans in the future. Blundell knew that at that time the British government was considering the principle of multiracial representation in the structure of the colonial government. This means that at some point in the near future he would have to work with Africans. Therefore, Blundell was forced to be cautious in adopting his position on the question of the Mau Mau movement.

In September 1952 the Mau Mau escalated its activity by assassinating Chief Waruhiu. In October the Mau Mau suddenly burst on the scene. For the next four years the killing, the brutality, and the suffering caused by both sides of the conflict were unimaginable. Before it finally came to an end in 1956 the Mau Mau movement and the colonial response to it cost the British government enormously. On October 20, 1952, Baring finally invited Blundell to a meeting at which he told him that a British battalion was on its way to help restore law and order, a state of emergency would soon be declared, and 187 of the ringleaders of the Mau Mau would be arrested and placed in detention. He also asked Blundell to serve on the war committee to put a quick end to the rebellion. Blundell was extremely pleased with these measures and pledged his full support and cooperation. In 1954 Baring named Blundell minister without portfolio and member of the emergency war council. His principal responsibility was to direct the campaign against the Mau Mau. As Blundell's role became more directly involved in the fight against the Mau Mau, he knew that his relationships with Africans had been dealt a severe blow at least for the time being.

SUMMARY AND CONCLUSION

This chapter began with a discussion of the crisis that evolved in 1948 when Blundell was first elected to the legislative council in the demand of Africans to eliminate *kipande*, a national system of registration that was so discriminatory against Africans. The colonial government, especially Philip E. Mitchell, the governor, did not understand that the demand was part of the rise of African consciousness that began at the conclusion of the war in 1945. Blundell's position was that from the African perspective the crisis was understandable. He did not wish to alienate the settler voters who had put him in the seat of power, but at the same time he did not see any reason why settlers opposed the proposed system of registration.

Then in 1952, when the Mau Mau rebellion started, Blundell abandoned his usual liberal position on issues and became actively involved in efforts to bring it under control. It is important to note that various examples and theories have been espoused to address the causes of the Mau Mau rebellion. But none of these theories addressed its three major causes: land distribution, economic deprivation, and the rise of African nationalism. Failure to understand these causes has always been a characteristic behavior of the colonial government anywhere in the world. Blundell's response to the Mau Mau was typically colonial. But he, unlike his fellow settlers, understood the Mau Mau rebellion from the perspective of the liberal ideas and ideals that he had inherited as he was growing up in Britain.

NOTES

1. The requirement to have Africans carry registration certificates was a common policy in all British colonial Africa in order to ensure effective control of the Africans. In colonial Zimbabwe the registration certificate was notoriously known among the Africans as *chitupa*.

2. In order to ensure that African workers did not desert their place of employment, the system of *kipande* was introduced in 1919. A metal identification card which was worn around the neck, *kipande* was designed for African workers only. On it there were details about the bearer's labor history of employment, just like *chitupa* in colonial Zimbabwe, his personal details, wages earned. In colonial Zimbabwe the holder of *chitupa* surrendered it to the employer instead of wearing it around the neck.

3. Tabitha Kanogo, *Makers of History: Dedan Kimathi* (Nairobi: East African Educational Publishers, 1992), p. 3.

4. Michael Blundell, *A Love Affair with the Sun* (Nairobi: Kenway Publications, 1994), p. 86.

5. Ibid., p. 89.

6. Bethwell A. Ogot, *Historical Dictionary of Kenya* (London: The Scarecrow Press, 1981), p. 141.

7. In 1954, two years after he had retired as governor, Mitchell published a book, *African Afterthoughts*, in which he admitted that his failure to resolve this controversy was the first step toward the Mau Mau uprising.

8. King George VI, who was on the British throne from 1937, when his brother, Edward VIII, abdicated to marry Wallis Simpson, a twice-divorced American woman, until 1952.

9. Blundell, *A Love Affair with the Sun*, p. 87.

10. Ibid., p. 86.

11. Ibid., p. 87.

12. George Bennett, *Kenya: A Political History* (London: Oxford University Press, 1963), p. 129.

13. Ogot, *Historical Dictionary of Kenya*, p. 135.

14. Wunyabari O. Maloba, *Mau Mau and Kenya: An Analysis of a Peasant Revolt* (Bloomington: Indiana University Press, 1993), p. 1.

15. Ibid., p. 2.

16. Basil Davidson, *Africa in Modern History* (Middlesex: Penguin Books, 1978), p. 263.

17. Edward VII, the oldest son of Queen Victoria, was on the British throne from 1901 to 1910.

18. Lord Elgin, The Land Policy of the British Government in Kenya: Section 8, March 9, 1908. Kenya National Archives.

19. Duke of Devonshire, State Paper on Land Policy in Kenya (Ref. Mcd 1922/23). Kenya National Archives.

20. Creech Jones, "Land Policy of the British Government," address to the House of Commons, March 7, 1949. Kenya National Archives.

21. James Griffiths, "British Land Policy in Kenya," address to the House of Commons, December 12, 1950. Kenya National Archives.

22. Alan Lennox-Boyd, "Land Policy of the British Government in Kenya," address to the House of Commons, February 22, 1952. Kenya National Archives.

23. Queen Elizabeth II, who succeeded to the British throne in 1952 when her father, King George VI, died suddenly.

24. *East African Standard* (Nairobi), October 8, 1954.

25. Oliver Lyttleton, "The Land Policy of the British Government in Kenya," address to the House of Commons, November 7, 1952. Kenya National Archives.

26. Bennett, *Kenya: A Political History*, p. 124.

27. The author saw this system in action as he was growing up in colonial Zimbabwe. One particular settler farmer, B. D. Goldberg, a wealthy tobacco farmer near Odzi, so successfully exploited this practice that the Africans all over the area knew him by his nickname, Magoboza (the one who exploits).

28. Robert B. Edgerton, *Mau Mau: An African Crucible* (New York: The Free Press, 1989), p. 18.

29. Fenner Brockway, *African Journey* (London: Gollancz, 1955), p. 175.

30. Ibid., p. 19.

31. In May 1997, when the author was in Kenya to conduct research for this study, the rate of exchange was 50 shillings to $1.00.
32. Edgerton, *Mau Mau: An African Crucible*, p. 18.
33. Ibid., p. 19.
34. Ibid.
35. Ibid., p. 20.
36. Isaac Leigh, *In the Shadow of the Mau Mau* (London: W. H. Allen, 1955), p. 16.
37. Edgerton, *Mau Mau: An African Crucible*, p. 21.
38. Maloba, *Mau Mau and Kenya*, p. 73.
39. Philip E. Mitchell, *African Afterthoughts* (London: Hutchinson, 1954), p. 252.
40. Ronald Webber, *The Peasant Revolt* (Lavenhow, Britain: Terrence Dalton, 1980), p. ix.
41. Paul Avrich, *Russian Rebels, 1600–1800* (New York: Schocken Books), p. 6.
42. Albert Memmi, *The Colonizer and the Colonized* (Boston: Beacon Press, 1965), p. 119.
43. Ibid., p. 120.
44. Paulo Freire, *Pedagogy of the Oppressed* (trans. M. R. Ramos) (New York: Continuum, 1983), p. 89.
45. Ibid., p. 70.
46. Ibid., p. 31.
47. Mao Tse-tung, *On Guerrilla Warfare* (New York: Frederick A. Praeger, 1961), p. 42.
48. Ibid., p. 843.
49. Samuel Popkin, *The Rational Peasant* (Berkeley: University of California Press, 1979), p. 5.
50. Ibid., p. 6.
51. Ibid., p. 8.
52. Allen Isaacman, "Peasants and Rural Social Protest in Africa," *African Studies Review*, Vol. 33, No. 2 (September 1990), p. 2.
53. Edgerton, *Mau Mau: An African Crucible*, p. 9.
54. Godfrey Huggins, "Taking Stock of African Education," address to the Southern Rhodesia Missionary Conference held at Goromonzi, August 26, 1954. Zimbabwe National Archives. For the entire address see Dickson A. Mungazi, *Colonial Policy and Conflict in Zimbabwe: A Study of Cultures in Collision, 1890–1979* (New York: Taylor and Francis, 1991), p. 167.
55. Lipscomb, *We Built a Country* (London: Faber and Faber, 1955), p. 19.
56. Leakey, *Defeating the Mau Mau* (London: Methuen. 1954), p. 59.
57. Edgerton, *The Mau Mau: An African Crucible*, p. 110.
58. Michael Blundell, *So Rough a Wind* (London: Weidenfeld and Nicholson, 1964), p. 88.
59. Ibid., p. 91.

6

Garfield Todd's Role in the Political Crisis in Zimbabwe

> There is a spirit of urgency in African development. Take that spirit, guide it, give it assistance, and there will develop a people who will be a credit to this country. Disregard or hinder that spirit, and an adverse effect will result with severe consequences for the country.
> —Garfield Todd, 1947

THE CHARACTER OF THE RHODESIA FRONT GOVERNMENT

From December 16, 1962, to March 3, 1979, Zimbabwe (then known as the British colony of Rhodesia) was ruled by the Rhodesia Front Party (RF), which espoused a racial philosophy which the Africans, many members of the white community, and the Christian Church[1] considered so oppressive that a major conflict became inevitable on two fronts: with the Africans, and with Britain on institutional issues. The leading members of the RF—Ian Smith, Winston Field, Clifford Dupont, Peter van der Byl, Andrew Skeen, John Mussett, William Harper, Lord Graham, Lance Smith, Arthur Smith, David Smith[2]—all lived and operated by the philosophy that the Africans must never aspire to achieve a social equality with the white man regardless of the level of their education.

Not since the inception of the colonial government in September 1890 was Zimbabwe subjected to such a political behavior of the extreme views of a group of white men who were so obsessed with sustaining white political power that nothing else seemed to matter. In their own way these men became the Don Quixotes of the new era of white supremacy, tilting at the giant windmills of the rising wave of African nationalism. They had, in effect, also become the Pied Pipers of the old colonial objectives to the extent that they led their white followers, not from the city of their dreaded fear of the advent of an African government to their envisaged utopia of absolute white political power, but to the cave of their political oblivion because a major national conflict which became inevitable as a result of their policies also led to the end in 1979 of the RF government and the colonial system it represented.

In the context of a political environment that had produced the RF, Ian Smith's political dictum, *No black majority government in Rhodesia in my lifetime, not in a thousand years*, became an obsession, a mission that he believed only he was called upon to accomplish as the only legitimate disciple, and, indeed, the vicar, as well as the rightful successor to Cecil John Rhodes, Leander Starr Jameson, Earl Grey, and Godfrey Huggins. From 1890 to 1961 these men had operated by a political philosophy that the RF adopted as its own modus operandi. It is a strange coincidence that the notion of a thousand years was first expressed by Rhodes in 1896, and then by Adolf Hitler in 1934. For Smith and his RF government there was no other course of action to follow, no other policy to define and pursue, and no other perspective from which to view the perilous nature of the problems they were creating as a government for itself and the country.

It is important to understand that in this drama, a form of tragedy in human existence, the RF declared Zimbabwe independent unilaterally on November 11, 1965, in an attempt to foil the effort of the Africans toward self-actualization. In doing so Ian Smith believed that he was, in effect, staging a *kamikaze* assault on the rising tide of African nationalism, because he believed that he only could do it. He regarded his own objectives as a mission that no other colonial official had accomplished in the past. Under Smith the RF also wanted to advise Britain in no uncertain terms that its decolonization process must be halted above the Zambezi. Therefore, in refusing to initiate dialogic interaction with Africans, Smith failed to realize that this action would turn out to be an ill-conceived strategy that meant his own ultimate self-deception and, thus, his own political demise, because it proved to the lull before the storm.

WHITEHEAD'S POLITICAL GAMBLE AND THE RISE OF THE RF

The stage for the worst political crisis in the history of colonial Zimbabwe was set in two critical events that began to unfold in 1959. The first event is that Edgar C. Whitehead, prime minister from 1958 to 1962, felt so threatened by the growing influence of the African National Congress (ANC) that he outlawed it on February 28. Whitehead's reason for taking this action—that the ANC had criticized the inadequacy of the political and educational policy of his administration "because it was designed to promote and protect the political and socioeconomic interests of the settlers and keep the black majority in a subservient position"[3]—must be viewed as arising from the knowledge that the Africans needed better education than they were receiving to realize their aspirations. Whitehead was unable to tolerate this kind of criticism from a group of people he and his predecessors considered not qualified to pass such a judgment. This demonstrates the extent of his intolerance toward the development of the Africans outside his control. The Africans' refusal to subordinate themselves to the educational and political policies of the government combined with Whitehead's own determination to nip this threat in the bud and, thus, set the two racial groups on an unprecedented confrontation course.

The second event that took place in 1959 is the enactment of the African Education Act, which, for the first time in the history of African education, created a unified teaching service for African teachers. Under its provisions African teachers with college educations would serve under the same conditions as white teachers with college educations.[4] Whitehead had reasons to consider this legislation a milestone, a major improvement in the education of the Africans. He believed it would resuscitate his own failing political heartbeat and restore the fast-disappearing confidence of the Africans in his government. But to his surprise and dismay this legislation was opposed on two fronts. First, the Africans opposed the fundamental principle that played a major role in producing it, namely Whitehead's view that he knew best what the Africans wanted in their education. "The fundamental Victorian attitude that the white man knew what the Africans wanted is why we rejected it."[5]

The African Education Act was also opposed by the Dominion Party (DP), the forerunner of the RF, for an entirely different reason. The DP was outraged by what it considered a threat to the principle of white political power and the thinking that Africans should receive an education that would help them claim social equality with whites. The DP believed that for Whitehead to allow African teachers with college educations to serve under the same conditions as white teachers with college educations was to erode the philosophy that whites must remain superior to Africans. The DP considered it inconceivable that anyone in the country should think that racial equality in the educational process could become a reality simply because Whitehead appeared to suggest that it should.

Therefore, the DP concluded that the enactment of the African Education Act of 1959 would signify the eventual reduction and loss of white political power to put the Africans at a political advantage. This is why it did every thing in its power to stop it before it became law. That the DP made no secret of its plan to have the government retain absolute power to control African education is quite evident in its own policy. This is also why the DP argued that for Africans to receive equal educational opportunity would mean that whites would have no basis to claim that the government must remain in what it called responsible, meaning white, hands for all time. Because the DP did not wish to see a transfer of power to the Africans, it tried to mobilize all its resources as members of the opposition in Parliament to kill the bill before it became law. While it failed in this fundamental objective, the political bitterness and hatred of the educational advancement of the Africans became the hallmark of its political behavior in the future.

With only 13 seats in a Parliament of 30 seats,[6] as opposed to 17 seats for the United Federal Party (UFP), which Whitehead led, the DP had no chance of stopping this bill. However, the anger and fear of what was likely to happen in the future were so intense that the DP took it upon itself to send Whitehead into the cave of political oblivion and wipe out the political and educational aspirations of the Africans before they became a reality. But the DP had to wait to fight an election in 1962 before it could put its own philosophy into action as an RF government. The fact that the African Education Act was opposed by both the Africans and the DP suggests that Whitehead faced a problem which no previous colonial government leader had faced before.

THE CONSTITUTION OF 1961 AND THE DP'S POSITION ON AFRICAN EDUCATION

The political crisis arising from the African Education Act of 1959 was really minor when compared to the crisis that the constitution of 1961 caused. What the DP did not know at the time is that the British government had told Whitehead in 1959 in no uncertain terms that it was impatient with the negative attitudes of the government and the white community toward the political and educational development of Africans and the suffering they had endured under the infamous Land Apportionment Act of 1929.[7] It was only natural that the Africans should have mixed reaction to this gesture on the part of the British government. This is why some members of the RF argued that the constitution of 1961 was designed to bring about a black government. But the Africans themselves felt that having been denied representation in the legislature since 1890, 15 African seats to represent an African population of 3.8 million against 50 white seats to represent 0.25 million whites, was a slap in the face.

To make sure that the white voters fully understood both the terms of the new constitution and the implications of their vote, Britain required that the constitutional proposals be submitted to a national referendum before they were adopted. What sent shock waves through the political spine of the DP members was the key provision of the new constitution that the government demonstrate its unquestionable commitment to the political and educational development of Africans. Political reality forced Whitehead, so he thought, to accept this requirement as a condition of his continuation in office. But in doing so he created a dilemma for white voters: to reject the new constitutional proposals and deny themselves an opportunity for their future political security, or to approve them and so help indirectly accelerate Africans' political and educational advancement. A former member of the RF commented to the author in July 1983:

Either way we knew that whatever we did, we could not win. Britain had made it clear that the exploitation that it believed we subjected the Africans through a self-serving political and educational policy had to stop. The granting of independence to Ghana in 1957 was a clear signal of what Britain intended to do in its African colonies. We thought that we were fighting only the African desire for advancement, we did not know that we were, in effect, caught between a rock and a hard place, a dilemma which we could not resolve.[8]

For the DP the referendum posed a formidable political problem of how to react. Without the leadership that would help put forth its views in a way that the voters would understand, it was still struggling to recover from the shock of the passage of the African Education Act of 1959, and so could not demonstrate a thorough grasp of the importance of this issue. Indeed, the DP was in a state of decay, unable to overcome its anger at the passage of the African Education Act. This helps to explain the agonizing situation that it now faced in what it believed was an even greater threat from Britain in demanding that the government demonstrate its commitment to the political and educational development of the Africans.

The DP's conclusion that the African Education Act of 1959, the constitutional proposals of 1961, and the British requirement for a rapid political and educational advancement of the Africans combined to constitute a set of conditions which its members could not accept. This shows the difficulty of the problem the DP was facing. The DP never conceived the thought that this was, indeed, the beginning of a decisive struggle between the colonizer and the colonized. Its preoccupation with the desire to retain power in white hands closed the minds of its members to the constructive analysis of the situation in order to come up with a possible alternative solution to a complex problem that it had, in fact, created through its political philosophy.

Aware that the DP espoused a political philosophy that the voters would not support, Whitehead tried to exploit the situation to maximize his own political advantage. He therefore vigorously campaigned for the approval of the constitutional proposals, presenting a point-by-point argument to persuade the voters to approve them. This is why he received wild applause on February 8, 1961, when he argued, "Southern Rhodesia will of course not have achieved complete independence in the international sense, but the United Kingdom participation in our internal affairs will have ceased."[9] But William Harper, the unpopular and emotional DP spokesman, was booed as he attempted to rebut, "I do not believe it is possible to achieve independence under these proposals."[10] Of course Harper was, in fact, right, but that the white voters did not believe him cast a longer shadow on the DP's credibility than the one that trailed it during the debate on the African Education bill in 1959

Rapidly moving events quickly established the knowledge that, indeed, the DP had earned its reputation as the members of the colonial establishment who opposed the advancement of the Africans, as it appeared unable to bounce back from the verge of political extinction following the announcement of the referendum results on July 27, 1961. Showing 41,949 "yes" votes and 21,846 "no" votes, Whitehead scored a resounding victory and sank the DP's hopes to a low point. The euphoria which characterized Whitehead's reaction to the results of the referendum can be understood in terms of his argument that the extreme elements of both white and African politicians had been dealt a death blow. Of course, with Africans accounting for 5 percent of the total vote, the outcome of the referendum was obvious.

The excitement of his victory carried Whitehead a little too far when he promised that racial discrimination in both society and education would be ended by repealing the infamous Land Apportionment Act. But in making this promise he created a bigger problem for himself than the DP had faced in opposing the African Education bill. However, in the wake of the demise of the DP, Whitehead was riding the crest of the wave of popularity among the white voters. All that the DP could do, for the time being, was to pick up the pieces of its shattered political philosophy, not the mantle which its members claimed Cecil John Rhodes, Leander Starr Jameson, and Earl Grey had left behind, swallow its pride, and nurse the painful wounds of a humiliating defeat. But the anger of both the thought of equality with Africans and the lost referendum became even more intense with the passage of time and reached a new height by the time of the elections of December 1962.

Three key issues must be raised at this point with respect to the DP's attitude toward the political and educational development of the Africans. The first key issue is that its members included men of extreme racial views, which forced them to lay claim to being the only true disciples of Rhodes, Jameson, Grey, and Huggins. These included Desmond Lardner-Burke, William Harper, Andrew Skeen, Winston Field, Ian Maclean, William Cory, Ian Smith, Desmond Frost, Clifford Dupont, John Mussett, John Gaunt, Lord Graham, Lance Smith, David Smith, and Arthur Smith. They all believed that keeping political power in the hands of whites was a necessary condition of limiting the political advancement of Africans. This could not be ensured if they were educated in the same way as whites. Therefore, the DP saw educational development of Africans as a major issue in the election campaign of 1962.

A liberal white man told the author in July 1983 the extent of the problem which the DP faced as a political party:

The DP's racial views and educational philosophy were too extreme to offer a realistic alternative solution to the conflict which was rising faster than most people realized. For us the choice between the UFP and the DP was really a choice between two evils, a steady progress to an African government under the UFP and a steady progress to racial confrontation under the DP. Given the attitude of the British government and the avalanche of African nationalism, we felt that we were better off to risk our future with the UFP. This is why we voted "yes" in the national referendum of 1961. But by the time of the general elections of 1962, new realities had come into play. It was a different ball game.[11]

By 1962 the DP had succeeded in having the white voters wonder if Whitehead was leading them along the road to their future political security or to the dreaded African government. This leads to the second key issue—namely, that the DP showed an intense dislike of the British principles regarding the place of Africans in the colonial society, especially the requirement that they be given an equal political and educational opportunity. That Britain reserved the responsibility of protecting the Africans by the constitutional provision of 1923 added a sinister twist and increased the intensity of the dislike the DP had for anything that the British government did or tried to do. This is why Britain's decision to retain this responsibility in the constitution of 1961 infuriated the DP. In addition to the increasing tension caused by the rising African nationalism, this aspect of the colonial situation had set the British government and the DP apart. This in turn set them on a confrontation course beginning in 1962 when the RF became the government.

The breakdown in communication between the DP and the British government would later prove crucial in the Africans' struggle for political development and independence. In 1962 the British government saw things from an entirely different perspective from that of the DP, demonstrating the critical nature of the conflict. Although the Africans were opposed to Whitehead's educational policy, they had no respect for the DP itself. Therefore a triangle of badly strained relationships emerged among the Africans, the UFP, and the DP, with the British government playing the role of an umpire, calling the plays from the Whitehall dugout. The DP thought the referendum was the bottom of the 9th inning with bases loaded with UFP players. The Africans watched this game between two white teams with an intense interest, hoping to catch the home-run fly ball before they became players themselves.

The third key issue that must be raised at this point is the difference in perception of the educational development of the Africans held by the UFP and the DP. This difference furnishes yet another example to illustrate that whites could no longer regard Africans as mere spectators of a political game that only white politicians played. Remembering that this kind of conflict existed in 1958 between Todd and Whitehead, the situation between Whitehead and the DP in 1962 acquired more powerful and perilous dimensions. As the election campaign of 1962 got under way, the views of the voters slowly changed from enthusiastic support to doubts and misgivings about Whitehead's policy.

AFRICAN DEVELOPMENT AS A MAJOR ELECTION CAMPAIGN ISSUE OF 1962

Wishing to consolidate the victory he had scored in the referendum of 1961 and to regain the confidence of the Africans which he had lost by declaring the state of emergency of 1959, Whitehead called a snap election in 1962. With a sense of self-confidence and, thus, a sense of self-deception, he suddenly announced in April 1962 that new general elections would be held in October. He believed that because the stricken DP was in a state of total disarray, it would never be able to launch an effective campaign against him. Whitehead also concluded that because the DP had failed to attract any support of the white voters in the referendum of 1961 by its argument that the constitutional proposals were a sellout to white interests, it was unlikely to succeed in raising any new issues that would attract their interest and support in the general election of 1962. Events later proved that he was wrong. However, he believed he had never had it so good, everything seemed to go his way. He did not know that he was about to play his last card and that his political career was about to end.

To conclude that the announcement of the impending elections added insult to the DP's injured feelings and shattered political objectives is to recognize the sorry state in which it found itself, "a political rubble, a bunch of subdued white racists whose obsession with the myth of white supremacy was leading them to a political dead-end street."[12] When William Harper resigned from the DP following the announcement of the impending general election, it precipitated a major crisis within the ranks of the party. No person was willing to risk his political career by assuming its leadership or associating himself with it in any way because its reputation had been damaged beyond repair.

Indeed, in his quiet and subtle way, Garfield Todd had been working behind the scenes to convince white voters that to belong to the DP or to support it in any way was to secure a one-way passport to political extinction, because since its demise from the referendum of 1961, it had been associated with everything that was wrong and negative in the white man's political behavior. As a result of Todd's initiative, the political fortunes of the DP were turning into ashes in the incinerator of the conditions of the times. Its members relentlessly flogged the dead horse of an issue that more moderate whites had accepted as a necessary condition for their continued political survival, the political and educational advancement of the Africans.

These were the circumstances in which Whitehead, in a state of euphoria, announced a series of changes he believed would satisfy the demands of the British government, pacify the Africans, and silence his critics and political opponents, especially Garfield Todd, who by this time had been building a solid base to play his role in the political transformation of colonial Zimbabwe. Whitehead convinced himself that if he succeeded in carrying out his agenda, his political career would be secured for many years to come. But before he knew it, public opinion began to change in favor of the DP. When he announced that the Land Apportionment Act of 1929 would be repealed in order to integrate the educational systems and society, the DP went into a state of panic. When he promised to end racial discrimination in employment and public facilities, and to open the public service to the Africans for the first time since they were excluded in 1931 by the provision of the Land Apportionment Act, the DP was outraged.

When Whitehead promised to include African junior ministers in his next administration, the DP felt insulted. When he predicted that an African government was possible within 15 years because the government would guarantee an effective system of education to produce well-trained Africans to run it, the DP thought he had gone too far. When he announced that he was naming a high-level commission of inquiry into African education[13] to remove all elements of racial discrimination as required by Britain, the DP thought he must be removed from office because he had become a political romantic adventurer.

There is no doubt that Whitehead sincerely believed that the white man's future in Zimbabwe would only be secured by giving the Africans a reasonable opportunity for advancement through education. The rise of African nationalism combined with British demands must have convinced him that the philosophy of white government for a thousand years and of regarding the Africans as uncivilized, fit only to train to function as servants of the white man, must belong to the past, along with its founder Cecil John Rhodes, and his disciples, Leander Starr Jameson, Earl Grey and Godfrey Huggins. We were living in a new era where the white man had to choose, to recognize that his own security was invariably linked with the advancement of the Africans within the framework of a genuine spirit of equal partners or to try to perpetuate his rule and face the possibility of strained race relationships.[14]

Whitehead's apparent advocacy of the kind of political and educational reform he was under British pressure to introduce suggests that he was indeed at least sensitive to the demands of the times. But how does one explain his change of views from maintaining white political power during the time that Todd was advocating moderation to advocating radical change in favor of the Africans during the election campaign of 1962? That he refused to operate "under colonial principles of privileges"[15] made his conflicting positions questionable to both settler voters and Africans.

Because of the sorry state in which it found itself, the DP felt it necessary to disband. Its members recognized their inevitable fate, knowing they had to shake off the negative image that was associated with their extreme racial philosophy. Fearing the political malaise that had brought about Todd's demise in 1958, the DP adopted a totally different strategy. They dissolved the DP in May 1962 and appealed to the number of small fragmented parties, including the United Group, the Southern Rhodesia Association, and even the conservative members of Whitehead's own UFP, to unite and form a new political party known as the Rhodesia Front (RF). The formation of the RF was an event that was destined to alter forever the course of politics and the character of race relationships in Zimbabwe. It was destined to lead the country to one of Africa's bitterest conflicts which resulted, not in a thousand years of white rule, as Smith had predicted, but in the advent of an African government. Behind the scene Todd played his role well.

The change of name from the Dominion Party to the Rhodesia Front had a psychologically boosting effect as the members of the new party struggled to create a new dynamic party which the white voters could trust and support. But the RF needed time to reorganize itself and to structure an election platform that would demonstrate not only familiarity with the critical issues of the day, but also a degree of moderation that would appeal to the voters. That the RF drew its membership from various splinter political parties whose members had divergent political views made it much harder for it to have a unified platform. The only thing its members shared in common was their uncompromising opposition to the educational advancement of the Africans. This is why they made Whitehead's educational policy a major election issue and the focus of their ire.

As the campaign got more heated, the RF began to grow from weakness to strength. Its rallying point was its unqualified opposition to Whitehead's educational policy. Fearing to expose its own ignorance of the issues, the RF simply elected to focus its major attention on attacking the education of the Africans as the greatest threat to white political power since 1890. It therefore presented a slate of candidates who had the emotional appeal and the ability to express themselves in a way that had the appearance of moderation. Slowly, as the RF struggled to present itself as a party capable of understanding the critical issues the country was facing, the negative image that had trailed and tarnished the DP began to fade.

When it felt strong enough, when its members knew that public opinion was slowly shifting from supporting Whitehead in favor of itself, and when it drew larger crowds to its political rallies than the DP had done, the RF launched a vicious campaign against Whitehead's educational policy. John Gaunt, Ian Smith, Winston Field, Desmond Lardner-Burke, Lord Graham, John Mussett, all wealthy and powerful, provided the leadership the RF needed to earn the respect of the white voters. However, none of these men comprehended the serious implications of their extreme racial philosophy on the future of the country. Their only concern was to do everything in their power to halt and reverse the educational course that Whitehead had charted for the expected political advancement of Africans.

The difference between the UFP and the RF relative to their respective election platforms was as clear as the difference between day and night. In a move that was intended to convince both the Africans and the British government of his sincerity, Whitehead vigorously courted the African vote, even though he knew that in accordance with the constitutional provisions of 1961, it counted for no more than 5 percent of the total white vote. He warned the white voters that their understanding of the issues was critically important to their long-term security and interests.

Whitehead also argued that to extend equal educational opportunity to Africans would demonstrate the goodwill of whites and the racial harmony and cooperation essential in building a politically stable society. He also showed why he believed that race was no longer a criterion to determine a person's place in society. This is why he warned that the alternative to this course of action would be the extreme racist government of the RF, which would drag the country toward a major racial conflict from which whites would emerge losers and Africans winners. But the postponement of the election from October to December did two things that worked against Whitehead. First, it gave the RF more time to present itself to the voters as a party that understood the issues. Second, it showed Whitehead and his UFP to be in a state of disarray, unsure of themselves and of the issues facing the country. In urging the white voters to reject the racist policies of the RF, Whitehead invited both races to work together for a secure country in which everyone was free to pursue his own goals. He even promised that he would use the two-thirds majority he had received in the referendum to build a strong administration that would ensure the interests of all people.[16]

As expected, the RF took the exact opposite position on all issues. It argued that the critical problem whites faced was a rapid educational advancement of Africans as a result of the misguided policy of the Whitehead administration. It argued that for Whitehead to consider the possibility of an African government within 15 years was a betrayal of the principles that had elevated whites to a position of power over the Africans. It concluded that for him to promise the Africans to repeal the Land Apportionment Act was to surrender the Magna Carta of white political power and security in the country.

While Ian Smith, Winston Field, and John Gaunt were not dynamic speakers, they augmented their political limitations with the intensity of their beliefs, the poignancy of their feelings, and the depth of their convictions. Suddenly it was a new ball game. The fortunes of the UFP and the RF were being reversed in a way that no one could have conceived only a few months earlier. However, the irony of the RF's political behavior is that it was contesting an election under a constitution that it had vigorously opposed as members of the DP. To add a touch of pathos to this tragic situation, the Africans also opposed the UFP but for an entirely different reason. The conflict between Whitehead and the Africans regarding the UFP's educational policy succeeded in persuading the voters to believe that they had a sacred mission to rescue the country from the vicious jaws of African nationalism and from Whitehead's appeasement of the British government's demands. The Africans believed they had a duty to take their country back from their colonial usurpers who had ruled it with impunity since 1890. They were not interested in anything else. They obtained support and inspiration from white liberals like Garfield Todd. Thus, Whitehead became the target of both the Africans and the RF, each firing political rounds in rapid succession, from two different strategic points.

As the RF grew from weakness to strength, the white voters listened to its message closely. That the RF focused on a single election issue, the education of the Africans, and ignored the rest forced Whitehead to play the political game according to his own rules. Whitehead's argument that his educational policy would lead to an African government within 15 years was a strategy the RF used effectively to persuade the voters that if he was returned to power they would have no future in the country. Indeed, the RF shared the view expressed by Ethel Tawse Jollie, a member of the legislature back in 1927, that the settlers had no intention of handing over the country to the African population or to admit them to the same social and political position that they themselves were enjoying, and that they should therefore make no pretense of educating Africans in exactly the same way they were educating white students.[17] Todd regarded the RF strategy to resort to policy and political behavior of the past as an act of desperation totally irrelevant to conditions of the times of 1962.

However, in speech after speech and at rally after rally, the RF invoked the memory and the claimed political wisdom of earlier leaders whose views and ideas were considered infallible. That infallibility was equated with the educational process and the view that integration must never be considered. Indeed, this is why Ian Smith told the author during an interview in July 1983, "We were advised that the standards would fall if we integrated the two systems of education."[18] The standards which Smith was referring to were really not educational at all, they were political. In the view of the RF members, the more the Africans were educated, the more they would demand equal treatment in society and the more they received equal treatment, the less could the whites lay a claim to exclusive political and socioeconomic superiority on the basis of education alone. This was Smith's definition of the fall of standards, which he and his RF government wanted to prevent at all costs.

With the strong financial support given by the wealthy and more radical members, the RF went on the offensive and presented candidates for all 50 white seats. It exercised extreme care and caution in selecting each candidate from men whose loyalty to party principles was absolute in every way, and carefully trained them to refrain from discussing any issue, other than the education of Africans, and thus avoid mistakes which might cost them the election. The RF candidates were also trained to arouse the passion and hatred of the possibility of educating the Africans beyond capability for manual labor. They were also trained carefully to arouse fear of the consequences of reforms which they believed Whitehead was trying to introduce in order to appease the Africans and the British government. Indeed, in basing its entire election campaign on the single issue of the education of Africans, the RF set out to prove that this was the most important issue of the election. This is why it adopted the uncompromising position that since the Africans "must at all times be subservient to the white man, they must never be educated in the same way as the whites."[19]

There is no doubt that the RF had a perfect plan of having the whites use the educational process to retain absolute political power. Since 1958, when the Africans began to claim their right to vote under the provision of the federal constitution of 1953, the government designed an effective method of restricting the number of African voters to no more than 5 percent of the total vote. Therefore, it put into place two voter rolls. The

"A" roll was for those voters who earned an annual income of $2,300 and who had four years of secondary education. The "B" role was for those who earned an annual income of $900 and who had ten years of schooling.[20] On the one hand, due to limited educational opportunity for the Africans, very few ever qualified for even the "B" roll. On the other hand whites had no difficult meeting the voting qualifications for the "A" roll.

By 1961 a new racially discriminatory practice had come into being. When the number of voters on the "B" roll reached 20 percent of the number of voters on the "A" roll, no one else would be allowed to register until the next election.[21] But there was no limit to the number of voters who could register on the "A" roll. Because all of the voters on the "A" roll were white, and all voters on the "B" roll were black, the government instituted racism in the electoral process itself. This remained in practice until 1979, the year that the RF collapsed. During the election campaign of 1962, the RF promised that it would make it harder for Africans to meet the educational qualifications which they needed to claim their right to vote, even on the "B" roll, where each ballot cast counted only 20 percent of the ballot cast on the "A" roll. This shows just how determined it was to uphold its educational policy as an essential tenet of its political philosophy. There is no doubt that the RF saw this as an effective strategy of increasing the number of white voters and decreasing that of the African voters. Educational opportunity was the key to it all.

While this plan was totally repugnant to both the British government and the Africans themselves, the RF managed to convince the white voters to believe that it was in their best interests to support it by returning it to power. By the time the elections were held on December 14, 1962, the white voters had been converted to the RF's line of thinking. Thus Whitehead and the British government were stunned when the RF won 35 seats and the UFP won only 15 seats. The remaining 15 seats were won by the Africans in accordance with the provisions of the constitution of 1961. The RF went into a state of euphoria as it found itself in a position of power to determine the course of development of the country. But in returning the RF to power the settler voters had no idea of the extent of conflict that would soon follow. The battle lines were being drawn as Todd was now beginning to get more involved in the struggle for the political transformation of Zimbabwe.

TODD AS A FACTOR IN THE TRANSFORMATION OF ZIMBABWE

Perhaps it is appropriate at this point to give a brief account of the phenomenon of Garfield Todd and the environment that motivated his involvement in the political transformation of Zimbabwe. Born in Waikiwi, Invercargill in New Zealand, Todd was the second son of Thomas and Edith Todd, a pioneer family who landed at Dunedin from Scotland in 1865. He studied at Southland High School and then spent five years with the family brick- and tile-making business beginning in 1926. He then decided to train for missionary work and spent the next two years at Otaga University and another three years at the Glen Leith Theological College, from which he graduated with a diploma in theology, first class, in 1931.[22] Todd was then ordained and spent the next two years as minister of the Omaru Church of Christ.

In 1932 Todd married Jean Grace Wilson of Southland, a trained teacher who had graduated from Dunedin College and Otaga University. In 1934 they volunteered for overseas work with the Church of Christ. After a few months at Fort Jameson in Northern Rhodesia (now Zambia) they arrived at Dadaya Mission outside Shabani (Zwishavane), in what was then Southern Rhodesia, on July 13, 1934, his 26th birthday. There he was appointed superintendent and came into direct contact with Africans whose personality, charm, and hard work he began to admire. He taught them good methods of agriculture and provided an education that inspired them with a vision of the future. One of these students was Ndabaningi Sithole, a man would later play a major role in the political transformation of Zimbabwe. From the moment he arrived at Dadaya, Todd and the Africans developed a unique relationship that translated into broad understanding of the meaning of human cooperation and friendship. He never knew what race was as he saw Africans as precious human beings who demonstrated a quality of life that made them special. In turn the Africans saw Todd as a man whose Christian principles and values extended far beyond the ordinary level of a human being. Given the conditions of the times, such a relationship between a white man and the Africans was rare in the quality of the message it carried for the country.

In carrying his duty at Dadaya Todd did what he did, not because he wanted publicity, but because he had embraced the Asquith-Lloyd George philosophy that those in a position to serve their fellow human beings need to understand a basic tenet of their responsibility that the development of society depends upon the commitment of those in positions of leadership to give nothing less than their best to serve human needs. When Todd went into politics in 1946 he never forgot the Africans who had been part of his mission and work at Dadaya. He built his home there and came to know more Africans as he represented them in Parliament. In 1954, 20 years after Todd had arrived at Dadaya, enrollment in the school system he was responsible for had increased more than three times 700 to more than 3,000 students.[23]

In 1944 Todd spent a year at a refresher course at the University of the Witwatersrand in Johannesburg. During that time he was elected class representative and held a seat on the student council. For many years he served as a member of the executive council of the Southern Rhodesia Missionary Conference, where his dedication to purpose and objectives of the Conference was absolute in every way. The introduction of free and compulsory education for white students in 1935 deeply troubled Todd because he saw Godfrey Huggins's action as blatant discrimination against the African students. For the next 11 years he struggled to give African students a hope for the future under very difficult circumstances.

In 1946 he decided to enter national politics and ran for the seat representing Insiza district as a member of Huggins's United Party. As Judith Todd, his daughther, said, he did this "because Godfrey Huggins thought he could make a positive contribution in Parliament."[24] He won. It was quite an acknowledgment of Todd's potential that Huggins, an ultraconservative, should invite Todd, a liberal, to join the political party that he led. With the formation of the Federation of Rhodesia and Nyasaland in 1953, Todd was elected leader of the United Party, and, thus, prime minister of Southern Rhodesia. Thus began the political career of a man whose contribution has left an important imprint on the history of Zimbabwe. Todd had other factors to work with.

BISHOP DODGE'S CRITICISM OF THE RF

The arrival of Methodist Bishop Ralph E. Dodge to assume his episcopal duties in Zimbabwe in 1956 coincided with a number of events that indicated that indeed the colonial society was drifting into the shadows of political uncertainty. The retirement of Godfrey Huggins from the office of prime minister of the Federation of Rhodesia and Nyasaland and the erratic behavior of his successor, Roy Welensky, the limitations of Garfield Todd's new education policy for the Africans, the resurgence of the right-wing Dominion Party, and the formation of the African National Congress were all events that made 1956 a unique year. Even the colonial government itself recognized this fact.[25]

Dodge was a unique leader in his perception of the role of both the missionary and the church in the struggle of Africans for development. Since his arrival in Angola in 1936, Dodge and the colonial governments never agreed on the place of Africans in colonial society. He was always revolutionary in both his thinking and action.[26] When it came to the application of principles of justice and fair play for Africans, Dodge was no compromiser. That the colonial society disregarded these basic principles in its treatment of Africans inevitably led to church-state conflict. This was the kind of environment that marred relationships between Dodge and the RF as soon as it assumed office in December 1962.

It seems that neither the colonial government nor Dodge's missionary colleagues fully understood the background that was so crucial to his endeavor. There was something in his early life that cast him in a mold in which he remained totally intolerant of injustice in society. This was the quality brought out of him by poverty, his struggle to secure a good education, a near-fatal illness—all combined to harden his spirit and to see society from a perspective that would not allow him to tolerate injustice of any kind.[27] In all his action to give Zimbabwe a new perspective from which to look at itself, Dodge believed that injustice was a result of human action that could be eliminated for the benefit of all.

The painful experience of his own background allowed him to see colonial Zimbabwe from a more realistic viewpoint than any of his colleagues. Having identified poverty, lack of adequate education, and a lack of political participation as the lot of the African masses, Dodge shared Todd's view that these conditions translated into outright oppression which the colonial government deliberately used to sustain its own position of power and domination.[28] Dodge and Todd were now operating from the same basic principles.

From this vantage point Dodge concluded that the Africans were also oppressed by a combination of four forces: ignorance, poverty, disease, and denial of political participation. All were directly related. This is why he argued, in 1964, "He who is dominated by another spiritually, economically, academically, or politically, will never develop his full potential."[29] In arguing that any effort to end the power of these forces of oppression must be directed at ending the colonial conditions that produce them, Dodge was in effect suggesting that the colonial government itself must be brought to an unconditional end "as a final outcome of freedom from domination"[30] of the Africans.

Therefore, like Todd, Dodge had no apology for arguing that freedom of conscience did not imply only religious, but also "speech, thought to develop different types of political organizations reflecting the wishes of the majority."[31] Both Todd and Dodge saw this freedom as essential to constituting a wholesome intellect that could not be achieved under the limitations imposed by the colonial condition. This perspective led both men to conclude that as long as the colonial condition continued, the Africans would remain oppressed and the church would not have the people of a free will to lead it into the future. They also concluded that the same colonial condition that oppressed the Africans also oppressed the church. This is why they argued that the colonial government had to go.

Recognizing the delicate balance they felt they had to maintain between sustaining the momentum for their crusade for fundamental social and political change and trying to avoid a confrontation between them and the RF government, Dodge and Todd attempted a Vatican-style diplomacy. But faced with a Machiavellian reaction, they were forced to change their strategy in order to continue their crusade. This is essentially why Dodge warned:

The Church finds itself in a dilemma when it recognizes that there are certain archaic or unjust laws on the statute books of a nation which it cannot conscientiously uphold, but which it is not able to alter through the legal process. Then the Church is in the embarrassing position of trying to maintain and encourage the enforcement of laws which it sincerely feels should not be observed. The most common area the Church finds itself in such a dilemma is in respect to discriminatory legislation.[32]

But in attempting a diplomacy Dodge and Todd quickly gave way to the demands of their conscience and the urgency of their call for rapid social change. In stating the position of both men that "the Church should not fail to call the attention of those in responsible positions in government to the urgency required in replacing archaic and discriminatory legislation with legislation which is fair and just to all racial groups. The time is past when the minority can hope to legislate with impunity against the majority,"[33] Dodge was, in essence, calling for the end of the RF government itself because it had outlived its usefulness.

The criticism that Dodge and Todd relentlessly leveled against the injustice of colonial Zimbabwe and the action that they suggested to end it led to three conclusions regarding their philosophy of society. The first is that they felt the Christian Church had both a historical right and a social responsibility to create a forum for public opinion to express itself in total support for its call for justice and fairness. They believed that unless the public accepted and lived the church's message, its call for constructive social change would be meaningless. This is why they offered a grim warning when Dodge wrote "seeds of oppression and discrimination will inevitably produce an undesirable harvest."[34]

The second conclusion is that Dodge and Todd held the view that all Christian leaders must embrace specific action beyond their religious pronouncements in order to arouse a popular passion for meaningful social change. This action may include nonviolent demonstrations that may be necessary to mobilize common constructive emotion giving cohesion to a popular demand for progressive and meaningful change. But in colonial Africa, as was demonstrated by events in South Africa since the Soweto uprising of June 16, 1976, nonviolent demonstration implies confrontation with the powers that be. The question was: To what extent were Dodge, Todd, and other Christian leaders who shared the importance of their crusade prepared to face the consequences of this confrontational strategy?

The third conclusion is that both Dodge and Todd argued that it was the duty of the people to force those who made the laws, meaning the RF, to remember that they had a right to disobey those laws that were discriminatory. They argued that civil disobedience and conscientious objection were forms of social action that Christian leaders historically urged their followers to adopt as a means of fighting injustice. This is why, the two men argued, the church must support "its members who defy existing laws which are unfair and discriminatory."[35] The problem that church leaders faced in this religious belief and teaching is that the RF saw it as nothing less than urging the people to break the law. Therefore, the interpretation that Dodge and Todd went by, of freedom of conscience, and their understanding of the purpose of law were in direct conflict with the interpretation and purposes of the RF government itself.

Serious as these differences were, they were not the only events that paved the road to a crisis between the church and the RF government. One fundamental difference between the two sides is the way they saw the Africans' place in society. On the one hand, from the time that Cecil John Rhodes characterized the Africans in 1896 as having the brain of children[36] to the time when Ian Smith expressed his view to the author in 1983 that the Africans did not believe in education because they thought "it was something that belonged to the white man,"[37] the colonial government persistently framed its national policy based upon this Victorian myth. On the other hand, Dodge argued on behalf of Christian leaders, including Todd, "My dealing with African people leaves me with very high appreciation of their natural ability. Make no mistake about it, world leaders will come from Africa."[38] This belief compelled him to argue that there was "a tremendous potential among the Africans, but it will never come to full fruition until the opportunities of training are comparable with those received by other people of the world, and only when the Africans have attained full nationhood."[39] From these differences of perception, especially regarding the place of Africans in society, it is fairly easy to see how neither the RF government nor Dodge and Todd were prepared to give up the philosophy that was central to their respective positions as a foundation for the future. Dodge and Todd intensely disliked the thought that in submitting to the power of the RF government, Christian people would not be able to fulfill their important functions in society. They made this clear when Dodge concluded, "Nothing more tragic could happen to the Church than to allow itself to fall under the control of a political party."[40] For Dodge and Todd to give up this view would be to surrender a cardinal principle they needed to develop in order to enable the church to exert its appropriate influence on society. For the RF government to reevaluate a policy that had been at the inception of the colonial government in 1890 would be to admit that it was wrong. The difference of perception in this regard is yet another example of the inevitable conflict that was so common between church and state during the mid-20th century. This conflict reached an ominous level during the time the RF was in power.

This church-state conflict also shows something more important. The view that Dodge and Todd held—that Africans possessed intellectual potential equal to that possessed by whites—was, in effect, a practice of religious belief in the total equality of all people. This is why they expressed their conviction that "God has divided His gifts fairly evenly among his various children of all races."[41] This was the first time since Rev. William Wade Harris, an official of the Aborigines Protection Society based in London, openly challenged the colonial educational policy in 1921 that Christian leaders openly challenged it again.

While the road to a final showdown between Dodge and Todd and the RF government began to appear in 1959, it took a perilous turn in 1963 and 1964. During the annual conference of the Methodist Church held at Murewa in May 1963, Dodge delivered one of his best episcopal addresses in which he argued that the church had a responsibility to start a social revolution. Comparing the situation in Zimbabwe under the RF with that in ancient Palestine, Dodge drew a striking similarity:

It was those in top positions in synagogues, society and government who resisted change. They undoubtedly looked with pity on the beggars, the outcasts. But their very pity revealed the fact that they felt themselves superior beings. People who live comfortably do not agitate for change. There is a great need for change in Southern Rhodesia. Those who have power and wealth must be willing to share. They must be aware that there is a dynamism of change.[42]

This was the first important event that took place in 1963 that became part of the cause of the crisis between the church and the RF government. The second important event was that the RF began to formulate its policy soon after it assumed power following a bitter election campaign in which it made race a major campaign issue. The RF promised the white voters that if elected it would elevate the white race to the pinnacle of absolute political power enshrined in the philosophy of racial superiority of the white man and the inferiority of the Africans. It also promised to do this by amending the notorious Land Apportionment Act of 1929 to make it more effective.[43] The RF also promised the white voters that if elected it would seek independence from Britain by either legal or illegal means.[44] In making this promise the RF neither tolerated the church's opposition to its policy nor appreciated the Africans' determination to realize the political aspirations.

A political crisis within the RF itself helped to precipitate a crisis between church and state. In April 1964 Winston Field was removed from the office of prime minister in a political ambush that was led by Ian

Smith because Field had shown some signs of respecting the British demand of African political and educational advancement. He had also released the African political prisoners who had been arrested under the state of emergency declared by Edgar Whitehead on February 28, 1959. When Smith assumed office on April 24, 1964, the character of the relationship between the church and the RF took a turn for the worse. Smith proved to be a politician who cared little for the condition of life of the people he governed. His political philosophy that there would never be a black majority government in Zimbabwe in his lifetime, not in a thousand years, became an obsession, a political religion that he worshipped with the devotion of a saint. Nothing else mattered.

Both the RF's victory in the general election of December 1962 and Smith's assumption of the office of prime minister in 1964 were received with measured feelings of dismay by both the Africans and the church leaders. Three weeks before Smith became prime minister, the Methodist Church held its annual conference at Murewa. Instead of addressing social issues in his episcopal address, as he had done in 1963, Dodge opted for an alternative approach. He entertained a motion from the floor, and after a considerable debate mainly on the wording, the conference passed a resolution stating, "Any unilateral declaration of independence would constitute an act of rebellion and create a grave situation in which we might find it necessary to advise our people that they are under no moral obligation to carry out the commands of an illegal government."[45]

There are two possible reasons to explain why Dodge entertained the motion that led to this resolution. The first is that he had been in the spotlight since he opposed the state of emergency of 1959 and wanted the RF government to know that other Methodists shared his views. The second reason is that the RF government would have no justification for singling him out for vindictive action. This would protect his position and so enable him to continue his crusade for social change. Of course this was a miscalculation because the RF was not guided by this kind of rationale and reasoning. The resolution ended with a grim warning, "Therefore we earnestly appeal for the convening of a constitutional conference which would make provision for a majority government,"[46] and was signed by the committee secretary, Reverend Robert Hughes, another uncompromising foe of the RF policy. The support that Todd received from Hughes added considerable strength to Todd's struggle against the RF government.

The crisis that was rapidly building up in 1964 was a climax of events that began to take place in 1959. When Edgar Whitehead declared the state of emergency of February 28, 1959, his predecessor, Garfield Todd, opposed it, arguing that the action was more likely to aggravate the situation than solve it. Todd also felt that in taking this action Whitehead was trying to limit the effect of the rise of African nationalism, and that this was the wrong way of dealing with this new phenomenon. In supporting Todd, Dodge was aware that he was adding fuel to an already raging fire. Writing a letter to Todd in March 1959, Dodge praised him for taking a stand against Whitehead's action, saying "although I have not had the privilege of meeting you, still I wish to express my appreciation to the stand which you have taken during the present emergency. Certainly there is a place in this great continent of Africa for a multiracial society based on mutual respect and full partnership. May you have strength and wisdom to carry out the task ahead."[47]

At that time little did Dodge know that he would need Todd's support before the end of 1964. The alliance between Todd and Dodge was noted by Ian Smith and William Harper, who, in 1959, were then members of the extreme Dominion Party, which was the opposition in Parliament. The alliance also sent a message early in the RF administration that Dodge and Todd intended to provide a leadership that envisaged a total social transformation of Zimbabwe. As soon as it became the government, the RF began to watch both men very closely.

DODGE'S DEPORTATION AND TODD'S REACTION

The cumulative effect of these developments can be measured in terms of a series of rapidly moving events that caught Dodge, Hughes, and Todd by total surprise and shock. Unwilling to take any criticism of RF's racist policy and frustrated by the persistent demand of the British for the advancement of the Africans, Ian Smith found an easy target for his vengeful action. On July 16, 1964, his government served Dodge and Hughes with deportation orders, requesting them to leave the country within 15 days. Dodge's request of July 17 for "an extension of forty days to allow me to complete my assignment as President of the Southern Rhodesia Christian Conference which terminates with the Biennial Conference September 5–9 and to permit Mrs. Dodge and me to attend the wedding of our daughter on August 15th"[48] was denied with the exception that William Harper, the RF minister of internal affairs told him, "I am prepared to authorize the issuance of a temporary permit to enable you to visit Southern Rhodesia on the 14th, 15th, and 16th of August, for the sole purpose of attending your daughter's wedding."[49]

But the letter dated August 13, 1964, written by D. E. Shephard, private secretary to Harper, and addressed to Mrs. E. Griffin, interim secretary to the Methodist Church's board of finance and coordination (BOFAC), demonstrates the serious nature and extent of the conflict that existed between the church's religious principles and the RF's political philosophy. The letter stated, "The severe action taken against this gentleman is, in the Government's opinion, fully justified. It was taken after very careful and deep consideration of the facts and circumstances which clearly show that it was in the interests of the country that such action be taken."⁵⁰

One is compelled to ask two questions: What were these facts and circumstances? What were the interests of the country that forced the RF to take this high-handed action? Answers to both questions must be furnished. The truth of the matter is that the RF was considering its own political interests and nothing else. On the top cover of his pamphlet, "The Church and Freedom," written in 1963, Dodge included a picture of a prison fence, implying correctly that as far as the Africans were concerned, Zimbabwe under the RF was nothing less than a political prison. This is exactly what Shephard meant when he said that Dodge threatened the interests of the country, because the RF had known all along that he and Todd had joined hands in waging a crusade to end all forms of colonialism. The only threat that the RF faced came from increasing African opposition to its policies. By refusing to disclose what it claimed were facts and circumstances, the RF demonstrated its inability to deal with the problems of its own creation.

One might add that the facts and circumstances that forced the RF to take this dramatic action amounted to nothing more than fear that indeed the Africans were responding to a call for a fundamental social change as a condition of a new society to emerge in order to enable the people to have a more meaningful life. That the RF did not see things from this perspective closed the minds of its leader members to the hard realities that they faced. The RF refused to acknowledge that "the fight against ignorance, intolerance, disease and poverty,"⁵¹ which Dodge and Todd were waging through their crusade, demanded a new political approach. In reality, these were the facts and circumstances that the RF did not want anyone to criticize it for.

Where then did Dodge's deportation lead the country, and what were some of the consequences of this action? Since Rev. William Wade Harris demanded involvement in the formulation of a national policy in 1921, Dodge was the most popular church leader among the Africans.⁵² Because of irreconcilable differences between him and Todd and the RF, the RF concluded erroneously that their action threatened national interests. Everyone knew that this argument was indeed a galaxy of absurdities. A study of the reaction, both African and white, furnishes enough evidence to show that indeed the RF feared that Dodge's and Todd's influence among the Africans would increase their political consciousness.

Among the first people to send Dodge messages of support and encouragement was Garfield Todd, the prime minister who was removed from office in 1958 for attempting to initiate a progressive policy toward the Africans, and whom Dodge praised in 1959 for expressing opposition to the state of emergency of February of that year. In a telegram Todd wrote "DEEPLY GRATEFUL FOR CONTRIBUTION YOU HAVE MADE. EXPRESS MY APPRECIATION TO YOU AND YOUR CHURCH. HOPE NOT LONG UNTIL WE WELCOME YOU BACK WITH HONOR."[53] Neither Dodge nor Todd was aware that his return to independent and free Zimbabwe would have to wait until 1980. Indeed, when Dodge returned in that year, he *was* welcomed with honor.

On July 27, 1960, believing that the situation was critical, Todd was among a group of individuals who signed a letter to the British Colonial Office, urging that the constitution that had been in operation since 1923 be suspended and substituted for by a truly democratic constitution that allowed Africans' equal role. He concluded, "I say solemnly that our house is on fire. It is on fire with racial feelings and racial aspiration. Southern Rhodesia faces the harsh reality of depression and unemployment."[54] Todd shared the Africans' view that any constitution must envisage the advent of an African government if peace must prevail in the country. This was the position that most settlers rejected outright, making Todd a villain and a social outcast. From that time to the advent of an African government in April 1980, Todd never compromised that position. This is why he and Dodge had a place of honor in independent Zimbabwe.

Beyond the fact that Todd was supporting Dodge in 1964 in the same way that Dodge had supported him in 1959 was an unquestionable hope and wish that the RF would soon be eliminated from the political scene of Zimbabwe, because its policies were totally out of tune with reality and the conditions of the time. Although Todd and Whitehead had serious political differences, those between Todd and Smith were so serious that they could not be restored. Could this mean that Smith feared there was something more than an alliance of religious and political ideology between Dodge and Todd against him? It is difficult to resist the temptation to reach this conclusion. But Todd clearly believed that Dodge's influence among the Africans was what the RF feared most.

A day after Todd had sent his telegram to Dodge on July 18, Joshua Nkomo, the veteran president of ZAPU which Smith outlawed in April, and who was now in detention at Gonakudzingwa, sent a letter of support to Dodge, saying as he added another dimension to the meaning of the deportation, "Christ died on the cross, not because those who were responsible for His crucifixion believed that He was doing wrong, but because he was an unusual leader doing the unusual thing. But His physical death has not gone with His unusual influence. In this same way your influence in this country will live forever."[55] What Nkomo was in effect saying is that Smith and his RF government were ill-advised to think that Dodge's role in the crusade for fundamental social change would suddenly come to an end with his deportation. If anything at all, it was likely to intensify that demand. Nkomo correctly concluded that the deportation was an attempt to find an easy way out of the problems that RF was creating.

Now that Dodge was out of the country, the RF turned its vengeful action against Todd. From October 18, 1965, to October 20, 1966, the RF placed him and his daughter Judith under house arrest because of his persistent argument that it was inflicting a severe damage to the future of the country by the pursuit of its policy. It is clear that the RF took this action to prepare for the unilateral declaration of independence on November 11, 1965. He was arrested on the eve of leaving for the University of Edinburgh where he had been invited to give a lecture. It was reported that the reason for the arrest was that the RF feared he was going to form a government in exile.[56] Todd remained an outspoken critic of the RF throughout the years of the war of liberation from April 1966 to December 1979, giving as much help as he could to the African guerrillas. It was only after the end of the RF in December 1979 that Todd began to live like a free human being.

SUMMARY AND CONCLUSION

This chapter has presented evidence leading to the conclusion that Todd's role in the political crisis in Zimbabwe came in two forms. The first form was his response to Whitehead's initiative. The second was his reaction to the RF policy. From the discussion in this chapter one can see that Whitehead's political demise came from his inability to reconcile himself to the conflicting positions he took. When he first recognized that Whitehead was in trouble, Todd tried in vain to help him see how contradiction in his political behavior was hurting him. This explains why only a few Africans believed Whitehead when he said on December 10, 1961, "Our constitution (of 1961) demands the spirit of tolerance. We are determined to have a society in which every body can express his own views without fear."[57] In this broadcast to the country, Whitehead was explaining why he was outlawing the National Democratic Party (NDP), which the Africans formed after Whitehead had outlawed the ANC in February 1959. When he launched his "Build a Nation" and "Claim Your Vote" campaigns, only 8,000 of the 50,000 qualified Africans responded. It is evident that Whitehead became a victim of his own gross miscalculations.

That Whitehead refused to discuss the educational system with the members of Parliament and with Africans themselves demonstrates the bad faith with which he approached this deeply emotional issue. He did not have to go far to find the reasons why the Africans were rejecting his policy. The banning of the NDP, and the arrest of its interim president, the charismatic and popular Michael Mawema on December 10, 1961, brought 25,000 Africans into the streets to demonstrate against him and in support of Mawema. When he ordered the armed forces to fire on the demonstrators, killing 36 Africans in Harare alone, any form of rapport he may have had with the Africans disappeared. At this point Todd felt that Whitehead could no longer be helped.

These were the reasons behind the Africans' rejection of Whitehead's policies. They could not in good faith support him because his entire program, especially his educational policy, did not reflect their aspirations. At the same time Africans could not make a choice between the UFP and the RF because neither represented their interests. This is why James Barber quotes Willie Musarurwa, a brilliant African political thinker in Zimbabwe, as saying during this crisis with reference to both the UFP and the RF,

Both parties want to prevent the advent of majority rule. Both believe that the end justifies the means. Both have low regard of the Africans. Both believe in white supremacy, which they euphemistically call "white civilization." Both use brutal methods to suppress the legitimate aspirations of 95 percent of the country's population. The Africans will not vote for a white supremacist party because it is led by a white man who dislikes the Africans less than another.[58]

Todd had long recognized this fact.

Todd's reaction to the RF was even stronger than his reaction to Whitehead. Todd recognized the fact that the RF failed to see things from any perspective other than from seeking a mandate from the white voters to enshrine its political philosophy as a major error in the course of human interaction. Todd would not remain silent in seeing the RF operate by its belief that its victory signaled the end of African hope for an education that would enable them to realize their ambition. He warned that the RF was setting a new stage for a bitter racial confrontation which was destined to create wounds that would not be healed. But what hat kind of relationship did the RF have with the Africans as it took office?

In 1983 Ian Smith admitted that he knew that the RF's educational policy would lead to a confrontation with the Africans, saying "we knew that the Africans were apprehensive about our educational policy. But we felt we had to fulfill the promises that we had made to the voters. There were other priorities more important than education."[59] This is why Todd fully supported Dodge's conclusion that the RF was "teaching to hate rather than to build human love, to destroy, rather than to save lives, to encourage ignorance and prejudice, rather than to gain knowledge; who in uncontrolled emotion takes the sword is still in danger of perishing by the sword."[60] During a speech to the Bulawayo National Affairs Association in February 1947, Todd said something prophetically that would have a direct message to the RF. He predicted: "There is a spirit of urgency in African development. Take that spirit, guide it, give it assistance, and there will develop a people who will be a credit to this country. Disregard or hinder that spirit, and an adverse effect will result with severe consequences for the country."[61] If the RF had listened to this warning and tolerated criticism, especially from those like Dodge and Todd who made it responsibly, then solutions to the problems that it had created would have been found peacefully. But what is even more tragic about the RF policy is that after Dodge's deportation, the church-state crisis took a more dangerous turn, just as Todd had predicted.

NOTES

1. The term *Christian Church*, as it has been used in Zimbabwe, carries the universal and collective definition of religious organizations, both Catholic and Protestant. This is the definition used in this study unless otherwise stated.

2. There were four Smiths in the RF government: Ian Smith, the prime minister and leader of the party; Lance Smith, minister of internal affairs; Arthur Smith, minister of education; and David Smith, minister of agriculture. There was also A. J. Smith, secretary for African education. They were not related by blood, but a political philosophy that the African must never hope to reach social equality with whites.

3. Ndabaningi Sithole, during an interview with the author, in Harare, Zimbabwe, July 22, 1983. Sithole was a founding member of the African National Congress and served as its vice-president.

4. Southern Rhodesia, The African Education Act, 1959.

5. Sithole, interview.

6. The magic number of 30 had been stipulated in the constitution that was introduced in 1924 until the constitution was changed in 1961, when the number of seats in Parliament was increased to 65 including 15 Africans. In 1962 the RF was the first government to sit in the legislature with Africans.

7. David Martin and Phyllis Johnson, *The Struggle for Zimbabwe* (Harare: Zimbabwe Publishing House, 1981), p. 68.

8. Interview with the author in Harare, July 15, 1983. The white man declined to be identified because, he said,

I do not wish to appear to excuse myself from the policies the RF pursued and try to give the impression that we were a bunch of racists. We did some things that were right, but because neither the Africans nor the British government trusted us, we were portrayed as insensitive oppressors interested only in sustaining our political power structure. Because were not able to erase this misconception, I resigned from the RF. I have no regrets. We had gone too far as a political party and in our desire to sustain our presumed superiority over the Africans.

9. James Barber, *Rhodesia: The Road to Rebellion* (London: Oxford University Press, Institute of Race Relations, 1967), p. 95.

10. Ibid., p. 96.

11. Interview with the author, in Harare, July 17, 1983.

12. A white political observer, during an interview with the author, in Harare, July 14, 1983.

13. The Judges Commission, which Whitehead named in 1961, submitted its report shortly after the RF assumed the government in 1962. The RF made no secret of the fact that it did not like the report because it was fundamentally opposed to it in principle.

14. A white man during an interview with the author in Mutare, Zimbabwe, July 21, 1983.

15. Albert Memmi, *The Colonizer and the Colonized* (Boston: Beacon Press, 1965), p. 21.

16. Martin and Johnson, *The Struggle for Zimbabwe*, p. 68.

17. Southern Rhodesia, *Legislative Debates*, 1927.

18. Ian Smith, the last colonial prime minister of colonial Zimbabwe who served from 1964 to 1979, during an interview with the author in Harare, July 20, 1983.

19. A white man during an interview with the author in Harare, July 29, 1983.

20. Franklin Parker, *African Development and Education in Southern Rhodesia* (Columbus: Ohio State University Press, 1960), p. 60.

21. Ibid., p. 61.

22. Garfield Todd: Biographical Note. Zimbabwe National Archives, July 28, 1997.

23. Ibid.

24. Judith Todd, letter to the author written from Bulawayo, Zimbabwe, May 9, 1997.

25. Southern Rhodesia, *The Annual Report of the Director of Native Education, 1957*, p. 2.

26. For a detailed discussion of Dodge's philosophy of the role of the church in Africa, see his *The Revolutionary Bishop: An Autobiography* (Pasadena, CA: William Carey Library, 1986).

27. R. Dodge, "Biographical Sketch," an unpublished introduction to *The Unpopular Missionary* (Westwood, NJ: H. Revell, 1964).

28. R. Dodge, "The Church and Freedom," an essay, 1963, p. 3.

29. Ibid., p. 3.

30. Ibid., p. 4.

31. Ibid., p. 4.

32. R. Dodge, "The Church and Law and Order," an essay, 1963, p. 3.

33. Ibid., p. 4.

34. Ibid., p. 6.

35. Ibid., p. 6.

36. Stanlake Samkange, *What Rhodes Really Said About Africans* (Harare: Harare Publishing House, 1982), p. 30.

37. Ian Smith, interview.

38. R. Dodge, "The African Church Now and in the Future," an essay, 1964, p. 9.

39. Ibid., p. 10.

40. Dodge, *The Unpopular Missionary*, p. 165.

41. Ibid., p. 86.

42. Ralph Dodge, "The Church in Africa," an episcopal address in *The Official Journal of the Methodist Church* (Old Mutare, Rhodesia Mission Press, 1963), p. 43.

43. Indeed, in 1969, the RF fulfilled its promise by enacting the Land Tenure Act, which was more oppressive than the Land Apportionment Act of 1929.

44. Indeed, the RF kept this promise also. When it found that it was unable to secure independence from Britain on its own terms, the RF unilaterally declared Rhodesia independent.

45. The Methodist Church, "A Warning against the Declaration of Independence," a press release, May 17, 1964.

46. Ibid.

47. R. Dodge, in a letter dated March 18, 1959, addressed to Garfield Todd.

48. R. Dodge, in a letter dated July 17, 1964, addressed to William Harper.

49. William Harper, in a letter dated July 22, 1964, addressed to Dodge.

50. D. E. Shephard, in a letter dated August 13, 1964, addressed to Mrs. E. Griffin.

51. Lois Stewart, "Response to Questionnaire," June 20, 1986.

52. See Chapter 10 of Dickson A. Mungazi, *The Honored Crusade: Ralph Dodge's Theology of Liberation and Initiative for Social Change in Zimbabwe* (Gweru: Mambo Press, 1991) for evidence leading to this conclusion.

53. Garfield Todd, in a telegram sent to Dodge, July 17, 1964, from his home in Shabani.

54. A. J. Peck, *Rhodesia Accuses* (Boston: Western Islands Press, 1966), p. 107.

55. Joshua Nkomo, in a letter dated July 18, 1964, addressed to Dodge from Gonakudzingwa Restriction Area where he was kept as a political prisoner.

56. Garfield Todd: Biographical Note.

57. Southern Rhodesia: *Parliamentary Debates*, 1959–1961.

58. Barber, *Rhodesia: The Road to Rebellion*, p. 165.

59. Ian Smith, interview.

60. R. Dodge, "A Statement on the Deportation Orders," July 18, 1964, p. 2.

61. Garfield Todd, "African Education in Southern Rhodesia: The Need for a Commission of Inquiry," an address to the Bulawayo National Affairs Association, February 18, 1947. Zimbabwe National Archives.

7

Blundell's Relations with Africans

> Unless the African himself can carry forward the conviction that what we have to offer him is a real way of life, something really to work for, then I believe that we have lost the battle for the continent of Africa.
>
> —Michael Blundell in 1957
> [cited in Blundell, 1994]

IMPACT OF MAU MAU LEADERSHIP

In his book, *So Rough a Wind*,[1] Blundell gives a fascinating account of his response to the Mau Mau movement in a manner that was so typical of the reaction of the settlers who were affected by the rebellion. At the beginning of the Mau Mau rebellion, settlers produced the kind of literature that reflected a mixture of anger because they saw it as an act of savagery, guilt because they felt that the colonial condition they created cheated the Africans of their land and livelihood, and fear because they did not know what the Africans would do next. This literature, therefore, is an account of the kind of relationships settlers had with Africans in varying forms. As the Mau Mau rebellion started, many settlers began to think it was a result of their failure to initiate dialogue that would have led to improved relationships with Africans for the good of the country.

Now that the rebellion had started, was it still possible to initiate that dialogue in order for both sides to have an understanding of the issues that had brought this tragedy about? But once the colonial government took the position that the Mau Mau rebellion was the work of barbarian people bent on destroying Western civilization, the opportunity to understand why it broke out was lost. All the settlers did was adopt the hostile attitude and policy of the colonial government. However, there was a nagging feeling among them that this tragedy could have been avoided if an effort had been made to reach out to the Africans to understand and appreciate their concerns. Because this feeling would not go away, settler writers began to play the survival game by producing literature that denigrated the Mau Mau instead of attributing the rebellion to their own failure to communicate with Africans on issues that divided the two sides.

This is the context in which one must read Blundell's *So Rough a Wind*. Apart from telling his life story in this book, Blundell also recorded the extent of his activity, particularly during the state of emergency following the outbreak of the Mau Mau, when the colonial government declared an open war on it. Consistent with the general purpose of the settler literature about the Mau Mau, *So Rough a Wind* is also a detailed account of the strategy Blundell was proposing to defeat the Mau Mau, rather to seek understanding of its causes. It does not do what would have been expected of a liberal national leader that Blundell was, and that is to rise above the fray to exert real leadership in seeking a meeting of the minds between the colonial establishment that he represented and the Africans. As an influential member of the war council, Blundell had a major role to play in seeking to fulfill the objectives of the colonial establishment.

However, Blundell completely ignored the legitimate concerns of the Africans and the causes that had brought them about. He also neglected a very important part of all this: that the Africans were fighting not against Western civilization, as the argument was being made, but against the oppressive system of the colonial government. How could Blundell, a man who was raised by the standards of fairness and application of reason, ignore this critical fact? How could he be part of a system that even refused to try to see if the Africans had reason to resort to the method that they did to have their problems addressed? This is not to suggest the conclusion that the Mau Mau rebellion was justified, but to suggest that there were alternative approaches to it as a response to the crisis other than military reaction.

As the chief spokesman of the settler community Blundell was quite forceful in characterizing the Mau Mau as "debased creatures of the forest."[2] This dark portrait of the Mau Mau was so widespread among settlers that only a few individuals, most of them from countries other than Kenya, felt that the Mau Mau rebellion was a form of African nationalism that must be responded to in a positive manner. These individuals included Louis S. St. Laurent, the liberal prime minister of Canada from 1948 to 1957. St. Laurent embarrassed Britain and angered settlers in Kenya by advancing his thinking that the Mau Mau was a legitimate nationalist movement fighting against the injustice of the colonial system.[3] Because of St. Laurent's rare views of the Mau Mau, it is necessary to give a brief account of this remarkable leader to see what there was in his background that enabled him to see things from the perspective that he did.

Born on February 1, 1882, in the small town of Compton, a few miles north of the Canadian border with Vermont, St. Laurent was one of six children born to Jean Baptiste Moise St. Laurent, a storekeeper, and Ann Mary Broderick St. Laurent, a former schoolteacher. His father was a descendant of the French settlers, and his mother's parents were Irish immigrants. He learned to speak both English and French as a boy, and both the English and the French worlds gave him his distinct liberal perspective of viewing issues. During the elections of 1896, St. Laurent became involved in the campaign of the Liberal Party, led at the time by Wilfred Laurier, and took tremendous pride in its victory in that year. In 1903, while he was a law student, St. Laurent became involved in the liberal causes in Quebec, such as the rights of workers to organize to protect their economic interests, reminding political leaders that they held office in order to serve the needs of the people, and to protect the freedom of individuals to engage in self-fulfilling activities. In his efforts to bring about these changes, St. Laurent quickly earned a reputation as a brilliant lawyer and politician.

In 1914 St. Laurent became a professor of law at Laval University and went on to serve as the president of the Canadian Bar Association from 1930 to 1932. Laval University provided an ideal academic and political environment for an aspiring politician. Founded in 1663 as a Catholic seminary, Laval University is the oldest institution of higher learning in Canada. It received a royal charter in 1852. Over the years Laval University has attracted outstanding individuals who have played major roles in the development of Canada. St. Laurent's tenure as law professor there helped him become ranked as one of the top Canadian authorities on constitutional law. From 1937 to 1939 he served as counsel to the Royal Commission on Canadian federal matters.

When Ernest Lapointe, Canadian minister of justice, died in November 1941, Canada lost an effective voice on the French Canadian Liberal Party. Mackenzie King, then Canadian prime minister, asked the 59-year-old St. Laurent to replace Lapointe. The following year St. Laurent was elected to the seat that Lapointe had held. He immediately attracted national attention by the quality of his service to Canada. On September 4, 1946, King appointed St. Laurent secretary of state for external affairs in which he effectively represented Canadian interests in international affairs. On August 7, 1948, St. Laurent was elected leader of the Liberal Party, a position that qualified him to become prime minister on November 15, 1948. During his term of office Canada's reputation soared as he distinguished himself as a champion of freedom of all people in the world. From 1948 to 1952 St. Laurent had considerable differences of opinion with Winston Churchill on British colonial policy in Africa.

In carrying out his duty as prime minister of Canada, St. Laurent operated under the Asquith-Lloyd George traditions that required national political leaders to place the interests of the people above their own. This is why in 1949 he succeeded in persuading Britain to grant the Canadian Parliament power to amend its constitution in order to address issues of concern to Canada. In the past only Britain had power to amend the Canadian constitution. This power enabled Canada in 1952 to have the first Canadian-born leader, Vincent Massey, appointed governor-general of Canada. St. Laurent felt strongly that the unfair treatment of people under colonial settings was detrimental to human development wherever it occurred, and that colonial systems existed only for purposes of exploiting resources, both human and material, for the sole benefit of the colonizing nation.

Under St. Laurent's leadership Canada took an increasingly important part in international affairs, including his role in the founding of NATO. St. Laurent also persistently argued that in all their forms colonial systems operated on institutionalized violence. Colonized people are often denied an effective voice in political matters and are always exploited economically, as they are forced to endure the harshness of laws that are passed to protect the interests of the colonizer. In 1948 he became an outspoken critic of the introduction of the system of apartheid in South Africa as one of the worst forms of colonial violence.

As soon as he became prime minister in 1948, the same year that Blundell was elected to the legislative council in Kenya, St. Laurent warned the colonial governments in Africa that they were likely to experience new and unprecedented problems because the Africans would no longer continue to allow themselves to be subjected to humiliating treatment so common under colonial systems. This is the position that Garfield Todd took in 1947 with direct reference to the African response to conditions in colonial Zimbabwe. This is also why, in 1952, St. Laurent argued that the Mau Mau was a legitimate form of African nationalism that the colonial government must acknowledge.[4] St. Laurent also suggested that the best way to resolve the conflict caused by the Mau Mau rebellion was not military, but dialogue. However, the colonial establishment declined to accept this suggestion. He also advised the colonial government in Kenya that it was in its own best interests to initiate contact with the leaders of the Mau Mau movement in order to establish lines of communication based on understanding the issues that had caused the rebellion.⁵

To counteract what it considered a campaign by St. Laurent to discredit it, the colonial government launched a vicious propaganda campaign against the Mau Mau. Because of the effectiveness of this campaign and the fact that only a few of the Mau Mau leaders were literate, the Mau Mau failed to mount an effective countercampaign of its own to prove to the outside world that it was fighting against the injustice and oppression imposed by the colonial conditions, and not against Western civilization, as the colonial government claimed. Blundell blundered in assuming the same attitude and position as his fellow settlers did, that because the Mau Mau represented barbarism at its worst it was not possible to initiate contact with its leaders for purposes of establishing lines of communication between the two sides.

Unless one was an African living in Kenya at this time, one is not likely to understand the Africans' anger at the colonial system and determination to eliminate it. Tabitha Kanogo concludes that the colonial condition that these and other Africans saw as oppressive consisted of denial of an opportunity for economic development, injustice of land distribution, labor practice, unfair tax system, the practice of *kipande*, unrepresentative political system, and racial discrimination.⁶ With respect to the first cause of anger among the Africans, the lack of opportunity for economic development, it is important to remember that in 1901 the railway line from Mombasa had reached Kisumu on the shores of Lake Victoria. Its construction cost the British government over five million pounds sterling.

Therefore, the British government wanted to ensure that the railway line should pay for its maintenance and must therefore contribute to the economy of the country. Because Kenya did not contain large deposits of minerals, the British Colonial Office decided that the development of the economy should be based on agriculture and that the railway should be used to transport food from one part of the country to another. To successfully do this, a critical policy element had to be implemented in accordance with provisions of the Berlin Conference that required Africans to fulfill functions as cheap labor. Once this policy came into being, Africans had no opportunity for meaningful economic development. After the end of the war in 1945 Africans recognized the basic need to force a change in this economic practice. This meant confrontation with the colonial system

The second cause of anger among Africans was the injustice of land distribution. In order to make it possible for settlers to undertake agricultural operation on a large commercial scale, the colonial government found it imperative to acquire large areas of land from the Africans.

Prospective setters were attracted to Kenya by offers of cheap land, cheap labor, and large profit. They came from Britain, New Zealand, Australia, and Canada. Settlers streamed into Kenya from the beginning of the century to the beginning of the Second World War.[7] This is why Blundell, at the age of 18, decided to go to Kenya in 1925. Cecil John Rhodes was about the same age as Blundell when he moved to South Africa in 1870. By the time of his death on March 26, 1902, Rhodes had become a millionaire many times over.

In Kenya nearly 8 million acres were confiscated from Africans without any compensation and were given to settlers during the first 50 years of the 20th century. The availability of land was a bonanza for settlers. The central highlands, which settlers wanted more than any other part of the country, were among the most fertile in Africa. This part of Kenya became an exclusive domain for settlers; Africans and Asians were not allowed to occupy land there.[8] By the beginning of the war in 1939 Africans had become foreigners in the land of their ancestors. Without land they had nothing to call their own, they had lost everything. By 1952 the colonial government had still not been able to understand that those who had been deprived of their most valued possessions were left with no choice but to fight to regain what had been stolen from them. This is why, by 1952, the Africans turned their anger into a determination to fight.

For the settlers to engage successfully in commercial agriculture they needed a constant and abundant supply of labor. Because most settlers did not have sufficient capital to invest in agricultural enterprises, they felt that labor, which only the Africans could supply, should be cheap. By formulating its policy the colonial government made this possible. In addition to those Africans who were deprived of their land by the colonial government, the vast majority of Africans had simply no desire to supply the cheap labor that the settlers needed to make a profit. The colonial government utilized various methods to compel Africans to seek employment as cheap labor. For example, in 1913, the year of the notorious Land Act in South Africa, Lord Delamere,[9] a settler who later served as chairman of the National Farmers Union, proposed that "the Native reserves should be cut in order to prevent Africans from having sufficient land to make them self-supporting. If the Africans had enough land and therefore stocked and produced for sale, they would not be obligated to supply labor for settler farmers."[10] While this strategy had the desired effect, it came at a high cost of conflict after the war in 1945.

The colonial government also employed a number of measures to force Africans to seek employment in settler establishments. One of these measures was the imposition of taxes on Africans. In 1902 and 1910, respectively, the hut and poll taxes were introduced. Africans were forced to make a choice between selling their limited livestock to pay the taxes or to seek employment in settler agricultural operations to raise enough money to pay the required taxes. Many Africans were forced to seek employment in order to save the limited numbers of their livestock. But conditions of work were so oppressive and the pay so low that many Africans deserted their employment, forcing the colonial government to introduce in 1919 the even more oppressive and humiliating *kipande* system. After the war in 1945 the Africans could no longer take this unjust practice. In their struggle for development, the Africans were undercut by the forces that came out of this practice. It is very easy to understand their anger and the desire to eliminate the colonial condition that this system represented. For Africans there was no escape from the tentacles of an old octopus except to fight.

The unrepresentative political system and the racial discrimination were closely related. Until Eliud Mathu was named by the governor to the legislative council, Africans had no representation in the body that made laws to govern them. The Africans bitterly resented the fact that their interests were represented in the legislative council by liberal whites and missionaries, who barely understood what their needs and aspirations really were. Kanogo concludes that in the political settings that existed under colonial system

Africans had no say in the formulation of economic, political or social policies within the country. Their participation was restricted to local Native councils. These were created in 1924 and were very limited in what they could achieve. This lack of political muscle was one of the key grievances which Africans sought to eliminate.[11]

Directly related to the lack of political representation was racial discrimination, which was pervasive and applied to every aspect of national life. By the end of the war Africans became acutely aware of the need to eliminate these forms of injustices as a condition of their development.

In spite of the belief that most members of the Mau Mau were illiterate, it became known that there were some very intelligent leaders with whom it was possible to negotiate. We have only enough space to discuss three of these leaders here: Waruhiu Itote, Dedan Kimathi, and Jomo Kenyatta.

Waruhiu Itote was born in 1921 in the Nyeri district. His early life was a constant struggle because, like most Africans, his parents were poor and so could not afford to provide what he needed to lead a normal life as a young African. Bright and highly ambitious, Itote excelled in his studies at the primary school. Always at the top of his class, Itote was, however, embarrassed by the extent of poverty that was part of his life. Unable to finance his education further, he left school to look for work. But unable to find a more meaningful employment opportunity, Itote was employed as a farm laborer and a houseboy, the kind of work that Masirero did for Bronco Bill. His intelligence impressed his employers, who did not knew that anger ran deep in his mind because the settlers had the best land and paid their African workers very low wages.

Itote left his employment to try his hand in business in Nairobi. In 1941, at the age of 20, Itote responded to the promise of the Atlantic Charter, an eight-point statement issued by President Franklin D. Roosevelt and Prime Minister Winston Churchill on August 11, 1941, stating that they respected the right of all people to live as they wished and pledged after the war was over to work toward the restoration of all human rights for those who had been deprived of them by force.[12] Although, after the war when Churchill reneged on that promise, saying that he was not appointed chief minister of His Majesty's Government to preside over the dissolution of the British empire, the Africans held him and other colonial systems to his word. Itote had joined the Kenya African Rifles (KAR) in Nairobi. From there he and other African volunteers were posted to the 36th KAR in Tanzania; they were sent to Ceylon and then to Burma, where they saw service.

The war had a profound impact on the Africans. The possibility of an instant and violent death in a foreign country and in a white man's war brought new realization that, contrary to his claim, the white man himself suffered from serious limitations in terms of human thought processes. However, Itote distinguished himself as a soldier, learning guerrilla warfare methods and survival in the jungle. At the conclusion of the war in 1945 Itote had become a new person. His confidence in himself was aroused to a point where he lost respect for the white man's claim of his superiority over the Africans. Upon his return to Kenya Itote tried to get back into business again, this time as a charcoal burner. But due to limitations imposed by the economic policy of the colonial government led at the time by Philip E. Mitchell, Itote found it very hard to be successful. After only a few years of frustrating efforts and unfulfilling hard work, he joined the East African Railways and Harbours as a fireman.[13] Although the work was hard and unsatisfying, Itote once again served with distinction, believing in himself and in the promise of the future. But the colonial government was not willing to gratify him and other Africans in the way promised by the Atlantic Charter.

In 1951 Itote resigned from Railways and Harbours and joined the Forty Group, a cultural and militant organization formed by Africans who were disillusioned with the policy of the colonial government and which tried to apply pressure to have it changed, either by political action or by threat of military force. He became an oath administrator in Nyeri, where he enjoyed the respect and following of the African masses who believed in what he was asked by his organization to do. Itote developed powerful communication skills and intense political feeling that led him to believe that the colonial government must be forced to make major changes in its policy and concessions to accommodate African aspirations.

Itote's charisma, his faith in the ability of the Africans to define and realize their goals, his dedication to principle, his discipline, and his ability to arouse a passion in the Africans about the need for their development placed him right at the top of the rapidly rising African nationalism. He began to believe more solidly that if conflict between the colonial government and the Africans must be avoided, then the colonial government must recognize the oppressive nature of its policy and do something to change it. This was not a call that Mitchell was likely to answer, but a challenge his administration would accept. As the Mau Mau movement began in 1952, the central committee ordered selected units to set up guerrilla camps in the forest. On August 16 Itote presented himself as General China and as a member of a party of eight young men who visited Jomo Kenyatta at Gatundu after receiving instructions to do so from the central committee.[14]

The meeting with Kenyatta proved to be the turning point in the decision of the Mau Mau leadership to launch a struggle for freedom. The eight young men found Kenyatta in his garden, dressed in an open shirt and a pair of baggy pants. He told them that it was a matter of time before he was arrested and spoke at length about the need to continue the struggle to eliminate the oppression to which the colonial system subjected them. He also spoke about the importance of leadership now that the movement was under way. He reminded them that by deciding to be members of this party they had demonstrated their commitment to the African cause, and they placed themselves in a position of leadership that was needed to lead Africans from the colonial land of Egypt to the promised land of freedom. Kenyatta then made an impassioned appeal, saying to the eight young men, "Some of you, too, will be imprisoned, and some of you will be killed. But when these things happen, my sons, do not be afraid. Everything in this world has to be paid for and we must buy our freedom with our blood."[15]

Itote listened intensely and was greatly moved. This simple speech, by a man who was revered and had learned so much from the political conditions in Kenya, was a reassurance and a personal commitment to a national cause. Kenyatta then turned to Itote to give him his charge and commission as General China. He talked about the struggle for freedom for which men throughout human history made great personal sacrifice for a cause. He told him of the African slave Toussaint L'Ouverture, who rose against the French on the island of Haiti in 1791.[16] He told him how, through suffering, the people of Kenya would one day gain their freedom. But to have freedom they would need courage, determination, and great personal sacrifice. Kenyatta reminded Itote that when Kenyatta himself first arrived in Britain in 1929 he promised to dedicate himself to the freedom of Kenya and that he would never lose sight of that objective. Kenyatta told Itole that he was prepared to go to prison or to die in the cause of freedom for Kenya and that even if he died his blood and heart would remain with the people of Kenya.

For both Kenyatta, the fatherly figure who had mellowed with experience, and Itote, the young man who had learned so much about the value of human life from the cruelty of war and colonial oppression, this time and place were a defining moment of their lives. This was no longer the twilight zone of African aspiration, but the sunrise of their determination on a cloudless tropical sky to get rid of the colonial condition that had engulfed the African existence for so long. Both men knew that the future of the country lay on their shoulders. They became totally convinced that they had a mission and a responsibility to ensure the destiny of their people and country. Each man knew that he needed the other to fulfill his assigned mission. For each man there was no going back. Instead they mapped out their strategy in total conviction that if they did not rise to the occasion Kenya would continue to develop as a settler paradise, and a passage to "the other way,"[17] as Charles Dickens saw conditions of life in his society, for Africans.

After the emotions aroused by the meeting subsided somewhat, Kenyatta, with dignity and majesty, turned to Itote and solemnly said to him,

You learned things in the army, my son, and now you can lead our people. If you had died in Burma no one would have remembered you, for you were fighting for the British. But should you die tomorrow in our struggle, you will die for your people and your name will live in the hearts of your people forever. You will become an important part of our history as a great leader.[18]

Kenyatta then gave each of the other seven young men their individual charges. All eight young men were now ready to assume their leadership roles in the struggle for Kenya. Itote, as General China, was assigned to lead a group of fighters into the Hombe area of Mount Kenya. He established a camp in the forest from which he effectively organized and carried out raids that paralyzed the settler community in the area. His military experiences in Burma served him well. The settler community, unable to contain the guerrilla fighters on its own, appealed to the colonial government in Nairobi for help, forcing the British battalion to spread thin and making it vulnerable to concentrated efforts by the Africans.

Following the declaration of the state of emergency, Itote established two more guerrilla camps in the area to broaden the base of operation. On January 15, 1954, Itote was wounded and captured in an engagement near Karatine. On February 1, 1954, he was charged with the crime of consorting with persons carrying firearms and being in possession of two rounds of ammunition without permit. Itote was found guilty as charged and was sentenced to death. But the sentence was postponed because Itote agreed to assist the colonial authorities in organizing cease-fire talks with the guerrillas.[19] It is an amazing fact that the colonial government decided to make this initiative after conflict had started and not before.

This action is what Louis S. St. Laurent saw as detrimental to human relationships in colonial conditions. However, given the opportunity, Itote showed rare leadership qualities that colonial governments had not recognized in the past as they manifested themselves in powerful ways. He demonstrated unusually high levels of negotiation. Whether the colonial authorities wanted it or not they could not pass up an opportunity to understand the reasons that had caused the Mau Mau rebellion. As much as he disliked to talk to those "debased creatures of the forest," Blundell had no choice but to do so in total knowledge that discussions with the Africans would determine the fate of the country. Whatever reason Blundell saw as the purpose of these discussions, the Africans themselves had reached a decision that they must be directed toward independence for Kenya. On March 4, 1959, Evelyn Baring was so impressed with Itote as a leader that he commuted his death sentence to life imprisonment.

Itote was released from prison on June 14, 1962, because there was a new constitution for Kenya that paved way for independence on December 12, 1963. Itote was immediately nominated for military training in Britain. On his return to Kenya he was admitted to Lanet, a training school for social workers, graduating with the rank of second lieutenant in Kenya's army reserve. In 1964 Itote joined the National Youth Service as section commander, rising later to the position of deputy director of the service, a position he held for many years. Today Itote's place in history is secure as he is recognized as a dedicated son of Kenya whose vision for the future of his country remained untarnished by the forces that tried to detract his attention from seeking to fulfill the goals the Africans had set for the liberation of their country.

Dedan Kimathi was known during the Mau Mau as Field Marshall Dedan Kimathi. He was born on October 31, 1920, and was therefore a year older than Waruhiu Itote. He grew up in the Nyeri district and attended school at Karumini in Tetu. His friends and close associates concluded early in his life that he was born a natural leader. He exhibited charisma and personality that made him unique. His friendly smile, his sharp and piercing eyes, his majestic poise and composure constituted characteristics that made him a unique person in every way. His struggle for formal education made a lasting impression on those close to him about his determination to pursue goals.

Like most Africans of his day, Kimathi encountered serious difficulties in his quest for education. His mother, the only person he depended upon to meet his needs, was not in a position to raise the finances that he needed to continue his formal education, which was often interrupted by periods of financial difficulties that forced him to take odd jobs to raise the money that he needed to pay for his education and related expenses.[20]

Throughout his school days Kimathi was a top student, excelling in every study he undertook. He showed unusual ability in English language and poetry. He was an excellent debater. In an effort to raise money to pay for his education, Kimathi opened a night school at his home where he taught simple writing and reading skills to those who, for one reason or another, could not attend day school. Some of his students paid in cash, others paid in various forms of materials, such as foodstuffs which he sold to get some hard cash. All the proceeds went toward the cost of his own education. Kimathi's desire for education took him to Wandumbi Primary School, where he paid his expenses by selling tree seeds to the forest department that was located near his home. He collected the seeds from the Aberdare Forest during his spare time. By the time he completed his primary schooling, Kimathi had become better educated than most Africans of his day. He was therefore in a position to try to secure employment, unaware that the colonial conditions would not permit him to fulfill his quest for meaningful employment opportunity.

Kimathi held several unfulfilling positions, ranging from clerk to business ventures. Between 1944 and 1952 he worked in Nyeri, in the Aberdare Forest, and at Thompson's Falls. He then returned to teaching at his first school at Karunani. He succeeded in motivating his students by example of his own self-reliance, creativity, and determination. His students developed tremendous admiration for him. Before long Kimathi turned his anger for the problems he and other Africans were facing in their struggle for both education and meaningful opportunity in life toward the settlers. He began to see them as callous usurpers of their land and opportunity. He regarded them as a selfish group of people who denied them better opportunity than they were actually receiving to earn a decent income and get better education. He held them responsible for the misery he and his people endured in every way. He began to see more clearly that the Africans would always be oppressed by the colonial condition until they decided to fight to bring it to an end.[21]

Kimathi designed a strategy that he utilized to seek the elimination of all forms of injustice to in a way that no one had thought of in the past. He decided to write letters to some leading black people he thought were influential in the Pan-African movement, which had been founded in 1919. These leaders included Kwame Nkrumah of Ghana, W. E. B. Du

Bois of the United States, and George Padmore of Britain.[22] Kimathi's ability to articulate concepts of the Pan-African movement impressed those he communicated with as he came through as an uncompromising and dedicated individual whose commitment to end the colonial conditions was absolute. When he joined the Forty Group, the military wing of the defunct Kikuyu Cultural Association in 1947, Kimathi proved to be an effective leader and a powerful strategist. Settlers, including Blundell, feared him more than they feared other Mau Mau leaders. He revived the Forty Group and sharpened it into a formidable military force that sent many settlers away from their farms into urban areas during the height of the Mau Mau rebellion. Nairobi, Kisumu, and Nakuru were crowded with settler refugees.

In 1951 Kimathi was a rising star in the activities of the Kenya Africa Union, exerting leadership influence that elevated the consciousness among Africans as a group of people trying to carve a new identity for themselves for the future. In 1952 he was elected branch secretary of the KAU in the Thompson's Falls area. In October that year he was appointed chief administrator of the Mau Mau branch in the area. Immediately Kimathi launched a campaign to publicize the image of the Mau Mau and to portray its campaign as a struggle to end the colonial condition that had oppressed the Africans since 1895. In a countercampaign to discredit the Mau Mau and to portray it as nothing more than a terrorist organization run by a group of barbaric individuals with no cause, the colonial government characterized it as motivated only by a desire to eliminate all the white people from Kenya in order to return to traditions of the past that no longer had an relevance to conditions of life of the present. This is the position that well-informed individuals like Louis S. St Laurent rejected, because it did not make sense as Africans persistently argued that they were fighting against the oppressive policies of the colonial government, not against Western civilization.

The colonial government also argued that the Mau Mau suffered from a "mental illness resulting from Kikuyu inability to cope with Western civilization and development introduced by the colonial government."[23] Kimathi stressed the fact that the Mau Mau was not a terrorist organization, nor were its members mad people who killed indiscriminately. Rather, he argued, the guerrillas were freedom fighters who wanted to regain their land and freedom from colonial oppressors. He stressed the fact that the colonists had reduced Africans to the status of slavery in their own land. He also stressed the fact that in human history no group of people willingly submitted to colonial oppression and that the Africans must not be asked to be the first people to do so.

In 1954, when Itote was wounded and captured in an engagement, he tried to persuade Kimathi to end the fighting as a condition for starting negotiations with the colonial authorities. But Kimathi would have none of it. He also opposed any move that the colonial government made that fell short of turning the country and the government over to the Africans. He argued that Africans all over the continent were struggling for freedom from colonial rule and those in Kenya had an obligation to do the same. Because of his determination and uncompromising position, Kimathi became the major target of the colonial government forces. The colonial government also suspected him of complicity in the murder of Chief Nderi Mangombe of the Thengeu Village in Nyeri. On October 22, 1952, soon after the Mau Mau rebellion started, the colonial government made a concerted effort to capture Kimathi, hunting him like a dangerous animal. The decision of some Mau Mau leaders to cooperate with the colonial government created some confusion among the ranks of the fighters.

On October 21, 1956, deserted by many of his supporters and people at a critical point in the struggle and without food and little ammunition, Kimathi made a gallant effort to continue the war. However, he was severely wounded and captured. On November 19, 1956, when he was charged at the supreme court in Nyeri with being in unlawful possession of firearms and six rounds of ammunition, Kimathi was as defiant as ever. Responding to the charges he faced he said,

If fighting for our land and freedom is a crime, then we shall fight to the last drop of our blood. We shall never give up until we have driven away those foreign murderers from our beloved country. We reject colonialism in Kenya because it has turned us into slaves and beggars. I do not lead terrorists, I lead Africans who want their self-government and land back.[24]

On February 18, 1957, Kimathi was executed in prison in Nairobi. But his death fired up the determination of the Africans in the way Jomo Kenyatta had predicted. Bethwell A. Ogot concludes: "The greatest of the Mau Mau leaders, Dedan Kimathi, refused to accept defeat, and his name lives on as one of the greatest freedom fighters of Kenya."[25] Indeed, for example, the New Stanley Hotel, located in downtown Nairobi, where the author stayed several times while conducting research for this study, is located on Dedan Kimathi Street, a fitting tribute to the gallant fighter who refused to give up hope for his people.

The return of Jomo Kenyatta to Kenya in 1946, following years of educational safari in Britain, was an event that his fellow Kenyans celebrated with great enthusiasm. Like Kwame Nkrumah in Ghana and Benjamin Nnamdi Azikiwe and Tafawa Balewa in Nigeria, Kenyatta became an instant folk hero and legend upon his return to Kenya. There was something about these men that the colonial governments did not fully understand about Africans in general: after spending years studying in Europe they acquired new levels of ability to understand the thought processes of the white man and to express aspirations of their people in most effective ways. Their studying the novels of Charles Dickens, interpretation of history of Edward Gibbons, the social implications of the plays of William Shakespeare, the political philosophy of John Stuart Mill, Thomas Hobbes, and Benjamin Disraeli, all combined to place the emerging Africans in a position of understanding Western thought process far more than the Europeans would understand the African mental processes. In clearer terms than they did in the past, these African nationalists had learned about the strategies designed by the impoverished European masses during the turbulent period of the Industrial Revolution to improve their lot. They had read with enthusiasm the works of Karl Marx, Rudyard Kipling, Victor Hugo, and Jean-Paul Sartre. How could the colonial governments pretend that Africans did not have minds capable of restoring themselves?

Kenyatta was as brilliant a student as he was politically savvy in an era of a people struggling for political independence and development. Back in Kenya his people had learned about his role in the Fifth Pan African Congress. They had known about his years of struggle to gain an opportunity for meaningful education in the art of politics. They knew about the political philosophy he expressed in his book *On Facing Mount Kenya*, which critics concluded was brilliantly written. They had heard of his restless and imaginative mind creating and dreaming of conditions that never were. They knew of his simple and unassuming personality anchored in the sharpness of his mind and the unshaken strength of his character. They knew of his ability to articulate issues in a composite fragile colonial environment in which his mind was cast. Such was the character of a man whose vision of his country and people transformed a basic thought process into action. An African graduate student from Kenya said in 1991 about Kenyatta:

In many ways Jomo Kenyatta was the African Bobby Kennedy of 1946. He saw some Africans viewing the colonial conditions as they were and asking why. But he dreamed of conditions that never were and asked why not.[26] Indeed, Kenyatta's mind was a bustling creature of enthusiasm. It was revolutionary to the core. It enabled him to grasp the adverse character of the colonial system and the need to end it without further delay. The African people listened to his message and supported him in giving it a new meaning. His dedication to the restoration of the African personality manifested the quality of the African mind at its very best.[27]

Martin Meredith agrees with this assessment of Kenyatta when he writes, "His life abroad, the knowledge and the experience he had gained of British politics had earned him great prestige and his return home now aroused a sense of great expectation. The nationalist campaigns he had waged abroad he was now bringing home to Kenya."[28]

As Kenyatta arrived back in Kenya, huge crowds of Africans came to see and greet him. In Mombasa the harbor was packed with Africans, and porters crowded around him. The harbor security system had a difficult time trying to control the crowds. During his train journey to Nairobi huge crowds waited to catch a glimpse of the man who symbolized everything they had dreamed of. As soon as he arrived in Nairobi, crowds carried him shoulder high as the people cheered and roared their acceptance of their folk hero. Was Kenyatta larger than life? No, he had a mind and ability to grasp the reality of things that never were and helped to ask why not. For Kenya this was a new day, the coming of age of the Africans in a way the colonial government, led by the arrogant and flamboyant Philip E. Mitchell, could not fully understand. The African world and the colonial world that had engulfed the African existence since 1895 were about to collide with such a force that a new world would emerge to give new meaning to the rise of African nationalism.

Wishing to determine his appropriate role in shaping the political development and mapping out the course to independence, Kenyatta wasted no time in seeking a meeting with Mitchell. That Mitchell was highly regarded at the Colonial Office at Whitehall in London raised fundamental questions in the minds of the Africans about the character of the colonial mind itself. Since 1944 Mitchell's policy and approach to the problems of colonial administration in Kenya had endeared him to his superiors as a man whose views and advice received more weight than those of any other colonial official. With a sense of his popularity, authority, and claimed knowledge of the Africans, Mitchell decided to hold the meeting with Kenyatta under the glare of enormous publicity both in Kenya and in Britain. Mitchell's main purpose was to reduce Kenyatta's ego to size and to remind him of his real place within the colonial society. Arrogant and sure of himself, Mitchell had no respect for Kenyatta, simply because he was returning home from Britain. Mitchell figured that if he could reduce Kenyatta's ego to the level of thinking no higher than that of other Africans, then he would stand out as a giant in the history of British colonial Africa as the man who demonstrated to the Africans that they were, indeed, inferior to the white man. He would be disappointed. However, the battle lines were being drawn for one of the most serious conflicts between the Africans and the colonial government ever to ensue.

Kenyatta, conscious of the availability of a rare opportunity to demonstrate the high quality of the African mind, was equally determined to dispel both the myth and the cultural and colonial arrogance that Mitchell represented and were behavior patterns so typical of colonial officials all over Africa. That Mitchell had arrived to assume his office as governor of Kenya in 1944, two years before Kenyatta, gave him no advantage in understanding the effect the surging African mind was having on the character of the colonial society. Mitchell was surprised to discover that Kenyatta demonstrated not only the brilliance, but also clearly articulated positions on pertinent issues such as African representation in the legislature, setting a specific agenda to ensure the political advancement of the Africans, the question of land distribution, especially relocating some Africans back to the fertile central highlands from which they were evicted in 1904, and a timetable to independence. For Mitchell to listen to an African he considered inferior espouse a political philosophy similar to that of Edmund Burke constituted a nightmare, an illusion that the colonial government would not be able to grasp. Mitchell was infuriated, not by Kenyatta's understanding of the issues, but by the brilliance that he demonstrated.

The drama of conflict between the Africans and the colonial authorities took a perilous turn in the events that followed. That Mitchell regarded the position and views of the African nationalists as "an emotional movement, rather than a result of rational thought process,"[29] reflected his failure to measure up to the level of understanding of the Africans. This accentuated differences of opinion about national policy. Mitchell's attitude and response also demonstrated the colonial culture of ignorance as an insult to the African intellect. This widened the chasm between the two sides instead of narrowing it so that it could be bridged. Such is the character of the colonial system anywhere: the colonizer refuses to understand the plight of the colonized. Mitchell's Victorian views of the African mind did not play well in the forthcoming struggle of wills between the colonial mind and the African mind. Given the nature of this irreconcilable difference, the meeting between Mitchell and Kenyatta achieved nothing except to strengthen their respective positions—Kenyatta arguing that Africans were capable of assuming national responsibility outside the control of the colonial system, and Mitchell holding on to his views that Africans were incapable of assuming such a responsibility because they did not have a recognized civilization. What was the world to make out this deadlock of minds?

These were the circumstances that invoked the resentment and indignation as a reaction among the Africans, especially those of the Kikuyu tribe, to which Kenyatta belonged, who were forcibly removed from the fertile central highlands to make room for settler farmers. Although a sense of guilt among some of these farmers compelled them to treat their African servants with a paternal attitude, such as Blundell did, to the Africans this attitude represented scorn and contempt of their potential and an insult to their ability to conceptualize issues of human interaction. Within a few years, the Kikuyu would play a decisive role in the drama of the conflict to follow. The Africans all over Kenya received Mitchell's position that the Africans must not be allowed to reclaim the central highlands with derision, suggesting the gathering of the clouds of that conflict. They also regarded with contempt any suggestion that the white man should retain possession of the best land in the country.

Jomo Kenyatta was thrust into this kind of political setting where compromise and understanding were virtually impossible. For him, maintaining the political status quo represented a painful reminder of what things once were. As a boy he had watched the white man usurp the land of his ancestors and forced him and his family to relocate in desolate places. The colonial entrepreneurs also forced the Africans to work for them to ensure their own socioeconomic and political security. He had watched the white man make fun of his culture and society and castigated them in such a manner that the vast majority of Africans began to doubt their own abilities. Kenyatta was determined to turn things around to revitalize the African mind engulfed by the colonial conditions so that it would restore itself to the position of greatness similar to that prior to 1895. Like Nkrumah, Kenyatta felt that these principles could not be compromised. He could not digress from the course that he had set for his people.

In 1949 a group of settler politicians, sensing what was likely to happen in the near future, published the *Kenya Plan*, which affirmed the presumed inferiority of the African mind. The group went on to add a clause that shattered any hope of racial cooperation:

Any attempt to hand over political power to an immature race must be resisted. To the Africans we offer sympathetic tutelage and guidance because they have a mind still to be developed. In time they will participate in government and in the affairs of the country. The white race is here to stay and other races must accept this premise with all that it implies.[30]

From this Victorian attitude, increasingly political restrictions and socioeconomic hardships were imposed on the Africans. Agricultural production was controlled to allow white farmers to sell their produce without any competition. Africans were required to carry identification cards they considered a symbol of colonial oppression. It is one of the most puzzling aspects of colonialism to think that the culture of ignorance became persistently a major influential factor of the colonizer. Since the end the Second World War the white man had seen activity surrounding the political thought process among Africans as coming from a group of primitive people, and totally refused to accept or acknowledge the fact that the African mind had reached a level of development unequaled by that of any other period in history. There is no question that this culture of ignorance became a major cause of conflict between the colonial governments and the Africans, and events in Kenya would substantiate this conclusion.

In this increasing climate of conflict and the refusal of the colonial government to acknowledge the coming of age of the African mind lay the elements that manifested Kenyatta's call for political action to realize the fact that the African mind had finally reached a new level of maturity. He reactivated the faltering Kenya African Union (KAU) originally formed in 1944, but which, without proper leadership and activity because nearly 8,000 Africans were participating in the war, lacked an effective political agenda to convince the colonial government that it must be taken seriously. This is what Mitchell had in mind when he suggested just before he retired in 1952 that the Africans were incapable of initiating an action based on rational planning independent of the influence of the white man. A parting of the minds had been reached and everything pointed to a protracted struggle of wills. This was the setting in which Kenyatta and other African nationalists rose to the occasion to play a decisive role in this unprecedented conflict of the minds.

As thousands of Africans returned home at the conclusion of the war in 1945, they were faced with enormous socioeconomic and political problems that were worse than before the war. Nairobi was crowded with thousands of unemployed Africans, including those who were returning from the war, as they watched their former white comrades assume positions of power. In July 1951 Eliud Mathu sent an urgent memo to Mitchell, warning of an impending major national confrontation between the Africans and the government unless Mitchell did something soon to resolve the causes of discontent among the Africans. In characteristic fashion Mitchell dismissed the warning, arguing that the Africans had neither the will nor the capability to wage a confrontation along the lines Mathu suggested in his memo. This allowed the Mau Mau leaders to plan their strategy for action more effectively. As soon as the Mau Mau rebellion started, Kenyatta was arrested and put on trial on December 3, 1952. Although he was defended by a team of legal experts led by the eminent British jurist, D. N. Pritt, Q. C., a former member of the British Parliament, who argued that Kenyatta and his four associates were being tried for their political activity and nationalism,[31] Kenyatta was found guilty and sentenced to imprisonment with seven years of hard labor. He was released in 1962 just in time to assume leadership of the preindependence government.

BLUNDELL'S RESPONSE AND THE NATURE OF HIS RELATIONS WITH AFRICANS

Although Blundell and other settlers had no communication with Africans at the beginning of the Mau Mau rebellion, they simply could not ignore their determination to bring the colonial condition to an end. While the settlers launched a campaign to discredit them as a group of people without a cause, they acknowledged their belief in seeking to fulfill their goals. While the settlers characterized the Mau Mau leaders as barbaric and uncivilized, they recognized the strength of their conviction in what they were seeking to accomplish. While the settlers minimized the military knowledge of the Mau Mau leaders, they realized that their courage could be utilized to influence new directions of racial relations in the post-Mau Mau period. While the settlers argued that the Africans had no intellect equal to that of the white man, they readily accepted the reality that the Africans had intellectual potential that would become the basis of national leadership in the future.

These were the considerations that Blundell later used to admit that

the forest fighters were courageous, tenacious and suffered immense hardships for the cause they believed in. The whole movement was well organized, had the benefit of several years of secret planning, and was divided into the active wing in the in the forest and passive wing in towns and villages which supplied information, recruits, supplies, and firearms.[32]

Indeed, the Mau Mau achieved military success such that colonial forces were taken by total surprise when the guerrillas captured offices and seized guns and ammunition with relative ease. Blundell concluded that it was a mystery why the Mau Mau guerrillas elected not to disrupt the colonial government itself at the time they were much stronger than it was. This may indicate what the Mau Mau leaders had argued from the beginning: that the Africans were fighting against the injustice of the colonial system, not Western civilization

The knowledge that the Mau Mau guerrillas had about the vulnerability of the colonial government was also the reality that forced the settlers, soon after the rebellion started, to seek the assistance of Waruhiu Itote in trying to initiate negotiations with the Mau Mau leaders. But, as Dedan Kimathi said in response, at that time the only condition the Mau Mau leaders would observe as terms of the cease-fire was for the colonial government to turn over the government to the Africans.[33] Because the colonial government was unwilling to do this, it created a major problem for the future. Blundell and other settlers knew that sooner than later they would have to concede to the demands of the Africans and concluded that it was better to start negotiating with the Africans under conditions of conflict than to wait to do so later, when the Africans would be in a much stronger position reinforced by the increase in consciousness throughout the continent.

The increasing tension between the Africans and the colonial government coincided with the elections in Britain in 1951 from which Winston

Churchill, the leader of the Conservative Party, defeated Clement R. Attlee, leader of the Labour Party, the man who had defeated him 1945. As soon as he assumed the office of prime minister Churchill named Oliver Lyttleton secretary of state for the colonies. Lyttleton had impressive credentials. He served as president of the British Board of Trade from 1940 to 1941, and chairman of Associated Electrical Industries from 1945 to 1951. He had the reputation of making radical decisions in situations that were difficult or controversial. In appointing Lyttleton to the Colonial Office Churchill was aware of his part in the Atlantic Charter of August 1941.

That Churchill did not feel bound by the pledge he made in the charter created serious problems for both Lyttleton and his successor, Alan Lennox-Boyd, as they tried to wrestle with constitutional issues relative to colonial policy following the end of the war. Also in 1951 the first colony under British rule, the Gold Coast (Ghana), was about to have its first African leader, Kwame Nkrumah. Although in theory the British stipulated different conditions for different colonies to imply that one was ready for independence while the other was not at any one given time, the Colonial Office had to observe consistency in the application of its policy in all its colonies. By making it possible for the Gold Coast to have an African government, Britain was implying that all its colonies in Africa would have African governments within a reasonable period of time. As leader of the settler community in Kenya, Blundell was quite aware of this development. He also knew that although in 1952 Kenya was in the grip of the Mau Mau rebellion, there was need to initiate dialogue with the Africans to ensure a stable future for the settlers. The major consideration he took into account was that while the governor served only a limited term of office, he would return to Britain while the settlers were permanent residents of Kenya.

Unknown to the settler community, Lyttleton went to work as soon as he was appointed. Through intermediaries he established contact with the African representatives for purposes of working out a new constitution that would start the process to independence. The departure from Kenya of Philip E. Mitchell in 1952 gave Lyttleton the opportunity he needed to carry out his agenda. Although Lyttleton and Evelyn Baring, Mitchell's successor, had mutual respect for each other, Lyttleton kept the core of his plan from Baring, fearing that he would expose it before details were developed. For the next three years Lyttleton diligently worked on a new constitution that he intended to set Kenya on the road to rapid change. From 1952 to 1954 settlers thought that Lyttleton had no policy for Kenya.[34]

In an effort to carry out his responsibility as leader of the settler community, Blundell tried to obtain all relevant information on what was happening in and about Kenya. He was so frustrated by Lyttleton's secrecy that he simply did not know what was happening and so did not know how to respond. In an effort to find out what was going on in the Colonial Office, Blundell tried to approach Baring but found him just as uninformed as the settler community. He concluded that Baring knew some things he did not want to let him know about. Humphrey Slade, an associate of Blundell's and a member of the legislative council, was so upset with Baring's attitude that he suggested to Lyttleton to remove him from the war council. Blundell presented the proposal to Lyttleton, "but it was obviously one which no Secretary of State could accept."[35] What was the purpose of making a suggestion he knew would be rejected? Blundell must have known that the governor was the top administrative officer of any colonial system and that the secretary of state for the colonies was above him. He and Slade made the suggestion out of frustration

Something strange happened in this saga of colonial political maneuvering. In 1952, as soon as the settlers knew that Lyttleton was working behind the scenes with Africans to introduce a new constitution for Kenya, Slade and Blundell made a surprise move to establish contact with what they regarded as moderate Africans. These included Daniel arap Moi, Tom Mboya, James Gichuru, Ronald Ngala, and Mbiyu Koinange. There were two reasons for this move. The first was to convince the British government, especially Lyttleton, that in the midst of the Mau Mau rebellion settlers and Africans would work together for the common good of the country.

The second reason for the move was convince the public that whatever plan Lyttleton developed for the future of Kenya, he could not do so without the involvement of the people of Kenya as a whole, and that any plan the secretary of state for the colonies developed must have its origin in Kenya. Slade and Blundell did their best to take advantage of this propaganda ploy to enhance their own political fortunes. But in 1953 they found out that Lyttleton was his own man and he would not be so easily manipulated into doing other than what his office demanded. It turned out that the African leaders to whom Slade and Blundell turned in order to stage a political "coup" against Lyttleton placed their confidence in him more than in them. For both men this was an embarrassing experience in their effort to establish functional relations with Africans. It was apparent that the move was made out desperation to have some influence on the course of developments in Kenya. But both men also knew that by this time the settler community was steadily losing the influence that its members might have had in the past.

During his term of office Lyttleton made three visits to Kenya. The last visit was in March 1954. As soon as he returned to London he informed the settlers in Kenya of his intent to introduce a new constitution for Kenya that paved the way for further constitutional development that eventually led to independence. During the three visits Lyttleton presented the key components to the settlers only for their information. For the first time a British government official indicated that from this point on any plan for the future of Kenya would not be subject to veto by the settler minority community, but take the interests of the African majority into account. Representing the settler community Blundell expressed surprise to hear Lyttleton say this. Blundell, who had an opportunity to discuss the plan with Lyttleton later, recalled Lyttleton's unwillingness to discuss details of the plan:

At my first meeting with Oliver Lyttleton we discussed the views and wishes of the European elected members on the issue of constitutional advance and their desire for greater part in the activities of the government. Lyttleton was cautious and did not want to commit himself to any changes during the emergency situation. He made it quite clear that any constitutional development in the future could not be built on a small European minority only, but would have to embrace all races.[36]

At a meeting that was held between him and Blundell, Slade, and Wilfrid B. Havelock,[37] Lyttleton advised the settler community to take the Africans into their confidence, saying that someday they will run the government. For the first time the settler community came face to face with the reality that Britain intended to grant independence to Kenya under African majority government. Therefore what appeared to be a surprise move made by Blundell and Slade to establish contact with moderate Africans was, in fact, their acceptance of the suggestion that Lyttleton made. Blundell, Slade, and Havelock seemed to understand the suggestion differently from the manner in which Lyttleton had made it. Said Blundell, "He (Lyttleton) had suggested that after the emergency greater local responsibility might be achieved by an existence of the membership system, but with the individuals concerned answerable as ministers to the electorate which should be based on elective franchise."[38] But the franchise that Lyttleton was talking about was broad enough to give the Africans a decisive majority, and, thus, the government. Blundell, Slade, and Havelock thought that widening the franchise would allow the settler legislative council more autonomy.

Given the terms that Britain was outlining for the independence of Ghana in 1957, just three years away, it was unlikely that Lyttleton would even consider granting autonomy to Kenya on terms decidedly favorable to settlers, with a clear knowledge that the Mau Mau rebellion was partly caused by the unrepresentative character of the colonial government. It is quite possible that Blundell, Slade, and Havelock heard from Lyttleton what they wanted to hear in what he said in his suggestion. Throughout colonial Africa misunderstanding between British principles and settler wishes became a serious problem in communication between the two sides. It was for this reason that Lyttleton decided to put a quick end to the speculation among settlers of what he was going to do by announcing in 1954 that there would be a new constitution for Kenya different from any that had been worked out in the past.

After a few preliminaries Lyttleton announced a new constitution for Kenya that he knew would be opposed by both the settlers, because it went too far in taking away their political power and by the Africans, because it did not go far enough in recognizing their legitimate demands for more political power. This is why Lyttleton refused to have the new constitutional proposal subjected to veto by either group The Lyttleton constitution, as it was known, was indeed radical in its clauses. It provided for a multiracial principle. It established a council of ministers, to whom were transferred most of the functions of the executive powers. All ministers were to be members of the executive council together with three additional nominated members, of whom two were to be Africans and one an Arab. The powers of the governor remained unchanged,[39] but the composition of the council of ministers was three settlers, two Asians, and two Africans. This was the first time in the history of Kenya that Africans and Asians were assigned to the executive council by constitutional clauses.[40]

Blundell did not mind that the Africans received two members to represent them on the executive council. This was a big gain since only one had served since 1944, when Harry Thuku was nominated to the legislative council. Blundell's reaction was: "The Africans had only one minister, B. A. Ohange, an arrangement which did not truly represent their interests, and also was unfair to Ohange himself as he had no one from his culture with whom to discuss cabinet matters."[41] As long as the constitution was put into effect, Lyttleton did not mind about Blundell taking credit for it for publicity of his own. The constitution was designed to last until 1960, when it would be reviewed. However, the eight African members of the legislative council that were elected on the new franchise in 1957 refused to cooperate because they thought it was unfair as Blundell had indicated.

Blundell was therefore pleased to know that the Africans shared his views of the Lyttleton constitution. Among these eight Africans there were four who were quite strong in their belief that the new constitution was unfair: Ronald Ngala, Daniel arap Moi, Masinde Muliro, and Oginga Odinga. They directed the African response to Lyttleton's initiative and settler reaction. All eight were quite active in nationalistic politics. Blundell, Slade, and Havelock did not quite know how to approach them in order to have meaningful relations with them in terms of Lyttleton's advice.

In 1954, believing that he had made a major contribution in the constitutional development of Kenya, Lyttleton resigned to chair the British Associated Electrical Industries, a position he held until 1963. Churchill named as his successor Alan Lennox-Boyd, a technocrat and savvy politician who had served in Churchill's administration as minister of transport and civil aviation from 1952 to 1954. In 1954 Churchill appointed him secretary of state for the colonies. Lennox-Boyd was known for his forthrightness, honesty, and candor in dealing with critical issues. When Churchill retired in 1955 he was succeeded by Anthony Eden as prime minister. The following year, Eden was faced with a major crisis when Gamal Abdel Nasser, president of Egypt since 1952, seized power in a coup that overthrew King Farouk. Nasser seized the Suez Canal, opened in 1869, and nationalized it. Eden asked Lennox-Boyd to handle the delicate matter of the constitution for Kenya while he was attending to the crisis of the Suez Canal.[42]

The British government did not want change of leadership from Churchill to Eden and the crisis over the Suez Canal to delay the constitutional development for Kenya that Oliver Lyttleton had initiated. However, faced with an international opposition to possible hostile recapture of the Suez Canal, Eden was forced to resign in 1957 and was succeeded by Harold Macmillan, who served as prime minister until 1963. Therefore as much as Lennox-Boyd wished to maintain the momentum that Lyttleton had built, delay became inevitable because he wanted to make sure that he had Macmillan's total support.[43]

The knowledge that the Africans, including the eight that were elected to the legislative council in 1957 as a result of the Lyttleton constitution, were unhappy gave Lennox-Boyd an opportunity to introduce his own constitution. In 1958 he was instrumental in passing the Kenya Constitution Order-in-Council, in order to avoid lengthy discussions with both Africans and settlers of provisions of the new constitution he was working on and wished to introduce as soon as possible. Suddenly in that year, when he thought all the elements were in place, Lennox-Boyd imposed his own constitution. The Lennox-Boyd constitution increased the number of elected Africans in the legislative council from eight to 14. This was equal to the number of elected settlers. Although this latest constitution did not reflect the principle of majority, it went much further than any previous constitution. Again, the settler community thought that the constitution had gone too far in giving the Africans more seats than they had ever had. But the Africans themselves felt that the principle of majority rule should have been honored.

The Lennox-Boyd constitution also created a category of elected members known as especially elected members. Under this category four members were Africans, four were settlers, and four were Asians including Arabs. The third clause was that a council of state consisting of a chairman and ten members appointed by the governor was established to protect the racial communities against discriminatory legislation. Its major function was to study bills to ensure that none was discriminatory. Blundell's response to the Lennox-Boyd constitution came in 1957, a year before it was introduced. He felt that the Lennox-Boyd "no longer reflected the agreed representation in the legislative council"[44] because, he concluded, he thought that the principle of majority rule must prevail without any safeguards for settlers. Blundell also spoke for the settlers when he argued that they were disturbed by the piecemeal erosion of the existing position which disregarded the need to ensure the position of minority settlers and individual rights and the need to move away from racial representation.

There is something that one needs to understand about how Blundell reacted to developments in Kenya, beginning with the Lyttleton initiatives. When he spoke as a representative of the settler community he said what he knew they wanted him to say. But when he spoke as an individual he seemed to be free to express his true feelings. For example, on September 12, 1957, during a visit to Britain, Blundell spoke as an individual to the English Speaking Union in Edinburgh:

It is the fashion to say in some quarters that white civilization must be preserved in Africa and the implication is that only white people can preserve that civilization. Well, I do not believe it for one moment. I think that the real challenge to us is how to give Africans conviction and force to carry forward our own ideas and our civilization And not to be solely dependent upon us to carry it forward for them. Unless we can do this, unless the African himself can carry forward the conviction that what we have to offer him is a real way of life, something really to work for, then I believe that we have lost the battle for the continent of Africa.[45]

This is the Michael Blundell the Africans had come to know over the years, not the one the settlers wish to have speak on their behalf. Because he was a political figure, Blundell often said some things he did not believe in. Because the increased number of elected Africans represented a basic change in the structure of political representation in Kenya, Blundell saw an opportunity for settlers and Africans to cooperate in building a country for the future. He was convinced that the changed political circumstances allowed the settler community in Kenya to accept the inevitability of an African government in the very near future

Blundell felt that instead of fighting against trends and opposing British policy, settlers must recognize that because they could not stop change, they must make sure to adjust their political objectives and strategy. In speeches to the settler community Blundell warned in 1957, "We cannot avoid the African majority government and therefore our policy should simply and clearly be designed to see that this great mass of people is as educated as possible. This can be accomplished by the removal of barriers and discrimination between us while we still have the protection of the British colonial rule."[46] In October 1959 Lennox-Boyd was succeeded by Iain N. Macleod, who served until 1961. Macleod was a man far more radical and impatient for rapid progress toward the achievement of independence in colonial Africa than any of his predecessors. Harold Macmillan, the man who appointed Macleod, was just as radical and impatient.

Speaking on February 3, 1960, to the Joint Session of the South African Parliament in Cape Town, the legislative capital city of the citadel of the notorious policy of apartheid, Macmillan warned of the consequences of refusing to acknowledge the rise of the African mind and the need to accommodate it, saying "the wind of change is blowing through the continent of Africa. Whether we like it or not, the growth of nationalistic consciousness is a political factor and we must accept it as a fact. Our national policy must take account of it."[47]

With this position the British government had finally come to acknowledge the coming of age of the Africans and was on its way to dismantle its colonial empire in Africa. In the House of Commons Fenner Brockway, James Callaghan, Harold Wilson, and Dennis Healey, all members of the Labour Party, were highly critical of what they regarded as delaying tactics in seeking solutions to the crisis in Kenya and in moving toward independence. In November 1959 Macleod ordered the colonial government to end the state of emergency in order to convene a new constitutional conference that the Africans had demanded. Although Blundell did not like the pace with which Macleod was moving, he came to recognize the inevitable and changed tactics, which implied that he supported the new British initiative.

Two conferences were held at Lancaster House in London in 1960 and 1962 to work out details of the independence constitution. The delegates to the Lancaster House conference fell into three groups: the Africans led by Ronald Ngala and Tom Mboya, the United Group led by Puck Briggs, and the New Kenya Group led by Michael Blundell. At that point Blundell, Slade, and Havelock, representing the settler interests, decided to seek active relations with the Africans. This is why Blundell and his group were not opposed to the African demands for independence under the principle of majority rule. But Briggs and his United Group were opposed to such a move. After one month Macleod made his move. The legislative council was to have 65 elected members. Of these, 53 were to be elected on a common voters roll giving the Africans the majority they had always argued in favor of. Kenya was now set for independence. The elements were in place, the climate was right. The Africans expected it.

SUMMARY AND CONCLUSION

Two major events have been presented in this chapter as being influential to the kind of relations that Blundell had with Africans to indicate how they shaped developments that finally led to independence for Kenya in December 1963. The first event was the Lennox-Boyd constitution of 1958. From the position that he adopted in 1957 that the settlers could not prevent the advent of an African majority government, Blundell saw the need to reach out to the Africans in order to structure new relations with them as a condition of settler security in the future. It was this constitution that finally convinced the settlers that Britain had decided to move rapidly along the road to granting independence to Kenya. After the Lyttleton constitution was introduced, settlers still hoped that Kenya would gain autonomy under their control. But the Lennox-Boyd constitution put an end to that hope. Instead Lyttleton advised them to seek better relations with Africans to ensure their own future in the country. Blundell knew that this was the wisest course of action to take.

The second event that had a profound impact on Blundell's relations with Africans was the naming of Iain N. Macleod as secretary of state for the colonies by Harold Macmillan in 1959. Both men had long come to believe that Britain must move rapidly to decolonize its African empire. The convening of the second Lancaster House conference in 1962 left no room for doubt that Kenya was heading toward independence under an African government. As liberal as he was, Blundell found Macleod too radical for his liking and took the occasion to tell him so.[48] A letter that Blundell wrote on February 29, 1960, to Roy Welensky, the emotional and erratic prime minister of the ill-fated Federation of Rhodesia and Nyasaland, shows the extent of his distrust of Macleod. Welensky had written to Blundell on January 8, 1960, asking for his advice on how to deal with Macleod. Blundell's advice was that Macleod "is an aggressive, tough, and ruthless character, very ambitious with a first class brain and very close to his prime minister. As far as you are concerned I would not trust him an inch."[49] But in following Blundell's advice, Welensky made such major errors in his attitude and behavior toward Macleod that Britain dissolved the federation in December 1963, two weeks after Kenya had gained independence.

It is important to remember that in seeking to improve relations with Africans, especially toward the end of the colonial rule of Kenya, Blundell was influenced by three major factors. The first was that he had to respect British policy and principles. No colonial leader who defied British policy and principles succeeded in his own action. Both Roy Welensky and Ian D. Smith found this the hard way. They lost everything they were fighting for. The second factor is that because Blundell represented settler interests, he needed to respect their views only to a certain extent. But since Blundell and his fellow settlers did not often agree on policy, he refrained from speaking on their behalf as time went on. The third factor was his own belief system. For quite some time Blundell operated by the liberal traditions that had been part of his upbringing. However, he appears to have abandoned these traditions during the Mau Mau rebellion, making it very difficult to have meaningful relations with Africans for the good of the future of Kenya. But after the Lyttleton constitution was introduced, he decided to revive his old liberal values to ensure that settlers had a meaningful future in Kenya.

NOTES

1. The title of the book comes from lines by William Shakespeare's *Henry IV*, "We shall be winnowed with so rough a wind that even our corn shall seem as light as chaff and good from bad find no partition."

2. Robert B. Edgerton, *Mau Mau: An African Crucible* (New York: The Free Press, 1989), p. 107.

3. Ibid., p. 105.

4. Ibid., p. 106.

5. Ibid., p. 108.

6. Tabitha Kanogo, *Makers of History: Dedan Kimathi* (Nairobi: East African Educational Publishers, 1992), p. 1.

7. Ibid., p. 2.

8. Ibid., p. 1.

9. In a letter dated March 30, 1962, Blundell expressed disagreement with Delamere's position of the question of land distribution. In this letter he argued that the land that settlers were vacating to return to Britain must be given back to the Africans.

10. Lord Delamere, during presentation of evidence before the Native Labor Commission, 1912–1913. Kenya National Archives.

11. Kanogo, *Makers of History: Dedan Kimathi*, p. 3.

12. The Atlantic Charter was issued in order to attract African volunteers to join the Allied forces against the Axis powers. The Africans understood it as a solemn promise to eliminate or to ease the colonial condition that had oppressed them for so long.

13. Bethwell A. Ogot, *Historical Dictionary of Kenya* (London: The Scarecrow Press, 1981), p. 80.

14. Jeremy Murphy-Brown, *Kenyatta* (London: George Allen and Unwin, 1979), p. 245.

15. Ibid., p. 246.

16. Kenyatta had read about L'Ouverture during his studies in London. C. L. James's book, *Black Jocobians*, appeared on the dust coat of the first edition of *Facing Mount Kenya* (Nairobi: Kenwey Publications, 1938). James, who met Kenyatta in London, had as profound an influence on Kenyatta as his book. The two men remained close friends for the rest of their lives.

17. In 1859 Charles Dickens published his classic book, *A Tale of Two Cities*, in

which he described the contradiction in his society, saying "It was the best of times, it was the worst of times. We had every thing before us, we had nothing before us. We were all going direct to heaven, we were all going direct the other way."

18. Murphy-Brown, *Kenyatta*, p. 246.
19. Ogot, *Historical Dictionary of Kenya*, p. 80.
20. Kanogo, *Makers of History: Dedan Kimathi*, p. 9.
21. Ibid., p. 10.
22. Ibid., p. 19.
23. Ibid., p. 23.
24. Ibid., p. iii.
25. Ogot, *Historical Dictionary of Kenya*, p. 107.
26. In 1968, Bobby Kennedy, then U.S. Senator from New York, during a campaign for president of the United States, made the now-famous remark, "Some people see things as they are and ask why. I dream of things that never were and ask why not." Kennedy was killed in Los Angeles in June of that year.
27. An African graduate student from Kenya attending Northern Arizona University, during an interview with the author in Flagstaff, Arizona, September 3, 1991.
28. Martin Meredith, *The First Dance of Freedom: Black Africa in the Post-War Era* (New York: Harper and Row, 1984), p. 53.
29. Ibid., p. 54.
30. Embassy of Kenya, in response to the author's request, Memo, Ref. Row/Edu/5/Vol. 25, July 16, 1991.
31. Wunyabari O. Maloba, *Mau Mau and Kenya: An Analysis of a Peasant Revolt* (Bloomington: Indiana University Press, 1993), p. 99.
32. Michael Blundell, *A Love Affair with the Sun* (Nairobi: Kenway Publications, 1994), p. 102.
33. Kanogo, *Makers of History: Dedan Kimathi*, p. 24.
34. Michael Blundell, *So Rough a Wind* (London: Weidenfeld and Nicholson, 1964), p. 160.
35. Ibid., p. 151.
36. Ibid., p. 139.
37. Sir Wilfrid B. Havelock was a member of the legislative council from 1947 to 1963. He served as chairman of the elected settler members of the legislative council from 1950 to 1954, minister of local government from 1954 to 1961, and minister of agriculture from 1961 to 1963. Like Blundell, Havelock was an influential settler politician among settlers but had no meaningful relations with Africans. In 1954 Lyttleton did not have any respect for any settler politician who failed to develop relations with Africans. That is why he tried to persuade these three politicians to make a fresh start in developing such relations for the good of the settler community in the future.
38. Blundell, *So Rough a Wind*, p. 139.
39. The British government knew that with steady progress toward independence the position of the governor became irrelevant. It was therefore not necessary to address it in the new constitution.
40. Ogot, *Historical Dictionary of Kenya*, p. 126.

41. Blundell, *A Love Affair with the Sun*, p. 105.

42. History seems to indicate that Eden was preparing to retake the Suez Canal by military force, but U.S. President Dwight David Eisenhower intervened on behalf of a peaceful resolution.

43. This means that Lennox-Boyd served under three Conservative administrations under the leadership of Winston Churchill, Anthony Eden, and Harold Macmillan.

44. Blundell, *So Rough a Wind*, p. 241.

45. Ibid., p. 242.

46. Ibid., p. 246.

47. Harold Macmillan, "Commonwealth Independence and Interdependence," an address to the Joint Session of the South African Parliament, Cape Town, February 3, 1960.

48. The letters Blundell wrote to Macleod on August 24, 1960, and January 26, 1961, blame him for the rapid pace of events toward independence and for the loss of confidence among settlers in the future. Macleod ignored both letters.

49. Michael Blundell, letter to Roy Welensky, February 29, 1960. See Blundell, *Love Affair with the Sun*, p. 207.

8

Michael Blundell and Garfield Todd as the Last British Liberals in Africa: Summary, Conclusion, and Implications

> There is no doubt that the younger settlers who had fought in the war with the African had an entirely different outlook on African political advance and the African himself from those who had remained behind and were still cocooned in the old colonial image.
> —Michael Blundell, 1964

> If we keep off the rolls our 6,000 Africans with ten years of education we would be so betraying the spirit of Rhodes that I would not continue to lead my party.
> —Garfield Todd, 1957
> [cited in Blake, 1978]

BLUNDELL AND TODD IN HISTORICAL PERSPECTIVE

This book has presented materials concerning the roles that Michael Blundell and Garfield Todd played in the political transformation of Kenya and Zimbabwe, respectively. When Blundell arrived in Kenya in 1925, the administration of Robert Coryndon as governor was coming to an end, and that of Edward Grigg was just beginning. Grigg came face to face with Harry Thuku, an intelligent and powerful African political leader who gave the Africans a new level of self-pride and the Kikuyu a new sense of collective identity. Bethwell A. Ogot concludes that when the East African Association was formed in July 1921, Thuku was a natural choice as its president.¹ Thuku was an articulate African whose own sense of destiny was unmarred by the corruptive influences of the colonial society. Blundell was introduced to this high-level intellect of the world of Harry Thuku in a way that shaped his own attitude toward Africans in general coming from opposite ends of the European perspective of the Africans.

Grigg and Blundell found themselves at odds on how to approach the influence that Thuku was exerting on the awakening of African consciousness cast in colonial settings.² As a candidate for governor Grigg had impressive credentials. He was a disciple of the charismatic Lord Milner, who was himself a graduate of the Asquith-Lloyd George school of thought. After serving on the staff of *The Times* from 1903 to 1910, Grigg served in the British Parliament as a member of the Liberal Party. His contribution to parliamentary debate and general performance greatly contributed to the high reputation of the quality of leadership of the Liberal Party.³ He was one of those who learned early the value of service to the people as a cornerstone of national development and greatness.

When Coryndon retired, Grigg was a natural choice to succeed him. He accepted his appointment with an image of a rising star within the hierarchy of the Liberal Party. On arriving in Kenya Grigg was unaware that he would soon come into conflict with a rising African star in the name of Harry Thuku. As a high-level colonial official Grigg also compromised his liberal views in order to give the impression of an authority who knew what he was asked to do to run an efficient system of government. In 1926 he and Thuku were each trying to assert his influence in a way that showed that they had an ego larger than themselves. The demands of his office forced Grigg to assert his superiority over Thuku. Grigg remembered that he was appointed to bring about closer union between Uganda, Tanganyika, and Kenya, three British colonies that were vital to the sustenance of British interests in East Africa.⁴ Grigg failed partly because of opposition from Donald Cameron, then governor of Tanganyika, and Harry Thuku, who saw possible closer union between the three colonies as contrary to African developmental interests.⁵ In 1922, when Thuku advocated civil disobedience as a method of protesting the injustice of the colonial system, Coryndon ordered his arrest and Grigg extended his term of imprisonment because of his unrepentant attitude. Thuku was detained for nine years, causing riots that inflicted severe damage to property. Grigg and Thuku saw each other as a threat to the welfare of the country. Upon his release in 1930, the year Grigg's tenure as governor came to an end, Thuku was elected president of the Kikuyu Central Association.

Although Grigg did not blame Thuku for the failure of his mission to bring closer union between the three British colonies, he criticized him for his role in opposing the union. While he blamed Cameron and Philip E. Mitchell, who was secretary of native affairs in Tanganyika at the time Cameron was governor from 1926 to 1934, he took the position that if Thuku had supported closer union between the three colonies, Cameron might have softened his opposition. On the eve of his retirement Grigg wrote about Mitchell and Cameron, saying that both men sabotaged a plan that would have brought benefit to the people of the three colonies, both settler and African.[6] Although Grigg ordered the release of Thuku in 1930, he had ordered that he remain in prison for most of his tenure as governor. This did not sit well with Michael Blundell, who thought that sending African nationalists to prison because of their protesting against colonial policy gave them a badge of honor among their people. Blundell advocated dialogue with them, just as Louis S. St. Laurent suggested at the beginning of the Mau Mau rebellion.

In 1929 Grigg faced a national crisis that he did not have to face very long. There was serious controversy generated by the traditional female circumcision among the Kikuyu. In that year the Church of Scotland Mission in Kikuyuland issued an order demanding that all members of their church who wished their children to attend school should promise that they would not participate in the practice of female circumcision, and that if they did their children would not be allowed in school.[7] Unwilling to discard this practice, the Kikuyu leaders decided to found their own schools. In August 1934 the Kenya Independent Schools Association was formed at Gituamba in the Muranga district. Johana Kunyiha from Nyeri and Hezekia Gachi were elected president and vice-president. In 1935 Archbishop Alexander of the African Orthodox Church based in South Africa visited Kenya under the auspices of the Kikuyu Independent Schools Association. He founded a seminary at Gitumba where he trained candidates from different districts.

In 1937, when Archbishop Alexander was leaving, having ordained Daudi Maina, Harrison Gachakia, and Philip Kiandi on June 27, 1937, disagreement developed between him and the leaders of the Kikuyu Independent Schools Association. The archbishop wanted the Kenya Church to be subordinated to his African Orthodox Church and to remit funds to him in South Africa. This proposal was unacceptable to the Kikuyu Independent Schools Association. The association then developed its own church and opened over 200 schools.[8] For the first time in the history of Kenya, Africans, especially the Kikuyu, felt a sense of independence in founding their own schools. However, with the declaration of the state of emergency in 1952 these schools were closed down. Blundell played a major role in the events that followed. This crisis had a direct impact on the recommendations of the Kerr Commission in Zimbabwe not to grant permission to African councils to open schools. The school crisis in Kenya was of a major interest among settlers in Zimbabwe.

While 1934 was a year of crisis in Kenya, rapidly moving events were taking place in Zimbabwe. When Garfield Todd arrived there that year to assume his missionary responsibility at Dadaya under the sponsorship of the Church of Christ based in New Zealand, Godfrey Huggins was slowly building himself as the kingpin of colonial politics. Huggins's background had a tremendous impact on the policy that he defined and pursued as leader of the colonial government from 1933 to 1952. Born at Bexley in Kent on July 6, 1883, Huggins was the son of a mediocre stockbroker.[9] At the age of ten Huggins suffered from an acute mastoid in his left ear. In spite of several operations he never fully recovered his hearing in that ear. For the rest of his life Huggins felt this was a political liability that he was not able to overcome. Robert Blake concluded that when there was a crisis in the colonial legislative assembly, Huggins would remove his hearing aid because he did not want to hear what was being said.[10] His health was handicapped by illness and he had no hope of following the footsteps of his father as a stockbroker. However, he managed to graduate from high school and barely qualified for admission into Malvern, a school for students of average academic ability.

Due to his many operations Huggins developed an interest in the study of medicine as a boy. But he was afraid of examinations that were part of the admission and graduation process. Blake concludes, "He only managed to qualify as a medical student through an obscure backdoor which soon afterwards closed."[11] Upon his graduation as a general medical practitioner, Huggins was employed by Appleyard and Cheadle at a monthly salary of 50 pounds sterling. But his relationships with the medical establishment were less than satisfactory. In 1911 he sought an opportunity in Africa, and Zimbabwe seemed to offer him what he was looking for. But on his arrival there Huggins developed new interests in politics, hunting, and polo. He also acquired some skills as a speaker, although he was monotonous and dull. Soon he attracted the attention of Charles Coghlan who persuaded him to run for a seat in the legislative assembly in the elections of 1924. At that time a new constitution came into being as a result of the referendum of 1922. Huggins was a principal political figure for many years in what became known as Central Africa.

The year 1934 also represented the beginning of events that had a tremendous impact on the future of Zimbabwe. Huggins won election as leader of the United Party. From that time on he maintained the office of prime minister of the Federation of Rhodesia and Nyasaland without interruption until he retired in 1956.[12] During these years Huggins defined and pursued a policy in a way that systematically reminded Africans that they had no place in the society that the white man controlled.

It was only after he retired from politics and only a few years before his death that he realized the damage that his policy had inflicted on the country. In an effort to leave a more positive image of himself, Huggins admitted to Blake: "Rhodesia is a black man's country. People used to talk about the Native problem. What they ought to talk about now is the European problem."[13] Blake concluded that Huggins could afford to say this when he no longer needed the white vote. If Huggins had recognized this reality while he was still in need of this vote, he would have joined Todd in placing Zimbabwe on a different course of development that would have eliminated the devastating war of independence from 1966 to 1979, and Ian Smith would not have a chance to lead the country astray by his extreme political views of Africans.

The year 1934 is also important to Zimbabwe in that Aaron Jacha founded the Bantu Congress of Southern Rhodesia. Although the Congress became an elitist organization, it created a new level of consciousness among Africans in a way that set the stage for the political transformation of Zimbabwe beginning in 1957. Jacha was educated in Methodist schools and after teaching for some years he turned to politics in 1931. He was inspired by the activities of the African National Congress of South Africa founded in 1912, led by John L. Dube. Beginning in 1941 the Bantu Congress of Southern Rhodesia was led by Thompson D. Samkange, a Methodist minister and nationalist. Both Jacha and Samkange went on to become successful in other areas of work. Jacha became leader of the African Farmers Union and Samkange became president of the Rhodesia Missionary Conference. Both men raised African consciousness to a new level that changed the nature of politics in Zimbabwe.

The year 1934 is also when Garfield Todd arrived in Zimbabwe. For the next 12 years Todd struggled against formidable odds to provide the kind of education that he thought Africans needed to ensure a better future. The effect of the Great Depression and the negative attitude of Huggins combined to complicate the problems all schools for Africans were facing. Todd did not have sufficient funds to operate an effective educational system. In 1946 he resigned from the missionary service to go into politics. He was elected to the legislature as a member of the United Party that Huggins led. His entire purpose was to seek an improvement in the conditions that controlled the life of Africans. He became what the *African Weekly* called "the Moses of our age."[14] Todd, the liberal former missionary, joined the Rhodesia United Party, not because he shared Huggins's conservative views, but because he needed an operational base and Huggins's ruling party was that base. Todd became his own man. He brought to the legislature an important agenda that he only sought to accomplish.

ISSUES BLUNDELL AND TODD ADDRESSED

There are three major issues that Blundell and Todd felt they must address in order to bring about change for improvement: the attitudes of settlers toward Africans, how the colonial governments should respond to the rise of Africans nationalism, and the unrepresentative character of the colonial governments themselves. The end of the war in 1945 created a new situation that the colonial governments did not anticipate. The rise of African political consciousness came as a total surprise to the colonial governments, but not to the Africans themselves. This consciousness had a serious impact on relations between the settlers and the African population. Africans began to see that discriminatory policy and practice were placing them at a disadvantage, giving the settlers a protected advantage at their expense. Some settlers, especially those who had participated in the war, were compelled by the war experience to recognize the dramatic change the war had brought in the attitude of both settlers and Africans. Blundell observed on this critical development, "There is no doubt that the younger settlers who had fought in the war with the African had an entirely different outlook on African political advance and the African himself from those who remained behind and were still cocooned in the old colonial image as it were."[15]

This acknowledgment suggests the conclusion that there were two groups of settlers who had to deal with Africans after the war: the settlers who stayed home during the war, and the settlers who, like Blundell, went to war and fought side by side with Africans. These came to know the Africans better than the settlers who remained home. That is why Blundell adopted an entirely new attitude after the war. By the time he was elected to the legislative council in 1948, Blundell had mellowed with new knowledge of the aspirations of Africans. By the time he was elected to the legislative assembly in 1946, Todd had also mellowed with new knowledge of the needs of the Africans. Throughout their political careers Blundell and Todd always spoke on behalf of the Africans.

It is quite an interesting phenomenon that the first issue in the relations between settlers and Africans that both Blundell and Todd addressed was the need for change of attitude among settlers toward Africans. Both men felt that if settlers had to create for themselves a secure future in Africa, then they had to accept Africans as equals in every respect. Both men did not have to wait to retire from politics, as Godfrey Huggins told Robert Blake after he retired from politics that Zimbabwe belonged to Africans, to recognize this hard fact. They even needed the settler vote to make their message go through. In this endeavor Blundell was far more successful than Todd. However, Todd, far more than Blundell, remained solid in his conviction even if it cost him his political life. Having been threatened and after receiving abusive telephone calls,[16] Todd and his daughter, Judith, remained unmoved from their conviction. Not even imprisonment and house arrest would shake their belief in the rightness of their cause. Father and daughter put the interests of the country before their own. They were always motivated by the needs of the African people as their understanding of their response as a prerequisite of national development.[17]

One must also remember that the Rhodesia Front government from 1964 to 1979 selected some leading church officials against whom to carry out a vendetta. For example, in addition to the deportation of Bishop Ralph E. Dodge of the Methodist Church, Bishop Donal R. Lamont of the Catholic Church was arrested, placed under house arrest, and finally deported in March 1977.[18] In 1964, the year that Bishop Dodge was deported, Bishop Kenneth Skelton of the Anglican Church was subjected to a similar threat by supporters of the RF. He recorded one such incident as follows:

The telephone was ringing as I walked into the Archdeacon of Salisbury's (now Harare) home. "It's for you, Bishop." A man's voice at the end of the line said, "Just a moment, my wife wants to speak to you." There was a pause, then a woman's voice with the threat said, "If Mr. Smith does not shoot you, I will." And in the background the husband's encouragement: "Tell him he's like Michael Scott."[19]

The second issue that both Blundell and Todd addressed was how the colonial government should respond to the rise of African nationalism. During the height of the Mau Mau rebellion in December 1954 and January 1955, Blundell knew that the rebels were considering the possibility of ending the conflict if the colonial government was willing to accept certain conditions, such as recognizing the existence of various forms of inequality that controlled society, and do something to end them. Blundell managed to hold informal talks with the Mau Mau leadership.

As soon as Blundell was satisfied that some progress was achieved, he "was able to announce in the legislative council that terms of a cease-fire had been offered."[20] He gave an account of the events that had led to this critical development. As Blundell had expected, his announcement triggered an explosion of indignation among members of the settler community who thought he had betrayed the decision not to talk to the Mau Mau because it was a terrorist organization. The understanding that he thought came from an effort to establish some form of communication between the two sides was used to demonstrate rage, as most settlers called for his arrest and trial on charges of treason. Although this action was never initiated, it shows the extent of distrust and displeasure the settlers expressed about Blundell's liberal views in critical national issues.

In 1957 Todd found himself in a similar position. On December 28, 1956, he announced the naming of Robert C. Tredgold, chief justice of the Supreme Court of the Federation, chairman of a commission to study ways of increasing African participation in the electoral process. Tredgold's mother was the daughter of John Smith Moffat, the son of Robert Moffat (of the London Missionary Society). This background had a tremendous influence on Tredgold's liberal views. When Tredgold published his report at the end of April 1957, the settler community was outraged because it blamed Todd for the manner in which the report recommended broadening the franchise to include more Africans with education. By the end of June Todd had been under so much attack he felt compelled to respond by paraphrasing Cecil John Rhodes's statement of 1896 that his policy was to extend equal rights for civilized men:

To the north and south of us racial politics are a fashion. Southern Rhodesia finds itself the custodian of Rhodes's liberal dictum of equal rights for all civilized men regardless of color. If legislation to implement that policy is passed when it is introduced to the House in July, and if we keep off the rolls our 6,000 Africans who have had ten years of education and who work as teachers, agricultural demonstrators, medical orderlies and so on, we will be so betraying the spirit of Rhodes that I would not continue to lead my party. However, I am confident that our legislators will meet the challenge of the spirit of the Tredgold Report, whatever will be the eventual letter of the law.[21]

In January 1958 differences of opinion between Todd and members of his administration were so serious that they could not be resolved in the ordinary political process. Todd accepted the recommendation of the Tredgold Commission to lower the voting qualifications to allow more Africans to vote. His entire cabinet resigned in protest, arguing that accepting the report as it was would lead to an African government much sooner than any white person would accept. Todd argued that allowing more Africans to vote would be the best way to ensure the security of the settlers in Zimbabwe. Failure to resolve the difference of opinion about this critical issue led to Todd's fall from power, creating by 1962 a national situation that led to the beginning of a major national crisis. Robert Blake concludes that Todd's fall from power was the major reason "for the alienation of African nationalists from the white electorate which gathered momentum after 1958."[22] Edgar C. Whitehead, who succeeded Todd, aggravated the situation by the manner in which he treated the African nationalists.

The formation of the African National Congress in 1957 enabled the African nationalists to see Whitehead as a faithful disciple of Godfrey Huggins, whose policy and attitude they detested intensely. They regarded him as an instrument by which settlers removed Garfield Todd from the sane course he had charted for the improvement of racial relations by designing a policy that was intended to promote the development of Africans. Two years later the pace of African nationalism was gathering momentum in a manner that so frightened Whitehead that he outlawed it on February 28, 1959, setting the stage that Todd had correctly predicted would lead to a major conflict. Todd argued that the state of emergency came at the worst possible time. When Methodist Bishop Ralph E. Dodge supported Todd's position, a major crisis was created between church and state.

The third issue that the two men discussed was the unrepresentative character of the colonial government in both Kenya and Zimbabwe. In Kenya the creation of the unofficial majority in the legislative council in 1948 was in response to the need settlers had expressed to form a broadly based representative system that adequately protected their rights. The argument was that this was necessary in order to ensure that the government remained in good hands against the pressure that the Africans were exerting to have them represent themselves. At that time an Asian member of the legislative council, A. B. Patel, had made a name for himself in representing his own interests instead of those of the Indian community. This is why the settler politicians liked him. But since 1944 Eliud W. Mathu demonstrated that he represented the interests of his people. Settler politicians feared that if more Africans like Mathu were allowed into the legislative council, they would paralyze its operations by their excessive demands.

Blundell recognized that as an appointed member of the legislative council Mathu found himself in a difficult situation. He concluded that if Mathu seemed too aggressive in representing African interests, he would lose the support and confidence of the governor who had appointed him to a position of influence. But if Mathu seemed to represent the views and position of the governor in order to remain in office, he could lose the confidence of his people and his effectiveness. Blundell concluded that the difficult position in which Mathu found himself demonstrated the unrepresentative character of the colonial government itself and must be changed.[23]

Indeed, from 1944 to 1957 Mathu tried to carry out his responsibilities as a chief spokesman of the Africans in a legislative body that was dominated by settlers who did everything in their power to promote and protect their own interests. Bethwell A. Ogot concludes that while Mathu tried to display courage in a difficult situation by trying to lay a solid foundation for more meaningful change to meet the needs of the Africans, he often ran into conflict with the colonial establishment.[24] Blundell argued that direct representation in which members were elected to the legislative council would eliminate the dilemma that Mathu found himself facing. The unrepresentative character of the colonial government was the main reason why the Lyttleton constitution was introduced in 1954.

Although the settlers protested, the Colonial Office in London had long recognized that the situation had to be addressed. Because Blundell supported such a move, he stood condemned by the very people whose interests he thought he was representing. When such a constitutional change made it possible to hold elections in 1957, Mathu lost his seat in the legislative council because he had been considered a representative of the colonial government. Although Mathu lost the election the Africans gained a new level of political power they did not have in the past. Blundell felt that his efforts were gratified in a meaningful way. Mathu, the gallant warrior who waged a lonely battle for the good of his people, accepted the outcome of the election in the knowledge that his role had made it possible.

Blundell was so pleased with Mathu's efforts that he began to push for more constitutional change to allow direct representation of the Africans as the only realistic way to ensure the future of settlers. Blundell himself concludes that the execution of Dedan Kimathi and the end of the Mau Mau rebellion in 1957 created a political climate that made new initiatives possible to change the character of the colonial government by constitutional advancement of the Africans.[25] These initiatives included the Lennox-Boyd constitution of 1958, because the Africans had rejected the clauses of the Lyttleton constitution of 1954. The success of the Lennox-Boyd constitution led to the two Lancaster House conferences in 1960 and 1962 to pave way for independence on December 12, 1963.

Blundell used his influence to advise various colonial officials, both in Africa and in Britain, on various aspects of colonial policy. For example, in the letter he wrote to Roy Welensky on February 29, 1960, in response to his of January 8, 1960, Blundell advised him to get tough with Iain Macleod. However, he concluded by saying that the presence of 60,000 Europeans against 6 million Africans in Kenya was not really a firm base to grant self-rule to settlers. Blundell advised Welensky that since 1957, when Britain granted independence to Ghana, the underlying principle that the Colonial Office considered was the principle of majority rule. He stressed the fact that the settlers in Kenya had accepted that reality. By implications Blundell was advising Welensky to be cautious about how to respond to British government policy. Welensky knew that his administration was facing the same situation in the Federation of Rhodesia and Nyasaland that settlers were facing in Kenya. For the first time in his political career, Welensky knew that the fate of the Federation was sealed. When Britain was forced to dissolve the Federation on December 31, 1963, Welensky remained in Zimbabwe for a few years, then returned to Britain where he died on December 5, 1991, still bitterly disappointed, like Godfrey Huggins, by the turn of events he could not control in Africa.

While Kenya was celebrating its independence on December 12, 1963, the drama of conflict was taking ominous turns in Zimbabwe. From its formation in 1962 to the end of its administration in 1979, the Rhodesia Front did not hesitate to show disrespect toward any display of intellect among the Africans. In this regard, its members remained loyal to the philosophy of their mentor, Cecil John Rhodes, who believed that the Africans had the minds of children.[26] Thus, as members of the Dominion Party (DP), they vigorously opposed the constitution of 1961 because it was incompatible with its political philosophy that the Africans belonged to an inferior place in society. Soon after winning the general elections held in December 1962, the RF was tormented by the reality that this was the first Parliament to have black faces sit opposite white faces in a chamber, which, up to that point, had been an exclusive club and a sacred shrine for the settlers. Aware that its opposition to a constitution which made this possible had been futile, the RF now felt it should launch its crusade directly against the African members of Parliament themselves.

The presence of 15 Africans in Parliament also constantly reminded the RF about the real possibility of a black government in the future. The RF members never attempted to hide the fact that they were outraged by the British insistence that Africans take their place in Parliament, and never forgave Edgar C. Whitehead for agreeing to a constitutional provision that made it possible for Africans to question the absoluteness of the political power of whites.[27] This is exactly why the RF detested the thought of engaging in parliamentary debates with Africans. The RF was not aware that to Africans the unrepresentative character of its government was totally unacceptable. However, from the very beginning of its administration, the RF introduced a new element of racial prejudice in Parliament itself. This dimension of human interaction had a profound impact on the ability of the African members to function effectively and hence to fulfill their responsibilities to their constituencies.

One of these 15 African members explained to the author in 1983 the effect of the RF's attitude towards them:

The 15 of us began to feel belittled, ridiculed, and out of place. No white members ever came to chat with us during intercessions, they all avoided us. They hated our presence in parliament, and even made fun of us. They laughed at us for what they claimed was a lack of experience on our part in parliamentary procedures. The Rhodesia Front used our presence to practice political target shooting and make cheap shots at what its members considered a notion that 15 black persons could engage in a debate with 50 white men on issues of national importance. This is how the RF made us feel small and out of place. Its negative attitude towards us impaired our ability to discharge our proper parliamentary and constituent responsibilities.[28]

In one way or another, the RF repeatedly humiliated the 15 African members of Parliament under the various provisions of the Land Apportionment Act. For example, they stayed in separate hotels. The white members and the African members had nothing in common outside the Parliament building. Even in Parliament itself when the African members tried to speak during a debate,

some RF members left the chamber in disgust, others shouted us down. Some continued their own private conversations, others simply laughed. We began to ask ourselves what we were doing in a colonial parliament. Who could expect 15 Africans to change things when there were 50 white men? We began to realize that our presence was nothing more than a token show of democracy which the RF successfully exploited for its own political gains and to reduce us to the level of being misfits.[29]

Although the number of African seats was increased to 16 by the RF constitution of 1969, that number was still so small that the attitude of the RF toward the African members even worsened. For example, in June 1979, when he learned that some African members suggested wearing formal wigs as a symbol of the respect they believed must be shown their office, Peter van der Byl, RF minister of information, immigration and tourism, did not hesitate to show his disrespect of both the suggestion and the Africans themselves when he reacted, "What do they want wigs for? They can just sprinkle a little powder on their heads."[30]

If the RF had the audacity to belittle the African members of Parliament only six months before the end of its political power, then common sense would suggest that it was even more abusive of the African members during the height of its power from 1966 to 1978. To belittle the African members of Parliament was part of the RF's strategy of making light of the issues that they tried to address. In this manner the African members were either completely silenced or intimidated. The following were the 16 African members of parliament and the constituencies they represented as of 1970:

Name	Constituency	Name	Constituency
Bhebe, M. M.[31]	Ntshonalanga	Masenda, L. P.	Mabvazuwa
Chikonyera, T. M.	Highveld	Moraka, W. S.	Motojeni
Gandanzara, N. A.	Manica	Mungate, A. T.	Zambezi
Gondo, J. M.	Kunyasi	Namate, D. M.	Tuli
Hove, J. B.	Pioneer	Ndhlovu, L. A.	Insukamini

Name	Constituency	Name	Constituency
Khabo, J. M.	Pagati	Sadomba, R. T.	Nemakonde
Mahlangu, L. J.	Mpopoma	Sifuya, E. G.	Kariba
Makaya, R. C.	Lowveld	Watungwa, E. G.	Harare

Source: Rhodesia: *Parliamentary Debates*, August 19, 1970.

To conclude that the African members of Parliament during the RF administration suffered from the effects of an identity complex is to recognize the political dilemma they faced. On the one hand, the RF resented their presence without reservation. On the other hand, the Africans whose interests they thought they represented did not appear to have placed any trust and confidence in them because, as one former member told the author,

We were considered to be in full cooperation with the RF in the pursuit of its policies. They wanted to know how we could easily allow ourselves to be used by the RF against their interests. They did not know that parliamentary decisions are determined by vote. How could 16 Africans influence the outcome of the vote against 50 racist white men? It actually turned out that their concerns were based on solid ground. We offered nothing more than a token opposition as the RF used our presence to strengthen its political power. Where would we go from here?[32]

THE EFFECT OF BHEBE'S MOTION

Just as the RF had converted its opposition to the constitution of 1961 into an instrument with which to serve its own political ends, so also did it make major capital political gains out of the presence of the African members of Parliament. Every time it passed a legislation, even though it was against the interests of the Africans, it claimed that it had the support of the African people expressed through the chiefs. However, the African members of Parliament repeatedly argued that they had opposed the entire RF legislative agenda. The more the Africans failed to play any meaningful role in Parliament, the more the RF took advantage of the situation to bolster its position.

A case in point: in 1969 Parliament introduced a new constitution which entrenched racial segregation in every aspect of national life. The African members voted against it while all white members voted in favor. The RF used the outcome of the vote to claim that it had the support of the African members as a whole. The RF had never had it so good. Indeed, the RF was having the best of both worlds. From 1969 to 1979, all white seats in Parliament were held by RF members; it had become absolute in every way. There was no white opposition since the United Federal Party suffered a humiliating defeat in the special election held in 1964. Any semblance of opposition came from the African members.

Indeed, during the RF tenure, Zimbabwe was an absolute one-party state.

Once the RF took office in December 1962, the education of the Africans continued to decline and was in total disarray. The RF did not care because the African political leaders and nationalists were in political prison or detention camps. The Africans did not have much hope that things would improve anytime soon. With its perception of invincibility, the RF launched a $3 million campaign in 1968 to attract a million new white immigrants from Europe by promising them the best education in the world. This caused the *Rhodesia Herald* of November 12, 1968, to mourn the deterioration of African education and urged the government to do something to reverse the trend. In its editorial the paper argued, "Of all the new things Europeans have brought into the lives of Rhodesian Africans, none is more appreciated, none more welcomed, none more sought after than schooling. Since the Second World War, the African desire for schooling has been insatiable."[33]

These were the factors that produced an environment in which the African members of Parliament tried to arouse a new nationalistic feeling against what they saw to be harmful effects of the RF's educational policy. But, distrusted by their own people and belittled by the RF, they knew that the odds were heavily against them. For them the choice was to swim or sink in the troubled political water which threatened to wreck their fragile political boat. They were caught between the futility of their cause and an avalanche of African criticism of their failure to influence the direction that they believed their education must take. They felt that they had to do something to regain the trust and confidence of the people they represented and to register their protest against the RF's educational policy.

After spending several weeks in designing their strategy and carefully checking the accuracy of their facts, the African members of Parliament felt they were ready for a showdown with the RF by making an assault on its educational policy. The day was Wednesday, August 19, 1970. After a thorough preparation and rehearsal, all 16 members took their seats some 30 minutes before the beginning of the session. The visitors' gallery was packed with whites and a few Africans seated in a remote corner. His voice quivering and almost choking with emotion, M. M. Bhebe, the member for Ntshonalanga, having been recognized by the Speaker in accordance with parliamentary procedure, stood up at 2:24 p.m., and, as if unsure of himself, straightened out his tie and buttoned his jacket. With a tense and serious look on his face, he said, "Mr Speaker,[34] I move that this House take note that there is widespread alarm and despondency among the African population of this country about the administration of African education."[35]

As usual, the RF members belittled the motion and saw Bhebe as a

Sancho Panza of the African political Don Quixote urging him to tilt at the giant windmills of the RF invincibility. The RF had neither an appreciation of the intensity of his feeling nor any understanding of the seriousness of his motion. However, as soon as Bhebe made the motion and before he even took his seat, J. M. Khabo, the member for Pagati, seconded it. Therefore, the Speaker had no choice but to have it debated. There was a mixed reaction from the RF members:

Some inwardly expressed an outrage: how dare the Africans question the absoluteness of its power and the right to design an educational policy for the Africans in accordance with its philosophy? Others responded with laughter and wondered why the African members decided to waste their time on such a futile endeavor. Some looked puzzled, others appeared angered by the whole thing. Some were making inaudible sounds as if they were in a pub.[36]

Bhebe spared no efforts to register what he believed was the root cause of alarm and despondency among the Africans about the RF's educational policy, and he took special exception to the fact that it had used the excuse of limited financial resources to curtail their educational development. Bhebe argued that this was the reason it was withdrawing a number of grants which had been traditionally paid to African schools. In addition to this the RF arbitrarily imposed a policy of 5 percent cut in salary grants for African teachers of primary schools, adding, "I do not think that the $1.25 which the Minister of Education now requires of each primary student will meet the requirements of African education. It will result, instead, in reducing the number of students from primary schools because their parents will not be able to pay."[37]

Bhebe cautiously touched upon an issue that was central to the RF's educational policy, that of expansion in African education in general. Making sure that the Africans understood this, he carefully and slowly let his intense anger and frustration take control of his emotion when he said "expansion of primary schooling is necessary for the expansion of secondary education. It is disturbing to find that the government deliberately withholds funds needed to make this expansion possible."[38] Bhebe must not have been fully aware that since it took office, the RF did not see the importance of expanding African education in the way he was discussing. While everyone else thought that education in 1970 had changed sufficiently to require a corresponding change of thinking about African advancement, the RF never lost sight of its vision of building a white utopia in an African setting by controlling the educational development of the Africans.

Quoting the recommendation of the Judges Report of 1962 that "marriage should not bar a woman teacher from the privilege of permanent appointment. Special regulations should apply in the event of childbirth,"[39] Bhebe had raised a point which was close to the cause of the Africans' unhappiness with the RF policy. Since Victorian times, women teachers all over the world suffered a disability through educational inequality, which in turn made them second-class citizens. But in Africa, including colonial Zimbabwe, an additional hardship was imposed and perpetuated because it added a dimension which deprived them of both an opportunity for education and for employment.

While he still had the floor, Bhebe wished to maximize the opportunity he had to cover as much ground as possible. This is why he relentlessly criticized the RF for not allowing African children to start school until they reached the age of seven. This is why he decried the practice of keeping enrollment at 45 for each class in the primary school. Because it was hard for the teacher to pay full attention to all the students, Bhebe argued, they were inadequately prepared to undertake secondary education. This in turn provided the RF a good excuse to conclude that the Africans could not benefit from academic secondary education. This is why it was pushing 37.5 percent of the graduates of the primary schools to vocational education and industrial training in the same way which Earl Grey and William Milton had done during the formative years of the colonial government. In essence, Bhebe was saying that the RF's educational policy was compatible with traditional colonial educational policy toward the Africans.

In concluding that "these are the facts that have caused alarm and despondency among the African people,"[40] Bhebe was saying in effect that because the RF was doing nothing right, either its whole policy must be overhauled, or the RF itself must be replaced, not by another white colonial government, but by an African government. That the RF did not appreciate his indictments indicates that there was no solution to the problem. For Bhebe to suggest the possibility of replacing the RF government with an African government is indicative of the reality of the conclusion that the colonized will continue to endure the agony of colonization and suffer a lack of educational development as long as the RF policy continued.

But for all his outrage and unreserved condemnation of the RF's educational policy, Bhebe demonstrated serious limitations and contradiction in his political action over the next two years. For example, on February 10, 1972, Bhebe wrote a letter to this author urging him to support the lop-sided agreement that had been reached on November 24, 1971, between Ian Smith and the British government on terms of ending the constitutional crisis caused by the unilateral declaration of independence (UDI) on November 11, 1965. Many observers concluded that approval of the agreement would have legalized UDI and would have taken 50 years for the Africans to have control of the government. The key requirement for the Africans to claim their right to vote was,

"You have been at a secondary school for two years or more and you have been earning $25.00 a month for the last two years, or own a house, building, farm, or land worth $600.00."[41]

In his letter Bhebe listed eight reasons why he thought the writer should support the proposals. Three of these reasons relate to the education of Africans:

1. There will be improved schooling facilities for Africans.
2. There will be improved teacher training facilities for Africans.
3. There will be equal pay for African teachers who have the same qualifications as white teachers.[42]

But as we have noted, the development of education for the Africans was the last thing that the RF wanted to see. He also did not take into account the fact that Britain acquiesced to the provision that "you own a house, building, farm or land worth $600.00," when, in fact, under the terms of the Land Tenure Act of 1969, which strengthened the racial character of the Land Apportionment Act of 1929, Africans were not allowed to buy land at all.

Responding on March 1, 1972, the author wished to remind Bhebe of the major flaws of the proposals and stated why he would not support them. "All the eight reasons you gave for asking me to support the proposals are merely secondary, and not important at all. The most important element of the proposals which has been left out is the question of a black majority government. When is it coming? I find myself unable to help legalize UDI by giving the proposals my support."[43] However, no one would wish to deny Bhebe the opportunity to put on record his total opposition to the RF educational policy. He would not be denied the publicity that he needed to prove to his constituency that he was representing their interests well. The charges that he made against the RF educational policy were sufficient to arouse the indignation of Africans all over the country. Therefore, Bhebe, indeed, succeeded in his efforts.

Bhebe's ability to articulate the concern of Africans about their opposition to the RF educational policy set the stage for the other African members of Parliament to support the motion. This is why J. M. Khabo, the member for Pagati, who seconded the motion, was also the first to speak after Bhebe in support of it. Wishing to highlight the charges that Bhebe had made and at the same time level new ones, Khabo listed a number of reasons why he seconded the motion. Pointing out the inconsistency in the RF educational policy, he reminded the House that the successive colonial governments had argued that the Africans were uncivilized and irresponsible. He wanted to know if, in forcing the local communities to assume the responsibility of finding the 5 percent balance in the primary teachers' salaries, the RF now thought they were in fact civilized and responsible enough to be entrusted with the responsibility of financing part of their own education.[44] This is the kind of thinking and talking that the RF feared would come from the African members of Parliament.

There is no doubt that Khabo intended this rhetoric to register his displeasure with the RF's attempt to perpetuate the Victorian myth that the Africans were uncivilized. Ian Smith himself had acquired a unique notoriety for repeatedly insulting the African culture by characterizing it as uncivilized and primitive.[45] Angered by A. L. Lazell's remarks that the African members were irresponsible for supporting the motion, Khabo was even more blunt in expressing his outrage against what he considered an RF conspiratorial action. He, of course, was referring to the partnership between the notorious Ministry of Internal Affairs and the Ministry of Education in formulating an educational policy that he believed was against the educational development of Africans.

That Khabo expressed his belief that the educational policy introducing the 5 percent cut in salary grants for African primary teachers was intended to mislead the Africans into believing that there was a positive cooperation between the two ministries in developing their education shows how well the Africans understood the seriousness of the issue they were debating. When he concluded that the real intent of this unholy alliance was to coordinate the RF's efforts in curtailing the educational development of Africans,[46] the debate had aroused deep emotions which neither side could control.

Khabo concluded that in enforcing provisions of the Land Apportionment Act of 1929, the Native Land Husbandry Act of 1951, and the Native Councils Act of 1957 in a way that reduced the Africans to the level of bare existence, the RF government used the Department of Native Affairs to effectively control the lives of Africans and force them to endure the educational agony that made it possible for the whites to profit from the cheap labor they supplied.[47] Khabo was even more vehement in expressing his belief that the Africans were now fully aware that the Department of Native Affairs under the RF had become a new symbol, even an agent of their oppression. Wishing to reduce the effect of this negative reaction from the Africans, Khabo argued, the RF changed the name from Department of Native Affairs to Department of Internal Affairs in 1965. But this new department instituted an oppression of its own. Like Bhebe, Khabo wanted to remind his fellow Africans that in the partnership between the two departments in designing their educational policy, the Africans had jumped from the frying pan into the fire.[48]

To substantiate his argument, Khabo pointed out that the African parents were already responsible for erecting and maintaining school buildings, teachers' houses, buying school furniture, paying fees, and meeting other expenses. He concluded by arguing that for the RF to impose the 5 percent cut in salary grants for African primary teachers was to add insult to injury, adding, "We feel that this is unfair to the Africans."[49] Questioning the policy of a government that did everything for white students and nothing for African students, Khabo particularly wanted his fellow Africans to remember that white students had enjoyed free and compulsory education since 1935.

Like Bhebe, Khabo warned the RF that in pursuing its educational policy in the way that it did, it was, in effect, creating an environment for a major conflict. Of course, some RF members laughed at this suggestion, while others were irritated by what they regarded as an incitement of hostility against the whites. But what really angered them was "the thought that the Africans could challenge the RF's authority and power and resented the constitutional provision which made it possible for the Africans to do that."[50]

Khabo reserved his severest attack of the RF's educational policy for his discussion of the effect of the salary scale for the African teachers who were paid 60 percent of what the white teachers were paid. Of course, the RF would argue that the African teachers had a different educational background and training from the white teachers. That is what Khabo argued was basically wrong with the entire system of education under the RF. A commencing salary of $77.00 per month for primary teachers carried a message that for any African to decide to become a teacher was to indicate his wish to live in poverty.

Concluding that the ultimate effect of this policy was to discourage Africans from becoming teachers so that the RF would have a good excuse that it was not expanding African education because there were not sufficient funds and too few teachers, Khabo put the RF on the defensive. This had a profound effect on the Africans' decision to confront the RF itself. Appealing to the RF to reconsider its policy, Khabo concluded, "We must consider the educational interests of the child. If we do not, we will not achieve a satisfactory objective."[51]

In accordance with the strategy which the African members had designed, Khabo left it to his colleagues to oppose other aspects of the RF educational policy that was causing alarm and despondency. E. G. Sifuya, a member for Kariba, argued that in forcing the Africans to pay taxes, the RF was in fact having the lion's share of the educational pie. In arguing that this was a strategy to perpetuate the RF power of the Africans, Sifuya actually recognized the real intent of the total RF educational policy, namely to condition the Africans to accept the view that after UDI, they must stop hoping that Britain would one day come to their rescue. Sifuya also argued that it was clear that the RF wanted the Africans to know that their future lay in their cooperation with the RF policies. "I would like the Minister of Education to know that this is what has caused alarm and despondency among the Africans,"[52] said Sifuya as he urged the RF to rescind its policy before it was too late.

One after another the African members of Parliament added indictments against the RF educational policy. In stating that the policy was designed to serve its own interests, the Africans mounted a united effort, not just to influence the change of policy, but also to alert the Africans of the danger to come if they failed to do something soon. Disregarding an interjection from Jack Christie, an RF member, R. T. Sadomba, the member for Nemakonde, argued that the overall effect of the RF educational policy was that it would create second class citizens out of the Africans.[53]

Completely aware that the RF did not take what they were saying seriously, the African members did everything in their power to let it know that they were not playing games. This is why N. A. Gandanzara, the member for Manica, began by cautioning the RF members as he began to speak in support of the motion when he said,

When we speak of these concerns, we are not wasting time, but we are stating the reasons why there is alarm and despondency among the Africans about the government policy towards their education. It is true that the Africans are unhappy about the disparity in the educational process. The government policy is either intentionally designed to retard African education or it is designed to trigger the reaction from the Africans so that it uses tear gas tactics against its opponents.[54]

Gandanzara raised two critical points that no previous speakers had discussed. The first was his argument that because the RF was the first colonial government to have Africans in Parliament, it insulted their intelligence in order to intimidate and silence them. He warned the RF that it was in its own best interests to respect the Africans and their ability to contribute to a crucial national debate about an important national policy. Its persistent disregard of the Africans would cost it dearly.[55] Gandanzara's second point was that in trying to force the Africans to accept its policy of community development, the RF was forcing its educational policy on them, and it would backfire. If the RF was still hoping that it would succeed in this direction, it would be well advised to direct its efforts toward a reevaluation of its entire policy instead. The Africans had made it clear that they had rejected its definition of their development. Gandanzara, as well as his 15 African colleagues, had neither the patience nor the tolerance of the RF's excuses for not providing the Africans an equal educational opportunity. All 16 African members of Parliament felt they had a mission to accomplish: to advise the RF in no uncertain terms that if confrontation came between it and the Africans, it could not say that it had not been warned.

In appealing to the RF to start all over in designing a more realistic educational policy for the Africans, Gandanzara concluded, "I appeal to the Minister of Education to make a serious reconsideration of his policy and take our views into account because if a 5 percent cut is implemented, it will mean a cut not only in teachers' salaries, but also in educational facilities in general."[56] In implementing its policy Gandanzara said that the RF demonstrated its lack of sensitivity to the concerns of the Africans. If this insensitivity continued, why should the Africans be asked to exercise reason and moderation? He urged the RF to demonstrate moderation by taking the views they had expressed into consideration in the interest of good racial relationships.

L. A. Ndhlove, the member for Insukamini, attempted to convince both the Africans and the RF that the most serious problem they encountered was the RF's negative attitude toward the educational development of the Africans, and that the RF had gone further than any other previous administration in not only promoting this attitude among whites, but also in basing its educational policy on it. Expressing his view that the Africans would expect meaningful educational change only through a change of government from the RF to the Africans, Ndhlove was in effect urging the Africans to coordinate their efforts in seeking an unconditional end of the RF government itself. The only other viable alternative was for the RF to end all forms of racial discrimination in the educational process.[57] Of course, Ndhlove had no illusions that the RF would even consider doing this.

In terms of colonial parliamentary procedures, it was not possible for every African member to put on record his opposition to the RF educational policy. However, for those who spoke this was an opportunity of a lifetime: no one would want to be left out of this great cause. But the Speaker of the House of Assembly felt that the African members had their space in the sun and, on August 25, 1970, allowed Arthur Smith, the minister of education, to respond to the charges. To conclude that his performance was less than satisfactory is to recognize that he failed to convince the Africans of the wisdom of the policy of his government.

It is quite clear that Smith wanted the Africans to know that the policy of a 5 percent cut could not be reconsidered, adding

If the Church authorities feel that they must hand over their schools on account of their inability to meet the 5% cut and there is no council to whom they can hand over, then, the government will take over the responsibility until such a time that a properly formed and efficient council can assume the responsibility. I have therefore difficulty in appreciating the mover's motion.[58]

In arguing that the reason for the 5 percent cut was that the RF wanted to save money toward establishing secondary schools, Smith must have forgotten that he told Geoffrey Atkins of Rhodesia Television on January 31, 1968, that the real reason for the policy was to force the African to accept the idea of community development.

The conviction with which Arthur Smith defended the policy of his government demonstrated a negative attitude of the RF which Ndhlove recognized as the main problem in the relationship between the Africans and the government itself. That Smith preferred to make his remarks in terms of generalities, and that he showed no feeling for the concerns the Africans had expressed, did irreparable damage to future interactions between the two sides. It is from this attitude that the Africans, both in the colonial Parliament and in general, concluded that the only way for them to have meaningful educational opportunity was to end the RF itself. This is not the position the Africans wanted to take, but it was one that the RF forced upon them as a condition of colonization.

SMITH VERSUS TODD: A FIGHT TO THE FINISH

While the drama of conflict was going on in Parliament, the intensity of conflict outside it reached new levels. The strange thing about Ian Smith's political behavior from the moment he assumed the office of prime minister in April 1964 to the time of the collapse of the RF in December 1979, was his belief that if he deported Dodge and continued the state of emergency to keep the African nationalists in detention his problems would go away. He did not know that they were just beginning. From July 1964 he began to make elaborate plans to seize power and declare Zimbabwe independent unilaterally. However, Smith delayed this action for one year due to a statement that British Prime Minister Harold Wilson made at the time:

An illegal declaration of independence in Southern Rhodesia would bring to an end relationships between her and Britain would cut Rhodesia from the rest of the Commonwealth, from most foreign governments and international organizations, would inflict disastrous economic damage upon her and would leave her isolated and virtually friendless in a highly hostile continent.[59]

When Smith finally took the action of declaring Zimbabwe independent unilaterally on November 11, 1965, he argued wrongly that the international community would come to his aid, that other nations would recognize his government because they wanted colonial governments to end. He thought it would be a matter of time before the country would get back on its feet to ensure development. He believed that the economic embargo the international community would impose would last only a short period of time. He blamed individuals like Todd for campaigning against his government and felt that these individuals would be dealt with severely. He then carried a campaign of terror against Todd and his daughter Judith to discredit them as unpatriotic individuals. In his turn Todd launched a successful campaign to discredit Smith and his RF government, that they were racists who wanted to oppress the Africans forever to protect the privileged position of settlers. Smith was so angry with Todd that he decided to have him arrested and tried for treason.

In 1971 the political and economic situation in Zimbabwe had become critical as Smith was losing the struggle to maintain his grip on the country. Having failed in 1966 and 1968 to reach an agreement with Britain, a new start was made in 1970 leading to an agreement in 1971 on the five basic principles that successive British governments had formulated. These principles stated that no independence will be attained before majority rule. In 1971 Sir Alec Douglas-Home seemed willing to abandon this basic principle but required that any agreement between Smith and himself should be subjected to approval by the people of Zimbabwe as a whole. This included the Africans. Smith did not know that he was put in a trap. Douglas-Home named Lord Pearce chairman of the commission to test acceptability. Lord Pearce and his commission arrived in Zimbabwe on January 11, 1972, to allow people to express their views on the proposals. Todd launched an intense campaign from his detention, forcing members of the Pearce Commission to visit him there to hear his views. Todd clearly carried the day by the strength of his conviction and argument that Smith and the RF had become the worst dictatorship Zimbabwe had ever known.

Todd was also quite candid in arguing that the Africans would not support any agreement between Britain and Smith in which they had no part. He added, "The only document we could accept is one agreed between the present administration and representatives of the African people and then ratified by Her Majesty's Government. But if Africans voted 'Yes' then absolute power will be given to white people to rule over 5 million African people. I believe that such power will corrupt us absolutely. That is why I must say 'No.' "[60] On January 18, 1972, Smith ordered the arrest of Todd and his daughter Judith. He was sent to prison in Kadoma and she was sent to a prison for women in Morondera. The battle lines between Smith and Todd had been drawn, it was now a fight to the finish. The news of the arrests was flashed across the world immediately. In Britain civic and political leaders called for military action to remove Smith from power and turn over the country to the Africans. In Africa the Organization of African Unity (OAU) intensified its support of the African nationalist guerrillas who were now waging a military campaign to end the RF government.

On October 28, 1970, the British Council of Missionary Society issued a statement saying, "In spite of the great moral difficulties fighting for a just cause has been accepted by the Christian conscience as justifiable. Those who are themselves in comfort and security cannot urge armed rebellion on others who would face death or suffering they do not have to bear."[61] In 1975 the World Council of Churches donated $479,000 toward organizations fighting against racism in southern Africa. By December 1979 Smith and his RF stood virtually isolated from the world, just as Harold Wilson had predicted in 1964. Economic embargo, military action by the nationalist guerrillas, and condemnation by the international community forced Smith to sue for peace and began negotiations with Britain and the Africans that finally led to the collapse of the RF and the advent of an African government on April 18, 1980.

CONCLUSION AND IMPLICATIONS

The purpose of this book was to discuss the roles that Michael Blundell and Garfield Todd played in the political transformation of Kenya and Zimbabwe. The evidence presented indicates that both men played their roles well. Both men were raised by liberal traditions and values that became part of their lives. They would refuse to compromise their basic approaches to national politics. Both men went into politics in an effort to make a difference in the lives of the people. Both men operated by the principles that had been adopted by leading liberals in Britain because they had seen tangible benefits that accrued to society.

Throughout the time they were involved in politics, Blundell and Todd recognized the imperative of service to the people as a prior condition of national development. Both men made great sacrifices for the beliefs. Both men were misunderstood by their fellow settlers in what they attempted to accomplish. Both men went into politics at a time when both countries were going through a period of great national crisis. Both men accomplished what they did because they were liberals. No other settlers of British origin accomplished as much as these two men did. Indeed, Blundell and Todd were the last British liberals in Africa.

Because of the roles that Blundell and Todd played, Kenya and Zimbabwe would never be the same again. Although Blundell retired from active politics in 1962, his legacy remained a major factor for the future. In Zimbabwe Todd never retired from politics until the advent of an African majority government in 1980. He was appointed senator by the government of President Robert Mugabe in recognition of his unique contribution to the political transformation of Zimbabwe. Until his death on February 1, 1993, Blundell demonstrated commitment to principles of fairness and justice that remained a distinctive hallmark of his political belief system. Until he moved into a retirement home in Bulawayo in 1997, Todd remained a gallant soldier for the rights of the deprived African masses. The two men never met nor communicated with each other, but they did follow similar paths in African history.

Something interesting has happened to both Kenya and Zimbabwe in recent years. When President Jomo Kenyatta died in 1978, he was succeeded by his vice-president, Daniel arap Moi. Two years later, in 1980, when the RF came to an end, the African majority government that succeeded it was led by Robert G. Mugabe. Both Moi and Mugabe experienced some political problems that came as an effort to change the political process that both Blundell and Todd believed must be based on solid principles of democracy. Both men considered the introduction of a one-party system of government, causing both countries to go through a difficult period of internal political conflict. In that initiative both Moi and Mugabe seemed to ignore an important fact about Blundell and Todd: if they had worked toward a one-party system of government, Moi and Mugabe would never have had a chance to lead their respective governments in a healthy climate of democracy. However, both men recognized their error and quickly abandoned thoughts of one-party systems.

In July 1989 fate cast both Moi and Mugabe into a continental spotlight they did not invite. In that year all countries in southern Africa were experiencing serious social, economic, and political problems that required an immediate solution to avoid national disaster. By 1989 Mozambique, which gained independence from Portugal in 1975, was going through a painful period of disintegration caused by a brutal civil war that inflicted an incalculable loss of human life and damage to national institutional programs.[62] In 1976 the Mozambique National Resistance (Renamo), which was led by Afonzo Dhlakama, began engaging in rebel and terrorist activities whose destruction and plunder defied comprehension. Renamo did not define its objectives in launching a campaign of destruction and killing. This suggests the tragic nature of the political situation that pervaded southern Africa at that time. Renamo utilized the military assistance it received from South Africa[63] to carry out raids into Mozambique and Zimbabwe, killing at least 100,000 and maiming many more in 1989 alone.[64] This was an attempt by Renamo terrorists to destabilize the new African government as part of South Africa's strategy to maintain apartheid in Mozambique.

The knowledge that the political crisis in Mozambique posed serious developmental problems for the region of southern Africa as a whole is why, in August 1989, the Organization of African Unity appointed Presidents Daniel arap Moi[65] and Robert Mugabe cochairmen of a commission charged with the responsibility of finding solutions to the political problems that Mozambique was experiencing as a nation. Suddenly Moi and Mugabe were thrust into a continental responsibility that required the action of statesmen. There is no question that this recognition was a result of the contributions that Blundell and Todd had made to the transformation of Kenya and Zimbabwe. They had no choice but to accept their responsibility toward Mozambique and the OAU in a manner that respected the contribution that Blundell and Todd had made to the development of their nations.

It is not surprising that the two leaders fully shared OAU's commitment to political reform of Mozambique to stabilize it and set it on the road to national reconstruction and development. The OAU recognized the fact that while the Moi-Mugabe mission carried short-term outcomes, it also carried a long-term solution. In a communiqué issued in Nairobi on August 8, 1989, the OAU stated:

The aim of the mission is to put an end to this inhuman situation. The first action is to stop all terrorist action. The acceptance of these principles could lead to a dialogue for ending the violence that has destroyed Mozambique and to establish peace for normal life so that national developmental programs can be reinitiated. Unless the scourge of violence is terminated, all other forms of national development cannot take place.[66]

While Mugabe was on a mission to find a formula for peace in Mozambique, political events in his own country suggested a potential for a major national crisis. Elements of such a crisis began to unfold in 1988. In that year Edgar Tekere, a leading member of the ruling ZANU-PF Party, resigned in protest against the possibility of the introduction of a one-party state.[67] Following Mugabe's election in 1980, Mugabe stated that his government would prefer a one-party government rather than the multiparty system that was currently in operation and that had put him in office. Britain had stipulated the existence of a multiparty political system as a condition of independence. Tekere was also protesting against what he said was widespread corruption among top government officials. Indeed, in April 1989, a commission of inquiry appointed by the government under the chairmanship of Justice Sandura uncovered widespread corruption by six senior government officials.[68] The aftermath of this inquiry resulted in fines, resignations, and one suicide. In this environment, Zimbabwe was poised for the most serious political crisis it had experienced since it gained independence on April 18, 1980.

Prior to these events, *Parade News Magazine* reported that "the students called for academic freedom and their inalienable rights and demanded the university administration to lift its tacit ban on the student magazine, *Focus*."[69] Relations between the university and the government were becoming strained. Students were calling for the same educational reform that Mugabe had proposed for Mozambique. The irony in Zimbabwe is that the president is also the chancellor of the university.

Displeased with the efforts the government was making to restore the confidence of the public, students at the university engaged in a variety of activities that the government considered defiance of the law. On August 9, Joshua Nkomo, senior government minister, and Faye Chung,[70] the minister of education, went to the university in an effort to diffuse the situation. They held a meeting with the students and tried to establish dialogue. In an impassioned and emotional appeal, Nkomo pleaded with the students, saying "We do not want a confrontation with our children. We have gone gray because we have a heritage to protect, and that heritage is yourself. Therefore, dialogue must be started. You cannot solve problems by shouting. Knowledge is not just shouting. Some of your behavior is not Zimbabwean."[71]

About 2,000 students responded by demanding that Nkomo give them assurances that the government would not turn the country into a one-party state. They also demanded that the Zimbabwe Unity Movement (ZUM), which had been recently formed under the leadership of Edgar Tekere, be allowed a platform to express its political views. Chung's patience ran out as she responded: "Senior Minister Nkomo has been invited here not to be insulted. If this is what we call our future leaders, then I must say that this university is full of rubbish, and the government will not waste money on rubbish."[72] This exchange of views created a situation that posed a new potential for a confrontation leading to an explosive outcome and threatened the democratic process.

Since that time President Mugabe has made a commendable effort to maintain democratic principles. His policy of inclusion, in which the Ndbele and the Shona work together for the development of their country, is the envy of many countries in Africa. Experience in postcolonial Africa indicates that those countries that seek to eliminate tribal differences in the pursuit of national policy stand a much better chance of success than those that maintain tribalism. In May 1997 a young Luo woman, Mellyse Otieno, told the author in Nairobi her hope for Kenya:

The greatness of Kenya lies in the cooperation of all its people. The Luo have made an outstanding contribution to the development of Kenya. Tom Mboya, Oginga Odinga, S. M. Otieno,[73] to name only a few have played a major role in the development of Kenya by their cooperation with leaders of other ethnic groups in maintaining democratic system of government for the benefit of all people. This is my hope for Kenya.[74]

This view suggests the implication that a truly independent nation can arise only from a truly independent population. A truly independent population can emerge only from educated individuals who understand the importance of sustaining democratic principles. Many nations of Africa have yet to realize this truth. Without an educated population, nations will always be oppressed by a combination of forces such as social ills, racial bigotry, tribal or ethnic conflict, and political dissent, all of which many nations of Africa have experienced. One reaches the conclusion, therefore, that observing democracy is in the best interest of the nations. The important thing for Kenya and Zimbabwe to remember is that political transformation cannot be initiated in a climate of a one-party system of government, it requires a collective action based upon common interests and a system to communicate ideas among the people. About this important principle of political development in the Third World in general is the conclusion that Paulo Freire reaches that the "ability to communicate ideas of self-consciousness"[75] forms an essential part of any system designed to ensure self-fulfillment as an important step toward creating an environment of national development. This means that cooperative efforts at the political, economic, and educational levels must constitute a viable channel to successful national development.

Therefore instituting a one-party system of government is often an indication that the government has something either to hide or to fear in its own people. Thus, the introduction of a one-party system cannot be considered a step in the direction of national development. After 45 years in office, the Nationalist Party of South Africa found this to be true the hard way. While the Nationalist Party ruled supreme since 1948, both the democratic process and human interactions suffered a severe setback. It is therefore important that Kenya and Zimbabwe reject once and for all a one-party system. The sustenance of democracy is too important to be tampered with because the survival of nations and the course of national development depend on it if waves of national conflict are to be avoided.

No matter how government officials see it, a one-party system is nothing less than a dictatorship. This is why, for example, massive demonstrations staged against the government of Kenneth Kaunda in Zambia led to an attempted military coup in June 1990 and his defeat in 1992. Since he assumed the office of president in October 1964, Kaunda not only instituted a one-party rule in 1971, but he also alienated Zambians by creating a political environment that denied them a role in the affairs of their country. This is not an environment that creates conditions of national development. The people of Zambia, as those of Malawi and South Africa, have come to recognize the fact that their development must not be compromised by government leaders who seek to realize their own personal ambitions. Kenya and Zimbabwe, be well advised and be wise!

NOTES

1. Bethwell A. Ogot, *Historical Dictionary of Kenya* (London: The Scarecrow Press, 1981), p. 202.
2. Ibid., p. 203.
3. Ibid., p. 66.
4. By geographical definition Tanganyika—Tanzania today—is south of the Equator, and therefore part of southern Africa, not part of East Africa. Thuku's opposition to closer union of the three colonies provided a historical precedent that Hastings Banda of Nyasaland and Kenneth Kaunda of Northern Rhodesia used to lead opposition to the Federation of Rhodesia and Nyasaland (1853–1963) because they thought it would stand in the way of African development in those two colonies.
5. Ogot, *Historical Dictionary of Kenya*, p. 67.
6. Edward Grigg, *Kenya's Opportunity: Memories, Hopes, and Ideas* (London: Faber and Faber, 1956), p. 239.
7. Jomo Kenyatta, *Facing Mount Kenya* (Nairobi: Kenway Publications, 1938), p. 130.
8. Ogot, *Historical Dictionary of Kenya*. p. 128.
9. Robert Blake, *A History of Rhodesia* (New York: Alfred A. Knopf, 1978), p. 217.
10. Ibid., p. 218.
11. Ibid., p. 219.
12. R. Kent Rasmussen, *Historical Dictionary of Rhodesia/Zimbabwe* (London: The Scarecrow Press, 1979), p. 119.
13. Blake, *History of Rhodesia*, p. 227.
14. Ibid., p. 312.
15. Michael Blundell, *A Love Affair with the Sun* (Nairobi: Kenway Publications, 1994), p. 85.
16. Judith Todd has recorded a number of incidents that clearly show that both she and her father were subjected to abuse by those settlers who opposed their views. Here is an example:

A young white man rang my father. I listened in to the call on an extension phone. "I want to speak to Todd." "Speaking: What can I do for you?" "You couldn't do anything for me," the young man in an rather uncertain voice said. "You haven't the brain of kaffir. You couldn't help anyone." "I see. Then why are you ringing me?" "Because we're coming to get you."

Judith Todd, *The Right to Say No: Rhodesia 1972* (Harare: Longman, 1987), p. 92.

17. In a letter to the author from Judith Todd dated August 6, 1997, she said, "Thank you indeed for the money which came at an extremely useful time. A young and poor friend of mine is just going to university overseas and so this will be a nice present to pass on to him for the journey." That is what Todd would do, consider the needs of other people first. There is no question that Judith was operating under the influence of the Asquith-Lloyd George philosophy, which her father had accepted as his own. Over many years she had seen her father operate from the same perspective, a fitting tribute to two great people Zimbabwe is proud of.

18. Rasmussen, *Historical Dictionary of Rhodeisia/Zimbabwe*, p. 145.

19. Kenneth Skelton, *Bishop in Smith's Rhodesia* (Gweru: Mambo Press, 1985), p. 5. Michael Scott, along with John Stonehouse and Fenner Brockway, was a member of the Labour Party who was known to oppose the RF government.

20. Blundell, *A Love Affair with the Sun*, p. 87.

21. Blake, *History of Rhodesia*, p. 303.

22. Ibid., p. 320.

23. Michael Blundell, *So Rough a Wind* (London: Weidenfeld and Nicholson, 1964), p. 145.

24. Ogot, *Historical Dictionary of Kenya*, p. 134.

25. Blundell, *So Rough a Wind*, p. 146.

26. Stanlake Samkange, *What Rhodes Really Said About Africans* (Harare: Harare Publishing House, 1982), p. 46.

27. A. J. Peck, *Rhodesia Accuses* (Boston: Western Islands Press, 1966), p. 16.

28. A former African member of Parliament who served from 1969 to 1978, during an interview with the author in Harare, July 15, 1983. The man declined to be identified because, he said, "I do not want to give the impression that we were a total failure because we accomplished some things for the good of the Africans. One wonders. However, in 1980, when there were 80 African members of Parliament as opposed to 20 white, it was now the Africans' turn to ridicule the white members, calling them, among other things, monkeys." For details see PBS, *Not in a Thousand Years: From Rhodesia to Zimbabwe*, a documentary film, 1981.

29. Ibid.

30. *Newsweek*, July 2, 1979.

31. See Appendix 9 and Appendix 10 of Dickson A. Mungazi, *The Fall of the Mantle: The Educational Policy of the Rhodesia Front Government and Conflict in Zimbabwe* (New York: Peter Lang, 1993) for the correspondence Bhebe and the author had on the political crisis in Zimbabwe during this time. The reader should note that the use of initials is a common practice among Africans, because the white masters often used their first names in a derogatory fashion.

32. A former African member of Parliament, during an interview with the author, July 15, 1983.

33. *The Rhodesia Herald*, November 12, 1968, p. 3.

34. In accordance with the colonial practice the Speaker of the legislature was considered a nonpartisan office. He often resigned either his seat in Parliament or from his political party to assume the prestigious position of Speaker. At that time the Speaker was Albert Stumbles, a former member of Whitehead's United Federal Party. The Speaker only cast a ballot in the case of a tie. Of course, under the RF this would never happen.

35. Rhodesia: *Parliamentary Debates*, August 19, 1970, p. 1864.

36. A former African member of Parliament, during an interview with the author, July 15, 1983.

37. *Parliamentary Debates*, August 19, 1970, p. 1865.

38. Ibid., p. 1870.

39. Ibid., p. 1871.

40. Southern Rhodesia, The Report of the Commission of Inquiry into Native Education [V. A. Judges Chairman], 1962, p. 138.

41. *Parliamentary Debates*, August 19, 1970, p. 1866.
42. Britain and Rhodesia: *Settlement Proposals, An Explanation* (London: H. M. P., 1971), p. 2.
43. M. M. Bhebe, in a letter dated February 10, 1972, addressed to the author.
44. M. J. Khabo, during the debate on the no-confidence motion, *Parliamentary Debates*, August 19, 1970.
45. Indeed, after five African members had supported the motion, A. L. Lazell, the RF member for Milton Park (named after William Milton), reacted, "I think that the supporters of this motion have been very irresponsible." Rhodesia: *Parliamentary Debates*, August 19, 1970, p. 1867.
46. For example, see Ian Smith, "Rhodesia's Finest Hour: Unilateral Declaration of Independence," November 11, 1965.
47. *Parliamentary Debates*, August 19, 1970, p. 1868.
48. Ibid., p. 1873.
49. Ibid., p. 1847.
50. Ibid., p. 1876.
51. M. J. Khabo, during debate on no-confidence motion, in *Parliamentary Debates*, August 19, 1970, p. 1877.
52. E. G. Sifuya, in ibid.
53. R. T. Sadomba, in ibid., p. 1887.
54. N. A. Gandanzara, in ibid., p. 1889.
55. Ibid., p. 1890.
56. Ibid.
57. L. A. Ndhlove, in ibid., p. 1891.
58. Arthur Smith, in ibid., p. 1892.
59. Blake, *History of Rhodesia*, p. 368.
60. Todd, *The Right to Say No*, p. 96.
61. British Council of Missionary Society, "Violence in Southern Africa: A Christian Assessment," October 28, 1970 (Mutare: Old Mutare Methodist Archives).
62. ABC-TV, *20/20: The Agony of Mozambique*, March 2, 1990.
63. On February 15, 1990, this author wrote a letter to President F. W. de Klerk, advising him that his overtures of peace to ANC in South Africa would be futile if he did not stop supporting UNITA (Angolan Independence Union) and Renamo activities.
64. *The Washington Post*, August 1, 1989.
65. Indeed, in July 1990 Kenya was rocked by violent demonstrations against the Moi government. That the demonstrators demanded an end to one-party rule, which Moi instituted in 1982, suggests a critical need for innovation in Kenya itself.
66. OAU, A Communiqué on Mozambique (Nairobi: August 8, 1989).
67. While the author was in Zimbabwe in May 1997 he learned that the ruling ZANU was trying to have Edgar Tekere rejoin the party.
68. For the names of these officials and the extent of their involvement in the scandal, see *The Herald*, April 13, 1989, p. 1.
69. Ibid., p. 45, *Parade* magazine section.
70. Faye Chung became minister of education on August 4, 1989, when Dzin-

gai Mutumbuka was forced to resign from the government following his conviction on charges of gross corruption, ibid.

71. *The Herald*, August 11, 1989, p. 15.

72. Ibid.

73. For a discussion of this remarkable leader, see Dickson A. Mungazi, *Gathering Under the Mango Tree: Values in Traditional Culture in Africa* (New York: Peter Lang, 1996).

74. Mellyse Otieno, during a conversation with the author in Nairobi, May 17, 1997.

75. Paulo Freire, *Pedagogy of the Oppressed* (trans. M. B. Ramos) (New York: Continuum, 1983), p. 62.

Selected Bibliography

BOOKS

Altrincham, Lord. *Kenya's Opportunity: Memories, Hopes and Ideas.* London: Faber and Faber, 1956.
Andrews, F. C. *John White of Mashonaland.* New York: Negro Universities Press, 1935.
Anglin, Douglas (ed.). *Conflict and Change in Southern Africa: Papers from a Scandinavian Conference.* Washington, DC: University Press of America, 1978.
Ashlay, Eric. *African Universities and Western Tradition.* New York: Alfred A. Knopf, 1964.
Atkinson, Norman. *Teaching Rhodesians: A History of Educational Policy in Rhodesia.* London: Longman, 1972.
Austin, Reginald. *Racism and Apartheid in Southern Rhodesia.* Paris; Unesco, 1975.
Awooner, K. *The Breast of the Earth: Survey of History, Culture, and Literature of Africa South of the Sahara.* New York: Anchor-Doubleday, 1975.
Ayadelette, F. *The American Rhodes Scholar.* Princeton; NJ: Princeton University Press, 1946.
Azunuino, Bragance. *The African Liberation Reader.* London: Rex Collins, 1979.
Banana, Canaan. *Theology of Promise: The Dynamics of Self-reliance.* Harare: The College Press, 1982.
Barber, James. *Rhodesia: The Road to Rebellion.* London: Oxford University Press, 1967.
Bate, H. M. *Report From Rhodesia.* London: Melrose, 1953.
Battle, Vincent M., and Charles H. Lyons (eds.). *Essays in the History of African Education.* New York: Teachers College Press, 1970.

Bennett, George. *Kenya: A Political History*. London: Oxford University Press, 1963.
Berens, Denis, and Albert B. Planger (eds.). *A Concise Encyclopedia of Zimbabwe*. Gweru: Mambo Press, 1988.
Bergman, Edward (ed.). *African Reaction to Missionary Education*. New York: Teachers College Press, 1975.
Biglew, F. *White Man's Africa*. London: Harper and Brothers, 1898.
Blake, Robert. *A History of Rhodesia*. New York: Alfred A. Knopf, 1978.
Blundell, Michael. *A Love Affair with the Sun: A Memoir of Seventy Years in Kenya*. Nairobi: Kenway Publications, 1994.
Blundell, Michael. *So Rough a Wind*. London: Weidenfeld and Nicholson, 1964.
Boggie, J. M. *First Steps in Civilizing Rhodesia*. Bulawayo: Belmont Press, 1940.
Bond-Stewart, Kathy. *Education*. Gweru: Mambo Press, 1986.
Bordolph, R. *The Civil Rights Record: Black Americans and the Law, 1848–1970*. New York: Thomas Crowell and Company, 1970.
Bowman, Larry W. *Politics in Rhodesia: White Power in an African State*. Cambridge, MA: Harvard University Press, 1973.
Brooks, Edgar. *Native Education in South Africa*. Pretoria: Van Schaik, 1930.
Brownlee, Margaret. *The Lives and Work of South African Missionaries: A Bibliography*. Cape Town: University of Cape Town, 1952.
Bull, Theodore. *Rhodesia: Crisis of Color*. New York: Quadrangle Books, 1967.
Carter, Gwendolyn, and Patrick O'Meara. *Southern Africa: The Continuing Crisis*. Bloomington: Indiana University Press, 1978.
Cash, Wilbur Joseph. *The Mind of the South*. New York: Alfred A. Knopf, 1941.
Chambliss, J. E. *The Life and Labors of David Livingstone*. Westport, CT: Negro Universities Press, 1875.
Chidzero, B. T. *Education and the Challenge of Independence*. Geneva: IEUP, 1977.
Chirenje, Mutero. "The Afro-American Factor in Southern African Ethiopianism, 1890–1906." In *Profiles of Self-determination: African Responses to European Colonialism, 1652 to the Present*, edited by David Chanaiwa. Northridge: California State University, 1976.
Christie, Ian. *Samora Machel: A Biography*. London: Panof Books, 1989.
Clark, E. *Quebec and South Africa: A Study of Cultural Adjustment*. London: Oxford University Press, 1934.
Clatworthy, Frederick. *The Foundations of British Colonial Education Policy, 1923–1938*. Ann Arbor: University of Michigan, 1971.
Clements, Frank. *Rhodesia: A Study of the Deterioration of a White Society*. New York: Frederick A. Praeger, 1969.
Clutton-Brock, Guy. *Cold Comfort Confronted: Rhodesia and the Black Struggle for Independence*. London: Oxford University Press, 1972.
Cohen, Robin (ed.). *Democracy and Socialism in Africa*. Boulder, CO: Westview Press, 1991.
Constantine, Stephen. *David Lloyd George*. New York: Routledge, 1992.
Cooper-Omer, J. D. *The Zulu Aftermath: A 19th Century Revolution in Bantu Africa*. Evanston, IL: Northwestern University Press, 1966.
Cory, Robert, and Dianna Mitchell (eds.). *African Nationalist Leaders in Rhodesia's Who's Who*. Bulawayo: Books of Rhodesia, 1977.
Cousins, H. *From Kaffir Kraal to Pulpit*. London: S. Patridge, 1899.

Cowan, Lang, James O'Connell, and David Scanlan (eds.). *Education and Nationbuilding in Africa*. New York: Praeger, 1966.
Cox, Courtland. *African Liberation*. New York: Black Education Press, 1972.
Crouse, Casper. *Rhodesian Independence and the Security Council of the United Nations*. Alice: Fort Hare College Press, 1966.
Curle, Adam. *Education for Liberation*. New York: John Wiley and Sons, 1973.
Curry Robert. *African Nationalist Leaders*. London: Rex Collins, 1971.
Curtin, Philip. *African South of the Sahara*. Morristown, NJ: Silver Burdett, 1970.
Curtin, Philip (ed.). *The Images of Africa: British Ideas and Action, 1780–1850*. Madison: University of Wisconsin Press, 1964.
Dacks, A. J. *Christianity South of the Zambezi*. Gweru: Mambo Press, 1973.
Daniels, C. (ed.). *Drums of War: The Continuing Crisis in Rhodesia*. Chicago: The Third World Press, 1974.
Davidson, Basil. *The Black Man's Burden: Africa and the Curse of the Nation State*. New York: Times Books, 1992.
Davidson, Basil. *Modern Africa: A Social and Political History*. New York: Longman, 1985.
Davidson, Basil. *The Search for Africa: History, Culture, Politics*. New York: Randon House, 1994.
Davidson, Francis. *South Africa and Central Africa: A Record of Fifteen Years of Missionary Labors Among the Primitive Peoples*. Elgin, IL: Brethren Publishing House, 1915.
Davies, Horton (ed.). *South African Missions, 1800–1950*. London: Thomas Nelson, 1954.
Davis, A. *The Native Problem in South Africa*. London: Chapman and Hall, 1902.
Davis, Richard. *Bantu Education and the Education of Africans in South Africa*. Athens: Ohio University Center for International Studies, 1972.
De Kieweit, C. W. *The Anatomy of the South African Misery*. London: Oxford University Press, 1956.
Demon, Donald, and Balam Nyeko. *Southern Africa Since 1800*. London: Longman, 1984.
Diffendorfer, Ralph (ed.). *The World Service of the Methodist Episcopal Church*. Chicago: Council of the World Board of Benevolences, 1928.
Dodge, Ralph E. *The Revolutionary Bishop: An Autobiography*. Pasadena, CA: William Carey Library, 1986.
Drake, Howard. *A Bibliography of African Education South of the Sahara*. Aberdeen, TX: University of Aberdeen Press, 1942.
Du Bois, W. E. B. *The Soul of Black Folk*. Greenwich, CT: 1902.
Dugard, John. *The Southwest Africa/Namibia Dispute*. Berkeley: University of California Press, 1973.
Dumbutshena, Enock. *The Zimbabwean Tragedy*. Nairobi: Oxford University Press, 1975.
Edgerton, Robert B. *Mau Mau: An African Crucible*. New York: The Free Press, 1989.
Eicher, J. C. *Educational Costing and Financing in Developing Countries*. Washington, DC: World Bank, 1984.
El-Ayouty, Yassin. *The Organization of African Unity: Ten Years After. Comparative Perspective*. New York: Praeger, 1975.

Fafunwa, Babs. *History of Education in Nigeria*. London: George Allen and Unwin, 1974.
Fletcher, Basil. *The Background of Educational Development in the Federation*. Salisbury: University of Rhodesia and Nyasaland, 1959.
Fortune, George. *African Languages in Schools: Select Papers from the 1962 and 1963 Conferences on Teaching African Languages*. Salisbury: University College of Rhodesia and Nyasaland, 1964.
Fraser, D. *The Future of Africa*. Westport, CT: Negro Universities Press, 1911.
Freire, Paulo. *Pedagogy of the Oppressed* (trans. M. B. Ramos). New York: Continuum, 1983.
Fuglesang, Andrea. *About Understanding and Observations on: Cross-Cultural Communication*. New York: Decade Books, 1982.
Gale, William. *Heritage of Rhodesia*. New York: Oxford University Press, 1960.
Gauss, Christian (ed.). *Michiavelli's The Prince* (Trans. Luigi Ricci). New York: Signet Classics, 1952.
Gelfand, Michael. *African Background*. Cape Town: Juta and Company, 1965.
Gelfand, Michael. *Diet and Tradition in African Culture*. London: E. and S. Livingstone, 1971.
Gelfand, Michael. *Growing Up in Shona Society*. Gweru: Mambo Press, 1979.
Gelfand, Michael. *Gubulawayo and Beyond: Letters and Journals of Early Missionaries to Zambezia, 1879–1889*. London: George Chapman, 1968.
Gelfand, Michael. *The Sick African*. Cape Town: Juta and Company, 1957.
Genn, Lewis. *Central Africa: The Former British States*. New York: Prentice-Hall, 1934.
Genn, Lewis. *Huggins of Rhodesia: The Man and His Country*. London: Allen and Unwin, 1964.
Gibbs, Peter. *Flag for the Matebele: An Entertainment in African History*. New York: The Vanguard Press, 1956.
Good, Robert. *U.D.I.: The International Politics of the Rhodesian Rebellion*. Princeton, NJ: Princeton University Press, 1973.
Gordon, David F. *Deconlonization in Kenya*. Boulder, CO: Westview Press, 1986.
Gordon, Robert. *The Bushman Myth: The Making of a Namibian Underclass*. Boulder, CO: Westview Press, 1991.
Gray, Richard. *The Two Nations: Aspects of Development of Race Relations in Rhodesia and Nyasaland*. London: Oxford University Press, 1973.
Green, J. S. *Rhodes Goes North*. London: Bell and Sons, 1936.
Griffin, J. H. *Black Like Me*. New York: American Library of Literature, 1962.
Grigg, Edward. *Kenya's Opportunity: Memories, Hopes and Ideas*. London: Faber and Faber, 1956.
Grimston, Brian. *Survey of Native Educational Development in Southern Rhodesia*. St. Albans, 1938.
Grove, G. C. *The Planting of Christianity in Africa, Vol. II*. London: Murray, 1952.
Grundy, Kenneth. *South Africa: Domestic Crisis and Global Challenge*. Boulder, CO: Westview Press, 1991.
Hailey, William. *The African Survey*. London: Oxford University Press, 1957.
Hall, Richard. *Great Zimbabwe of Mashonaland*. London: Longman, 1967.
Hancock, Ian. *White Liberals, Moderates, and Radicals in Rhodesia, 1953–1980*. Kent: Croom Helm, Ltd., 1984.

Hapsgood, David. *Africa in World Focus*. New York: Ginn and Company, 1971.
Harden, Blaine. *Africa: Dispatches from the Fragile Continent*. New York: W. W. Norton and Co., 1990.
Hargreaves, John D. *Decolinization in Africa*. London: Longman, 1988.
Hassauig, Schioldberg. *The Christian Missions and the British Expansion in Southern Rhodesia, 1888–1923*. Ann Arbor: University of Michigan Microfilms, 1960.
Henderson, Lawrence. *Angola: Five Centuries of Conflict*. Ithaca, NY: Cornell University Press, 1979.
Herbstein, Dennis. *White Man, We Want to Talk to You*. London: Oxford University Press, 1979.
Herman, Herbert. *The Log of a Native Commissioner*. Bulawayo: Books of Rhodesia, 1971.
Hindley, George. *Fifty Years with Ford*. Bulawayo: Duly and Company, 1961.
Hirschman, David, and Brian Rose. *Education for Development in Southern Africa*. Johannesburg: South African Institute of International Affairs for the Foundation of Foreign Affairs, 1974.
Hirst, Paul. *Knowledge and the Curriculum: A Collection of Philosophical Papers*. London: Routledge and Kegan Paul, 1974.
Holleman, J. F. *Chief, Council, and Commissioner: Some Problems of Government in Rhodesia*. Essen, The Netherlands: von Garcun, Ltd., 1969.
Holleman, J. F. *Shona Customary Law*. Cape Town: Oxford University Press, 1952.
Hone, P. F. *Southern Rhodesia*. New York: Negro Universities Press, 1909.
Hopgood, David. *Africa in To-day's World Focus*. New York: Ginn and Company, 1971.
Hortrell, Muriel. *African Education: Some Origins and Developments in 1953*. Johannesburg: South African Institute of Race Relations, 1964.
Houtandji, Paulin. *African Philosophy: Myth and Reality*. Bloomington: Indiana University Press, 1982.
Huberman, A. M. *Understanding Change in Education in Africa*. Paris: Unesco, 1973.
Huddleston, Trevor. *Naught for Your Comfort*. New York: Oxford University Press, 1956.
Hyan, R. *Elgin and Churchill and the Colonial Office, 1905–1908*. London: Macmillan and Company, 1968.
Ingle, Clyde. *From Village to State in Tanzania*. Ithaca, NY: Cornell University Press, 1972.
Innes, Duncan. *Our Country, our Responsibility*. London: Africa Bureau, 1969.
Irvine, S. H. *Selection for Secondary Education in Southern Africa*. Salisbury: University College of Rhodesia and Nyasaland, 1965.
James, L. A. *Racism and Education: Aspects of Development in Former British Central Africa*. Dayton: Brown and Kroger, 1965.
Jaster, Robert. *The Defence of White Power: South African Foreign Policy under Pressure*. New York: St. Martin's Press, 1989.
July, Robert. *A History of the African People*. New York: Charles Scribner's Sons, 1974.
Kane, Norah. *The World's View*. London: Cassell and Company, 1954.
Kanogo, Tabitha. *Makers of History: Dedan Kimathi*. Nairobi: East African Educational Publications, 1992.

Kapenzi, Geoffrey. *A Clash of Cultures: Christian Missionaries and the Shona of Southern Rhodesia*. Washington, DC: University Press of America, 1978.

Kaplan, Irving. *Zaire: A Country Study*. Washington, DC: American University Press, 1979.

Kapungu, Leonard T. *Rhodesia: The Struggle for Freedom*. Mayknoll: Orbis Books, 1974.

Keatley, Patrick. *The Politics of Partnership*. Harmondsworth. Penguin Books, 1963.

Kenyatta, Jomo. *Facing Mount Kenya*. Nairobi: Kenway Publications, 1938.

Kenyatta, Jomo. *Harambe: The Prime Minister of Kenya's Speeches, 1963–1964*. Nairobi: Oxford University Press, 1964.

Kimble, H. T. *Emerging Africa*. New York: Scholastic Books, 1963.

King, Jr., Martin Luther. *Why We Can't Wait*. New York: New American Library, 1964.

Kitchen, Helen (ed.). *The Educated African: A Country Survey*. New York: Praeger, 1971.

Knight, Edward. *Rhodesia To-day*. Bulawayo: Books of Rhodesia, 1970.

Knorr Kenneth. *British Colonial Theories*. Toronto: University of Toronto Press, 1973.

Kopan, Hans. *Nationalism: Its Meaning and History*. London: van Nostrand Company, 1965.

La Guma, Alex (ed.). *Apartheid: Collection of Writings of South Africa by South Africans*. New York: International Publishers, 1971.

Lardner-Burke, Desmond. *Rhodesia: The Story of Crisis*. London: Albourne, 1966.

Lewis, Leonard. *Equipping Africa: Educational Development in British Colonial Africa*. London: Edinburgh House Press, 1968.

Lovejoy, Paul (ed.). *African Modernization and Development*. Boulder, CO: Westview Press, 1991.

Lugard, Frederick. *Dual Mandate in British Tropical Africa*. London: Blackwood, 1926.

Lyons, Charles. *To Wash and Aethiop White: British Ideas About Black African Educability, 1530–1960*. New York: Teachers College Press, 1975.

MacDonald, J. G. *Rhodesia: A Life*. Bulawayo: Books of Rhodesia, 1971.

MacPhee, Marshall. *Kenya*. New York: Frederick A. Praeger. 1968.

Makulu, Henry. *Education, Development and Nation-building in Independent Africa*. London: SCM Press, 1971.

Malherbe, Ernest. *Education for Leadership in Africa*. Durban: Natal Technical College, 1960.

Malherbe, Ernest. *The New Education in a Changing Empire*. Pretoria: Van Schaik, 1963.

Maloba, Wunyabari O. *Mau Mau and Kenya: An Analysis of a Peasant Revolt*. Bloomington: Indiana University Press, 1993.

Mandela, Nelson. *Long Walk to Freedom: The Autobiography of Nelson Mandela*. Boston: Little, Brown and Company, 1994.

Marshall, Charles. *Crisis over Rhodesia: A Skeptical View*. Baltimore: Johns Hopkins University Press, 1967.

Martin, David, and Phyllis Johnson. *The Struggle for Zimbabwe*. Harare: Zimbabwe Publishing House, 1981.

Mason, Philip. *The Birth of Dilemma: The Conquest and Settlement of Rhodesia.* London: Oxford University Press, 1958.
Mason, Reginald. *British Education in Africa.* London: Oxford University Press, 1959.
Maxey, Kees. *The Fight for Zimbabwe: The Armed Conflict in Southern Rhodesia since U.D.I.* London: Rex Collins, 1975.
Maxon, Robert M. *Struggle for Kenya: The Loss and Reassertion of Imperial Initiatves, 1912–1923.* London: Assocciated University Press, 1993.
Mboya, Tom. *The Challenge of Nationhood.* New York: Praeger, 1970.
McIntyre, W. D. *Colonies into Commonwealth.* New York: Walker and Company, 1967.
Meli, Francis. *South Africa Belongs to Us: The History of the ANC.* Harare: Zimbabwe Publshing House, 1988.
Memmi, Albert. *The Colonizer and the Colonized.* Boston: Beacon Press, 1965.
Meredith, Martin. *The First Dance of Freedom: Black Africa in the Post-war Era.* New York: Harper and Row. 1984.
Michie, W. D. *The Lands and People of Central Africa.* New York: Longman, 1981.
Mlambo, Ishmael. *Rhodesia: The Strugglke for a Birthright.* London: C. Hurst and Company, 1972.
Mnyanda, B. J. *In Search of Truth.* Bombay: Hind Kitabs, 1954.
Monroe, Walter (ed.). *Encyclopedia of Educational Research.* New York: Macmillan and Company, 1960.
Moore, Robin. *Rhodesia.* New York: Condor Publishing Company, 1977.
Morrell. W. *British Colonial Policy in the Mid-Victorian Age.* Oxford: The Clarendon Press, 1969.
Mtashali, B. V. *Rhodesia: Background to Conflict.* New York: Hawthorne Books, 1967.
Mugomba, Aggripah, and Mougo Nyaggah. *Independence without Freedom: The Political Economy of Colonial Education in Southern Africa.* Santa Barbara: ABC-Clio, 1980.
Mungazi, Dickson A. *The Challenge of Educational Innovation and National Development in Southern Africa.* New York: Peter Lang, 1991.
Mungazi, Dickson A. *Colonial Education for Africans: George Stark's Policy in Zimbabwe.* Westport, CT: Praeger, 1991.
Mungazi, Dickson A. *Colonial Policy and Conflict in Zimbabwe: A Study of Cultures in Collision, 1890–1979.* New York: Taylor and Francis, 1991.
Mungazi, Dickson A. *The Cross Between Rhodesia and Zimbabwe: Racial Conflict in Rhodesia, 1962–1979.* New York: Vantage Press, 1981.
Mungazi, Dickson A. *Education and Government Control in Zimbabwe: A Study of the Commissions of Inquiry, 1908–1974.* Westport, CT: Praeger, 1990.
Mungazi, Dickson A. *The Fall of the Mantle: The Educational Policy of the Rhodesia Front Government and Conflict in Zimbabwe.* New York: Peter Lang, 1993.
Mungazi, Dickson A. *Gathering Under the Mango Tree: Values in Traditional Culture in Africa.* New York: Peter Lang, 1996.
Mungazi, Dickson A. *The Mind of Black Africa,* Westport, CT: Praeger, 1996.
Mungazi, Dickson A. *The Struggle for Social Change in Southern Africa: Visions of Liberty.* New York: Taylor and Francis, 1989.

Mungazi, Dickson A. *To Honor the Sacred Trust of Civilization: History, Politics, and Education in Southern Africa.* Cambridge, MA: Schenkman Publishers, 1983.

Mungazi, Dickson A. *The Underdevelopment of African Education: A Black Zimbabwean Perspective.* Washington, DC: University Press of America, 1982.

Mungazi, Dickson A., and L. Kay Walker. *Educational Reform and the Transformation of Southern Africa.* Westport, CT: Praeger, 1997.

Mungeam, G. H. *British Rule in Kenya, 1895–1912.* Oxford: Clarendon Press, 1966.

Munro, Forbes. *Colonial Rule and the Kamba.* Oxford: Clarendon Press, 1975.

Murphree, M. W. *Village School and Community Development in a Rhodesia Tribal Trust Land.* Salibsury: Zambezia, 1970.

Murphy-Brown, Jeremy. *Kenyatta.* London: George Allen and Unwin, 1979.

Murray, Victor. *The School in the Bush: A Critical Study of the Theory and Practice of Native Education in Africa.* London: Longman, 1938.

Mutasa, Didymus. *Rhodesian Black Behind Bars.* London: Mowbrays, 1974.

Muzorewa, Abel. *Rise Up and Walk: An Autobiography.* Nashville: Abingdon Press, 1978.

Naylor, W. S. *Daybreak in the Dark Continent.* New York: The Young Peoples Missionary Movement, 1905.

Nelson, Harold. *Area Handbook for Southern Rhodesia.* Washington, DC: American University Press, 1975.

Nkomo, Joshua. *Rhodesia: The Case for Majority Rule.* New Delhi: Oxford University Press, 1966.

Nkrumah, Kwame. *Africa Must Unite.* London: Heinemann Educational Books, 1958.

Nyangani, Wellington. *African Nationalism in Zimbabwe.* Washington, DC: University Press of America, 1978.

Obasamjo, Olusegun, and Hans d'Orville (eds.). *Challenges of Leadership in African Development.* New York: Taylor and Francis, 1990.

O'Callaghan, Marcon. *Southern Rhodesia: The Effects of Conquest on Society, Education, and Culture.* Paris: Unesco, 1977.

Ogot, Bethwell A. *Historical Dictionary of Kenya.* London: The Scarecrow Press, 1981.

Olaniyan, Richard. *African History and Culture.* Lagos: Longman, 1992.

Oldham, James. *White and Black in Africa.* New York: Green and Company, 1930.

Omari, C. K. *The Family in Africa.* Geneva: World Council of Churches, 1974.

O'Meara, Patrick. *Rhodesia: Racial Conflict or Coexistence?* Ithaca, NY: Cornell University Press, 1975.

Palley, Claire. *The Constitutional History and Laws of Southern Rhodesia, 1885–1965.* London: Clarendon Press, 1966.

Palmer, Robin. *Land and Racial Domination in Rhodesia.* Los Angeles: UCLA Press, 1977.

Parker, Franklin. *African Development and Education in Southern Rhodesia.* Columbus: Ohio State University Press, 1960.

Passmore, Gloria. *The National Policy of Community Development in Rhodesia.* London: Clarendon Press, 1966.

Peck, A. J. *Rhodesia Accuses.* Boston: Western Islands Press, 1966.

Penny, J. E., and E. E. Thorpe. *Pioneers and Planters: Black Beginnings in America.* Middletown, CT: Xerox Publishing Corporation, 1974.

Pillard, James. *Twenty-Year Report of the Phelps-Stokes Commission, 1911–1931.* New York: Phelps-Stokes Fund, 1932.
Popkin, Samuel. *The Rational Peasant.* Berkeley: University of California Press, 1979.
Porter, B. *Critics of the Empire: British Colonial Attitudes Towards Colonialism in Africa.* New York: St. Martin Press, 1968.
Rake, Alan. *Tom Mboya: Young Man of New Africa.* New York: Doubleday, 1962.
Raner, William. *The Tribe and Its Successors: An Account of African Traditional Life and European Settlement in Southern Rhodesia.* New York: Frederick A. Praeger, 1962.
Ranger, Terence O. *The African Voice in Southern Rhodesia, 1898–1930.* Evanston, IL: Northwestern University Press, 1970.
Ranger, Terence O. *Revolt in Southern Rhodesia, 1896–1897.* Evanston, IL: Northwestern University Press, 1967.
Raphaeli, Nimroid. *Public Sector Management in Botswana.* Washington, DC: World Bank, 1984.
Rasmussen, R. Kent. *Historical Dictionary of Rhodesia/Zimbabwe.* London: The Scarecrow Press, 1979.
Raynor, William. *Tribe and its Successors: An Account of African Traditional Life after European Settlement in Southern Rhodesia.* New York: Frederick A. Praeger, 1962.
Rea, Frederick. *Missionary Factor in Southern Rhodesia.* Salisbury: Historical Association of Rhodesia and Nyasaland, 1962.
Reed, Douglas. *The Battle for Rhodesia.* Cape Town: Howman, 1967.
Rich, Evelyn. *Africa: Tradition and Change.* New York: Random House, 1972.
Riddell, Roger. *From Rhodesia to Zimbabwe: Education for Employment.* Gweru: Mambo Press, 1980.
Roberts, George. *Let Me Tell You a Story: Life as Lived by Pioneer Missionaries to Rhodesia.* Bulawayo: Rhodesia Christian Press, 1964.
Rogers, C. A. *Racial Themes in Southern Rhodesia: The Attitudes and Behavior of the White Population.* New Haven, CT: Yale University Press, 1962.
Rogers, C. A., and C. Franz. *Racial Themes in Southern Rhodesia: Attitudes of the White Population.* New Haven, CT: Yale University Press, 1967.
Rolin, Henri. *Les Lois et l'Administration de la Rhodesie.* Brussels: l-Etablissment Emil Bruylant, 1930.
Samkange, Stanlake. *Origins of Rhodesia.* New York: Frederick A. Praeger, 1968.
Samkange, Stanlake. *What Rhodes Really Said About Africans.* Harare: Harare Publishing House, 1982.
Scanlon, David. *Traditions of African Education.* New York: Teachers College Press, 1964.
Schweitzer, Albert. *Our Task in Colonial Africa.* New York: Harper Brothers, 1948.
Shamuyarira, Nathan. *Crisis in Rhodesia.* London: Audre Deutsche, 1964.
Shapera, I. *Livingstone's Missionary Correspondence.* Berkeley: University of California Press, 1961.
Sithole, Ndabaningi. *African Nationalism.* London: Oxford University Press, 1959.
Sithole, Ndabaningi. *The Roots of a Revolution: Scenes from Zimbabwe's Struggle.* London. Oxford University Press, 1977.
Skelton, Kenneth. *Bishop in Smith's Rhodesia.* Gweru: Mambo Press, 1985.

Skeys, F. W. *With Plumer in Matebeleland.* New York: Negro Universities Press, 1935.
Smith, William. *Nyerere of Tanzania.* Harare: Zimbabwe Publishing House, 1983.
Solarz, Stephen. *Rhodesia: Where Do We Go From Here?* Washington, DC: U.S. Government Printer, 1979.
Sparks, Allister. *The Mind of South Africa.* New York: Alfred Knopf, 1989.
Sparks, Allister. *Tomorrow Another Country: The Inside Story of South Africa's Road to Change.* Chicago: University of Chicago Press, 1995.
Sparrow, G. *Rhodesian Rebellion.* London: Brighton, 1966.
Stack, Harvey. *The Case for Rhodesia.* Syracuse, NY: Syracuse University Press, 1978.
Stack, Louise, and Don Morton. *Torment to Triumph in Southern Africa.* New York: Friendship Press, 1976.
Standing, T. G. *A Short History of Rhodesia.* London: Longman and Sons, 1935.
Steere, D. V. *God's Irregular: Arthur Shearly Cripps: A Rhodesian Epic.* London: S.P.C.K., 1983.
Steiner, Elizabeth. *Educology of the Free.* New York: Philosophical Library, 1981.
Sylvester, Christine. *Zimbabwe: The Terrain of Contradictory Development.* Boulder, CO: Westview Press, 1991.
Symonds, Jane. *Southern Rhodesia: Background to Crisis.* New York: Oxford University Press, 1965.
Taylor, R. *African Education in Rhodesia.* Salisbury: Government Printer, 1970.
Thiongo, Ngugi, and Micere Mugo. *The Trial of Dedan Kimathi.* Harare: Zimbabwe Publishing House, 1976.
Thompson, A. R. *Education and Development in Africa.* New York: St. Martin's Press, 1981.
Tichawapedza, Fungai. *The Zimbabwean Woman in the Struggle for Liberation.* Washington, DC: ZANU Office, 1978.
Tignor, Robert L. *The Colonial Transformation of Kenya: The Kamba, the Kikuyu, and the Masaai from 1900 to 1939.* Princeton, NJ: Princeton University Press, 1976.
Todd, Judith. *Rhodesia: A Study of Racial Conflict.* London: Oxford University Press, 1969.
Todd, Judith. *The Right to Say No: Rhodesia 1972.* Harare: Longman, 1987.
Tredgold, Robert C. *The Rhodesia That Was My Life.* London: George Allen and Unwin, 1968.
Tucker, L. L. *On Trek with Christ in Southern Rhodesia.* Mutare: Rhodesia Mission Press, 1935.
Turner, V. W. *Schism and Continuity in an African Society.* Manchester: Manchester University Press, 1957.
Vambe, Lawrence. *An Ill-fated People: Zimbabwe Before and After Rhodes.* Pittsburgh: University of Pittsburgh Press, 1972.
Vambe, Lawrence. *From Rhodesia to Zimbabwe.* Pittsburgh: University of Pittsburgh Press, 1976.
Walker, Eric. *The British Empire: Its Struggle and Spirit.* Cambridge: Bawes and Bawes, 1944.
Walker, L. Kay, and Dickson A. Mungazi. *Colonial Agriculture for Africans: Emory Alvord's Policy in Zimbabwe.* New York: Peter Lang, 1998.

Weaver, Thomas (ed.). *To See Ourselves: An Anthropology of Modern Social Issues*. Glenview, IL: Scott, Foresman and Company, 1978.
Weinrich, A. K. *Black and White Elites in Rural Rhodesia*. Manchester: Manchester University Press, 1973.
Weinrich, A. K. *Chief and Council in Rhodesia*. Columbia: University of South Carolina Press, 1971.
Widner. Jeniffer A. *The Rise of a Party-State in Kenya: From Harambe to Nyayo*. Berkeley: University of California Press, 1992.
Williams, G. Mennen. *Africa for Africans*. Grand Rapids, MI: William Eerdman Publishing Company, 1969.
Willis, A. J. *An Introduction to the History of Central Africa*. London: Oxford University Press, 1964.
Wilmer, E. T. (ed.). *Zimbabwe Now*. London: Rex Collins, 1973.
Windrich, Elaine. *The Rhodesian Problem*: London: Routledge and Kegan Paul, 1975.
Young, Kenneth. *Rhodesia and Independence. A Study in British Colonial Policy*. London: Dent and Sons, 1967.

GOVERNMENT DOCUMENTS, MATERIALS, AND ORDINANCES IN ZIMBABWE

Anglo-Rhodesian Proposals for a Settlement, 1971.
Campaign for Full Literacy in Five Years, Office of the Prime Minister, 1983.
Circular Number Six on African Education, 1970.
Department of Native Education. *Annual Reports of the Director of Native Education*, 1929–1975.
E/1/1/1: Correspondence from the Department of Native Education to Schools, 1924–1935.
E/1/840: Reports of Inspectors of Schools, 1901–1913.
E/2/11/1–60: Miscellaneous correspondence relating to schools for whites, 1910–1935.
E/2/2/2: Correspondence to British [Synod] Methodist Schools, 1906–1915.
E/2/4/6: Correspondence on intercolonial conference on education, 1906–1909.
E/2/7/1: Correspondence on Education Ordinances, 1902–1907.
E/2/9/2: Correspondence relating to materials supplied to teachers, 1918–1919.
Ministry of Native Education. *African Education Act*, 1959.
Ministry of Native Education. *The New Education Policy*, 1956.
Native Affairs Development Association, 1973
Ordinance Number 3: Responsibilities of the Director of Education, 1903.
Ordinance Number 5: Imposing the Payment of Native Taxes, 1894.
Ordinance Number 6: The Repression of Theft of Stock, 1893.
Ordinance Number 7: Control of Native Schools, 1912.
Ordinance Number 18: The Appointment of the Director of Education, 1899.
Policy Statement Number 5: Presidential Directive for the Development of Education in Zimbabwe, 1980.
Rhodesian Front. *The Dynamic Expansion in African Education*, Ref. Gen/1/1/11/21708, April 20, 1966.

Rhodesian Front. *The Land Tenure Act*. Salisbury: Government Printer, 1969.
Rhodesian Front Party. *Constitution of the Rhodesian Pront Party*. Salisbury: Rhodesian Front Headquarters, 1962.
Rhodesia Labour Party. *The Education Policy of the Rhodesia Labour Party*. Salisbury: The Labour Party, 1945.
Rhodesian Ministry of Education. *Annual Reports of the Secretary for African Education*, 1962–1975.
Rhodesian Ministry of Education. Correspondence with Church Organizations, 1969–1974.
Southern Rhodesia Government. *Official Year Books*, 1932–1939.
United Rhodesia Party. *The Education Policy of the United Rhodesia Party*. Salisbury: Government Printer, 1939
United Rhodesia Party. *The Five-Year Education Plan for Africans*. Salisbury: Government Printer, 1956

DOCUMENTS FROM ZIMBABWE NATIONAL ARCHIVES

Anglo-Rhodesian Relations: Proposals for a Settlement, Ref. Cmd/RR/46/71, November 25, 1971.
Beit Trust. Statement on the Operations of the Trust from date of operation to December 31, 1913.
British Colonial Office. The Constitution for Southern Rhodesia Conferring the Status of Responsible Government, Section 28, 1923.
British South Africa Company. The Diary of Leander Starr Jameson [Administrator from September 10, 1890 to April 1, 1896], Ref. AV/AJ/11: Folios 109–11.
British South Africa Company. Information for intending settlers in Southern Rhodesia, 1901.
British South Africa Company. Reports on Administration, 1899–1902 (2), Ref. SBR/711, 1902.
British South Africa Company Records. Alfred Beit, Ref. AV/5.
British South Africa Company Records, Charles Coghlan [Premier from October 1, 1923 to September 1, 1927], Ref. Co/8/1: Folios 13–17.
British South Africa Company Records. The Diary of Herbert Keigwin, Director of Native Development, 1920–1922.
British South Africa Company Records. Papers of Cecil John Rhodes, Ref. RH/1/1/1.
British South Africa Company Records. The Will of Cecil John Rhodes, Ref. RH/1/2/1–6.
Huggins, Godfrey. "The Education Policy of the Rhodesia United Party," a statement of policy and principles. Salisbury: Government Printer, 1939.
Jones, Creech. Land Policy of the British Government in Kenya, March 7, 1949.
Lennox-Boyd, Alan. The Land Policy of the British Government in Kenya February 22, 1952.
Lyttleton, Oliver. The Land Policy of the British Government in Kenya, November 7, 1952.

Milton [Administrator from December 5, 1898 to December 31, 1914]. Government Notice Number 177, the naming of the Graham Commission, letters dated July 5 and July 14, 1910.
Morris, S. E. (Chief Native Commissioner), "Chief Mangwende is Deposed and Banished," a statement explaining the government's action in deposing Chief Mangwende, January 14, 1960.
Native Commissioner for Mangwende Reserve. A Memo to the Head Office, February 18, 1951, Ref. 191/79.
Report of the Chief Native Commissioner for Matebeleland, 1901–1913.
Reports of the Chief Native Commissioner for Mashonaland, 1901–1912.
Rhodes, Cecil John, A Memo to the British South Africa Company, Ref. File: Ms/Lo/1/19, April 15, 1899.
Rhodesia. *African Education*, Ref. 738, 1973.
Rhodesia. *Education: An Act*, No. 8. Salisbury: Government Printer, 1979.
Rhodesia. *Report of the Commission of Inquiry into Racial Discrimination* (Vincent Quenet, Chairman), Ref. 27015/36050, April 23, 1976.
Southern Rhodesia. *Annual Reports of the Director of Native Education*, 1927–1960.
Southern Rhodesia. *Annual Reports of the Native Commissioners*, 1927–1961.
Southern Rhodesia. *Annual Reports of the Secretary for African Education*, 1962–1979.
Southern Rhodesia. *Legislative Debates*, 1923–1961.
Southern Rhodesia. *Parliamentary Debates*, 1924–1961.
Southern Rhodesia. *Ordinance Number 1*, 1903.
Todd, Garfield. Biographical Sketch. Zimbabwe National Archives, 1997.
Todd, Garfield. "New Education Policy for Natives," 1956.
Zimbabwe. *Annual Digest of Statistics*. Harare: Government Printer, 1988.
Zimbabwe. *Annual Report of the Secretary for Education*, 1980–1989. Harare: Government Printer, 1989.
Zimbabwe. B. T. Chidzero (Minister of Finance and Planning). *Budget Statement*, July 27, 1989.
Zimbabwe. *The Constitutional Amendment* No. 23, 1987.
Zimbabwe. *Constitution of Zimbabwe*, Harare: Government Printer, 1985.
Zimbabwe. Ministry of Education. *Arra Kis: School Library News*. Harare. Vol. 6, No. 60, July, 1986.
Zimbabwe. *Prime Minister Opens Economic Conference*, September 5, 1980.
Zimbabwe. *Prime Minister's New Year's Message to the Nation*, December 31, 1980.
Zimbabwe ZAPU. *Primary School Syllabus*, August, 1978.
Zimbabwe-Rhodesia. *Report of of the Constitutional Conference*, Ref. R2R3, London. Lancaster House, December 21, 1979.

DOCUMENTS FROM KENYA NATIONAL ARCHIVES

Duke of Devonshire. The State Papers on Land Policy in Kenya, Ref. Med. 1922–1923.
Elgin, Lord. The Land Policy of the British Government in Kenya, March 9, 1908.
Griffiths, James. Land Policy of the British Government in Kenya, December 12, 1950.

Jones, Creech. The Land Policy of the British Government in Kenya, March 7, 1949.
Lennox-Boyd, Alan. The Land Policy of the British Government in Kenya, February 22, 1952.
Lyttleton, Oliver. The Land Policy of the British Government in Kenya, November 7, 1952.

REPORTS OF THE COMMISSIONS OF INQUIRY IN ZIMBABWE

Commission of Inquiry into Education (Marshall Hole Chairman), Ref. A/5/08, 1908.
Commission of Inquiry into Industrial Development of Natives (Herbert Keigwin, Chairman), Ref. A/7/20, 1920.
Commission of Inquiry into Native Affairs (James Graham, Chairman), 1911.
Commission of Inquiry into Native Education (Alexander Kerr, Chairman), 1951.
Commission of Inquiry into White Education (Alexander Russell, Chairman), Ref. A/2/17, 1916.
The Report of the Commission of Inquiry into African Primary Education, (L. J. Lewis, Chairman), 1974.
The Report of the Commission of Inquiry into Discontent in the Mangwende Reserve (James Brown, Chairman), 1961.
The Report of the Commission of Inquiry into Native Education (A. V. Judges, Chairman), 1962.
The Report of the Commission on Higher Education in the Colonies (Justice Asquith, Chairman), the British Colonial Office, Ref. Cmd.6647, 1945.
The Report of the Land Commission (Morris Carter, Chairman), Ref. CSR/3/26, 1925.

PARLIAMENTARY DEBATES: ZIMBABWE

1964, 1955, 1960, 1962, 1963, 1964, 1967, 1969, 1970, 1971, 1972, 1973, 1977, 1978, 1983

PRESS STATEMENTS AND SPEECHES BY GOVERNMENT OFFICIALS IN ZIMBABWE

Chung, Faye (Minister of Primary and Secondary Education). "The Importance of Local Production of Science Textbooks." Ref. 80/89/CB/MA. March 9, 1989.
Chung, Faye. "Pre-school Training Graduates." Ref. 317/88/GB/SD/BJ, July 25, 1988.
Chung, Faye. "The Role of Booksellers in Educational Development." Ref. 223/89/CB/EM/SM, July 13, 1989.
Chung, Faye. "Women Are Educated Less than Men." Ref. 230/89/CB/SM/SR, July 25, 1989.

Culverwell, Joseph (Minister of State for National Scholarship). "Take Education Seriously." Ref. 59/88/SL/BC, February 23, 1989.
Culverwell, Joseph. "U.S. Sponsored Students Graduate." Ref. 78/89/CB/MA, March 1, 1989.
Hughes, Aminia (Deputy Minister of Transport). "Be Selfless and Dedicated Teachers." Ref. 482/88/SM, October 28, 1988.
Karimanzira, David. "Educate the People on the Dangers of Agrochemicals." Ref. 399/88/EMM/CB, September 14, 1988.
Karimanzira, David (Minister of Social Services). "Educate Farmers on Better Livestock Production." Ref. 472/88/EMM/SM, October 25, 1988.
Karimanzira, David. "Government to Provide More Extension Staff." Ref. 235/89/EMM/SM/SK, July 25, 1989.
Kay, Jack (Deputy Minister of Lands, Agriculture, and Rural Settlement). "Zimbabwe Is SADDC's Breadbasket." Ref. 384/EMM/SG, August 29, 1988.
Ministry of Higher Education. "Learner-Tutor Course Applications." Ref. 459/88/CB/SM, October 17, 1988.
Ministry of Information. "Vacancies for Zimbabwe-Cuba Teacher Education Course." Ref. 460/88/CB/SM, October 17, 1988
Ministry of Public Construction and National Housing. "Three Hundred Million Dollars Boost Rural Housing." Ref. 19/89/BC/SK, January 23, 1989.
Muchemwa, Felix (Minister of Health). "State Certificated Nurses Graduate in Masvingo." Ref. 29/80/RN/SD/BJ, July 21, 1988.
Mujuru, Joyce (Minister of Community and Cooperative Development). "Women's Role in Nation Building." Ref. 4/1/89/SG/SM, June 6, 1989.
Mutumbuka, Dzingai (Minister of Higher Education). "The Importance of Revising History." Ref. 15/89/CB/SK, January 23, 1989.
Mutumbuka, Dzingai. "Marymount Teachers Graduate." Ref. 365/88/03/MM, August 20, 1988.
Mutumbuka, Dzingai. "The Role of Professional Bodies in National Development." Ref. 427/88/CB/EMM, September 22, 2988.
Mutumbuka, Dzingai. "Training Institutions Play Vital Role in National Development." Ref. 447/88/CC/ES, October 7, 1988.
Mutumbuka, Dzingai. "The University of Zimbabwe Staff Development." Ref. 405/88/CB/ME, September 14, 1988.
Nkomo, John (Minister of Labor). "A Call for Educational Program." Ref. 356/88/SK/EM/SG, August 17, 1988.
Nyagumbo, Maurice (Minister of Political Affairs). "Zimbabwe Objects to Education of U.N. Transitional Assistance Group." Ref. 7/89/BC/SM, January 13, 1988.

CHURCH PUBLICATIONS, DOCUMENTS, LETTERS

Catholic Church. *Pastoral Letter: Violence in Southern Africa*. London: S.C.M., 1970.
Chimbadzwa, Josiah. "The Seed Is Planted." Tape recording made by Rev. E. Sells, 1968. Old Mutare Methodist Archives.
Christian Century Foundation. *Christian Century*, October 8, 1969
Christian Council of Rhodesia. *The Church and Human Rights*. Annual Report, 1965.

Dodge, Ralph E. "The African Church Now and in the Future." Essay, 1964.
Dodge, Ralph E. "The Church in Africa." Episcopal address in *The Official Journal of the Methodist Church*. Old Mutare: Rhodesia Mission Press, 1963.
Dodge, Ralph, E. "The Church and Freedom." Essay, 1963.
Dodge, Ralph E. "The Church and Law and Order." Essay, 1963.
Dodge, Ralph E. Letter dated March 18, 1959, addressed to Garfield Todd.
Dodge, Ralph E. Letter dated July 17, 1964, addressed to William Harper.
Dodge, Ralph E. Newsletter addressed to Methodist Missionaries, February 24, 1964.
Floyd, Jean. "A Kraal School in Uzumba Reserve." Essay on African Education. Old Mutare Methodist Archives (mimeographed), 1956.
Harper, William. Letter dated July 22, 1964, addressed to Dodge.
Hassing, Per. Letter addressed to Dr. James Matthews, an official of the Methodist Church in New York, written from Old Mutare Methodist Center, April 2, 1959. Old Mutare Methodist Archives.
Heads of Denominations. *Memorandum to the Ministry of African Education*. Salisbury, February 26, 1970
Kachidza, Henry. Letter dated August 1, 1964, addressed to the World Council of Churches in Geneva.
Lamont, Donal. *An Open Letter to the Prime Minister*: Old Mutare: Old Mutare Methodist Archives, October 26, 1976.
Methodist Church. *The Christian Advance* (2), Number 1, 1918.
Methodist Church. *Umbowo*. Old Umtali: Rhodesia Mission Press, 1964.
Methodist Church. "A Warning Against the Declaration of Independence." Press release, May 17, 1964.
Methodist Episcopal Church. *Official Journal of the Methodist Church*. Old Umtali: Rhodesia Mission Press, 1905, 1907, 1919, 1927, 1964.
Mungazi, Dickson A. Letter to Bishop Desmond Tutu, Chair, Truth and Reconciliation Commission, Pretoria, South Africa, June 9, 1997.
National Council of Churches. *Africa Is Here*. New York: Board of Foreign Missions, 1952.
Nkomo, Joshua. Letter addressed to Dodge, July 18, 1964.
Pelley, Donald. *A Short History of St. Augustine's Mission*. St. Augustine's School Records Office (Mimeographed), 1903.
Shephard, D. E. (private secretary to the Minister of Internal Affairs), letter to Dodge, July 22, 1964.
Stewart, Lois. Response to Questionnaire, June 20, 1986.
Todd, Garfield. Telegram dated July 17, 1964, sent to Dodge.
Todd, Judith. Letter to the Author, May 9, 1997.
United Methodist Church. *Annual Report*, Salisbury, 1969.
United Methodist Church. *Official Journal of the United Methodist Church*, 1969, 1970.
United Methodist Church. *Resolution to the Ministry of Education*, Salisbury, April, 28, 1970.
United Methodist Church. *Southern Africa*. New York: Board of Global Ministries, 1986.

ARTICLES IN NEWSPAPERS, JOURNALS, AND MAGAZINES

Alston, M. C. "Pioneer School in Southern Rhodesia." *United Empire*, 22 (1931), pp. 16–18.
Barr, F. C. "Native Education in Rhodesia." *Month* 35, June 1966, pp. 352–59.
Beit, Alfred. "Government Policy and African Development," *The African Weekly*, Vol. 1, No 28, December 13, 1945.
Bevan, L. E. "Education of Natives in the Pastoral Pursuits." NADA 2 (1924), pp. 13–16.
Birmingham, David. "The United Kingdom Studies Symposium on African Studies." *The Journal of Modern African Studies*, April 1970, pp. 138–40.
"Britain and Rhodesian Students." *Africa*, March 1971, pp. 24–26.
Cannon, J. "Cecil Rhodes and Religious Education." *The Methodist Quarterly Review*, October 1924, pp. 634–37.
Carruthers-Smith, E. E. "African Education in Bulawayo from 1892." NADA, May 1971, pp 81–93.
Charles, S. J. "Southern Rhodesia." *Practical Education and School Crafts*, July 1964, pp. 201–03.
The Christian Science Monitor. "Future Leaders Learn Next-door: Namibians Study at U.N. School in Zambia," September 7, 1989.
Currie, J., et al. "Indirect Rule in Africa and its Bearing on Educational Development," *Overseas Education*, August 1933, pp 82–84.
Davidson, Basil. "African Education in Bantu Central and Southern Africa." *Presence Africaine*, September 1956, pp. 106–12.
Fletcher, Basil. "Educational Enterprise in Africa." *School and Society*, May 23, 1959, pp. 242–43.
Fritz, Mark. "African Democracy Takes a Backward Leap." *Arizona Daily Sun*, Flagstaff, November 21, 1993.
Good, Kenneth. "Education for the Colonized." *New Society*, November 1, 1973, pp 268–70.
Good, Robert. "Intelligence and Attainment in Rhodesia." *Overseas Education*, April 1956, pp. 17–27.
The Herald (Zimbabwe). Various issues, July 9, 1983, through August 8, 1980.
———. April 13, 1989, "Mozambique Looks to the World for $450 million Aid."
———. July 10, 1989, "Apartheid Cannot be Condoned."
———. July 15, 1989, "Secondary Schools Hit by Shortage of Qualified Teachers."
———. July 17, 1989, "Worry over School Zoning."
———. July 20, 1989, "Mozambique Peace Drive a Concern."
———. July 24, 1989, "Concept of Education with Production Explained."
———. July 28, 1989, "Nkomo's Economic Objectives are a Priority in Resettlement."
———. July 28, 1989, "University of Zimbabwe gets $400 Million from Federal Republic of Germany for Developing Equipment."
———. August 11, 1989, "Nkomo Lectures University Students."
———. August 11, 1989, "Sanctions that Would Bite."

———. August 12, 1989, "President Calls for Revolutionary Land Reform Programs."

———. August 17, 1989, "Compensation for Teachers who Joined Freedom Struggle."

Huggins, Godfrey. "Rhodesia Leads the Way: Education for Europeans in Southern Rhodesia." *Times Educational Supplement*, February 14, 1931.

Irvine, Sanders H. "Education for Citizenship." NADA, March 1961, pp. 74–83.

Isaacman, Allen. "Peasants and Rural Social Protest in Africa." *African Studies Review*, Vol. 33, No. 2 (September 1990).

Jackson, H. M. "Native Education in Southern Rhodesia." *African Observer*, September 1934, pp 28–32.

Jowitt, Harold. "The Protectorate of Southern Africa." *The Yearbook of Education*. Salisbury: Government Printer, 1954.

Junod, H. A. "Native Language and Native Education." *The Journal of African Society*, 1905, pp. 1–14.

Kazembe, Phillip. "Shona in the Schools." *Teacher in New Africa*, June 1967, pp. 16–18.

Keystone, J. E. "Report on the Regional Organization of Research in the Rhodesias and Nyasaland." *Nature*, November 1949, pp. 911–13.

Lacey, C. "Christian Racism in Rhodesia." *Christian Century*, March 1972.

Lewis, Thomas. "The Problem of Semi-Educated Africans." *Overseas Education*, January 1942, pp. 265–73.

Lloyd, B. W. "School Library Facilities for Africans in Southern Rhodesia." *Overseas Education*, April 1960, pp. 36–41.

Los Angeles Times. "Africa's Future Riding the Train to Nowhere," July 17, 1990.

Maier, Karl. "Opponent May Thwart Mugabe's Bid for a One-party System." *The Washington Post*, March 29, 1990.

Milton, Alan. "Teachers for Rhodesia's Tomorrow." *South African Outlook*, August 1966, pp. 129–30.

Mungazi, Dickson A. "Apartheid in South Africa: Origin, Meaning, and Effect." A Documentary Film, Audio-Visual Services, Education, Northern Arizona University, Ref. AC/ECC/2/90, February 22, 1990.

Mungazi, Dickson A. "Application of Memmi's Theory of the Colonizer and the Colonized to the Conflicts in Zimbabwe." *The Journal of Negro Education*, Vol. 55, No. 4 (1986).

Mungazi, Dickson A. "Educational Innovation in Zimbabwe: Possibilities and Problems," *The Journal of Negro Education*, Vol. 54, No. 2 (Spring 1985), pp. 196–212.

Mungazi, Dickson A. "Educational Policy for Africans and Church-State Conflict During the Rhodesia Front Government in Zimbabwe." *The National Social Sceince Journal*, Vol. 2, No. 3 (June 1990).

Mungazi, Dickson A. "A Strategy for Power: Commisions of Inquiry into Education and Government Control in Zimbabwe." *The International Journal of African Historical Studies*, (Boston University), Vol. 22, No. 2 (1989).

Mungazi, Dickson A. "To Bind Ties Between the School and Tribal Life: Edu-

cational Policy for Africans under George Stark in Zimbabwe." *The Journal of Negro Education*, Vol. 58, No. 4 (1989).
Murphree, Betty Jo. "The Acculturative Effects of Schooling on African Attitudes and Values." *Zambezia*, January 1970.
Murphree, Marshall. "A Village School and Community Development in Rhodesia Tribal Trust Land." *Zambezia*, August 1970.
Murray, Victor. "Education under Indirect Rule." *The Journal of African Society*, September 1935, pp. 227–68.
The New York Times. "Higher Controls Seen in Zimbabwe," December 10, 1989.
The New York Times. "The Old Men versus the Public: Africa's Iron Hands Struggle to Hang on," July 15, 1990.
The New York Times. "Students Fail Zimbabwe and Pay Heavy Price," November 16, 1989.
Ngonyama, Suzan. "The Education of the African Girl." NADA, January 1954, pp. 57–58.
Orbell, S. F. "The Role of Environmental Factors in the Education of African Pupils." *Zambezia*, September 1970, pp. 41–45.
Parker, Franklin. "African Community Development and Education in Southern Rhodesia, 1920–1935." *International Review of Missions*, July 1962.
Parker, Franklin. "Early Church-State Relationship in African Education in Rhodesia and Zambia." *World Yearbook of Education*, 1966.
Parker, Franklin. "Education in the Federation of Rhodesia and Nyasaland." *The Journal of Negro Education*, September 1961, pp. 286–93.
Rea, Frederick. "The Future of Mission Education in Southern Rhodesia." *International Review of Missions*, May 1960, pp. 195–200.
Smit, D. L. "Black and White in Southern Africa." *The African Weekly*. Vol. 1, No. 28 (April 18, 1945).
Sunday Mail (Zimbabwe). "Teachers Form Union," August 1989.
Time. "South Africa Scan: Facts and Reports," 1989.

OTHER NEWSPAPERS AND MAGAZINES

African News, The, January 16, 1961; February 20, 1964
African Weekly, The, various issues in 1945 and 1964
Chicago Tribune, October 1, 1981
East African Standard, October 8, 1954
Economist, The, September 30, 1989
Journal of Social Change and Development in Southern Africa, January 1996
Moto, various issues, 1963–89
Newsweek, July 2, 1979
Parade (Harare), August 1989
Rhodesia Herald, The, various issues, 1902–89
Teacher in New Africa, various issues 1964–69
Time, various issues, 1990–97
Washington Post, The, August 1, 1989
World Almanac and Book of Facts, The, various issues, 1990–95

AFRICA IN GENERAL

ABC-TV: *20/20: The Agony of Mozambique*, March 2, 1990.
Africa Action Committee. *Uhuru for Southern Africa*. Kinshasa, December 15, 1984.
Afro-American and African Studies. *Africana* (College Park, MD), Vol. 2, No. 1, (1985).
Anad, Mohamed. *Apartheid: A Form of Slavery*. New York: United Nations, No. 37/71, 1971.
Ayittey, George. "In Africa Independence Is a Far Cry from Freedom." *The Wall Street Journal*, March 28, 1990.
British Council of Missionary Society. "Violence in Southern Africa: A Christian Assessment." Statement of policy on Southern Africa, October 28, 1970.
Carlson, Brian. "American Education: A South African Perspective in the Process of Desegregation." *Kappa Delta Phi*, Summer 1988.
Center for Applied Research. *Social Implications of the Lagos Plan of Action for Economic Development in Africa, 1980–2000*. Geneva, November 1981.
Central Committee for SWAPO. *Swapo: Political Program of the Southwest Africa People's Organization*. Lusaka, July 28–August 1, 1976.
Churchill, Winston, and Franklin Roosevelt. *The Atlantic Charter*, August 11, 1941.
Congolese National Liberation Front (CNLF). *The Struggle for Liberation: Continued Policy of Discrimination*. New York, 1975.
Davidson, Basil. *Africa: New Nations and Problems*. Documentary film, Arts and Entertainment Network, 1988.
Dodge, Ralph E. "The Church and Political Community." Essay, 1963.
Dodge, Ralph E. "A Political Community" Essay, May 1964.
Evans, M. *The Front-line State, South Africa and Southern African Security: Military Prospects and Perspectives*. Harare: University of Zimbabwe, 1989.
Gordimer, Nadine. *Gold and the Gun: Crisis in Mozambique and South Africa*. Documentary film, Arts and Entertainment Network, 1990.
Landis, Elizabeth. "Apartheid and the Disabilities of Women in South Africa." New York: United Nations Unit on Apartheid, 1975.
The League of Nations Covenant. Article 22, January 20, 1920.
The League of Nations. *The Mandate for Southwest Africa*, May 7, 1920.
M'Bow, Amadou-Mahtar, Unesco Director-General. "Unesco and the Promotion of Education for International Understanding." Address to the New York African Studies Association Conference, Albany, October 29, 1982.
Macmillan, Harold. "Commonwealth Independence and Interdependence." Address to the Joint Session of the South African Parliament, Cape Town, February 3, 1960.
Malianga, Washington (a spokesman for ZANU). "We Shall Wage an All Out War to Liberate Ourselves," April 1966.
Mandela, Nelson. Inaugural Address. Cape Town, May 9, 1994.
Mandela, Nelson. "Speech given in Soweto during a reception held in his honor," February 12, 1990.
Mandela, Nelson. "Statement made in Cape Town soon after his release from Victor Verster Prison," SABC, February 11, 1990.

Selected Bibliography 275

McNamara, Robert. "The Challenge of Sub-Sahara Africa." John Crawford Lectures, Washington, DC, November 1, 1985.
Mnegi wa Dikgang. *Education with Production.* Vol. 5, No. 2 (Gaberone), June 1987.
Molotsi, Peter (Fordham University). "Educational Policies and the South African Bantustans." Paper presented at the New York Association of African Studies, Albany, October 29–30, 1982.
Morton, Donald. "Partners in Apartheid." New York Center for Social Action, United Church of Christ, 1973.
Mungazi, Dickson A. Letter addressed to Bishop Desmond M. Tutu, Chair, Truth and Forgiveness Commission, February 20, 1997.
Mungazi, Dickson A. Letter addressed to President F. W. de Klerk of South Africa, on the effect of apartheid on Southern Africa, February 15, 1990,
Mutumbuka, Dzingai. "Zimbabwe's Educational Challenge." Paper read at the World University Services Conference, London, December 1979.
New York Friends Group, Inc. *South Africa: Is Peaceful Change Possible?* New York, 1984.
OAU. "A Communique on Mozambique," Nairobi, August 8, 1989.
Office on Africa Educational Fund. *The Struggle for Justice in South Africa.* Washington, DC February 1984.
PBS. "Not in a Thousand Years: From Rhodesia to Zimbabwe." Documentary film, 1981.
"Prospects of a Settlement in Angola and Namibia." Statement by the Parties Representives of the U.S.A, Angola, SWAPO, and Cuba, 1990.
Rhodesia Front Government. *The Dynamic Expansion in African Education.* Policy statement, Ref. INF/NE/Acc.40/2710, April 20, 1966.
Riddell, Roger. *From Rhodesia to Zimbabwe: Alternatives to Poverty.* Position paper. Gweru: Mambo Press, 1978.
Rubin, Leslie. "Bantustan Policy: A Fantasy and a Fraud." New York: United Nations, Unit on Apartheid, Number 12/71, 1971.
Smith, Arthur (Minister of Education in Rhodesia). Interview with Geoffrey Atkins of the Rhodesia Broadcasting Service, on Educational Policy for Africans, January 31, 1968.
Smuts, J. C. *The League of Nations: A Practical Suggestion,* 1918.
South African Ministry of Information. "South Africa Stops Native Students from Territories from Attending its Schools." Press release, November 2, 1950.
Southern Rhodesia. United Federal Party. *Information Statement,* Ref. UFP/SR/9, 1961.
Sullivan, Leon. "Meeting the Mandate for Change: A Progress Report on the Application of the Sullivan Principles on U.S. Companies in South Africa." New York, 1984.
Tanzania: *Basic Facts about Education.* Dar es Salaam. Government Printer, 1984.
Tanzania: *Education for Self-reliance.* Dar es Salaam. Government Printer, 1967.
TransAfrica. *Namibia: The Crisis in U.S. Policy Toward Southern Africa.* Washington, D.C., 1983.
UNESCO. "Education in Africa in the Light of the Lagos Conference," Paper Number 25, 1976.
United Nations. *A Crime Against Humanity: Questions and Answers on Apartheid.* New York, 1984.

United Nations. *Program of Action Against Apartheid*. New York, October 25, 1983.
University of Cape Town. "A Call for Post-doctoral Research Fellows, 1991." *The Chronicle of Higher Education*, March 16, 1990.
Washington Office on Africa. *Resources on Namibia*. Washington, DC, March 1982.
Watson, P. *The Struggle for Democracy*. Documentary film, PBS, 1988.
World Bank. *Accelerate Development in Sub-Sahara Africa: An Agenda for Action*. Washington, DC: World Bank, 1983.
World Bank. "Alternatives to Formal Education : Unesco Conference on Education." Harare, June 28–July 3, 1982.
World Council of Churches. Involvement in the Struggles Against Oppression in Southern Africa, 1966–1980.
ZANU. *Liberation Through Participation: Women in the Zimbabwean Revolution*. Harare: ZANU, 1981.
ZANU. *Zimbabwe: Election Manifesto*, 1979.
Zimbabwe Conference of Catholic Bishops. *Our Mission to Teach: A Pastoral Statement on Education*. Gweru: Mambo Press, 1987.

INTERVIEWS

Mazaiwana, Edward, former Inspector of Schools, Harare, May 31, 1989.
Muzorewa, Abel, Bishop of the United Methodist Church in Zimbabwe, July 27, 1983.
Nyongesa, H. K., Director, Kenya National Archives, December 13, 1995.
Otieno, Mellyse, Secretary, Nairobi, May 17, 1997.
Sithole, Ndabaningi, former President of ZANU, Harare, July 22, 1983.
Smith, Ian D., former Prime Minister of Rhodesia, July 20, 1983.

Index

Aborigines Protection Society, 180
Abrahamson, A. E., 129
Account of the Native Africans, An (Winterbottom), 53
Addams, Jane, 104
African Education Act, 163–64, 165
African Farmers Union, 227
African National Congress (ANC), 1, 14, 74–75, 130, 163, 185, 27, 230–31
African Orthodox Church, 225
Africans, 7, 99; control of, 4–5; cultural values of 117–18; education of, 64–66, 67–74, 75, 108, 109, 110–12, 113–14, 123–24, 163, 225–26; employment of, 147, 148–50, 159n27, 196–97, 198; equal opportunity for, 125–26; European attitudes toward, 27–28, 48n12, 52–54, 61–62, 76–77, 88–91, 149–50; in Kenya, 135–36, 137–38, 140–41, 191–93, 194–95, 197–209, 213–15, 216–17; land distribution and, 143–45, 195–96; nationalism and, 169–70; political awareness of, 92–93, 135–36; post-war personality of, 115–17, 119, 122; and registration certificates, 136–37; and Rhodesia Front, 234–35, 236–44; self-determination and, 5–6, 119–20, 135–36, 228; in World War II, 112–13, 126–27; in Zimbabwe, 15–16, 59–60, 241–42
African Weekly (newspaper), 111
Agriculture: in Kenya, 37–38
Alexander, Archbishop, 225
American Colonization Society, 3
American Dilemma: The Negro Problem and Modern Democracy, An (Myrdal), 1
Anderson, A. G., 32
Angola, 152
Apartheid, 1–2, 4, 7
Asquith, Herbert Henry, 33, 34, 84, 98, 104
Atkins, Geoffrey, 244
Atlantic Charter, 5–6, 112–13, 198, 211, 219n12
Attlee, Clement, 8, 211
Avrich, Paul, 151

Baldwin, Stanley, 44, 85, 98
Balfour, Arthur James, 33
Bantu Congress of Southern Rhodesia, 227

Baring, Evelyn (Lord Howell), photo 5, 17, 45–46, 142, 156, 211, 212
Bathe, Arthur, 65
Beit, Alfred, 119
Belfield, Henry, 36, 37
Belgium, 4
Bennet, George, 141, 147
Berlin Conference, 2, 3, 23, 25–26, 28, 53, 75
Bhebe, M. M. and Rhodesia Front, 236–44
Bismarck, Otto von, 25
Blair, Tony, 81, 82, 101n2
Blake, Robert, 226, 228, 230
Blixen, Karen: *Out of Africa*, 148
Blundell, Gerry, 94
Blundell, Michael, photo 2, 10, 17, 29, 33, 81, 84–85, 135, 148, 149, 223, 224, 225; and Africans, 89–90, 135, 140–41, 149, 218; and Kenya, 8–9, 21, 86–88, 196, 216–17, 218–19, 221n48, 228, 246; and Oliver Lyttleton, 211–12, 213; and Mau Mau rebellion, 142, 156–58, 209–11, 229; in politics, 94–100, 136, 214, 217, 231–32; and settlers, 139–40; in Solai, 91–92; *So Rough a Wind*, 191, 192–93, 219n1; and World War II, 93–94
Boers, 4, 104
Bowring, Charles, 37, 38
Briggs, Puck, 217
British Colonial Office, 31–32, 45, 46, 184, 232
British Council of Missionary Society, 245–46
British East Africa Association, 28
British South Africa Company, 12, 57, 58, 60, 65, 72
Brockway, Fenner, 148, 217
Brodhurst-Hill, Evelyn, 89, 91
Brodhurst-Hill, Timothy (Bronco Bill), 87–88, 89–91
Brooke-Popham, Robert, 44
Bruce, James, 23
Bulawayo National Affairs Association, 110, 186
Burton, Richard, 23
Byrne, Joseph , 42, 43, 44

Callaghan, James, 217
Cameron, Donald, 49n41, 224, 225
Campbell-Bannerman, Henry, 33, 34
Canada, 104–5, 193–94
Carothers, J. C.: *The Psychology of the Mau Mau*, 154–55
Carter, Morris, 41
Carter Commission, 41, 49n39
Carver, George Washington, 27–28
Cavendish-Bentinck, Ferdinand C., 94–95
Central African Federation, 43
Central highlands (Kenya), 29, 30, 37; settlement in, 95–96, 139, 143, 144–45
Chamberlain, Neville, 5, 44
Chaplin, Francis P., 107, 108
China, 151–52
China, General. *See* Itote, Waruhiu
Chou En-lai, 152
Christie, Jack, 242
Christianity, 23, 178, 187n1; acceptance of, 63–64; impact of, 24–25, 61–62
Chung, Faye, 249, 253–54n70
Churchill, Winston, photo 1, 5, 8, 21, 29, 34, 44, 112, 143, 198, 210–11; *My African Journey*, 144
Church of Christ, 226
Church of Scotland Mission, 225
Civil wars, 3–4; in Zimbabwe, 13, 14–16. *See also* Mau Mau rebellion
Cleveland, Ralph, 129
Clutton-Brock, Guy, photo 6,
Coffee Board of Kenya, 96, 100
Coghlan, Charles, 105, 106–7, 108, 226
Colonialism, 21, 26–27, 85, 194–95, 228; and education, 105–6, 109–12, 113–14, 119–20, 121–22; in Kenya, 8–10, 28–38, 42–47, 142–46, 195–97, 231–32; and Mau Mau rebellion, 155–56, 198–209; missionization and, 60–64; in Zimbabwe, 10–16, 54–77, 105–8, 118–19, 120–21
Colonial Office. *See* British Colonial Office
Colonies, 3, 4–5

Index 279

Communist Manifesto, The (Marx and Engels), 84
Conservative Party, 81, 82, 100n1
Constitution: Kenya's, 145–46, 211–16, 218, 232; Zimbabwe's, 165
Corfield, F. C., 155
Corn Laws, 151
Cory, William, 167
Coryndon, Robert, 9, 41, 42, 223
Council of Non-European Trade Unions, 125–26
Crown Colonies, 38
Crown Lands ordinance, 37
Cuba, 151
Cultural values: African, 117–18

Dadaya Mission, 108, 109, 175, 226
Darwin, Charles, 77n1; *The Descent of Man*, 3, 52; *Origin of Species*, 2–3, 52
Davidson, Basil, 143
de Gaulle, Charles, 8
de Klerk, F. W., 1
Department of Native Development, 74
Descent of Man, The (Darwin), 3, 52
Deutsche Koloniałbund, 4
Devonshire, Duke of, 144
Dhlakama, Afonzo, 247
Diefenbaker John, 105
Disraeli, Benjamin, 25, 82
Dodge, Ralph E., 15, 108, 229, 231; and Rhodesia Front, 176–82; and Garfield Todd, 182–85
Dominion Party (DP), 163–64, 165, 170, 182, 233; educational policy of, 166–67; and Great Britain, 167–68
Douglas-Home, Alec, 245
Dube, John L., 227
Du Bois, W.E.B., 202–3
Dupont, Clifford, 161, 167

East African Association, 9, 223–24
Economy in Kenya, 37–38, 147–48, 195
Edgerton, Robert B., 148, 149–50, 155
Education: of Africans, 64–65, 125, 163, 217, 226; colonial government and, 67–74, 75, 119–20, 121–22; Dominion Party, 166–67; missionaries and, 60, 61, 62–63, 66–67, 225; Rhodesia Front, 173–74; in Zimbabwe 105–6, 109–12, 113–14, 127–30, 236, 237–38, 239–44
Education Ordinance (1899), 68–70
Education Ordinance (1903), 71
Elgin, Lord, 34, 35, 143–44
Eliot, Charles, 28, 29, 31, 35
Ellman-Browne, George, 128
Embu, 22
Employment of Africans, 136, 147–48, 196–97, 198; and *kipande*, 147–48, 158n2
Engels, Friedrich: *The Communist Manifesto*, 84
Enlightenment, 51–52
Equal opportunity: promoting, 125–26, 136
Estado Novo, 4
Ethiopia, 3–4, 44, 93–94, 152
Ethnic groups, 22, 29, 36. *See also* various tribes by name

Facing Mount Kenya (Kenyatta), 89
Farm workers, 159n27; in Kenya, 42, 147–50
Federal Independence Party (FIP), 140
Federation of Rhodesia and Nyasaland, 176, 232
Field, Winston, 15, 161, 167, 171, 172, 180–81
Fletcher, Patrick, 128, 129
Forced labor, 37, 114–15
Fort Kericho, 32
Forty Group, 198, 203
Fourteen Points, 85
Fraser, Peter, 108
Freire, Paulo, 152–53, 250
French, Walter, 96–97
French Revolution, 151
Frost, Desmond, 167

Gachi, Hezekia, 225
Gandanzara, N. A., 242–43
Garvey, Marcus, 41
Gaunt, John, 167, 171, 172
Germany, 25

Ghana, 7, 14, 46, 165, 211, 213
Gibbs, Peter, 55
Gichuru, James, 212
Girourd, Percy, 35
Gituamba, 225
Gladstone, William, 83–84, 85
Goldberg, B. D., 148, 159n27
Graham, Lord, 161, 167
Graham Commission, 71, 73
Grant, Kennedy, 111
Great Britain, 4, 25, 103–4, 151, 165; colonialism of, 21, 213–14; and Dominion Party, 167–68; imperialism of, 75–76; and Kenya, 28–38, 39–44, 46–47, 210–13, 214–15, 217, 220n39, 231–32; liberalism in, 84–85; missionaries and, 60–64; political parties in, 81–84, 100–101n1; and Zimbabwe, 53–77, 169, 189n44, 238, 244
Great Depression, 91, 108–9, 112
Grey, Earl, 12–13, 65, 67, 70, 162, 166, 167, 170, 238
Griffin, Mrs. E., 182
Griffiths, James, 145
Grigg, Edward, 9, 40, 223, 224–25; *Kenya's Opportunity: Memories, Hopes and Ideas*, 42–43
Grogan, E. S., 32
Guerrilla warfare. *See* Mau Mau rebellion
Gweru, 127

Hadfield Commission, 74
Hardinge, Arthur Charles, 9, 28, 30, 31
Harper, William, 161, 166, 167, 168, 182
Harris, William Wade, 180, 183
Hatty, Cyril, 128
Havelock, Wilfrid B., 213, 220n37
Healey, Dennis, 217
Helm, Charles, 55, 56, 57, 78n15
Highlands Orders-in-Council, 144
Hilton-Young Commission, 39, 43
Hitler, Adolf, 5, 44
Hole Commission, 105, 106
Hope Foundation, 61

Hopkinson, Henry, 145
Huggins, Godfrey, 5, 13, 43, 108, 130, 148, 162, 167, 170, 176, 228; on African education, 51, 75, 123–24, 125; and African self-determination, 114, 115, 118, 120–21, 126; and Garfield Todd, 110, 111; on Mau Mau rebellion, 154–55; and United Party, 226–27
Hughes, Robert, 181
Hunt, James, 53
Hut tax, 35, 48n25

Imperial British East Africa Company, 28
Imperialism, 75–76
Independence, 3–4, 7, 247; of Ghana, 14, 213; of Kenya, 10, 46, 145–46, 217, 220n39, 233; of Rhodesia, 238, 244–45; of South Africa, 104, 107
Individuals, 2, 7–8
Industrial Revolution, 7, 21–22, 23, 62, 113
Intelligence, 53
Isaacman, Allen, 154
Itote, Waruhiu (General China), 6, 197–98; and Mau Mau rebellion, 199–201, 203–4, 210

Jacha, Aaron, 227
Jameson, Leander Starr, 12, 58, 59, 162, 166, 167, 170
Joint Select Committee, 43
Jollie, Ethel Tawse, 4, 73–74, 109, 172–73
Jones, Creech, 144–45
Jowitt, Harold, 74, 75, 108
Judges Commission, 188n13, 237–38

Kamba, 29, 36
Kangethu, Joseph, 41–42
Kanogo, Tabitha, 195, 197
Kapenzi, Geoffrey, 66–67
Kariba, 241
Kariuki, Jesse, 41–42
Katanja, Philip, 39
Kaunda, Kenneth, 250

Index 281

Kavirondo, 32
Kenya, 2, 6, 17, 18 (map), 22, 223, 247, 249, 250, 253n65; African consciousness in, 135–38; African politics in, 92–93, 140–41; Blundell and, 86–90, 246; colonialism, 8–10, 28–38, 42–45, 46–47, 49n46, 145–46, 231–32; employment in, 147–50; farming in, 91–92; independence of, 217, 220n39, 233; Kikuyu in, 39–42; land distribution in, 143–45, 195–96, 219n9; Lennox-Boyd constitution and, 215–16, 218; Oliver Lyttleton and, 211–15; Mau Mau rebellion in, 45–46, 153–56, 191–93, 194–95, 197–211; politics in, 94–100; registration certificates in 136–37; settler meetings in, 138–40
Kenya African National Union (KANU), 46
Kenya African Rifles (KAR), 198
Kenya African Union (KAU), 45, 142, 203, 209
Kenya Central Association, 44
Kenya Coalition Party, 95
Kenya Constitution Order-in-Council, 215
Kenya Independent Schools Association, 225
Kenya's Opportunity: Memories, Hopes and Ideas (Grigg), 42–43
Kenyatta, Jomo, photo 5, 7, 29, 43, 46, 142, 155, 219n16, 247; *Facing Mount Kenya,* 89; and Mau Mau rebellion, 199–200, 204–9
Kerr Commission, 225–26
Khabo, J. M., 237; and educational policy, 239–41
Kiamba Local Native Council, 39–40
Kikuyu, 22, 29, 30, 36, 225; and Kenyan politics, 38–42; and Mau Mau uprising, 45–46, 156–57
Kikuyu Association, 38, 40
Kikuyu Cultural Association (KCA), 41, 43, 142, 203
Kikuyu Independent Schools Association, 225
Kikuyu Loyal Patriots, 40

Kikuyu Provincial Association, 41
Kimathi, Dedan, photo 8, 232; and Mau Mau rebellion, 201–4, 210
King, William Lyon Mackenzie, 104, 105, 193
King's African Rifles, 93–94
Kipande, 36, 37–38, 136, 140, 147–48, 158n2
Kisii, 32
Knorr, Kenneth, 26, 54
Koinange, Mbiyu, 39, 40, 212
Kunyiha, Johana, 225

Labor: and education ordinances, 71, 72; in Kenya, 147–50, 195, 196–97
Labor Circular Number One, 37
Labour Party, 43, 81, 82–83, 100n1, 217
Laikipia, 30, 31
Lamont, Donal R., 108, 229
Lancaster House conference, 217, 218, 232
Land Apportionment Act (1929), 164, 166, 169, 172, 180, 189n43, 234
Land Commission (Kenya), 40
Land distribution, 240, in Kenya, 28–29, 31–32, 40, 143–45, 195–96, 219n9
Land Tenure Act, 15, 189n43, 239
Lapointe, Ernest, 193
Lardner-Burke, Desmond, 167
Laurier, Wilfred, 193
Lazell, A. L., 240
Leader of British East Africa (newspaper) 40
Leadership: and rebellion, 151–52; Mau Mau, 197–209
Leakey, L. B.: *Defeating the Mau Mau,* 155
Leigh, Isaac, 150
Lennox-Boyd, Alan, 46, 145–46, 215–17, 218
Lennox-Boyd constitution, 95, 215–16, 218, 232
Liberal Party, 33, 34, 35, 83, 84, 104
Liberal Party (Canada), 192, 193
Liberia, 3
Lipscomb, F. F.: *We Build a Country,* 155

Livingstone, David, 12, 23–24, 62, 67
Lloyd, A. D., 129
Lloyd George, David, 33, 84, 85, 98, 106
Lobengula, Khumalo, 54–55, 78nn15, 19; and Rhodes, 57–59; and Rudd Concession, 56–57
London Anthropological Society, 53
London conference, 13–14
London Missionary Society, 23, 55
Lotshe, 56
Louis XVI, 151
Lumumba, Patrice, 7
Luo, 22
Luthuli, Albert, 7, 27–28
Lyttleton, Oliver, 46, 146, 220n37; and Kenya's constitution, 211–15, 232
Lyttleton constitution, 10, 95, 232, 211–15, 232

MacDonald, Malcolm J., 46, 49n46, 144
MacDonald, Ramsay, 83, 98
Mackinnon, William, 28
Maclean, Ian, 167
Macleod, Iain N., 217, 218, 221n48, 232
Macmillan, Harold, 105, 217, 218
Maguire, Rochfort, 55
Malan, Daniel F., 1
Maloba, Wunyabari O., 142, 150
Mandela, Nelson, 1, 4, 104
Mangombe, Nderi, 204
Manica, 242
Mao Tse-tung, 152, 153–54
Margai, Milton, 7
Marx, Karl: *The Communist Manifesto*, 84
Masai, 22, 29, 30, 31, 36, 37
Mashonaland, 58
Masirero, 90, 101n16
Massey, Vincent, 194
Masters and Servants Ordinance, 36
Mathu, Eliud Wambui, 9, 10, 44–45, 47, 197, 209, 231–32
Mau Mau rebellion, 6, 10, 42, 45–46, 99, 151, 225; Blundell and, 156–58, 209–11, 229, 232; causes and interpretations of 142, 143–50, 153–56;

and Kenyan government, 191–93, 194–95; leaders of, 197–209
Mawema, Michael, 185–86
Mbagathi River, 30
Mboya, Tom, 212, 217, 249
Memmi, Albert, 152
Meredith, Martin, 205–6
Meru, 45–46
Methodist Church, 121, 180, 181, 182–83
Michell, Lewis, 107
Military, 32, 36, 44. *See also* Kenya African Rifles; Rhodesia African Rifles; World War II
Mill, John Stuart, 62
Milton, William Henry, 65–66, 68, 70, 238; government policies of, 105–7
Missionaries, 13, 23; impact of, 24–25; and Kikuyu, 39, 40, 225; in Zimbabwe, 60–67, 108, 109, 111–12, 226
Mitchell, George, 108
Mitchell, Philip E., photo 5, 9, 10, 45, 95, 135, 136, 156, 157, 158, 211, 225; and African politics, 137–38, 142, 206–8; and Mau Mau rebellion, 150–51, 155
Moffat, Howard Unwin, 108, 109
Moffat, Robert, 23, 24, 60, 61, 62, 230
Moi, Daniel arap, 212, 214, 247–48, 253n65
Mombasa, 28, 29, 44
Mondlane, Edwardo, 7
Moore, Henry Monck-Mason, 44, 45
Morris Carter Commission, 41
Mozambique, 152, 154, 247–48
Mozambique National Resistance (Renamo), 247
Mugabe, Robert, 246, 247–48, 249
Muliro, Masinde, 214
Mungeam, G. H., 33
Mussett, John, 161, 167
Mutare, 127
Mwamuka, Aldon, 126–27
My African Journey (Churchill), 144
Myrdal, Gunnar: *An American Dilemma: The Negro Problem and Modern Democracy*, 1
Mzilikazi, King, 55, 61

Nairobi, 28, 29
Nakuru: settler meeting at, 138–40
Namibia, 152
National Democratic Party (NDP), 14, 185
National Insurance Act (1911), 84
Nationalism: African, 11–12, 13, 14, 124, 152, 162, 167, 169–70, 181–82, 228, 229; and African National Congress, 230–31; Mau Mau rebellion and, 192–93
Nationalist Party, 1, 250
Native Areas Orders-in-Council, 144
Native Authority Ordinance, 36–37
Native Local Councils 42
Native Registration Ordinance, 37–38, 147
Nazis, 5, 44
Ndebele, 22, 54–55
Ndhlove, L. A., 243
Nemakonde, 242
New Kenya Group, 99, 217
New Zealand, 21, 103, 108
Ngala, Ronald, 212, 214, 217
Ngong, 30
Nicholas II, 151
Nile River, 23
Njonjo, Joseph, 39
Nkomo, Joshua, 7, 184–85, 249
Nkrumah, Kwame, 7, 14, 202, 211
Northern Rhodesia, 43
Northey, Edward, 9, 38, 41
Nyasaland, 43
Nyeri, 45
Nyongesa, H. K., photo 4

Odinga, Oginga, 214, 249
Ogot, Bethwell A., 34, 204, 223, 231
Ohange, B. A., 214
Old Age Pension, 84
Ordinance Number 7, 71–72
Ordinance Number 133 (1907), 71
Organization of African Unity (OAU), 14, 245, 248
Origin of Species (Darwin), 2–3, 52
Ormsby-Gore Commission, 39
Otieno, Mellyse, xv, photo 9, 249

Otieno, S. M., 249
Out of Africa (Blixen), 148

Padmore, George, 203
Paget, E. F., 120, 123
Pan-African movement, 202–3
Parliamentary Act (1908), 84
Patel, A. B., 231
Pearce, Lord, 245
Pearce Commission, 245
Peck, A. J., 129, 133n66
Peel, Robert, 83
Political parties, 81–82; in Zimbabwe, 161–64
Political representation: in Kenya, 29, 37
Politics, 29; Africans in, 140–41; Blundell in, 94–100; Kikuyu, 39–42 in Zimbabwe, 109–12, 119–21, 128–30
Popkin, Samuel, 154
Pritt, D. N., photo 7, 209
Psychology of the Mau Mau Rebellion, The (Carothers), 154–55

Quinton, H. J. 129

Race relations, 119, 130; after World War II, 122–23, 126–27
Racism, 35, 246; institutional, 68–70
Railways: in Kenya, 28, 195
Read, Wynwood, 27, 53
Rebellions: peasant, 151–54. *See also* Mau Mau rebellion
Reform Act (1867), 81, 82
Registration certificates, 136–37, 158nn1, 2. *See also* Kipande
Religion, 66. *See also* Christianity
Renamo. *See* Mozambique National Resistance
Renison, Patrick, 46
Rhodes, Cecil John, 7, 11, 27, 28, 47–48nn9, 12, 53, 76, 77n10, 162, 166, 170, 179, 230; colonization by, 54–58
Rhodesia, 244–45. *See also* Zimbabwe
Rhodesia African Rifles, 115, 126–27
Rhodesia Front Party (RF), 11, 13, 16, 161–62, 183, 186–87 187n8, 189n44, 229, 246; actions of, 170–74, 233–44;

and civil war, 14–15; and Ralph Dodge, 176–82; and education, 173–74; and Winston Field, 180–81
Rhodesian Missionary Conference, 227
Rift Valley, 30, 96–97
Rolin, Henri, 72
Rolin Report, 72
Roosevelt, Franklin D., 5, 112, 198
Rose, Emory, photo 3, 139
Royal African Society, 119–20
Royal Charters, 28, 57, 107
Rudd, Charles, 54–56
Rudd Concession, 56–57
Russian Revolution, 151

Sadler, James Hayes, 9, 31, 32, 33, 34, 35, 143
Sadomba, R. T., 242
St. Laurent, Ann Mary Broderick, 193
St. Laurent, Jean Baptiste Moise, 193
St. Laurent, Louis S., 105, 201; on Mau Mau rebellion, 193–95, 225
Salazar, Antonio, 8
Samkange, Stanlake, 28
Samkange, Thompson D., 227
Savage, Michael J., 108
Schools, 225–26
Scott, Lody Francis, 97
Selassie, Haile, 3
Self-determination, 114, 125; in Atlantic Charter, 5–6, 112–13; Huggins on, 123–24
Settler meetings: in Kenya, 138–40
Shelton, Kenneth, 108
Shepard, D. E., 182
Shona, 22
Sifuya, E. G., 241–42
Skeen, Andrew, 161, 167
Skelton, Kenneth, 229
Slade, Humphrey, 157, 212, 213
Slavery: and colonial society, 35–36
Smit, D. L., 119
Smith, Arthur, 161, 167, 187n2, 243–44
Smith, David, 161, 167, 187n2
Smith, Ian, 11, 13, 15, 76–77, 79n52, 124, 148, 167, 179, 181, 186, 187n2, 218, 238, 244; and Rhodesia Front, 161, 162, 171, 172, 246; and Garfield Todd, 182, 245
Smith, Lance, 161, 167, 187n2
Smuts, J. C., 122, 123
Socialism, 83, 84
Soemmering, S. T. von, 23, 27, 52
Solai, 91–92, 94
Soldier Settlement Scheme, 38
Somalia, 44
So Rough a Wind (Blundell), 191, 192–93, 219n1
South Africa, 1–2, 4, 7, 104, 107, 119, 152, 250, 253n63
Southern Christian Missionary Conference, 105
Southern Rhodesia. *See* Zimbabwe
Southern Rhodesia Association, 170
Southern Rhodesia Missionary Conference, 71, 72, 105, 106, 176
Speke, John Hanning, 23
Stark, George, 75, 121
Stewart, Donald, 30, 31, 32–33, 37
Stigand, Chauncy, 150
Stumbles, A. R., 128
Suez Canal, 25, 221n42
Swann, H. B., 90–91

Tanganyika, 28, 40, 42, 49n41, 251n4
Tapsell, Sir Peter, photo 10
Taxation: in colonial Africa, 35–36
Taylor, J. R., 130–31
Teachers: in Zimbabwe, 237–38, 239–40
Tekere, Edgar, 248, 249, 253n67
Thatcher, Margaret, 81
Thompson, Robert, 55
Thuku, Harry, photo, 9, 38, 47, 135, 214, 223–25, 251n4; political activism of, 40–42, 43
Tignor, Robert L., 29, 35, 36, 82
Todd, Jean Grace Wilson, 175
Todd, Judith, 17, 185, 229, 245, 251nn16, 17
Todd, Reginald Stephen Garfield, photos 3 and 6, 12, 17, 21, 33, 103, 114, 121, 161, 169, 172, 174–76, 186–87, 194, 223, 227, 228–29, 245, 246–47, 251n16; and African opportuni-

Index   285

ties, 15–16, 115–18, 120, 123, 230;
  Ralph Dodge and, 182–85; educa-
  tional policies of, 109–111, 127–30;
  fall from power, 128–30; as mission-
  ary, 108–9, 226; RF government
  and, 13, 177–82; and Whitehead,
  168, 230, 231
Tory Party, 82, 83
Trade unions, 125–26
Training: manual, 71, 72
Treaties, 26, 104
Tredgold, A. M., 122, 123
Tredgold, Robert C., 108, 230
Tredgold Commission, 230

Uganda, 40, 42, 95
United Federal Party (UFP), 164, 167–
  68, 170, 171–72, 174, 186, 235
United Group, 170, 217
United Party, 110, 226–27
United States, 41
Universal Negro Improvement Associ-
  ation, 41
University of Witwatersrand, 175–76

Vambe, Lawrence, 129
van der Byl, Peter, 161
Vereeniging, Treaty of, 104
Victoria, Queen, 28, 57
Victoria Falls, 23
Victorian era: scientific concepts of, 52–
  54
Vietnam, 152
Vincent, Alfred, 94–95

Wacuima, Charity, 149
War: in colonial Zimbabwe, 59–60. *See
  also* Civil war; Mau Mau rebellion
Ward, H. F., 97
Waruhiu, Chief, 45, 157
Waswa, Ruth, photo 4
Webber, Ronald, 151
We Build a Country (Lipscomb), 155
Welensky, Roy, 43, 176, 218, 232–33
Wellington College, 86
White, Charles, 23, 27, 52

Whitehead, Edgar C., 13, 14, 15, 129,
  162–63, 173, 185–86, 188n13, 233;
  and African nationalism, 181–82,
  230–31; and Dominion Party, 164,
  166, 167, 168, 169, 170; and United
  Federal Party, 171–72
Williams, Hugh, 74, 109
Wilson, Harold, 217, 244, 246
Winterbottom, Thomas: *An Account of
  the Native Africans,* 53
World Council of Churches, 246
World War I, 37, 82–83
World War II, 5, 13, 42, 44, 93–94; Afri-
  cans and, 112–14, 115, 118, 119, 122,
  126–27, 198, 219n12, 228
Wright, E. H., 138–39

Yamba, D L., 123
Young Kikuyu Association (YKA), 38,
  39, 40

Zambezi River, 23
Zambia, 250
Zimbabwe, 2, 5, 17, 19 (map), 22, 28,
  148, 152, 158nn1, 2, 185–87, 226,
  246, 249, 250, 252n34; African development in, 123–24; colonialism in,
  10–16, 48n25, 52, 54–77; Dominion
  Party in, 163–64, 168–69; education
  in, 67–74, 105–6, 109–12, 113–14,
  119–20, 127–28, 239–44; forced labor
  in, 114–15; government in, 106–8,
  167–69; Great Depression in, 108–9;
  The Kerr Commission in, 225–26;
  liberal views in, 122–23; missionaries in, 60–67; nationalism in, 169–
  70, 181–82; political parties in, 161–
  64; politics in, 118–21, 128–30, 229;
  protests in, 248–49; Rhodesia Front
  actions in, 161–62, 170–74, 233–44
Zimbabwe African National Union
  (ZANU), 14, 248, 253n67
Zimbabwe African People's Union
  (ZAPU), 14
Zimbabwe Unity Movement (ZUM),
  249

ABOUT THE AUTHOR

DICKSON A. MUNGAZI is Regent's Professor of History at the Center for Excellence in Education at Northern Arizona University. He is the author of numerous books on African political history and education, including *The Mind of Black Africa* (Praeger, 1996), and *The Last Defenders of the Laager: Ian D. Smith and F. W. de Klerk* (Praeger, 1998).